Shakespeare's *Hamlet* and the Controversies of Self

Shakespeare's *Hamlet* and the Controversies of Self

JOHN LEE

OXFORD
UNIVERSITY PRESS

OXFORD
UNIVERSITY PRESS

Great Clarendon Street, Oxford OX2 6DP

Oxford University Press is a department of the University of Oxford.
It furthers the University's objective of excellence in research, scholarship,
and education by publishing worldwide in

Oxford New York

Athens Auckland Bangkok Bogotá Buenos Aires Cape Town
Chennai Dar es Salaam Delhi Florence Hong Kong Istanbul Karachi
Kolkata Kuala Lumpur Madrid Melbourne Mexico City Mumbai Nairobi
Paris São Paulo Shanghai Singapore Taipei Tokyo Toronto Warsaw

with associated companies in Berlin Ibadan

Published in the United States
by Oxford University Press Inc., New York

First published 2000

British Library Cataloguing in Publication Data
Data available

Library of Congress Cataloging in Publication Data
Data available

ISBN 0-19-818504-9

3 5 7 9 10 8 6 4 2

Typeset by Regent Typesetting, London
Printed in Great Britain
on acid-free paper by
Biddles Ltd,
Guildford and King's Lynn

To my mother
PATRICIA M. LEE

Acknowledgements

Like dwarfs on the shoulders of giants

ANYONE writing on Shakespearian matters, let alone *Hamlet*, cannot but be aware of the debt owed to previous criticism. Here that debt is most obviously paid in disagreement, which may seem a rather poor return. I have been grateful for the chance to disagree.

Throughout the writing of this book, I have benefited from the advice of John Lyon and George Donaldson, and the support of Richard Beard. Dr Fay Fransella was kind enough to read and comment on Chapter 6. I would not have begun without the encouragement of Professor Marilyn Butler and Professor Howard Erskine-Hill. Grants from the Research Committee of the University of Bristol and the Sidney Perry Foundation helped me to continue. Subsequent support was provided by the Departments of English at the Universities of Bristol and Newcastle.

Part of Chapter 3, in a revised form, was published as 'The Man who Mistook his Hat: Stephen Greenblatt and the Anecdote' in *Essays in Criticism*, October 1995. (Please also see the correction to that article published in the July 1998 issue.) The Frick Collection, New York kindly gave permission for Van Dyck's portrait, *Sir John Suckling*, to be reproduced.

Contents

Abbreviations

EETS	Early English Text Society
EIC	*Essays in Criticism*
ELR	*English Literary Renaissance*
NYRB	*The New York Review of Books*
PMLA	*Publications of the Modern Language Association of America*
RES	*Review of English Studies*
SQ	*Shakespeare Quarterly*
SS	*Shakespeare Survey*
TLN	Through Line Numbers
TLS	*The Times Literary Supplement*

Introduction

Shakespeare's 'Hamlet' and the Controversies of Self has a three-part structure. Throughout, the focus of the argument is provided by the search for an answer to a critical issue: does Prince Hamlet have a self-constituting sense of self? In each part this search is driven by the question with which *Hamlet* opens: 'Who's there?'

Part I unfolds the contemporary academic drama surrounding the critical issue. The main roles are played by famous New Historicists and Cultural Materialists. Through the first three chapters, their answers to the question of 'Who's there?'—when asked of the Prince or similar persons—are examined. Often conflating terms such as 'self', 'identity', and 'human nature', they argue that neither the Prince nor any other English Renaissance dramatic person has a self-constituting sense of self, but are instead socially produced subjects lacking any meaningful sense of interiority. 'That Within' the Prince is an absence or gap, which critics have delighted in filling. However, although these critics' answers are similar, the arguments leading up to them and the implications leading off from them are not. To understand these arguments and implications as fully as possible, Part I also examines what defines New Historicists and Cultural Materialists respectively, for answers are best understood when their speakers are known. One point that emerges from this examination is the centrality of *Hamlet* to an understanding of both movements. In relation to New Historicists, the absence of *Hamlet* from their criticism is evidence of their tendency to banish the critical and historical past; for, given their concerns, *Hamlet* ought to be central to their debates. This logical centrality of *Hamlet* is recognized by Cultural Materialists, who focus on *Hamlet*, using the Prince as their point of attack on previous critical tradition and (rather grandly) on contemporary society.

Part II is set in the more distant past, its players drawn from Shakespearian critics of the seventeenth, eighteenth, and early nineteenth centuries. Intrigued by the absence of previous criticism from New Historicist accounts, dubious of the account given of that criticism by Cultural Materialists, this section recreates the first scenes and acts of this critical drama; it presents the various answers given in response to the question of 'Who's there?' during the first two hundred years of Shakespearian criticism. Key to these answers, and to the drama which they constitute, is the concept of character. Throughout this period, Shakespeare's ability or lack of ability to create character—that is, dramatic persons with a sense of interiority or inner life—is seen to be central to the valuation of his achievement as a whole. Shakespeare's defenders and his attackers both focus on this issue, their debate developing through a series of definitions of 'character', where such definitions gradually develop over time a greater emphasis on interiority. *Hamlet* was one of the standard examples of this debate from its outset; by the end of this period, the Prince had become the prime exemplar of what 'character' meant, and was central to the establishment of the worth of Shakespeare. Yet what interiority was remained vague and mystically defined; typically, critics would state that Shakespeare possessed that quality, and lapse into wonderment when they failed to describe what it was.

Part III opens, then, with a sense of the high stakes and long vistas that lie behind the controversies of self. Hamlet, the Prince, and *Hamlet*, the play, now take centre stage. The arguments of the New Historicists and Cultural Materialists cannot be easily refuted, since both *Hamlet* and English Renaissance culture lack the modern vocabulary of meaning through which interiority is described. An argument needs to be found in which the verbal text can be shown to express meanings which, in terms of the absence of the relevant modern vocabulary, might be thought to be inexpressible. Drawing on constructivist psychology and moral theory, a terminology and methodology is developed that is capable of advancing such an argument. The textual ways are traced by which 'that Within' Prince Hamlet is constructed. The Prince is shown to have a self-constituting sense of self, and this sense of self is central to his tragedy. In answering the initial question, this argument challenges one of the central tenets of New Historicist and Cultural Materialist criticism.

This sense of self is not, however, either essentialist or transhistorical; one aspect of its historical specificity is examined—its rhetorical nature, which the Prince finds unsatisfactory. Indeed, *Hamlet* can be seen to be unsatisfied with its notions of self; in a brief, final chapter two Prince Hamlets are identified, a Quarto Prince and a Folio Prince. The Folio's Prince is argued to be a revised version of the Quarto Prince, and a significant number of those revisions are seen to aim to create a greater degree of self-constituting interiority. The nature of the sense of self, then, is both an issue and at issue within the play. *Hamlet* debates the present critical debate; it has its own controversies of self.

Part I

I
The Changing of the Guard

Actus Primus. Scoena Prima.
Enter Barnardo and Francisco two Centinels.
Barnardo. Who's there?

(1. 1. 1[1])

BARNARDO opens *The Tragedie of Hamlet, Prince of Denmark* with a question which echoes through the play. Or rather, he begins with the play's particular form of that question—a challenge. Asked as a challenge, 'Who's there?' loses its everyday familiarity. Asked by Barnardo, the challenge itself becomes unusual; Barnardo is the relief guard and, as Francisco points out, the challenge is not his to make. Our attention focuses on the question. Barnardo's life may depend upon the answer. The fear of the unknown, implicit within the everyday question, becomes explicit, as does the question's aggressive desire to render the unknown known. The question's loss of familiarity, its importance, the fear and hostility that lie within it, all are sharpened when the audience learn that Barnardo is expecting the arrival of a ghost. From the first lines of the play, the importance of identity and identification is acknowledged, and the fact that neither needs be established is recognized. 'Who's there?' never becomes a simple question within *Hamlet*; identity, from the first line, is problematic.[2]

[1] Unless stated otherwise, all quotations are from a First Folio in the possession of the Elizabethan Club of Yale University, prepared in a facsimile edition by Helge Kökeritz. This edition is not used because it is thought to provide a purer access to a Shakespearian original, but because it is a (recreation of a) Renaissance edition, the material practices of which have substantial implications for critical interpretation. For a useful survey of these issues, see Margreta de Grazia and Peter Stallybrass, 'The Materiality of the Shakespearean Text', *SQ* 44 (1993), 255–83. The Folio is used in preference to Q2, as it is taken to be a revised version of Q2; Q1 is taken to be a 'bad quarto'. The arguments that underlie these opinions, and the large textual debates in which they are involved, are discussed further in Ch. 8. All three texts can be found in *The Three-Text 'Hamlet'*, ed. Bernice W. Kliman (New York: AMS Press, 1991). When quoting from the Folio, act, scene, and line numbers are provided for convenience, and refer to *William Shakespeare: The Complete Works*, ed. Stanley Wells, Gary Taylor, and others (Oxford: Oxford University Press, 1986). (This text is not the same as either G. R. Hibbard's single-volume Oxford edition or the Norton edition.) When quoting a passage that does not occur in the Folio, I follow Kliman's practice of counting the lines from the last Folio line. So e.g. the beginning of the Q2 soliloquy 'How all occasions doe informe against me' occurs at 4. 4. 9 + 26. Where Q1 is quoted, Kliman's TLN is used, and the corresponding Folio location indicated where relevant. So e.g. Hamlet's first speech in Q1, 'My lord, ti's not the sable sute I weare' occurs at Q1 179–85, 1. 2. 77–86.

[2] Leo Salingar makes similar points about the opening's concern with questions of identity,

The argument of Part I of this book is that 'Who's there?' would be a fitting opening line for some of the literary-critical dramas scripted by New Historicist and Cultural Materialist critics. These two critical movements have been remarkably influential over the last fifteen to twenty years, shaping many of the key literary debates of Renaissance studies. If 'Who's there?', and so identity, is seen to be a central issue for them, then *Hamlet* might have been expected to be a particularly important example and proving ground for their arguments. The drama of *Hamlet* would lie at the heart of New Historicist and Cultural Materialist thinking, and so the discussion of the one would address the central critical or interpretative debates of the other. Substantiating that this question is central to these critical movements, and understanding why this should be, requires a knowledge of what the two movements are, or—in other words—whose is the challenge.[3] This can be done in two very different ways: one is to examine what particular critics say these movements are; the other is to examine what they show themselves to be in their critical practice. I look at both, using what emerges as the disparity between the statements of critical theory and the actual critical practice as the basis of a critique of their arguments. A further distinction needs to be made between New Historicism and Cultural Materialism, a distinction insisted on by the proponents of each movement. Again there is a considerable disparity between their accounts of this difference and the difference that is seen in their work.

Part I, then, opens with some New Historicist accounts of New Historicism, goes on in its second chapter to treat the practice of the most famous New Historicist players, and draws to a close with a similarly twofold consideration of Cultural Materialism. New Historicists have often cast their account of their

and traces the play's repetition of the opening scene's question and action. See 'Shakespeare and the Ventriloquists', *SS* 34 (1981), 51–60 (55–6).

[3] Several critiques centred on these two critical movements have been published whose concerns at times parallel those of this book. In the examples that follow, New Historicism and Cultural Materialism are taken to be indicative of a present unhealthy state of literary criticism. Graham Bradshaw, in *Misrepresentations: Shakespeare and the Materialists* (Ithaca, NY: Cornell University Press, 1993), looks at the movements' self-interested misrepresentations of *Henry V*, *Othello*, and *The Merchant of Venice*. (He also examines the two movements' representations of Tillyard, but does not examine Tillyard himself.) Howard Felperin, in *The Uses of the Canon: Elizabethan Literature and Contemporary Theory* (Oxford: Clarendon Press, 1990), examines the shortcomings of the two movements from a deconstructive position. Brook Thomas, in *The New Historicism: And Other Old-Fashioned Topics* (Princeton: Princeton University Press, 1991), attempts to construct a theoretically coherent rationale for the use of literary texts within historicism, insisting on historiography's importance in bringing about the new. Brian Vickers, in *Appropriating Shakespeare: Contemporary Critical Quarrels* (New Haven: Yale University Press, 1993), amasses a large collection of arguments concerning the weaknesses of many of the theories of what he terms 'Current Literary Theory' and, in respect to New Historicism, concentrates on its ahistorical nature. Katherine Eisaman Maus, in *Inwardness and Theater in the English Renaissance* (Chicago: University of Chicago Press, 1995), approaches similar areas to those in this book and starts from a similar sense of dissatisfaction, though unlike this book she retains a Cartesian notion of self and explores the dramatic potential of a variety of 'gaps'. Her arguments are the greatest recent contribution to the controversies of self. (For definitions of 'Cartesian' and 'gap', see Ch. 6.)

movement in terms of a battle over the interpretative kingdom of literary criticism. Their account is analysed here in terms of parents (who tend to be a little hard to identify), friends and enemies—rather as if, in fact, the battle was for the kingdom of Denmark.

> *Fran.* Nay answer me: Stand & vnfold your selfe.
>
> (I. I. 2)

New Historicists, when they feel challenged, begin a standard description of their movement by an examination of their enemies, or—as they would term it—their 'others'. The first 'other' discussed is historicism, logically enough as this is the term New Historicism defines itself against. Both historicism and New Historicism are extrinsic, as opposed to intrinsic, forms of literary historicism; that is, they explore the relationship between literature and history, as opposed to the history of literature. Beyond that the resemblance is said to end. Historicism is always 'old' historicism, which must be the antithesis of 'new' historicism. If this was not so, then New Historicism would lose its distinctness, and might look remarkably like its enemy. New Historicism has, then, a dangerous name; and a paramount, often desperate need to prove itself new. Perhaps because of this its proponents have often declared their unhappiness with that name; none more so than Stephen Greenblatt, who, though he was not the first to use the term 'New Historicism', may be said to have been the decisive factor in the critical movement's adoption of that title.[4] The most commonly preferred term in such declarations of unease is 'cultural poetics', a variation of a phrase that Greenblatt had used before 'New Historicism'.[5] Given this unease, the reasons for New Historicism's success as a name become interesting, as Greenblatt notes, though he puts off an exploration of the reasons to 'some point' in the future.[6] Some of these reasons will emerge later in my account.

[4] Greenblatt claims that although he has 'never been very good at making up advertising phrases of this kind [i.e. New Historicism]', this name 'stuck much more than other names I'd very carefully tried to invent over the years'. He believes he invented the movement's title 'out of a kind of desperation to get the introduction done' to a special issue of *Genre*. This anecdote occurs at the beginning of 'Towards a Poetics of Culture', in *Learning to Curse: Essays in Early Modern Culture* (London: Routledge, 1990), 146. The introduction referred to is in *Genre*, 15 (1982), 1–6. However, as Louis Montrose points out ('Professing the Renaissance: The Poetics and Politics of Culture', in H. Aram Veeser (ed.), *A New Historicism* (New York: Routledge, 1989), 15–36, (32)), 'New Historicism' had already been used in the field of Renaissance studies (with reference to cultural semiotics) by Michael McCanles, in his 'The Authentic Discourse of the Renaissance', *Diacritics*, 10:1 (1980), 77–87.

[5] Greenblatt discusses what he means by the term at some length in the introduction to *Renaissance Self Fashioning: from More to Shakespeare* (Chicago: University of Chicago Press, 1980), 1–9. Here he refers to the phrase a 'poetics of culture' as he does in *Shakespearean Negotiations: The Circulation of Social Energy in Renaissance England* (Oxford: Clarendon Press, 1988), 5. Montrose uses 'New Historicism' without particular complaint in his 'Renaissance Literary Studies and the Subject of History', *ELR* 16 (1986), 5–12, but when he came to rethink and expand this essay he argued that 'cultural poetics' is a more descriptively accurate term. See 'Professing the Renaissance', 17.

[6] Greenblatt, *Learning*, 146.

What, then, is this 'old' historicism? By far the most common method of answering this question is to take E. M. W. Tillyard and his *The Elizabethan World Picture* (his other books are rarely mentioned) as representative of the 'old' historicism.[7] Indeed, the number of times Tillyard's name is invoked, in conjunction with *The Elizabethan World Picture*, is remarkable. But more remarkable is the way in which it is almost never obvious quite how he is meant to stand for 'old' historicism. Jean E. Howard provides a good example of this peculiarity in an article which is often taken as a central statement of New Historicism's aims. She is here beginning her description of what makes New Historicism new:

> To answer that question I want to sketch what must of necessity be a simplified picture of some of the assumptions underlying the historical criticism of a figure such as Tillyard.[8]

This may at first seem reasonable. After all, it has a scholarly disclaimer, being only 'a simplified picture'. But Howard is qualifying this 'sketch' further, for it will only give us a 'simplified picture of *some of* the assumptions'. In fact, 'assumptions' provides another level of qualification; Howard is now saying that she is partially sketching what she has deduced as 'underlying' the actual text. So she is sketching a partial picture of a subjective interpretation of what was never said. And then we come to Tillyard; only we don't. Instead we come to 'a figure such as Tillyard'. Howard is, then, sketching a partial picture of a subjective interpretation of what was not said by someone who never existed. She does not sketch from life, as her metaphor suggests (particularly when allied with scholarly qualification and the invocation of a particular critic), but rather is sketching creatively. Tillyard, in fact, has disappeared before he has been invoked, to leave a hollowed-out name which can be used to define the acknowledged enemy.

The peculiar convolutions of this sentence are all the more remarkable both as Howard usually writes with precision, and as such convolutions are found in other critics' writings. Indeed, the frequency of the use of Tillyard's name divorced from the historical body of Tillyard's writings makes the invocation a trope of New Historicist (and Cultural Materialist) writing. Even a critic such as Lee Patterson, himself intent on drawing attention to the methodological weaknesses of New Historicism, uses the device; in his essay on 'Literary History' he argues: 'the construction of a totalized past, whether as global as Hippolyte Taine's *History of English Literature* (1864) or as specific as E. M. W. Tillyard's *The Elizabethan World Picture* (1944) is a prominent result of old

[7] The relative absence of Tillyard's other works is rather peculiar; his *Shakespeare's History Plays*, for instance, would offer a better target for New Historicism's enmity. *The Elizabethan World Picture* may be chosen as Tillyard's representative book for its misleading and thus misrepresentable title, and for its introductory quality, which can be easily mistaken for a reductive approach.

[8] Jean E. Howard, 'The New Historicism in Renaissance Studies', in *ELR* 16 (1986), 13–43, 18.

historicism's beliefs.'[9] Lee Patterson goes on to demonstrate his arguments by quotations from Taine; he never once quotes from Tillyard.[10]

The Tillyard trope, then, is a rhetorical device which gives the illusion of specificity to the arguments in which it is employed, while in fact allowing the critic's description of the past to stand unchallenged. There are other versions of the same rhetorical strategy. Stephen Greenblatt recognizes that 'New Historicism' tempts readers to conflate it with (old) 'historicism'. This, however, would be a mistake, he asserts, for the two terms have antithetical meanings. Greenblatt substantiates this neatly, arguing that New Historicism can be defined simply as the antonym of 'historicism'—as that term's meanings are defined in *The American Heritage Dictionary*:

1. The belief that processes are at work in history that man can do little to alter.
2. The theory that the historian must avoid all value judgments in his study of past periods of former cultures.
3. Veneration of the past or of tradition.

'Most of the writing labelled new historicist,' Greenblatt says, 'and certainly my own work, has set itself resolutely against each of these positions.'[11] He goes on to demonstrate the ways in which his work, and that of other critics, has insisted on opposite beliefs, theories, and attitudes.

Greenblatt, by taking a dictionary definition of 'historicism', does not have to confront any real 'old' historicist literary critics. In their place he puts the authority of the dictionary, with the consequence that readers may assume that previous old historicists resolutely agreed with each of these positions. As with the Tillyard trope, the literary-critical past is being effaced, to be replaced with a description of the present critic's choosing. Greenblatt does at least use someone else's description of historicism. Yet the choice of dictionary is fortuitous. Had Greenblatt used the *OED* he would have found a more expansive definition, whose first sense would render void the argument that New Historicism was a straight antonym of historicism:

9 Similarly, see Greenblatt, 'Introduction', in *Genre*: 'The earlier historicism tends to be monological; that is, it is concerned with discovering a single political vision' (5).

10 Lee Patterson, 'Literary History', in Frank Lentricchia and Thomas McLaughlin (eds.) *Critical Terms for Literary Study* (Chicago: University of Chicago Press, 1990), 250–62, (251). Patterson's critique of New Historicism is to be found in his *Negotiating the Past: The Historical Understanding of Medieval Literature* (Madison, Wis.: University of Wisconsin, 1987), 57–74; he repeats his totalizing charge against Tillyard on p. 63, again without substantiation. Patterson is used here as an example of how thoroughly hollowed-out the name 'Tillyard' has become. *Negotiating the Past* otherwise presents a lucid discussion of historicism in the particular context of medieval literary studies. Patterson's sense of disappointment with, and his criticisms of, New Historicism parallel those advanced here at several points, particularly in seeing New Historicism as sharing large areas of continuity with 19th-c. literary historicism. Indeed, this thesis is supportive of Patterson's assertion of the need for categories of difference, and provides arguments for Patterson's assertion that 'The self may well be made, but it is also self-made' (74). Patterson is very worried by New Historicists' answer to the question of 'Who's there?'

11 Stephen Greenblatt, 'Resonance and Wonder', in *Learning*, 164–5.

1. The attempt, found esp. among German historians since about 1850, to view all social and cultural phenomena, all categories, truths, and values, as relative and historically determined, and in consequence to be understood only by examining their historical context, in complete detachment from present-day attitudes. 1895

This is problematic for Greenblatt's argument, as he and New Historicist critics generally place at the centre of their criticism the belief that 'all social and cultural phenomena, all categories, truths, and values' must be seen as 'relative and historically determined'. Or, as Greenblatt puts it as he rejects sense 1 of *The American Heritage Dictionary*: 'New historicism [. . . is interested] not in the abstract universal but in particular, contingent cases, the selves fashioned and acting according to the generative rules and conflicts of a given culture.'[12] 'Who's there?', Greenblatt and other New Historicists rightly insist, has significantly distinct meanings in different historical periods. This is not to say New Historicism can be defined by this *OED* sense of historicism; New Historicists would reject the belief that phenomena can be viewed 'in complete detachment from present-day attitudes'. However, to have included the *OED*'s definition (or that in Webster's *Third International Dictionary*) would have greatly complicated and weakened Greenblatt's attempt to distinguish the novelty of New Historicism.[13]

These two approaches to a definition of New Historicism begin, then, by moving to banish the literary-critical past. Such a banishment of the past is an odd trait for any kind of historicist movement and a dubious foundation on which to build one's self-definition. Why should New Historicists use such an approach? The answer, in part if not in whole, lies in what 'old' historicism was. As has been said, New Historicists need to be different from old historicists; their name demands such a difference. But what if they found they were not? They could either abandon their identity (an almost unthinkable course), or work towards creating the impression that they were different (adopting a different *nom de plume*—such as 'cultural poetics'—might be helpful here). The possibility that this line of reasoning raises is that Tillyard, far from being a good example of what distinguishes New Historicists from old, is a figure whose literary-critical practices are hard to distinguish from those of the New Historicists.

An analysis of Tillyard's practices and beliefs in *The Elizabethan World Picture* confirms this possibility. Lee Patterson used the Tillyard trope to introduce the

[12] Greenblatt, 'Resonance and Wonder', in *Learning*, 164.

[13] *The American Heritage Dictionary* is a particularly strange choice for Greenblatt to have made. It was published in 1969 to take advantage of the public reaction against both the breadth of sources and the recognition of the authority of usage displayed by Webster's *Third New International Dictionary* (1961). It is considered both reactionary and lacking authority, as noted in the *Encyclopaedia Britannica*'s summary: 'A "usage panel" of 104 members, chosen mostly from the conservative "literary establishment", provided material for a set of "usage notes". Their pronouncements, found by scholars to be inconsistent, were supposed to provide "the essential dimension of guidance," as the editor put it, "in these permissive times"' (xviii. 281).

assertion that Tillyard constructed a 'totalized past', a homogeneous and monolithic conception of culture. It is an assertion that is often repeated.[14] Yet *The Elizabethan World Picture* does not bear this out. Tillyard, in the first two sentences of his first chapter, states that what follows was written to correct those people who think the 'Age of Elizabeth' was homogeneously secular, though 'they admit indeed that the quiet was precarious'.[15] The central purpose of Tillyard's argument, then, is to show how much more precarious that 'quiet' is than has been thought. Tillyard does this by focusing particularly on the continued presence and dynamism of religious systems of explanation for the world, systems which he sees as competing with secular and humanist accounts. These 'two contradictory principles co-existed in a state of high tension' (p. 2), as they had done in the Middle Ages. The Age of Elizabeth is one characterized by competing discourses; indeed this is its true glory—'The greatness of the Elizabethan age was that it contained so much of new without bursting the noble form of the old order' (p. 6). Tillyard, then, addresses himself to the question of what the Elizabethan World Picture was, specifically to show that there was not any single, definitive order.

In fact, Tillyard goes out of his way to alert the reader to the partial nature of the discourse of order he describes. In his preface, he states not only that the idea of cosmic order he charts is '*one* of the genuine ruling ideas of the age' (my emphasis), but that it is an idea of a particular class, that of 'educated Elizabethans', and that within that class 'there were many variations of opinion about the way the universe was constituted impossible to record in a short book' (p. vi). His genuine caution extends yet further, as he warns the reader (through a polite indirect address) against any simple determinism; that is, against the idea that the currency of this particular idea might be thought to determine how an Elizabethan would think:

> To hold that the other world, because so persistently advertised, had it all its own way in the experience of medieval thinkers is as simple-minded as to hold that all Germans are merciless because their leaders have ordered them to be so . . . On reflection we can only conclude that many Germans must be obstinately kind. (p. 2)

The more you insist on a certain conception of cosmic order, the more likely it is that that order is under attack, questioned, or rejected. It is a simple point bravely made; for as *The Elizabethan World Picture* was first published in 1943, it must have been tempting to indulge in some simple-minded determinism. How appealing to conjure up a past of certainty and appointed order, in which to escape from the troubles of the present; similarly, how easy to misrepresent the Germans as Nasty Nazis, killing Brave Brits. I emphasize the courage with which Tillyard dismisses this 'simple-minded' point of view, since he is often

[14] e.g. Greenblatt, 'Resonance and Wonder', in *Learning*, 168–9; Montrose, 'Professing the Renaissance', 18.

[15] E. M. W. Tillyard, *The Elizabethan World Picture* (London: Chatto & Windus, 1943), 1. Further references to this work are given after quotations in the text.

argued to have held such a point of view as a result of his country's political position.[16]

Greenblatt's three senses of 'historicism' are no more successful in describing Tillyard's historicism. To begin with the third sense, Greenblatt argues that far from indulging in a 'veneration of the past or tradition' which is marked by seeing 'high culture' as a domain free of 'specific economic or political determinants', New Historicists are concerned to give a sense of the 'psychic, social, and material resistance, a stubborn, unassimilable otherness, a sense of distance and difference. New historicism has attempted to restore this distance.'[17] So has Tillyard. Like New Historicists, he is aware that concepts and systems of understanding change. In the final paragraph of his epilogue he makes explicit the distance between his age and that of Elizabeth, and acknowledges that it is, in the last analysis, insurmountable:

> Finally it must be confessed that to us the Elizabethan is a very queer age. No one can have understood the Elizabethan age who thinks *Orchestra* a poem exceptional to it. . . . When we are confronted with the notions that . . . while angels take their visible shapes from the ether devils take theirs from the sublunary air, we cannot assume, try as we may, an Elizabethan seriousness. (p. 101)

Yet, for Tillyard, that does not make the attempt at understanding purposeless, but simply acknowledges its limitations. In this he is again like Greenblatt, and, like Greenblatt, Tillyard does not exemplify the second sense of historicism as given in *The American Heritage Dictionary*. Greenblatt, in rejecting that sense, notes how his critical practice, and that of others, was decisively shaped by his opposition to 'the Viet Nam War'. At the time of that war,

> to study the culture of sixteenth-century England did not present itself as an escape from the turmoil of the present; it seemed rather an intervention, a mode of relation. The fascination for me of the Renaissance was that it seemed to be powerfully linked to the present both analogically and causally.[18]

Tillyard, who served as an infantry officer in the First World War, would agree whole-heartedly.[19] The attempt to understand, though never ultimately successful, must be made, he felt, because the past is always part of the present. *The Elizabethan World Picture* closes, as it opens, contemplating the Second World War. Having recognized that particular 'Elizabethan seriousness' cannot be recaptured, Tillyard concludes by arguing that the Age of Elizabeth is in some ways an analogue and perhaps even a cause of what is happening:

[16] Patterson's belief that Tillyard's historicism is motivated by a 'patriotic nationalism' ('Literary History', 251), is a development of his belief that all historicisms are the expression of political values (*Negotiating the Past*, p. x).

[17] Greenblatt, 'Resonance and Wonder', in *Learning*, 169.

[18] Ibid. 169.

[19] See *The Times*, 25 May 1962, 18. Tillyard was an infantry officer in the BEF during 1915–16; from 1916 to 1918 he was in the Salonica force, on account of his knowledge of Greek. There he worked as a liaison officer with the Greek High Command. He was mentioned three times in despatches and afterwards received the OBE. He was also awarded an MC by Greece.

Yet we shall err grievously if we do not take that seriousness into account or if we imagine that the Elizabethan habit of mind is done with once and for all. If we are sincere with ourselves we must know that we have that habit in our own bosoms somewhere, queer as it may seem. And, if we reflect on that habit, we may see that (in queerness though not in viciousness) it resembles certain trends of thought in central Europe, the ignoring of which by our scientifically minded intellectuals has helped not a little to bring the world into its present conflicts and distresses. (pp. 101–2)

As this paragraph also shows in its valuation of the power of reading and of the reader's agency, Tillyard is not a simple determinist; with Greenblatt he rejects the last remaining sense of historicism—'the belief that processes are at work in history that man can do little to alter'. Indeed, Tillyard's sense of literature's power is unconvincing in its Utopian naïvety. George Steiner's dark worrying over literature's moral ineffectiveness is far more understandable, and Tillyard's hopes (and perhaps it is significant that Tillyard is writing before the end of the war and the full realization of its horrors) need to be balanced with Steiner's recurring image of the German concentration camp commandant reading Goethe.[20]

There is not the simple opposition that Greenblatt suggests between the old literary historicism of Tillyard and the literary historicism of the New Historicists. But what of the older literary historicism of the nineteenth century, the historicism of *The American Heritage Dictionary*, which Tillyard was supposed to represent? Can New Historicism at least establish an opposition with that? In theoretical terms, the answer is yes. As Lee Patterson has argued, one of literary historicism's founding influences was the nineteenth century's (particularly German) scientific positivism.[21] Scientific positivism saw all phenomena as the effects of agents of causality (such as cultural traditions, social institutions, race, physical environment) and believed that the causes of the effects could be objectively identified. These causal agents were seen to be interrelated; the assumption being, as Patterson notes, that 'each part of a culture was governed by the values that informed the whole'.[22] These values were the *Zeitgeist*.

A positivist literary historicism, then, in theory saw literature as one more phenomenon, and set out to discover the agents of causality that produced it.[23]

[20] George Steiner, *Language and Silence: Essays 1958–1966* (London: Faber, 1967). See especially the preface (13–17) and 'Night Words' (89–99). His novel, *The Portage to San Cristobal of A.H.* (London: Faber, 1981) develops the argument concerning the dehumanizing potential of language and literature, as represented in the non-rational power of 'A.H.'s' (Adolf Hitler's) eloquence.

[21] See *Negotiating the Past*, 9–18; 'Literary History', 250–1.

[22] Patterson, 'Literary History', 251.

[23] Augustus Ralli later applied the same approach to literary criticism itself. In the preface, he states that he traces the 'course of aesthetic opinion on Shakespeare from his own time to the end of 1925' in the hope that this might provide 'an epitome of the movements of the human mind through three most eventful centuries'. This thought was suggested to him by a comment in the *TLS*. Augustus Ralli, *A History of Shakespearean Criticism*, 2 vols. (London: Oxford University Press, 1932).

In theory it is critically unselfconscious, deterministic, and profoundly anti-humanist. So Taine, in the introduction to his *History of English Literature* (1864), states: 'Vice and virtue are products, like vitriol and sugar; and every complex phenomenon arises from other more simple phenomena on which it hangs.'[24] Literature is not 'a mere individual play of imagination, the isolated caprice of an excited brain' (i. 1); for 'it is a mistake to study the document, as if it were isolated' (i. 2). Instead literature is 'a fossil shell', the missing link which allows the historian to reconstruct the causal agents of the age, owing to 'the law of mutual dependence' (i. 29). Taine explains this: 'A civilisation forms a body . . . religion, philosophy, the organisation of the family, literature, the arts, [these] make up a system in which every local change induces a general change' (i. 29). To enter this system is to reach, 'a new world which is infinite, because every action which we see involves an infinite association of reasonings' (i. 7). The literary historian must discover the underlying causal agencies of this world: 'in short, he works out its psychology' (i. 7). This psychology, informing and shaping the whole, creates a totalized picture of culture as coherent, stable, and consistent.

Yet, as Frank Lentricchia has argued, Taine's practice is often self-conscious (i. 6) and also betrays a profound 'humanistic and individualistic' impulse when it actually approaches the literary text; Taine 'grants literature', Lentricchia notes, 'precisely what historicist theory . . . is not supposed to grant to any distinct cultural form; the very power which formalist theory claims for literature, the unique privilege of putting us into authentic contact with the real thing through the medium of the "great writer" and his canonical texts'.[25] This is most noticeable in Taine's discussion of Shakespeare.[26] Taine's subversion of his theory in his practice threatens the clear-cut opposition that New Historicists desire. This is particularly so since, as will be seen later, New Historicist practice, as opposed to its theory, is often reminiscent of Taine's, especially in its 'humanistic and individualistic' impulses when confronted with Shakespearian texts.

This is not to argue that there is no difference between these two historicisms, and that New Historicism is simply the pretender that wants to be king. A second generation of New Historicist critics, while retaining the focus on Tillyard, have examined his historical methodology more attentively.[27] His

[24] Hippolyte Taine, *History of English Literature*, trans. H. Van Laun, 4 vols. (London: Chatto & Windus, 1877; first pub. 1864), i. 11. Further references to this work are given after quotations in the text.

[25] Frank Lentricchia, 'Foucault's Legacy—A New Historicism?', in Veeser (ed.), *The New Historicism*, 231–42 (233).

[26] See Taine, 'Shakespeare', ii. 50–141 (61–3).

[27] Simon Palfrey argues that Greenblatt sounded the death-knell for New Historicism 'mark one', 'in an apology for his "totalizing" practice and "monolithic entities"' in the introduction to his ironically 'mark one' *Shakespearean Negotiations* (1988). See Palfrey, *Late Shakespeare: A New World of Words* (Oxford: Clarendon Press, 1997), 9. However, even after that date parts of the Tillyard trope remain. Hugh Grady's critique of Graham Holderness's *Shakespeare's History* (New York: St

fault is now seen not to be his (supposedly) nineteenth-century historicism, but his reliance on the history of ideas. This history is argued to be no longer historical enough. One of its founding assumptions was that an idea can be distilled from its context. Arthur O. Lovejoy, one of the pre-eminent practitioners of the history of ideas, makes the quasi-scientific implications of 'distilled' explicit in the first chapter of his *The Great Chain of Being*:

> The initial procedure may be said—though the parallel has its dangers—to be somewhat analogous to that of analytic chemistry. In dealing with the history of philosophical doctrines, for example, it cuts into the hard and fast individual systems and, for its own purposes, breaks them up into their component elements, into what may be called their unit-ideas.[28]

Tillyard is happy to acknowledge that his debt to Lovejoy's work 'is obvious'.[29] New Historicists are not made happy by this acknowledgement; they argue that the dangers suggested by the parallel cannot be avoided. Rebecca W. Bushnell, in her *Tragedies of Tyrants*, presents the argument cogently.[30] Her starting-point is the insistence that the history of ideas is reductive, because of its sense that an idea can exist as a unit, detached from its context, and retain a significant or even fixed meaning, as if it had been an element in a mixture. In this, she shares Tillyard's later critical position; for he too had come to feel unhappy at the reductive nature of the history of ideas. In his introduction to his *Shakespeare's Problem Plays*, first published seven years after *The Elizabethan World Picture*, Tillyard warns of the danger of 'abstracting the thought too crudely from its dramatic context', urging contemporary criticism to concentrate on the local effect of the thought or image, what he terms the 'total poetic effect'. With his customary modesty he admits that this marks a change in his critical practice: 'It may not be for me to criticize, since I have probably done the same in writing of Shakespeare's History Plays. But for my present treatment I have tried to follow the poetic and not the mere abstracted significances.'[31] Tillyard is not, as often asserted by New Historicist critics,

Martin's Press, 1985), which points to the strong American influence on Tillyard's thought and his covert modernism, is still willing to praise Holderness for his insight into the topicality of Tillyard's *The Elizabethan World Picture* and *Shakespeare's History Plays*, a topicality (and jingoism) which Grady, following Holderness, believes is alluded to only once in an aside, and whose otherwise unmentioned nature explains the longevity of Tillyard's influence. The quotations already offered show Tillyard to be much more open about the topicality of his writing than Grady allows. (Later in the same book Grady also considers the historical accuracy of Tillyard's account as a reason for the longevity of his account of the history plays.) See Hugh Grady, *The Modernist Shakespeare* (Oxford: Clarendon Press, 1991), 165.

[28] Arthur O. Lovejoy, *The Great Chain of Being: A Study of the History of an Idea* (Cambridge, Mass.: Harvard University Press, 1936), 3.

[29] Tillyard, *The Elizabethan World Picture*, 105. Grady believes the acknowledgement only to be made retrospectively. See Grady, *The Modernist Shakespeare*, 170.

[30] Rebecca W. Bushnell, *Tragedies of Tyrants* (Ithaca, NY: Cornell University Press, 1990), pp. ix–xiv.

[31] E. M. W. Tillyard, *Shakespeare's Problem Plays* (London: Chatto & Windus, 1950), 10.

unselfconscious in his critical practice; he is no more or no less so, indeed, than the majority of contemporary critics. He is more accurately seen as impressively up to date in his interdisciplinary knowledge, allying this with a willingness to reconsider his fashionable critical theories.

Bushnell, in place of the history of ideas, urges the use of the more linguistic historical methodology of the contemporary school of history that Quentin Skinner and John Pocock are taken to represent. Their methodology represents, in Skinner's words, a move from the history of ideas to 'the histories of ideologies'. Instead of the idea being distilled from its context, it is recontextualized as fully as possible within the general systems or structures of its particular domain of language. Meaning is seen to stem from the interrelationship of the idea and its ideology, and so, Skinner argues, a fuller and non-anachronistic understanding of the performative quality of the social practice or literary text is achieved.[32] Thus Bushnell in her book is not primarily interested in 'theories of resistance or nonresistance', but instead is 'trying to uncover . . . the early modern "language" or rhetoric of tyranny'.[33]

This is a significant and productive distinction; yet its effect is not as significantly distinctive of New Historicist practice as Bushnell argues. The result of the attempt to recover languages must be, as Bushnell makes clear, the coverage of a 'wide range of texts of many genres'.[34] Bushnell takes this wide coverage to be a distinctive trait of New Historicism. (As Bushnell recognizes, the trait is rather theoretical; she is critical of New Historicist critics for having created their own canon of privileged texts.) She sets this wide coverage against the presentation of a narrow range of 'so-called classic texts as representative of universal culture' which she suggests typifies the history-of-ideas, old historicist approach (p. x). Yet this wide coverage of non-classical texts has an earlier precedent. Lovejoy, in recounting the academic resistance to his methodology, singled out the particular aspect that most puzzled students of 'literature departments'; it was the history of ideas' refusal to 'stick to the masterpieces . . . or at least to these *plus* the minor classics', and its belief that, 'your minor writer may be as important as—he may often, from this point of view, be more important than—the authors of what are now regarded as masterpieces'.[35] A wide range of texts, then, was a novelty not of New Historicism, but of Lovejoy's approach.

New Historicism is only able—at the level of theory—to make coherent distinctions between itself and previous extrinsic literary historicism at the expense of alerting the reader to the many continuities it shares with 'old' historicism. As a result, New Historicists who are willing to pay attention to their enemy are led to a much greater sense of not only self-consciousness (a

[32] Quentin Skinner, *The Foundations of Modern Political Thought*, 2 vols. (Cambridge: Cambridge University Press, 1978) pp. xiii–xiv.

[33] Bushnell, *Tragedies of Tyrants*, p. xiv.

[34] Ibid. p. xiv.

[35] Lovejoy, *The Great Chain of Being*, 19–20.

rather unfocused, easy aim) but self-critique. Bushnell talks of New Historicism as if it is at a slight distance, and recognizes that 'for every gain there is a loss'.[36] The enemy keeps on threatening to become the parent.

New Historicists are unable to define themselves—as their name urges them to do—through any simple opposition to 'old' historicism. But they have other enemies, who provide the more positive sense of why they want to be historicists. New Historicists object to the anti-historical determinism of structuralist and post-structuralist formalism.[37] This allegation of determinism, already made against Tillyard and nineteenth-century historicism, is much more convincingly made against these two varieties of literary approach. Under structuralism, because the subject (whether that be a person or a word) is given meaning or produced by the dominating structures, it is hard to envisage any meaningful independence for it, to envisage any place for subject-led change. New Historicism, then, sees structuralism and post-structuralism as producing by a different route the same effects as old literary historicism. Indeed, there seems to be a conspiracy, aided by the formalism of New Criticism, either to banish history, or to erode its difference, or to banish the subject from history.[38]

In picking these more obviously modern and respected theories as enemies, and especially in picking structuralism and post-structuralism, even if only in their formalist aspects, the danger is that New Historicism will be seen as a reactionary and anti-theoretical movement, a 'backlash phenomenon' as Howard puts it.[39] This danger adds yet another spur to New Historicism's need to distinguish itself sharply from old literary historicism. Yet, as has been seen, New Historicism's attempt to do that through a declaration of its 'insistence on agency', its insistence on 'value judgements', and its insistence on a complicating historical difference is not successful.[40] For though laudable, these aims are not distinctively new; Tillyard satisfied all three.

Bar. Long liue the King.
Fran. Barnardo?

(I. I. 3)

Barnardo's response demonstrates a second way of answering the challenge of identity. Instead of giving an account of his enemies, he declares his allegiance, by invoking the authority he serves. So doing, he gives an old answer to a new demand. For Francisco's 'Nay answer me: Stand & vnfold your selfe', develops the defamiliarizing effect begun by the use of a challenge.[41] It asks that the

36 Bushnell, *Tragedies of Tyrants*, p. x.

37 See e.g. Montrose, 'Renaissance Literary Studies', 5.

38 Frank Lentricchia's *After the New Criticism* is often quoted in this context. See Montrose, 'Professing the Renaissance', p. 20.

39 Howard, 'The New Historicism', 19.

40 Greenblatt, 'Resonance and Wonder', in *Learning*, 74, 75, and 76 respectively.

41 For an argument that such estrangement of the audience is a principle upon which *Hamlet* works (for *Hamlet* as a generator of 'indefinition'), see Stephen Booth, 'On the Value of *Hamlet*', in

response should be more than an external naming, a voicing of the respondee. 'Unfold' in the sense used here, *OED*'s '2. To disclose or reveal by statement or exposition; to explain or make clear', is not usually used reflexively. Indeed, the *OED* cites Francisco's demand as the first reflexive use. (Though this does not guarantee that it was a first use, it is likely that it would be novel.[42]) Prior to this, and often subsequently, deeds previously hidden, plans made or marvels unknown were 'unfolded'. Here, this sense of revealing the unknown (which Francisco hopes will turn out to be a disclosing of the known) is used of revealing identity; Shakespeare is shifting the use of a word from one domain to another. This employment of new vocabularies to talk about identity is evidence of what New Historicists would term 'negotiation'. Here Barnardo responds to Francisco's demand with an old-fashioned declaration, an explanation not of himself, but of his allegiance. For the second time in three lines, a defamiliarized challenge of identity is not directly answered.

New Historicism in its standard self-definition similarly follows up its account of its enemies with an account of its friends. These have, according to New Historicists, created a 'new philosophy [which] calls all in doubt'.[43] Many of these friends are practitioners of the French New Philosophy.[44] The most prominent is Michel Foucault, and New Historicism everywhere cites his *bon mots*. Howard again offers an example of this in her description of New Historicism. After she has rejected 'old' historicism, she considers the question of 'how is a contemporary historical criticism to proceed?' She founds her answer on 'one of Michel Foucault's central contributions to contemporary historical studies'.[45] She uses Foucault, then, as her authority; put another way, she is claiming Foucault not only as a friend, but as a parent, the defining source of the theory that determines aspects of her critical practice. Greenblatt, at the beginning of 'Towards a Poetics of Culture' (1987), puts forth a similar view: 'Certainly, the presence of Michel Foucault on the Berkeley campus for extended visits during the last five or six years of his life, and more generally the influence in America of European (and especially French) anthropological and social theorists, has helped to shape my own literary practice.'[46]

Norman Rabkin (ed.), *Reinterpretations of Elizabethan Drama* (New York and London: Columbia University Press, 1969), 137–76.

[42] This sense of novel usage is confirmed by a search of *English Verse Drama: The Full-Text Database* (Cambridge: Chadwyck-Healey, 1995; first release). Of the six plays that contain 'unfold' before *Hamlet*, in none is the verb used reflexively. The closest sense is *Jack Straw*'s 'vnfold my minde' (Act 4). This situation is repeated in plays after *Hamlet* and up to 1630. *English Verse Drama*, however, does not contain all verse drama.

[43] The quotation is from John Donne's 'The First Anniversary' in *An Anatomy of the World* (1611), l. 205, in *John Donne: The Complete English Poems*, ed. A. J. Smith (Harmondsworth: Penguin, 1971).

[44] For a summary discussion see Richard Wilson, 'Introduction: Historicising New Historicism', in Richard Wilson and Richard Dutton (eds.), *New Historicism and Renaissance Drama* (London: Longman, 1992), 1–18 (1–4).

[45] Both Howard, 'The New Historicism', 22.

[46] Greenblatt, 'Towards a Poetics of Culture', in *Learning*, 146–7.

Yet Foucault's 'central contribution' does not support this attempt at self-definition. In Howard's words, this contribution was his recognition of, and struggle against, 'the tendency to project the present into the past and so to construct narratives of continuity'.[47] But this awareness that investigators bring their own particular combination of the assumptions and interests of their time to bear on the objects they are studying is not a new perception to Foucault.[48] Montaigne, in his 'On Cannibals', works towards similar conclusions in his reflections on South American natives (the phrase 'narratives of continuity' eludes him). From the opening of the essay, Montaigne recognizes that cultures typically interpret other cultures through their own assumptions, and that language plays an instrumental role in such (mis-)interpretations. Montaigne illustrates this point by recalling the Greek King Pyrrhus' arrival in Italy, and Pyrrhus' surprised recognition that these *barbaroi* (as they were called in Ancient Greek) were not, as the word suggested, barbarians.

Montaigne does have more confidence than Foucault in the power of reason; Pyrrhus was able to realize his error. However, as Montaigne goes on to note, all knowledge, whether or not the product of reason, may be gross error; no European, he points out, knew of 'so infinite and vast a country' as South America until his lifetime. As Montaigne puts it, 'We embrace all, but we fasten nothing but wind.'[49] (Montaigne, indeed, believes the new continent to have East India on its west side.) His sense of the difficulty of interpretation, of coming to an accurate, impartial knowledge of the natives, increases towards the end of the essay, as Montaigne realizes that they are no longer as they were before the arrival of Europeans. The natives' cultures, from the moment of contact, have been changing—and as Montaigne sees it, have begun to be destroyed; 'their ruin shall proceed from this commerce, which I imagine is already well advanced'.[50] Montaigne, then, is well aware that the act of interpretation affects what is interpreted, as is he that the act of interpretation depends on one's point of view: Montaigne notes how different the natives' impressions of the Frenchmen are from the Frenchmen's impressions of the natives, and offers as some guarantee of the relative objectivity of his account the lack of intelligence of the man who described the native's culture to him. Intelligent observers, Montaigne argues, tend to shape what they see to fit their interpretation.[51]

47 Howard, 'The New Historicism', 22.

48 Many examples could be found; Lee Patterson, in arguing for the inescapability of subjectivity, chooses as example something Heidegger 'long ago said, in a classic statement': 'If, when one is engaged in a particular kind of interpretation, in the sense of exact textual interpretation, one likes to appeal to what "stands there," then one finds that what "stands there" is in the first instance nothing other than the obvious undiscussed assumption of the person who does the interpreting' (Martin Heidegger, *Being and Time*, trans. John Macquarrie and Edward Robinson (New York: Harper, 1962), 191–2. Quoted in Patterson, *Negotiating the Past*, 43).

49 Michael Montaigne, *The Essays of Montaigne*, trans. John Florio, 3rd edn., 3 vols. (London: David Nutt, 1892; first pub. 1632), i. 218 (Ch. 30).

50 Ibid. i. 231.

51 This may be a sophisticated joke on Montaigne's part. If, as has been suggested, the witness

Another founding contribution attributed to Foucault is his conception of power; Richard Wilson in his history of New Historicism declares Foucault's concept of power to be the movement's 'greatest single intellectual stimulus'.[52] Quite what Foucault's definition of power is has been, outside literary-critical circles, the source of controversy.[53] Within New Historicist circles, Foucault's conception of power is one that sees it not just as a palpable force to be wielded, usually from the apex of a society; but rather as present everywhere, the result of discourses which are themselves constitutive of, and constituted by, institutions. Greenblatt in his *Renaissance Self-Fashioning* aims to:

achieve a concrete apprehension of the consequences for human expression—for the 'I'—of a specific form of power, power at once localized in particular institutions—the court, the church, the colonial administration, the patriarchal family—and diffused in ideological structures of meaning, characteristic modes of expression, recurrent narrative patterns.[54]

Power acts in a capillary fashion, working everywhere, from the lowest level up, and may be gathered into one place by an institution. As Greenblatt's quotation suggests, power for Foucault (the Foucault of *The Order of Things* especially) was bound up with discourses. For discourses, as the result of historically specific social practices and conditions, give rise to epistemological systems—disciplines such as medicine. It is within these disciplines that subject-persons are able to be known, and so power gained over them. But at the same time, the subject-persons are the product of the disciplines acting upon them. Thus sexual desires, to take a famous example of Foucault's, are not latent to the subject-person, and so repressed by society, but are created by the human sciences as their means of attaining knowledge of and power over the subject-persons. The body politic creates the 'private' body; Foucault describes the body politic, one of the principle subjects within *Discipline and Punish*, as:

a set of material elements and techniques that serve as weapons, relays, communication routes and supports for the power and knowledge relations that invest human bodies and subjugate them by turning them into objects of knowledge.[55]

mentioned by Montaigne did not in fact exist; and if, as David Quint argues, Montaigne quite deliberately uses the native culture as an image of contemporary French culture, particularly in its too thoroughgoing stoicism; then Montaigne would here, as elsewhere, be doing just what he is describing. See David Quint, *Montaigne and the Quality of Mercy: Ethical and Political Themes in the Essais* (Princeton: Princeton University Press, 1998), ch. 3.

[52] In Wilson and Dutton (eds.), *New Historicism and Renaissance Drama*, 83.

[53] For an overview of this controversy see Barry Smart, *Michel Foucault* (London: Routledge, 1985), ch. 4.

[54] Greenblatt, *Renaissance Self-Fashioning*, 9.

[55] Michel Foucault, *Discipline and Punish: The Birth of the Prison*, trans. Alan Sheriden (Penguin: Harmondsworth, 1991; first pub. as *Surveiller et punir: Naissance de la prison* by Editions Gallimard, 1975), 28.

This concept of power takes power and the desire for power to be one of the fundamental human experiences. It owes much to Nietzsche, and Foucault is happy to acknowledge his indebtedness, believing Nietzsche to have recognized a similar relationship between power and knowledge.[56] In New Historicists' use of it, it is a rather Machiavellian concept; history is seen as an endless struggle for power.

This consequence of this model of power for New Historicist criticism has been profound. The playing-out on stage of subversive actions in Renaissance drama, far from being a dangerous liberation, is now seen—in a manner akin to sexual desires—as created by governing institutions as a means to attain knowledge and power over the subject-person. In New Historicist terminology, this process is termed 'containment'. So, for example, carnival, in its Bakhtinian sense, is now not seen as the liberating spirit of art contending with the austerities of Lent (the dominant culture), but rather carnival is one of the tools through which Lent establishes its dominance. Carnival becomes a form of psychologist's couch, on which the disruptive elements of culture are allowed to express themselves before submitting to an authority which can now claim even greater knowledge of, and so power over, them. There is an irony here. As may have been recognized, this model of power has a tendency to a deterministic view of history, and so sits uneasily with the first of New Historicism's three principles, as defined by Greenblatt: the refusal to believe 'that processes are at work in history that man can do little to alter'. This contradiction is usually resolved in favour of determinism, particularly in Greenblatt's work, as he admits: 'new historicism', he argues, 'does not posit historical processes as unalterable and inexorable, but it does tend to discover limits or constraints upon individual intervention'.[57] Or, as he puts it in another essay, adapting a comment of Kafka's, 'There is subversion, no end of subversion, only not for us.'[58]

This model of power, however, is not uniquely Foucault's, and he did not claim it to be. Foucault acknowledged that his rejection of a repressive model of power had been anticipated by the Frankfurt School of sociology's theory of 'repressive tolerance' and, in particular, the work of Herbert Marcuse.[59] This was of little account to Foucault, as he argued that origins were illusory. As Wilson notes in his history of New Historicism: 'The message Foucault brought to America was that there is no founding moment, because every utterance or

[56] See Michel Foucault, 'Nietzsche, Genealogy, History', in *The Foucault Reader*, ed. Paul Rabinow (Harmondsworth: Penguin, 1991; first pub. New York: Random House, 1984), 76–100. Simon During gives a more sophisticated account of the influence of Heidegger's appropriation of Nietzsche on Foucault. See Simon During, *Foucault and Literature: Towards a Genealogy of Writing* (London: Routledge, 1992), 104.

[57] Greenblatt, *Learning*, 164.

[58] Greenblatt, 'Invisible Bullets' in *Shakespearean Negotiations*, 39.

[59] Noted in Wilson, 'Introduction', 4. The work of Marcuse's mentioned is *One Dimensional Man* (Boston: Beacon Press, 1964).

event has to be understood as part of something else.'[60] Wilson is aware of the irony that this argument was itself seen as originating from Foucault, and used to construct Foucault's founding, paternal authority.

If Foucault is not (and would not claim to be) the originating source of the theoretical arguments by which New Historicism distinguished its critical practice, why do New Historicists constantly invoke him as if he were? As with their account of Tillyard, the answer lies in the use to which New Historicists put Foucault's name. For 'Michel Foucault!' is in many ways, for New Historicists, a modernization of Barnardo's 'Long live the King!' 'Michel Foucault!' is a watchword, the linguistic right of entry to a particular domain of argument. Such a watchword neatly complements the Tillyard trope; 'Tillyard' banishes one critical past, while 'Michel Foucault!' summons up another in its place.

While New Historicists' paternity suits are not convincing, neither are their other critical friendships, which show a decided lack of constancy in their affections. Take, for example, their relation to structuralist theory. New Historicists, as mentioned above, hold the formalist and deterministic tendencies of literary structuralism as important enemies. Yet at the same time, they take as one of their central truths the founding argument from which those formalistic and deterministic tendencies arise.[61] This is the literary structuralist argument that language constructs reality, with the result that everything may be considered discourse. This is Howard's version of the argument: 'everything from maternal "instinct" to conceptions of the self are now seen to be the products of specific discourses and social processes'.[62]

Leaving aside, at present, the world of debate in Howard's 'are now seen', it is clear that such a belief has little or no room for agency. If everything is 'product', how can any person be 'producer'? Literary structuralism follows this through, logically, to its deterministic conclusions, offering an anti-historical picture of timeless structures dominating their systems. New Historicists do not: on the one hand they insist that they reject determinism (and dislike literary structuralism); on the other they insist that everything may be considered discourse (and praise literary structuralism). It is all a little confusing, and no attempt at reconciliation is made; with a remarkable show of *fiat*, New Historicists insist on their right to use some aspects of a theory and dismiss other connected aspects which might complicate or resist their conclusions.

Greenblatt tells a story of how his teaching of 'Marxist Aesthetics' came to an end when,

[60] Wilson, 'Introduction', 2.

[61] This contradiction is explored at greater length by Howard Felperin, '"Cultural Poetics" versus "Cultural Materialism": The Two New Historicisms in Renaissance Studies', in his *The Uses of the Canon*, 142–69.

[62] Howard, 'The New Historicism', 20.

Someone finally got up and screamed out in class "You're either a Bolshevik or a Menshevik—make up your fucking mind," and then slammed the door. . . . I thought about it afterwards and realized that I wasn't sure whether I was a Menshevik, but I certainly wasn't a Bolshevik. After that I started to teach courses with names like "Cultural Poetics".[63]

Greenblatt's story is a humorous one, and generous in its acknowledgement of his student's charge. His refusal to align himself with a single, named Marxism is understandable; such an approach may be a strength in literary criticism, for literature is often far more complex and multi-faceted than the theory that is used to explicate it. Theories typically illuminate aspects of a text. Here, however, the sense of ease is a little too pronounced. The admission of contradictoriness stands in place of any attempt to puzzle further, to rectify or consider whether there is anything to change. Instead, Greenblatt begins to teach a different course with a new name. Here, as occasionally elsewhere in New Historicist writing, there is the sense that the New Historicist theory, for all its proclaimed theoretical sophistication, is simply that New Historicists need no coherent theory. As Greenblatt says, 'One of the peculiar characteristics of the "new historicism" in literary studies is precisely how unresolved and in some ways disingenuous it has been—I have been—about the relation to literary theory.'[64]

In employing such selectivity, New Historicists treat their friends badly. Indeed, 'friends' might seem too strong a word; New Historicists, in the imperialism of their choices, seem to treat their friends rather like servants. New Historicists (and Cultural Materialists) themselves tend to describe this imperialism as an exciting cross-disciplinary eclecticism.[65] Whichever term is preferred, the tendency generates the unwanted ironies that are often found in New Historicist criticism, as it leads New Historicist critics to misrepresent their friends, and—in breaking disciplinary boundaries—to enter fields in which their competence is limited. One last result of this is that New Historicists choose the wrong friends. Foucault, at first sight, would seem an obviously well-chosen and relevant friend. Though it is difficult to categorize Foucault's subject area, he is clearly involved in a particularly literary form of history.[66] His arguments, however, were aimed at explaining French histories (such as that of rationality and knowledge, and their interrelationship with power). How close, then, was seventeenth- or eighteenth-century France to England? Are the two cultures equivalents, as the New Historicist use of Foucault suggests?

[63] Greenblatt, *Learning*, 147.

[64] Ibid. 146.

[65] See Jonathan Dollimore, 'Critical Developments: Cultural Materialism, Feminism and Gender Critique, and New Historicism', in Stanley Wells (ed.), *Shakespeare: A Bibliographical Guide* new edn. (Oxford: Oxford University Press, 1990), 405–28 (406–7).

[66] In fact, Foucault, like New Historicism, had difficulty in distinguishing his history from the history of ideas. He also was led to invent his own title, that of 'Professor of the History of Systems of Thought'. See Smart, *Michel Foucault*, 13.

One way of producing evidence of the two cultures' similarity would be to look at the impact of Foucault's arguments on the social historians of this period of English history. David Cressy, a historian himself, has examined Foucault's influence on the most well-known of these—Keith Thomas, Peter Laslett, Jim Sharpe, and Keith Wrightson. He not only finds almost no evidence of influence, but also the 'fundamental objection . . . that [Foucault] is unhistorical'.[67] Such an objection, if true, is potentially devastating to New Historicists, in the light of their use of Foucault as the foundation of their historical practice in relation to *English* history. It is, in fact, shocking, and reveals another quality of their declarations of allegiance; New Historicists tend to establish the authority invoked as authoritative by their own invocation. Their purpose is to be unquestioned. 'Long live the King!'—to answer 'why?' or 'who?' to such a declaration is to be treasonous. And treason threatens the state, in this case, the New Historicist kingdom. Cressy dares to enlarge on why Foucault is unhistorical:

> First it is by no means certain that Foucault's account of power, the body, and the asylum is correct, even if it is persuasive, even for revolutionary France. Second, to argue from France to England, and from the 1780s to the 1610s is an exercise in anachronism and dislocation.[68]

Not only is Foucault not relevant to the historical period and place of Shakespeare's plays, but he may not really be relevant even to the history of his own country. Once again, New Historicism is advancing an authority which turns out not to be very authoritative.

If the New Historicists' king has no historical clothes, why have they not noticed? Perhaps New Historicism has, in fact, chosen its friends not wisely but too well. For the surprisingly unhistorical nature of Foucault suits New Historicist practice. Greenblatt moves from an analysis of the trial of Martin Guerre (or rather Arnaud du Tilh as Martin Guerre), a Frenchman who was 14 in 1538, to a consideration of the construction of identity in the Renaissance, and in the English Renaissance drama.[69] Greenblatt states his awareness of the complex and distinct histories of identity; and yet he moves from Guerre's trial in a French legal system to English dramatic and historical persons with little sense of the important distinctions between the various specific and complex, legal and dramatic discourses.[70] Such an undiscriminating approach is in turn particularly unsuitable for interpreting Shakespearian texts, where matters of identity and its relation to culture are discussed precisely and with complex

[67] David Cressy, 'Foucault, Stone, Shakespeare and Social History', in *ELR* 21 (1991), 121–33 (124).

[68] Ibid. 125.

[69] Greenblatt, 'Psychoanalysis and Renaissance Culture', in *Learning*, 131–45.

[70] Second-generation New Historicist criticism has again moved to remedy this imprecision. See Elizabeth Hanson, *Discovering the Subject in Renaissance England* (Cambridge: Cambridge University Press, 1998).

distinctions. For in Shakespeare's plays there is a significant difference between a Frenchman and an Englishman.

The New Historicists attempt at self-definition through a declaration of allegiance is no more successful than their attempt at self-definition through an account of their enemy. Their declaration of allegiance, like Barnardo's, is more useful to them than it is descriptive of them. It does not 'unfold' them. Francisco's uncertain reply is understandable. For a second time, their answer to the challenge of identity seems unsatisfactory.

Bar. He.
(1. 1. 3)

New Historicists have a third way of attempting coherently to identify themselves; with Barnardo, they simply assert their identity.[71] In place of accounts of their enemies or authorities, there is a declaration of their own beliefs, built up from their founding assumptions, the aims arising from those assumptions, and the expected consequent effects of those assumptions and aims—a changing of the guard. Clearly, these beliefs will draw on the positions of their friends, some of which have been described, but this section will, with one exception, simply follow the New Historicist declaration of identity, leaving aside questions concerning that identity's relationship to the tangled nexus of friends and enemies. A discussion of the actual (and often less positive) effects of New Historicist beliefs will follow in the next chapter, where the account of English Renaissance literature produced by New Historicists will be examined.

Before tracing New Historicists' assertion of their identity, a caveat is needed. No one single critical method will be found that can be labelled New Historicist, and it would be foolish to criticize New Historicists for this. A movement need not be homogeneous; New Historicism contains very many and different critics and critical approaches. It is unlikely that any one New Historicist will have all the friends and enemies that I have described above. However, most of the most influential, I believe, will recognizably fit within my description, even if they emphasize one relation and make light of another. To be considered a single movement, New Historicist criticism must yield beliefs which, though various, can be seen to be of a related nature and which constitute what is a recognizably new paradigm for critical writing.

Howard is also representative of this third method of self-definition. Having employed the 'Tillyard trope' in the first part of her article, she begins the second part by describing what New Historicism's founding assumption must be: 'In order to understand what does, or might, constitute the core of a truly new historical criticism one must begin, I believe, with the basic issue of what

[71] This bears out Lee Patterson's central argument that there can be no theoretical justification of historicism, and that the 'various forms of resolution at which historicist negotiations arrive' are governed 'by values and commitments that are in the last analysis political'. Patterson, *Negotiating the Past*, p. x.

one assumes to be the nature of man.'[72] Such an 'I believe' is honest and direct, and the choice of basic issue understandable. 'The nature of man' is a logical place to start, because what man's nature is thought to be determines the nature of the historical criticism that is practised. The Christian historiography of the Middle Ages, for example, tended to see history as the manifestation of God's purposes, and had less interest in particular persons, these tending simply to be present as examples of the workings of God's plan. The humanist historiography of the Renaissance began to focus on particular persons, stressing their ability to shape their city- and later their nation-states, and so to determine history. Man was seen to be able to accomplish more through his own nature.[73] Traditional Marxist historiography reversed this trend, seeing history (that is the living of it) as the product of economic forces that shape society and so the person. Man was again present as an example, not this time of God's purpose, but of the base structures of the state. Such an account of these historiographies is oversimple, but illustrates the logic of Howard's and the New Historicist position, as it shows the subject-person varying with the subject-discipline. Clearly, the linkage between the two kinds of subject is circular; one produces the other and is in turn produced by it. From this circularity comes much of the relationship's complexity and potential to generate argument.

What also becomes clear from this circularity, of which Howard is aware, is that her argument of a founding assumption is, precisely considered, a false straightening. One cannot decide the nature of man and then build a critical theory upon that, no more than a theory can be chosen which determines the answer to the question concerning the nature of man. The one produces the other, as before. There is nothing wrong with such straightenings; they are necessary to produce a clarity of argument. But it should be recognized that Howard's logic is an argumentative logic; and that her argument would look a lot less persuasive and attractive if the answer to the basic issue was seen to be a product of New Historicists' theoretical assumptions. Howard's basic issue, in fact, might be put another way, as a question. The answer to that question is what will, as she says, 'constitute the core of a truly new historical criticism'. It will be the first line of this new critical drama. And that question is 'Who's there?' This New Historicist 'Who's there?', like Barnardo's, represents a defamiliarization of the everyday use of the question; New Historicists are interested in the nature of the responding subject—'the nature of man' in Howard's words.

New Historicists give an Odysseus-like answer to this question: they respond 'nobody' or, less frequently, 'everything'. They do not usually put it so directly; Howard, for example, states that New Historicists share 'the notion that

[72] Howard, 'The New Historicism', 20.

[73] For a discussion of these two historiographies, see Irving Ribner, *The English History Play in the Age of Shakespeare* (Princeton: Princeton University Press, 1957), esp. ch. 1.

man is a construct, not an essence'.[74] While Greenblatt states: 'the very idea of a "defining human essence" is precisely what critics like me find vacuous and untenable'.[75] 'Construct', to unpack Howard's answer first, has the simple and radical sense of 'constructed'. Man's nature is seen as the product of forces external to him, and in New Historicist usage 'product' is an acceptable synonym for construct. So, as has been seen, Howard asserts that 'everything from maternal "instinct" to conceptions of the self are now seen to be the products of specific discourses and social processes'.[76] When someone comes knocking on the door, the answer to 'Who's there?' is 'a social product', or (as New Historicists believe that all culture is interconnected) 'everything', but no single body or person, no individual. Greenblatt has a similar sense of the caller's identity. In the introduction to *Renaissance Self-Fashioning* he lists the ten 'governing conditions' of the creation of identity. He then sums these up, in what is probably the most famous New Historicist definition of identity:

> We may say that self-fashioning occurs at the point of encounter between an authority and an alien, that what is produced in this encounter partakes of both the authority and the alien that is marked for attack, and hence that any achieved identity always contains within itself the signs of its own subversion or loss.[77]

The person is once again product, this time of 'an authority and an alien'. There is no sense of agency, of self-driven self-fashioning. 'Nobody' or 'everything' is again the answer.

Before examining the aims this belief gives rise to within New Historicist critical practice, Howard's 'are now seen to be' needs to be considered—this was the phrase which was previously said to contain a world of debate. Howard suggests, with the phrase, that the theory which she proposes is uncontentious. The theory was, as has been said, the literary structuralist argument that language constructs thought. (The theory is also of prime importance within literary forms of deconstruction, as epitomized by the reading of Derrida's 'il n'y a pas de hors-texte' as an ontological statement.[78]) The theory is, in fact, not only contentious but largely discredited, outside departments of literature. Literary structuralism drew for this theory on the structuralist[79] debate

74 Howard, 'The New Historicism', 23.

75 Greenblatt, 'Resonance and Wonder', in *Learning*, 165.

76 Howard, 'The New Historicism', 20.

77 Greenblatt, *Renaissance Self-Fashioning*, 9.

78 Jacques Derrida, *Of Grammatology*, trans. Gayatri Chakravorty Spivak (Baltimore: Johns Hopkins University Press, 1974; first pub. as *De la grammatologie*, Paris, 1967), 158. For the importance of Saussure see 'The Outside ~~Is~~ the Inside', 44–65. As Richard Waswo has pointed out, the quotation is more convincingly read as a methodological statement (with which New Critics might agree). See Richard Waswo, 'How To Be (or Not to Be) a Cultural Materialist', *The European English Messenger*, 6 (1997), 59–67 (62).

79 Assigning writers on cognitive development to schools—behaviourist, nativist, structuralist/constructivist—is an approximate exercise, and one with results which the writers themselves might contest. In the discussion that follows, I follow the attributions of Howard Gardner, in his *The Quest for Mind: Piaget, Lévi-Strauss and the Structuralist Movement* (London: Quartet, 1976).

concerning cognitive development. This debate developed between and from the positions of Claude Lévi-Strauss (1908–) on the one hand and Jean Piaget (1896–1980) on the other. Howard Gardner, in his *The Quest for Mind* (1976) analyses the positions of these two theorists. The role played by language in thought, far from being uncontentious, Gardner describes as 'perhaps the most controversial' area of a 'heated debate' over cognitive development.[80] Piaget's position was, simply put, that 'language makes at best only a small contribution to thought', while Lévi-Strauss, himself relying heavily on the work of structural linguists, 'attributes to language a determining role in thought'.[81]

Howard clearly prefers the position of Lévi-Strauss. Yet Lévi-Strauss does not hold that language determines thought, just that it has 'a determining role'; his position is, as Gardner puts it, 'at most, a diluted version of the Whorf–Sapir hypothesis, which would confer upon the actual categories of the language a determining role in the thought processes of individual speakers.'[82] Howard's 'are now seen' is thus presenting a contested theory ('the Whorf–Sapir hypothesis') as the consensus of structuralist accounts of cognition.[83] Indeed, she is in fact trying to present the strong version of that theory, for which it is very hard now to find any adherents. Gardner, whose book seeks to argue that a substantial degree of agreement exists between the approaches of these two men, describes a very different area of consensus in the structuralist account of cognition: 'Each of these scholars focuses particularly on Man, seeing him as a constructive organism, with generative capacities.'[84] Man, then, is a 'construct' for both Piaget and Lévi-Strauss, but he is not a constructed *product*. Rather he is a constructor, a *producer* of himself from his perception of what lies around him. For example, for Piaget, cognitive development occurs as the result of the individual's actions on the society around him or her. Personal identity is predominantly learnt: Piaget's picture of a child is of 'a seeking, exploring individual' who comes to understand his society by observing the effects of his actions upon it.[85] In effect, the child in his actions is constantly creating and testing his or her models of reality. Mental development comes as simple models (or concepts) are integrated to produce a more sophisticated understanding of both himself or herself and the surrounding world.[86] Such a degree of agency, nearly autonomy, for the 'I' has tended to be qualified by contemporary 'social constructivists', a group whose name

[80] Gardner, *The Quest for Mind*, 177. [81] Ibid. 178, 179. [82] Ibid. 181.

[83] Indeed, if there is any consensus, which for Gardner is devoutly to be wished, it probably lies in the fact that both Piaget and Lévi-Strauss are 'really interested in a level beneath the language that is spoken or heard—in the actions or precepts reflected in language' (181).

[84] Ibid. 242. [85] Ibid. 192.

[86] Piaget argued that this development took place in four stages: the sensorimotor stage (up to 2 years old), the preoperational stage (from 2 to 6 or 7 years old), the concrete operational stage (from 7 to 11 or 12 years old), and the formal operations stage (from 12 years onwards). For this reason he is technically categorized as a genetic epistemologist, though most people talk of him as a psychologist.

makes clear their greater recognition of the importance of society on the person's cognitive development.

Structuralist writing on cognition does, then, share Howard's belief that man is primarily a construct as opposed to an essence.[87] Man is historically and contextually various, not always the same. Yet this does not necessarily make him a product, constructed by something apart from himself. Instead he may be 'constructive', possessing considerable agency, with which he builds himself. Howard's, and New Historicists', adoption of the strong Whorfean (as it is now known) argument has led them to see the question of the nature of man in terms of a binary opposition; either man is an essence and has agency, or he is a construct and does not. This opposition constantly undermines New Historicists' declarations of their belief in agency; they may believe in it, but they will never, because they can never, find it—hence Greenblatt's appropriation of Kafka: 'There is subversion, no end of subversion, only not for us.' There is no need for this dilemma. The option that man is a construct and has agency is both intellectually coherent and persuasive. In Part III this option will be explored further, as part of the process of developing an intellectually coherent literary historicism.[88]

Returning to 'Who's there?' and the New Historicist answer of 'nobody' or 'everything', how does this answer affect the movement's critical aims? Within the text, dramatic persons become a kind of theatrical stage, on which are played out the various discourses that have produced them. As opposed to being of interest for themselves, they become a place in which to trace out the dynamics of their society; 'everything' can be seen through or in them. The text itself loses any sense of autonomy or unity. The New Critics' tendency to see texts as islands, as artistic objects or icons capable of being understood separately from their society, is reversed; instead a text gains its meaning through its relation to other social discourses and social practices. For this reason, New Historicists reject the notion of a canon of literary texts, intending instead to resite the canonical literary text among multiple forms of writing, and in relation to social practices and institutions.[89] The aim is to study as wide a variety of texts as is reasonable.

A similar loss of any sense of autonomous agency or boundedness is experienced by the author, who is seen as the mouthpiece of language, and not the creator of the text. Yet the text is not seen simply as a passive product, for it possesses social agency. For, as the literary text must be one of the discursive

[87] Though Piaget's sense of the importance of the biological structure of the brain, or a nativist's, Chomsky's for instance, belief in innate ideas (that is that man comes preprogrammed with hypotheses about what his world will be like) show a certain degree of essentialism.

[88] Basically, such a Piagetian position insists on a divide between language and reality, and so ruptures the circularity that the Whorfean hypothesis builds into many aspects of New Historicist argument; such circularity, for instance, as is seen in the inescapability of power and the inability to resist oppression.

[89] Montrose, in 'Professing the Renaissance', presents this argument well.

practices that construct man, it is socially productive and powerful. New Historicists are concerned with literature both as a social product and as socially productive. In this sense literature is a part of history, a shaping force within it, and this view confirms the New Historicist repudiation of the opposition between real, objective history and unreal, subjective literature. Instead New Historicists aim to explore the ways in which literature creates subjects and their society, and so takes part in history. Thus, although New Historicism believes in causality (otherwise it would not be a historicism), it does not believe in a hard determinism, where an external causal agent can be seen to produce a literary effect. Partly this is because the categories of internal and external have broken down, partly because there are no longer seen to be any monolithic causal agents, as there is no monolithic power wielded from the 'top' of society. Moreover, as the New Historicist critic is also a construct, a product of the present, that present must determine the view of the past. History is not a discovery of facts, but a product of someone's reading; New Historicists repudiate any sense of historical objectivity. Instead of there being a single history of, say, the subject-person, New Historicism expects to find and write various histories, reflecting differing points of view on the past. Two books are often cited as offering models for this approach: Edward Said's *Orientalism* (1978), which argues that the West's view of the East is a textual construct made up from fragments of quotations, and Tvetzvan Todorov's *The Conquest of America* (1982) which sees the conflict between the Spanish and the natives of Central America as a battle of interpretations.[90] This new understanding of the relationship of history and literary texts has been encapsulated by Montrose; New Historicism, in his phrase, insists on 'the Historicity of Texts and the Textuality of History'.[91] It is a widely quoted slogan.[92] In place of objectivity, a New Historicist critic's responsibility is to recognize and elucidate his or her biases as clearly as possible. Theoretical and political self-consciousness becomes highly valued. As New Historicist critics tend to be dissatisfied with their culture and discipline, this self-consciousness frequently becomes a despairing acknowledgement that the critic is part of the culture and discipline that is disliked; the critic is, him- or herself, part of the problem. Such a refrain is New Historicism's *mea culpa*.

The central movement of New Historicist criticism, then, the aim and consequence of their beliefs, is to diffuse the 'I'—whether that is the 'I' of dramatic person, text, critic, reader, or author. 'Decentring' is the name given to this movement and, in its decentring, New Historicists see themselves as

[90] Edward Said, *Orientalism* (Harmondsworth: Penguin, 1985; first pub. New York: Pantheon, 1978). Tzvetan Todorov, *The Conquest of America: The Question of the Other*, trans. Richard Howard (New York: Harper Collins, 1984). Said and Todorov are quoted in Wilson, 'Introduction', 5; Todorov in Howard, 'The New Historicism', 22.

[91] Montrose, 'Renaissance Literary Studies', 8.

[92] See, for instance, Greenblatt, 'Resonance and Wonder', in *Learning*, 170.

radically and innovatively anti-humanist.[93] As part of that decentring, humanist literary critics need to be 'decentred' from the critical kingdom, and in their place New Historicists enthroned. New Historicists ask 'Who's there?' as the opening line in what they hope will be a changing of the academic guard. In this, they are modest—compared to Cultural Materialists. This modesty is another consequence of their founding belief in man being a produced construct; the terminology drawn on to express this aspect of their declaration of identity is that of revised Marxism.

Central to New Historicists' belief in the purpose and abilities of their criticism is Althusser's definition of ideology, as given in his 'Ideology and Ideological State Apparatuses'.[94] The older, traditional sense of ideology conceived it to be a consciously held set of political beliefs, a false or dream consciousness, wielded by one group to dominate another. (Marx had used this sense, although, Althusser argues, it is un-Marxist.[95]) In its Althusserian sense, ideology is taken to be the way in which people interpret their relation to society (pp.160–5). Since this interpretation is carried out through social practices and social discourses, it is beyond the person's control. Ideology is not consciously held, and the notion of agency dissolves. Indeed, it is rather that ideology interprets people; in Althusser's phrase, 'Ideology Interpellates Individuals as Subjects' (p. 160). This needs explanation.

Althusser uses 'individual' to signify the person prior to his or her immersion in ideology. (In New Historicist debate the term 'individual' is typically used as the label for the essentialist notion of man.) For Althusser, the immersion in ideology makes the individual into a subject, in the sense of a subjected-person. However, this immersion, as the social discourses and practices exist before the individual, occurs before birth: so in fact, '*individuals are always-already subjects*' (p. 163). However, as with the relationship between the subject-person and subject-discipline, and as with the relationship between literature and history, the relationship between Althusser's individual and subject is circular; both are fundamental to each other. For the subject is both ideology's destination and its creation ideology's purpose, yet it is also the category through which ideology exists:

> There is no ideology except by the subject and for subjects. Meaning, there is no ideology except for concrete subjects, and this destination for ideology is only made possible by the subject: meaning, *by the category of the subject* and its functioning.

93 'Most necessary 'tis, that we forget', as the Player King says (3. 2. 183). Such anti-humanism, in fact, is one of New Historicism's chief points of continuity with 19th-c. historicism. See Lentricchia, 'Foucault's Legacy'; Patterson, *Negotiating the Past*, chs. 1 and 2. Lee Patterson also makes clear the ways in which the abandonment of categories such as intention and literature effectively preclude historicist criticism. See particularly pp. 57–74.

94 Louis Althusser, 'Ideology and Ideological State Apparatuses', in *Lenin and Philosophy and Other Essays*, trans. Ben Brewster (London: NLB, 1971), 121–73. Further references to this article are given after quotations in the text.

95 Althusser is here referring to Marx's theory of ideology as given in *The German Ideology* (149).

> By this I mean that, even if it only appears under this name (the subject) with the rise of bourgeois ideology, above all with the rise of legal ideology, the category of the subject (which may function under other names: e.g., as the soul in Plato, as God, etc.) is the constitutive category of all ideology. (p. 160)

For Althusser, then, ideology is inescapable: 'man is an ideological animal by nature' (p. 160). His conception of ideology sits well with other New Historicist beliefs, particularly their Foucauldian conception of power. Moreover, for Althusser, the question of 'Who's there?' becomes significant in a new way. It is not simply that he, like New Historicism, would answer 'nobody' or 'everything', with the caveat, 'that is to say, ideology'. For Althusser 'Who's there?' is the central and first question in the *drama* of ideology, a drama of the individual becoming a subject.

This becomes apparent as Althusser moves on to consider how ideology functions. Recognition is one of the two functions of ideology (the other being misrecognition). Recognition is what constitutes the individual as a subject. That this recognition is then held to be obvious is 'the elementary ideological effect' (p. 161). Althusser illustrates this function:

> To take a highly 'concrete' example, we all have friends who, when they knock on our door and we ask, through the door, the question 'Who's there?', answer (since 'it's obvious') 'It's me'. And we recognize that 'it is him', or 'her'. (p. 161)

This is one of 'the rituals of ideological recognition', a mystifying ritual which falsely convinces both parties 'that we are indeed concrete, individual, distinguishable and (naturally) irreplaceable subjects' (p. 162). Barnardo's challenge, then, made to Francisco through a door of darkness, shows ideology at its most profound moment of action—in its attempt to constitute the individual as subject. Yet this hailing at first fails; the elementary ideological effect of obviousness is lost. Identity is for a moment unfixed, on the loose, just as in a little while the Ghost will come walking across the stage. The Ghost in turn will refuse to submit to recognition. Ideology falters, or rather different ideologies compete. The Ghost, a subject of a residual ideology (in Raymond Williams's term[96]), calls into question the dominant political ideology of Denmark, and so disrupts the process of the constitution of subjects within it. This disruption will focus on the emergent Prince Hamlet; and in the play, the way in which he recognizes the Ghost literally dramatizes his constitution as a subject. Much of *Hamlet*, the play, takes place in the space of this moment when ideology is failing to constitute the subject; it is a play not of being, but of becoming.

In terms of New Historicist critical practice, this Althusserian sense of ideology has focused attention on the political implications of man's constructed nature and so of literary texts, as they are part of the production of that nature. However, New Historicists tend to focus on the inescapability of ideology, as

[96] The term is one of a trilogy, the other two being 'dominant' and 'emergent'. See Raymond Williams, *Marxism and Literature* (Oxford: Oxford University Press, 1977), 121–7.

they focus on the inescapability of Foucault's conception of power. New Historicists, therefore, see their task to be the demonstration of the ways in which man is constructed by ideology; but, in abandoning the sense of ideology as a false consciousness, New Historicists abandon the traditional Marxist belief that by exposing the gap between ideology and social reality the state which is built on that gap may be altered. New Historicists, in their political hopes, have tended to provide, in Catherine Gallagher's words, 'an amplified record of Marxism's own edgiest, uneasiest voices'.[97]

There are exceptions to this, but it is in this area of argument that New Historicists are most clearly distinguishable from Cultural Materialists. For Cultural Materialists retain the more traditional conception of ideology, allowing them to label notions of the nature of man which are essentialist as ideological; that is as false, politically implicated notions of man. Cultural Materialists then argue that this essentialist ideology of man is the false consciousness of the modern capitalist state in particular. They stress the circularity of the relationship between the subject-person, the subject-discipline, and the state. Catherine Belsey encapsulates this view in *The Subject of Tragedy*:

> Liberal humanism proposes that the subject is the free, unconstrained author of meaning and action, the origin of history. Unified, knowing and autonomous, the human being seeks a political system which guarantees freedom of choice. Western Liberal democracy, it claims, freely chosen, and thus evidently the unconstrained expression of human nature, was born in the seventeenth century with the emergence of the individual and the victory of constitutionalism in the consecutive English revolutions of the 1640s and 1688.[98]

New Historicists argue that by changing the notion of man, the notion of what the critical kingdom should be is changed. Cultural Materialists go much further; pointing to the circular relationship between the subject and the actual kingdom, contemporary 'Western Liberal democracy', they argue that by exposing the 'individual' (the essentialist notion of man) as a false ideology they can change the state; capitalism, paternalism, and militarism can all be overturned. For Cultural Materialists, asking 'Who's there?' is the prelude to a wholesale changing of the guard.

97 Gallagher, 'Marxism and the New Historicism' in Veeser (ed.), *The New Historicism*, 47.

98 Catherine Belsey, *The Subject of Tragedy* (London: Methuen, 1985), 8.

2
Fear and Wonder

'WHO'S there?', then, is central to New Historicists' self-definition; who they say they are, what they say they are about, and how they say they are going to carry that out. The question should provide the focus of their critical drama—a 'whodunnit' with a novel twist, if the notices are to be believed, in which the villain is not the butler but nobody. This second chapter turns to that critical drama, mindful that notices, particularly those written by the performing company, are not always accurate. To an extent this caution is seen to be justified; instead of being novel, many aspects of their performance are old-fashioned, the historical detective work being unpersuasive. Yet, overall, the notices do not mislead; for the play's old-fashioned aspects are themselves a result of the New Historicist desire to answer 'nobody' to the question of 'Who's there?' The question and answer remains as central to New Historicists' practice as it was to their theory. Believing in nobody's guilt, they tell the historical stories that substantiate that conclusion, ignoring evidence that might tend to point to a different answer. *Hamlet* is a particularly noticeable absence from their critical drama. *Hamlet* is so often and so obviously relevant to New Historicists' preoccupations that its omission can be used to define the critical movement. Chapter 2 closes by arguing that New Historicism is best seen as a style of argument, weakened by its lack of fear.

> *Mar.* Peace, breake thee of: [*Enter the Ghost*] Looke where it comes againe.
> *Barn.* In the same figure, like the King that's dead.
>
> (I. I. 38–9)

Turning from describing the criticism New Historicists expect their movement will produce, to examining the criticism that has actually appeared, is a disappointing experience. For far from a new critical drama, it seems that the new drama has the old kings. Most striking is the New Historicists' overwhelming interest in and emphasis on the Renaissance (or, as they might prefer, the early modern period). There is nothing in New Historicists' assertion of their beliefs and aims that leads us to expect such an emphasis. Why, then, is there this one? New Historicists, themselves disconcerted by such a congruence, have put forward various explanations for this. Montrose argues that New Historicists focus on the Renaissance because the literature in this period has no 'ideology of aesthetic disinterestedness'; that is, literary texts do not try to efface their political, socially productive nature.[1] He points to the effects of patronage, of

[1] Montrose, 'Renaissance Literary Studies', 12.

the competition between the different royal courts, and of a belief in literature's ability to persuade. Yet the notion that the absence of an ideology of aesthetic disinterestedness distinguishes the Renaissance is not convincing. Satirical writing, to take just one example, can be found both before and after the Renaissance, and is an obviously interested mode.[2]

Another and more frequent group of answers seeks to account for this emphasis by arguing that the Renaissance is a particularly twentieth-century and post-modern age; that is, that Renaissance England has many and particular similarities to contemporary culture. Howard again provides a useful description of this argument:

> But now, as critics and historians sense the modern era slipping away and a new episteme inchoately emerging, the Renaissance is being appropriated in slightly different terms: as *neither* modern nor medieval, but as a boundary or liminal period between two more monolithic periods where one can see acted out a clash of paradigms and ideologies, a playfulness with signifying systems, a self-reflexivity, and a self-consciousness about the tenuous solidity of human identity which resonate with some of the dominant elements of postmodern culture.[3]

Howard's descriptive phrases are not unapt when applied to English Renaissance literature; however, Howard's and other New Historicists' definitions of the Renaissance period through such an inchoate/monolithic discrimination rely on a picture of the medieval period that, far from being at the forefront of historical thinking, is out of date. David Aers, in his *Community, Gender, and Individual Identity*, sums up this 'traditional' view of the period to have held the medieval period to be 'unified by Christian faith and a common moral theory, the antithesis to a "modern" world riven by competing ideologies, conflicts and tensions'.[4] Such a view, for Aers, dates from the 1930s; he finds the continued use of it 'bizarre' (p. 184). Aers is concerned particularly with British Cultural Materialists, citing as examples Howard Barker and Catherine Belsey (p. 17). His comments, however, apply equally well to the New Historicists' use of history; both critical movements share a similar historical picture.

Aers is rather baffled as to why Cultural Materialists should want to invoke such an out-of-date, conservative picture of the medieval period, particularly as he feels these critics should be on his side; he shares their dislikes of the British state and their hopes of changing it. In fact, Aers provides the answer to his question without realizing; as he notes, this out-of-date picture of the Middle Ages 'seems to guarantee a world free from anything remotely like the individual subject found in the "modern" west' (p. 7). His bafflement arises from the ease with which he can repudiate this out-of-date picture of the

[2] If examples of works are wanted Langland's *Piers Plowman* (*c*.1367–86) and Dryden's *Absalom and Achitophel* (1681) might be mentioned, among countless others.

[3] Howard, 'The New Historicism', 16–17.

[4] David Aers, *Community, Gender, and Individual Identity: English Writing 1360–1430* (London: Routledge, 1988), 6. Further references to this book are given after quotations in the text.

Middle Ages through reference to 'the impressively detailed literature' which describes 'thirteenth century urban markets dominated by merchant entrepreneurs' (p. 13).[5] What he does not recognize is the paramount importance to Cultural Materialists and New Historicists of answering 'nobody' to the question of 'Who's there?' Other answers, such as 'an individual', are simply not acceptable (until after the English Renaissance), for they contradict the founding belief of both critical movements.

Aers closes his account with a moderate plea:

> What Raymond Williams calls 'singularity' or 'individualism' was not quite as 'new' in 1611 as he and the conventional chronology of cultural history maintains. Perhaps, too, it is thus time to put a self-denying ordinance on claims about the new 'construction of the subject' and its causes in allegedly new features of the sixteenth century. (p. 17)

Aers's quotation of Williams's *Keywords* is apposite, recognizing the immense importance Williams is accorded by Cultural Materialists. Within that critical movement, Williams is a kind of John the Baptist; he is constantly acknowledged as having prepared the way for the new movement. Jonathan Dollimore, for example, in a survey of recent developments in Shakespearian criticism, talks of Williams as a 'major influence' on Cultural Materialism, and a collection of interviews with Williams as the 'best introduction' to it.[6] Williams's influence, however, is also present in New Historicist writing, although he is named less frequently. One who does mention him, in an autobiographical aside, is Greenblatt. Greenblatt, recalling his two years at Cambridge as a Fulbright scholar, remembers how he was 'struck by what seemed to me the intellectual power and moral authority of one of my teachers, Raymond Williams'.[7] Returning to the United States, under Williams's influence he wrote a dissertation 'on the functions of writing in Ralegh's career'.[8] This eventually became *Sir Walter Ralegh: The Renaissance Man and his Roles* (1973); though not recognized as such by its reviewers, it was one of the first New Historicist works. A main part of its thesis, for instance, was the belief that 'at key moments in Ralegh's career, the boundaries between life and art completely break down'.[9] This belief is a variation of New Historicism's central assertion of the indivisibility between literature and history. At that time, this belief was greeted sceptically by some reviewers.[10] One, Joan Rees,

[5] As a literary example he quotes the complaint in *Dives and Pauper* (a prose dialogue written *c.*1405–10) that, 'every man wil ben his owyn man & folwyn his owyn fantasyys & despysyn her souereynys, her doom & her gouernance ne geuyn no tale of Goddis lawe ne of londys lawe ne of holy chirce ne han men of vertue ne of dignete in worchepe but for pride han hem in dispyt and ben besy to worchepyn hemself in hyndryng of othere' (p. 16).

[6] Dollimore, 'Critical Developments', in Wells (ed.), *Shakespeare: A Bibliographical Guide*, 407.

[7] Greenblatt, *Learning*, 2.

[8] Ibid. 2.

[9] Stephen J. Greenblatt, *Sir Walter Ralegh: The Renaissance Man and his Roles* (New Haven: Yale University Press, 1973), p. ix.

[10] See e.g. Tom Cain, 'Ralegh's Roles', *EIC* 24 (1974), 286–94; Joan Rees, '*Sir Walter Ralegh; The Renaissance Man and his Roles*', in *RES* 26 (1975), 70–1.

particularly disliked the book's moralistic comments.[11] Rees's criticism recalls Greenblatt's acknowledgement of his admiration of the 'moral authority' of Williams, an admiration that in turn reinforces and develops Williams's role as a kind of literary-critical John the Baptist. Williams, then, may be seen to have given an initial impulse to New Historicism, standing behind one of its first critical productions.[12] More, his influence is continually present in New Historicists' vigorous desire for, and pursuit of, moral authority, already apparent to Rees. In fact, if Williams's influence is combined with the acknowledged initial influence of the Warburg-Courtauld Institute,[13] then it would seem that the history of New Historicism cannot be differentiated from Cultural Materialism along North American–British lines as is commonly suggested.[14]

Williams's discussion of 'individual' in *Keywords*, then, may be another reason for New Historicists' promotion of a traditional and conservative picture of the medieval period. Indeed, it may have been formative of the cultural history of the subject which New Historicists have used and Cultural Materialists written. Since this history is rather absurd, as Aers points out, it is worth noting that Williams has little responsibility for it. For Williams is not discussing the history of the subject. Rather, he is discussing the history of meanings of the word 'individual', and the connections through which that word fits into a vocabulary of culture and society.[15] Williams does believe that the development of the meanings of words is linked to cultural development, but he is quite aware of the complexity of that relationship, and is not committed to the position that a concept cannot exist before it is named, let alone prior to the date of first recorded use.[16] Moreover, in this history of verbal meanings, Williams is correct. 'Individual', in its sense of a particular subject-person possessed of agency, is not used to describe the medieval subject-person that Aers correctly argues it fits very precisely. Similarly, the complex of meanings of words associated with this sense of individual does not exist until some years into the seventeenth century. This touches on what will become one of the central issues of this book. The critical implications of the lack of this vocabulary

11 Ibid. 70

12 Indeed, Raymond Williams seems to have anticipated most of the main terms of New Historicism in Section Two of *Politics and Letters: Interviews with New Left Review* (London: NLB, 1979), 95–185. Here he also rejects the Whorf–Sapir hypothesis as an idealist theory (182). Other important figures, I believe, are Anne Barton and C. L. Barber. See Anne Righter, *Shakespeare and the Idea of the Play* (London: Chatto & Windus, 1962), and Barber, *Shakespeare's Festive Comedy: A Study of Dramatic Form and its Relation to Social Custom* (Princeton: Princeton University Press, 1959).

13 See H. Aram Veeser's introduction to *The New Historicism*, pp. xii–xvi (p. xiii). David Norbrook provides another account of the impact of the Warburg Institute in the 'Introduction' to *Poetry and Politics in the English Renaissance* (London: Routledge & Kegan Paul, 1984), 1–17 (2–3).

14 See Dollimore, 'Critical Developments', in Wells (ed.) *Shakespeare: A Bibliographical Guide*, 407.

15 See Raymond Williams, *Keywords: A Vocabulary of Culture and Society*, rev. edn. (London: Fontana Press, 1983), 15.

16 Ibid. 15–25.

are significant; the vocabulary, as Part II shows, has been of particular importance to the development of notions of subjectivity within both Shakespearian and literary criticism in general. The absence of this vocabulary lends plausibility to the New Historicist and Cultural Materialist argument that the subject-person is a product within English Renaissance literature. Therefore, for those who wish to argue that the subject-person is a self-constituting construct (and so possessed of agency), an argument or arguments must be found in which the verbal text can be shown to express meanings which, in terms of the absence of the relevant modern vocabulary, might be thought to be inexpressible. This is attempted in Part III.

The determining role of the founding question and its answer, of 'Who's there?' and 'nobody', is not only evident in the picture of the Middle Ages, but is seen elsewhere in New Historicists' and Cultural Materialists' choice of sources for their English Renaissance history. It explains, for example, their use of Lawrence Stone for their social history of the period. Stone's statements are treated, like Foucault's, as having canonical authority. Yet, to a historian such as David Cressy, Stone's arguments represent 'a stage in historical analysis that may have peaked in the early 1970s, but which has been in retreat for more than a decade'.[17] This is not to belittle Stone, for his arguments were the spur to the subsequent work. The out-of-date nature of Stone's work, however, has not been noticed by New Historicist critics. Stone is a continuous influence, and in particular his *The Family, Sex and Marriage in England, 1500–1800* (1977).[18] That book argues that the English family underwent sharp changes in its structure and attitudes during the period 1500 to 1640. Summarily put, in 1500 family life was unemotional and authoritarian, and the extended family placed little importance on the individual member, instead concentrating on its relationship to kin and community. Only after 1640 did the 'closed domesticated nuclear family' begin to develop, characterized by the affection demonstrated between family members, and founded upon individualism and introspection.

This picture of the family, sex, and marriage has been thoroughly superseded by the work of a number of historians.[19] The family unit, at least as far back as to the fourteenth century, is now argued never to have been an extended one. Making slight allowances for variations between class, the family unit basically consisted of parents and their offspring, of which there were on

[17] Cressy, 'Foucault, Stone, Shakespeare and Social History', 26.

[18] Lawrence Stone, *The Family, Sex and Marriage in England, 1500–1800* (London: Weidenfeld & Nicolson, 1977).

[19] See for a direct response to Stone, Linda A. Pollock, *Forgotten Children: Parent–Child Relations from 1500 to 1900* (Cambridge: Cambridge University Press, 1983); and, more generally, Alan MacFarlane, *Marriage and Love in England: Modes of Reproduction 1300–1840* (Basil Blackwell: Oxford, 1986); Ralph Houlbrooke (ed.), *English Family Life, 1576–1716: An Anthology from Diaries* (Basil Blackwell: Oxford, 1988); J. A. Sharpe, *Early Modern England: A Social History 1550–1760* (London: Edward Arnold, 1987); Wrightson, Keith, *English Society: 1580–1680* (London: Hutchinson, 1982).

average two or three, with perhaps some household servants. Moreover, this family life is marked by affection and a sense of the importance of individual members.[20] Stone's arguments, then, are dated, but they are also amenable to an answer of 'nobody', as he sees individualism and introspection as post-1640 qualities of the family unit; and so his arguments continue to be used within New Historicist writing.[21] The body of work prompted by his pioneering studies, which has convincingly refuted his paradigm of the development of the family unit, is not amenable to the answer of 'nobody'; this work has not been used to any substantial degree by New Historicists (or Cultural Materialists) to test their founding assumptions. Stone has declared himself both unimpressed by 'Foucault's neglect of the historical context' and 'openly sceptical of the credentials of literary critics to pursue historical topics'.[22] This, however, seems to have had no impact on those literary critics who use him so certainly.

A similar situation is found with the New Historicist use of political history. Having used Foucault as a model for their historical methodology, and Stone as a source for a socio-historical account, they turn to Christopher Hill for an interpretation of the flow of history through the Renaissance period. Hill gives a Marxist interpretation of the events leading up to and culminating in the English Civil War.[23] In terms of the way he is used by New Historicists, the argument of his 1940 essay still holds sway: in the Civil War, 'An old order that was essentially feudal was destroyed by violence, and a new and capitalist order created in its place. The Civil War was a class war, in which the despotism of Charles I was defended by the reactionary forces of the established Church and feudal landlords.'[24] Central to this interpretation of the Civil War is the presence of long-term causes. In that, it is similar to the Whig-Liberal account, which sees the Civil War as a stage in England's slow, evolutionary progress towards parliamentary sovereignty. However, Hill's and the Whig-Liberal

[20] This is not to say that family and social life was much as it is today. One, perhaps surprising, difference is to be found in sexual activity; although marriage was legal, with parental consent, from the ages of 12 for girls and 14 for boys, in 1600 the average age at marriage was 26 for women and 28 for men. For the vast number of women, therefore, the most vigorous years of sexual maturity were passed over in a fairly asexual state. This provides a useful example of the constructed nature of behaviours which are often considered innate.

[21] As this use is implicit, structuring, and widespread it is hard to footnote. Looking through the bibliographies of many of the New Historicist works already mentioned is one way of tracing Stone's continued influence, and the absence of other social historians. For example, Jean E. Howard in her *The Stage and Social Struggle in Early Modern England* (London: Routledge, 1994), quibbles with the details of Stone's account but does not question the soundness of his paradigm (p. 161).

[22] In a paper delivered in May 1990. See Richard Dutton, 'Postscript', in Wilson and Dutton (eds.), *New Historicism and Renaissance Drama*, 222.

[23] In historical studies, to call the military, political, and other events of the mid-17th c. 'the English Civil War' is to enter into an argument about what those events were; other terms used are 'the English Revolution', 'the Great Rebellion', or 'the Puritan Revolution'. I use English Civil War as I believe it to be the presently most acceptable term.

[24] 'The English Revolution', in Christopher Hill (ed.), *The English Revolution 1640: Three Essays* (London: Lawrence and Wishart, 1940), 9–82 (9).

picture of this period have come under increasing criticism since the 1970s, as the historical school labelled 'revisionist' has challenged Hill's and the Whig-Liberal portrayal of Parliament's role and nature.[25] The histories of the institutions do not, they argue, support such long-term causal explanations. The reasons for the Civil War are at present seen to be much more localized and much more complicated, lying as much in the personalities of those involved and their short-term decisions as in any great structural changes in society; bipolar categories such as Crown versus Parliament or court versus country are no longer satisfactory.

These historians have emphasized the importance of the Privy Council and the court, rather than of Parliament, to Tudor and Jacobean government. In this newer, now dominant account, the court was the arena, or more appropriately (particularly in Elizabeth's reign with the cult of Gloriana) the theatre, through which the monarch ruled and communicated with his or her subjects.[26] The courtier's relationship with the monarch became of prime importance. He needed to attract the attention and gain the favour of the monarch, whether this was through the tiltyard, the hunting field, the masque, dance, or the discharge of official duties. What this meant was that, in D. M. Loades's words, 'competition was the essence of a courtier's existence'.[27] The rewards of success for such a 'homo ludens'[28] were great. There were lucrative positions in the gift of the monarch, but more regularly success came in the form of the monarch's granting of the courtier's petitions, or of petitions the courtier introduced. Through this ability to have petitions granted came the courtier's power and status. Tudor government was thus intimately personal. Indeed, so intensely personal was it that politics was scarcely even factional, groups being very scarce and usually based around family interests. 'The real

[25] Kevin Sharpe and Peter Lake argue that the revisionism was first systematically presented in this context by C. S. R. Russell, *Parliaments and English Politics, 1621–9* (Oxford: Clarendon Press, 1979); M. A. Kishlansky, *The Rise of the New Model Army* (Cambridge: Cambridge University Press, 1979); and K. Sharpe (ed.), *Faction and Parliament* (Oxford: Clarendon Press, 1978). See Kevin Sharpe and Peter Lake (eds.), *Culture and Politics in Early Stuart England* (London: Macmillan, 1994), 321.

[26] This account of the court draws on D. M. Loades, *The Tudor Court* (London: Historical Association, 1991). This pamphlet presents a summary account of Loades's far more detailed treatment of the subject in his *The Tudor Court* (London: Batsford, 1986). Loades takes the court to be everyone who, on a particular day, is surrounding the King or Queen. For the Jacobean and Caroline courts see David Starkey (ed.), *The English Court: From the Wars of the Roses to the Civil War* (Harlow: Longman, 1987). All accounts of the court and indeed of Tudor history as a whole, owe a huge debt to Professor G. R. Elton's *The Tudor Revolution in Government* (Cambridge: Cambridge University Press, 1953). For an account of the present standing of the thesis of 'the Tudor Revolution', and of the relationships between the court, Privy Council, and Parliament, see Christopher Coleman and David Starkey (eds.), *Revolution Reassessed: Revisions in the History of Tudor Government and Administration* (Oxford: Clarendon Press, 1986). For an account of the visual iconography of Elizabeth's court, and the optical principles on which it was based, see Roy Strong, *The Cult of Elizabeth: Elizabethan Portraiture and Pageantry* (London: Thames and Hudson, 1977).

[27] Loades, *The Tudor Court* (pamphlet), 18.

[28] Ibid. 21.

situation was far more anarchic and unpredictable than would be consistent with such a notion [of faction].'[29]

It is difficult, then, to see long-term causal influences shaping the political events of the Tudor and Jacobean period. Instead political decisions were taken to meet immediate problems; the short-term vacillations of Elizabeth's foreign policy are representative. What such a short-term view points to is the fact that the Tudor state was not able to generate a great degree of coercive force. Elizabeth's reign, thus, is now seen as an exercise in survival for the monarch, with far fewer major achievements than was once thought.[30] In fact monarchal survival was itself an achievement, and owed much to the Tudor success with the court system. Through it, the Tudors created displays of power, magnificence, and culture to overawe any dissidence and make the ideology of obedience unquestionable. Such a production and manipulation of magnificence, or *maiestas*, was immensely successful, allowing Elizabeth to gain for England an influence in diplomacy out of proportion to the nation's actual wealth and power, and to create a myth of imperial greatness that not only preceded the actual period of imperial expansion by some two hundred years, but which remains strong today.

By the end of the sixteenth century, however, the court was becoming isolated from the rest of the country, its members becoming a specialized ruling class. This gap between rulers and ruled was dangerous. As Loades points out:

> In creating distinctions of this kind . . . the court spelt danger to itself, because contact and communication were its lifeblood, and the measure of its political value to the monarchy. It needed to be both open and attractive, and if its mores became either too repugnant or too esoteric it would cease to perform its essential function.[31]

This is what happened during the reigns of James I and Charles II, allied to the development of factional groupings.[32] But even on this level, it could not be said that the failure of the institution of the court led inevitably to the Civil War. Rather, the personality and decisions of Charles, and his relationship with Parliament, are stressed as the decisive factors.[33] One argument is that the decisive moment came when Parliament had Charles's favourite, Strafford, beheaded, after which the King was set on achieving some form of revenge.[34] Another is that the war was inevitable once Charles had attempted to have five

[29] Ibid. 20.

[30] J. A. Sharpe argues that Elizabeth's reign contained two major achievements, the creation of the Church of England and the introduction of the poor law. See his *Early Modern England*, 10.

[31] Loades, *The Tudor Court* (pamphlet), 29.

[32] The account that follows draws on, in addition to the books mentioned above, Derek Hirst, *Authority and Conflict: England 1603–1658* (London: Edward Arnold, 1986); Roger Lockyer, *The Early Stuarts: A Political History of England, 1603–1642* (Harlow: Longman, 1989).

[33] The civil disturbances in Scotland and Ireland are seen in relation to their impact on the relations between the King and Parliament.

[34] Strafford was beheaded on 12 May 1641.

Members of Parliament and one peer impeached for treason.[35] As J. A. Sharpe argues in his summary account of the revisionist history of the period, one thing is sure: 'The outbreak of this war, as our account has implied, has little to do with a rising middle class or a transition from feudalism to capitalism.'[36] The newer account may not be correct, but the old account is definitely superseded.[37]

Yet New Historicists still use Hill's Marxist account of the English Civil War, even though the revisionist picture of the Elizabethan and Jacobean periods is in several ways suitably New Historicist: it insists on the complexity and lack of a causal hierarchy in a culture; it attempts to reconstruct the interrelated nature of that culture; it stresses the practical difficulties of political dissent.[38] Hill's view of history, however, is particularly valuable because it complements the New Historicist picture of the medieval period in terms of its chronology of the notions of man. (Hill, unlike Stone, believes that literary critics have recently been the best writers of seventeenth-century history.[39]) First, in stressing long-term causes, Hill's Marxist history leads to a diffusion of any sense of individual agency. Second, it removes an essentialist notion of human nature, the individual, from the medieval period, and places its arrival after the English Civil War with the installation of the capitalist state. By contrast, the revisionists' account, though emphasizing the inchoate, competitive, and fluid nature of the English Renaissance, gives to subject-persons a greater agency, and so (in New Historicist terms) individuality.

As with the use of Tillyard, a second generation of New Historicists have moved to rectify this use of out-of-date history, although this awareness of the detail of history has typically led them to distance themselves from New Historicism.[40] However, their famous predecessors did not simply ignore revisionist historians, or use only out-of-date historical studies; as with their use of theory, they exercised an imperialism of choice, selecting the details which did not trouble their overall picture. Take, for example, their tendency to use 'early modern' in place of 'Renaissance'. The use of 'early modern' is the result of the influence of contemporary historians. 'Renaissance' has always been a

[35] These were Viscount Mandeville, and Pym, Hampden, Haselrig, Holles and Strode.

[36] Sharpe, *Early Modern England*, 20.

[37] So, for example, revisionists have in turn been criticized for depoliticizing history in stressing the homogeneity of political culture; their critics have (as is the fashion) been referred to as post-revisionists. See Sharpe and Lake, *Culture and Politics*, 1–3. There is an interesting parallel between the antagonism of post-revisionists to revisionists, and that of Cultural Materialists to New Historicists.

[38] Sharpe and Lake suggest what the two movements might gain from each other; for revisionism this is particularly a greater sense both of the difficulty of establishing the boundary between the real and the represented, and of the ambivalence of discourses. See their *Culture and Politics*, 1–20.

[39] Quoted by Jonathan Dollimore in Wells (ed.), *Shakespeare: A Bibliographical Guide*, 413. Hill made the statement in a review in the *TLS*, 1–8 Jan. 1988.

[40] See Hanson, *Discovering the Subject*, 7.

difficult term because of its portmanteau quality; the Renaissance is the product both of developments in technology, knowledge, and scientific methodology, and the result of many specific renaissances from the fourteenth century to the sixteenth.[41] And then there is the Renaissance's densely packed relationship to the Reformation to consider.

Early modern England, by contrast, has far less connotations and is in this respect more precise, though still fluid. J. A. Sharpe makes the (necessarily arbitrary) choice of beginning his social history of this period in 1550. 'Early modern' also indicates a sense of the connectedness of this period with the present. Greenblatt, in his choice of titles for his books, is indicative of the development of 'early modern England's' dominance in literary criticism: his most recent collection of essays, *Learning to Curse*, has the subtitle, *Essays in Early Modern Culture*. (Greenblatt refers to early modern *culture* as his essays range across Europe; the risk in the practice and term is of homogenizing the differing cultural developments and pace of developments within three hundred years of European and European colonial history. A similar risk is taken in the title of *Renaissance Self-Fashioning*.)

'Early modern England', in its stress on continuity, is a useful term, though its usefulness has itself recently come under attack.[42] What it loses in comparison with 'Renaissance' is the suggestion of the age's self-consciousness, a self-consciousness that is of particular importance to the literary historian as it was created out of a literary and artistic dialogue with the classical past. Care must be exercised here; the notion of the Renaissance is a nineteenth-century historian's invention. The sense of self-consciousness to which I refer is that bound up with the terms 'humanist' and the 'studia humanitatis', and with the myth, actively promoted at the time, of a renaissance in these subjects. These two terms refer to a movement which was one of the shaping forces of the period, and which was in the nineteenth century given the label 'humanism'. Central to the humanist project was the revival of ancient learning (or at least its greater promotion). However, the humanists did not study classical authors in a simple, uncritical spirit of veneration. Rather, while they did grant immense prestige to classical authors, they also tried to understand these

[41] The often-quoted examples are the arrival of gunpowder, the invention in 1454 of movable-block printing, the discovery of the New World in 1492, and the replacement of Ptolemaic cosmology with various theories which put the sun at the centre of the solar system. In the arts, the Italian Renaissance is spoken about as having its roots in the 14th c., and is flourishing by the 15th c. The English Renaissance, however, which is later owing to England's northern position and insularity, is used to refer to the period beginning roughly with Henry VIII's rule in 1509 and running to about 1660. In literary journals of English literature the English Renaissance tends to refer especially to the Elizabethan and Jacobean periods.

[42] 'Early Modern' has recently been argued to be a term complicit in the banishment of the relation between subject and object, and so supportive of essentially Burkhardtian subject-orientated histories. 'Early Colonial' has been suggested as a preferable term. See Margreta de Grazia, Maureen Quilligan, and Peter Stallybrass (eds.), *Subject and Object in Renaissance Culture* (Cambridge: Cambridge University Press, 1996), 5.

authors' works through an understanding of their historical context. They were, in this sense, extrinsic historicists.

A result of this was that the humanist project limited, at the same time as it celebrated, the authority of classical figures. For those figures, and their wisdom, were constrained by the experiences of their times. Thus the relationship between reader and author or text became more personal; a dialogue not a lesson. The humanist could learn from the classical authority, but he could also use what he had learnt to express his own feelings in his own particular context. This use of classical forms and ideas to express one's own feelings was the process of 'imitatio'.[43]

Central to the humanist project was the production of distinct 'identity'. Montaigne, concentrating on ideas not literary forms, describes this process in 'Of the institution and education of Children':

> For if by his owne discourse he [the reader] embrace the opinions of Xenophon, or of Plato, they shall be no longer theirs, but his. He that merely followeth another, traceth nothing, and seeketh nothing . . . it is requisite he endevour as much to feed himselfe with their conceits, as labour to learne their precepts; which, so he know how to applie, let him hardly forget, where, or whence he had them. Truth and reason are common to all, and are no more proper unto him that spake them heretofore, than unto him that shall speake them hereafter. And it is no more according to Platoes opinion, than to mine, since both he and I understand and see alike. The Bees doe here and there sucke this, and cull that flower, but afterward they produce the hony, which is peculiarly their owne, then is it no more Thyme or Marjoram. So of peeces borrowed of others, he may lawfully alter, transforme, and confound them, to shape out of them a perfect peece of worke, altogether his owne . . . Let him hardly conceale, where, or whence he hath had any helpe, and make no shew of any thing, but of that which he hath made himselfe.[44]

Montaigne is here putting his precepts into practice, by borrowing unacknowledged from Seneca's *Letter* 84 the image of the bee plundering flowers. The humanist production of identity was, then, to be the production of a *distinct* identity; the child was to be able to express himself in a way 'altogether his owne'. It was also the production of a particularly literary identity; the unique expression of the subject-person was in fact a cloth woven to a considerable extent from the expressions of others. Indeed, the humanists' self-conscious sense of the circularity between literature and life, or, to put it in New Historicist parlance, of the literariness of life and the lifelikeness of literature, was acute.

Just as for New Historicists, the question of what the difference is between literature and life became paramount.[45] This sense of circularity, allied to the

[43] Sir Thomas Wyatt's Englishing of sonnets from Petrarch's *Rime* is one of the earliest examples in English.

[44] Montaigne, iii. 156–7 (Ch. 25). This essay is now usually known as 'On Education'.

[45] Sharpe and Lake, *Culture and Politics*, note this concern in relation to the importance within the English Renaissance of the figure of the evil machiavel, 'cynically manipulating the masks of contemporary rhetoric and moral suasion to conceal and realize his own corrupt ends' (p. 16).

spectacular nature of Elizabethan power and the personal dynamics of the court, created the sense of the theatricality of life which informed the Elizabethan age; as Anne Righter (later Anne Barton) puts it in *Shakespeare and the Idea of the Play*,

> In sermons and song-books, chronicles and popular pamphlets, Elizabethans were constantly being reminded of the fact that life tends to imitate the theatre. . . . The play metaphor was for Elizabethans an inescapable expression, a means of fixing the essential quality of the age.[46]

Yet this metaphor did not fix the quality of the relationship between acting, or literature, and life. 'For Elizabethans,' as Righter points out, 'the relation of illusion to reality was anything but simple. . . . Certain spectators in a theatre might, for a moment, mistake illusion for reality; other playgoers carried the language and gestures of the drama away with them . . . for use in the world outside.'[47]

The question of the difference between literature and life is seen particularly acutely in the question of 'Who's there?' Montaigne's confidence, in the opening of the passage quoted above, suggests that this relationship is a non-question; it is clear that the child makes the opinions his own: 'For if by his owne discourse he embrace the opinions of Xenophon, or of Plato, they shall be no longer theirs, but his.' But why, then, does Montaigne go on to emphasize the need for the child to disguise his borrowings? 'Let him hardly forget . . . Let him hardly conceale, where, or whence he hath had any helpe.' The repeated emphatic 'hardly' begins to draw attention to itself. The metaphor of the bees and honey does not hold on all levels; bees go to flowers to make honey, and the honey they make does not change what they are, or our perception of what they are. By contrast, the child, in expressing its personality through the flowers of literature, constructs its identity from its anthology; it becomes someone, perhaps someone else, by its reading.

Montaigne wishes to efface this process of construction. If this can be done, it then becomes difficult to tell the difference between what is life and what is literature; the one is productive of the other and vice versa. Is life a process of acting? In the sentence subsequent to the above passage, Montaigne justifies what he has said by giving examples of the naturalness of concealment: 'Pirates, filchers, and borrowers, make a shew of their purchases and buildings, but not of that which they have taken from others.' These examples are not the expected models for a child. Montaigne goes on to make clear, though a world of drama lies within his bracketed qualification, that 'The good that comes of studie (or at least should come) is to prove better, wiser, and honester.'[48] Yet

[46] Anne Righter, *Shakespeare and the Idea of the Play* (London: Chatto & Windus, 1962), 83–4. Interestingly, in the light of Montaigne's worries over identity and contemporaries' worries concerning Machiavelli's sense of the performative nature of identity, Righter argues that this notion was introduced to the stage through the figure of the Vice (pp. 68–75).

[47] Ibid. 83.

[48] For an introduction to this world of Elizabethan drama, and the particular relationship

proving cannot be dissociated from the piracy of theft and both are seen to bring profit, to gain power. 'It is the understanding power (said Epicharmus) that seeth and heareth, it is it, that profiteth all, and disposeth all, that moveth, swayeth, and ruleth all.'[49] The relationship between fiction, life, and power is once more at issue, as it had been for the classical authors whom the humanists studied. Cicero had given his answer to the relationship thus, describing orators as 'veritas ipsius actores [the players who act real life]'.[50] Using 'early modern' in place of 'renaissance' directs attention away from the self-conscious sense of the fictive, literary nature of the world possessed by Renaissance humanists. Once again, this will tend both to lessen New Historicism's obvious affinities to the past and to make the past more malleable and childlike, because it is less self-aware.

New Historicism, then, although it is determinedly anti-humanist, has many similarities to humanism, similarities that extend beyond an interest in the same debates and relationships. For humanism, as Paul Oskar Kristeller first made clear, was not defined by its concern with the study of classical authors. Rather humanism was a characteristic phase in the rhetorical tradition of Western culture. It was the humanists' rhetorical ideals, specifically the ideal of eloquence, which led them to the study of classical texts and not the other way round.[51] Classical texts were studied as a means of creating the orator, the man who might communicate persuasively. Eloquence was necessary in every field, and so humanists 'tried to assert the importance of their field of learning and to impose their standards upon the other fields of learning and of science' (p. 102). For this reason, there were humanists in every field, holding opinions and beliefs that were quite contradictory. They had no common philosophical doctrine, but instead represented a broad cultural and literary movement. New Historicism, then, might usefully be seen as a movement of the same sort as Renaissance humanism, that is as a phase in a rhetorical tradition. Like Renaissance humanism, New Historicism cuts across disciplinary boundaries and has no definable doctrine. Aram Veeser, in his introduction to *The New Historicism*, hints (unconsciously I imagine) at this parallel when he argues that the New Historicism 'threatens [the] quasi-monastic order' of conventional

between the city and the theatre, see Anne Barton, 'London Comedy and the Ethos of the City'; and 'Comic London', both in her *Essays, Mainly Shakespearean* (Cambridge: Cambridge University Press, 1994), 302–28 and 329–51 respectively.

49 Montaigne, i. 157.

50 Cicero, *De Oratore* 3. 214. This phrase would be highly charged for a Roman audience, who sought strenuously to keep acting and oratory separate. One of the emperor Nero's greatest sins was that he allied acting and life, being the actor emperor. See Catherine Edwards, 'Beware of Imitations: Theatre and the Subversion of Imperial Identity', in Jas Elsner and Jamie Masters (eds.), *Reflections of Nero: Culture, History and Representation* (Chapel Hill, NC: University of North Carolina Press, 1994), 83–97.

51 Paul Oskar Kristeller, *Renaissance Thought: The Classic, Scholastic and Humanist Strains* (New York: Harper & Row, 1961), particularly ch. 5, 'Humanism and Scholasticism in the Italian Renaissance', 92–119 (99). Further references to this work are given after quotations in the text.

disciplinary boundaries.[52] The monastic order was based on a profoundly scholastic philosophy, and it was this that humanists were seen as, and often saw themselves as, opposing. As Kristeller points out, it was in fact a false perception, for the humanists were no philosophers at all. They were rhetoricians (p. 100).

Stone's and Hill's histories, the term 'early modern', all these are complementary to New Historicist and Cultural Materialist answers to 'Who's there?'[53] They lend weight to the attempt, in Aers's words, 'to guarantee a world free from anything remotely like the individual subject found in the "modern" west'. Within Cultural Materialism, this has led to the establishment of chronological histories of the subject which are only drawn on in passing by New Historicists. Cultural Materialists intend to undermine the contemporary state by the exposure of the individual not as a transhistorical notion of human nature, but as the ideological construct of capitalism, a construct on which the modern state was founded. Cultural Materialists, then, are not only interested in what they regard as the true answer to the question of 'Who's there?' ('nobody'), but also in the varieties and dates of what they regard as a false answer ('an individual'). Their political project of changing the guard stands or falls on the argument that the false answer ('an individual') was installed by, and is a foundation stone of, a capitalist society after the time of the Civil War. For if, as Aers argues, the individual can be found in the medieval period, the link between the modern capitalist state and the individual is far less clear cut, and so exposing the individual as a false ideology becomes less significant. The English Renaissance thus becomes a time of particular importance to the Cultural Materialists because of its position immediately before the English Civil War.

The English Civil War is less important to New Historicist arguments, since, quite understandably, they are not greatly concerned with the contemporary British state. The English Renaissance has been central within their accounts because they see it as supportive of their answers to 'Who's there?', and because it illustrates one of Michel Foucault's central theses—the notion that power in the early modern period was spectacular. As has been said, the Elizabethan state had limited (by modern standards) mechanisms by which to control its members.[54] Thus, for example, it 'staged' its shows of power to create the impression of its invulnerability. Hence the English Renaissance state's punishment of those who stood against it was spectacularly visited

[52] Veeser, *The New Historicism*, p. ix.

[53] This can be seen explicitly (as the title suggests) in Stone's *The Causes of the English Revolution, 1529–1641* (London: Routledge and Kegan Paul, 1972).

[54] e.g. A. Plowden describes Elizabeth's secret service as being 'pitifully small and amateurish' with a maximum of twelve full-time agents. A. Plowden, *The Elizabethan Secret Service* (Hemel Hempstead: Harvester, 1991), 55. For an interesting description of the life and death of one such agent, see John Bossy, *Giordano Bruno and the Embassy Affair* (Vintage: London, 1992; first pub. 1991).

on the visible body of the transgressor—who was branded, maimed, or hanged.

The power of the state was in this way theatrical, even to the extent of depending on the audience's reaction; the condemned might upstage the state, and take control of the performance, as did Sir Walter Ralegh, who in his speech from the scaffold successfully (in terms of public perception) ascribed the reason for his death to the malice of certain other nobles, and ended by commanding the executioner when to strike.[55] Thus the theatre, which becomes in the Elizabethan period, in Greenblatt's words, the 'literalization and institutionalization of the place of art' has a natural affinity in the English Renaissance with the issues of power; it becomes 'particularly useful for an analysis of the cultural circulation of social energy'.[56] Indeed, it not only allows the theatricality of power to be studied, but also the power of theatricality. Leonard Tennenhouse's *Power on Display: The Politics of Shakespeare's Genres* is influential here. In 'Family Rites: City Comedy and the Strategies of Patriarchism', he begins by arguing that the condition of London is related to the nature of the city comedy that was written within it.[57] But this relationship was not one way; by the end of the chapter, he comes to the following conclusion over the battle to control London's development that he has traced between the patriarchy of the King and the paternalism of the twenty-six aldermen and 250 common councillors: 'Consequently, the whole strategy James proposed for dealing with the issue of a corrupt London can be viewed as an adaptation of the dramatic strategies enacted in the theatre over the preceding ten to twelve years.'[58] The theatre is thus explicitly concerned with the relationships that New Historicism aims to trace between the state, art, and the individual.[59] New Historicists' overwhelming concentration on not only the English Renaissance, but also English Renaissance drama, now becomes understandable. But there arises a secondary question: why, within English Renaissance drama, has the critical emphasis been on the works of William Shakespeare?

This emphasis derives especially from the fact that the most influential New Historicist books and articles have generally been on Shakespeare, though it can be enumerated. In Wilson's and Dutton's *New Historicism and Renaissance Drama*, for example, of the ten articles on literature five are specifically concerned with Shakespearian plays. This collection, in fact, focuses on the 'traditional' literary canon (three of the other essays are on Marlowe, Ben Jonson, Webster), and within that canon focuses on what are now seen as

[55] See Greenblatt, *Walter Ralegh*, 18–20.

[56] See Greenblatt, *Shakespearean Negotiations*, 13.

[57] Tennenhouse uses the term 'city comedy' interchangeably with 'Jacobean city comedy'. The latter term, however, seems to be what is meant by the former, and is used in the sense distinguished by Brian Gibbons in his *Jacobean City Comedy* (2nd edn.; London: Methuen, 1980).

[58] Leonard Tennenhouse, 'Family Rites: City Comedy and the Strategies of Patriarchism', in *Power on Display: The Politics of Shakespeare's Genres* (London: Methuen, 1986), 160–71.

[59] See e.g. Greenblatt, *Shakespearean Negotiations*, esp. 1–20.

patriarchal issues.[60] This has, unsurprisingly, brought protest from feminist critics. Carol Thomas Neely points out how the New Historicists' concern with power, politics, history, and the monarch, is specifically male-orientated; they show very little interest in women, marriage, and sexuality. Moreover, while keeping to the traditional canon, Neely argues that New Historicists have tended to elevate the marginal male over the dominant women.[61] Greenblatt's *Renaissance Self-Fashioning* is exemplary of this male-orientated interest; as it traverses the lives of More, Tyndale, Wyatt, Spenser, Marlowe, and the work of Shakespeare, it might be more accurately entitled 'Renaissance Male Self-Fashioning' (or more accurately still, 'English Renaissance Male Self-Fashioning'). The strength of this critical emphasis is seen well in a collection of essays on tragicomedy, *The Politics of Tragicomedy*, edited by Gordon McMullan and Jonathan Hope. The editors are quite aware of the New Historicist emphasis on Shakespeare, which they deplore; they seek to resist this by including only articles on works written between 1610 and 1650, so limiting Shakespeare's presence to 'only a handful of his late and collaborative plays'. However, they uncomfortably (but honestly) acknowledge that, 'Some of the best writing in this collection does concentrate on Shakespeare . . . This, we accept, may leave us at least partially susceptible to our own criticisms of the New Historicism with respect to the question of textual, generic, and authorial privileging'.[62]

The explanation of this critical emphasis is clear and remarkable. Greenblatt's 'Invisible Bullets', the first chapter of *Shakespearian Negotiations*, is illustrative.[63] As he often does, Greenblatt begins his account with an unusual, little-known, but interesting text; Harriot's diary recording his contact with the Algonquian Indians. Greenblatt thus gives his historicism a newness through his style; what could be more 'new' than approaching *The History of Henry IV* through Harriot's little-known recording of his life among the Indians? Greenblatt argues that Harriot and Hal are both involved in the same task—

[60] In the edition of *Genre* devoted to New Historicist criticism (in which Greenblatt believes he coins the movement's name), six of the twelve articles directly concern Shakespeare, two deal with Spenser, Jonson, and Donne, and three are not concerned with any particular writer (which leaves one on Elizabethan poetry). See Greenblatt, *Genre*.

[61] Carol Thomas Neely, 'Constructing the Subject: Feminist Practice and the New Renaissance Discourses', *ELR* 18 (1988), 5–18. For a more general critique of New Historicism's male-orientated concerns, and the suggestion that New Historicism to a large extent arose out of feminist theory, see Judith Lowder Newton, 'History as Usual? Feminism and the "New Historicism"', in Veeser (ed.), *The New Historicism*, 152–67.

[62] Gordon McMullan and Jonathan Hope (eds.), *The Politics of Tragicomedy: Shakespeare and After* (London: Routledge, 1992), 10.

[63] Much has been claimed for this essay. Vickers collects some comments in *Appropriating Shakespeare*: 'Robert N. Watson writes that "Stephen Greenblatt's wonderfully fresh and insightful 'Invisible Bullets' is of course a seminal document in the New Historicist Movement"'. Arthur F. Kinney, editor of *English Literary Renaissance*, has hailed it as 'perhaps the most important, and surely the most influential essay of the past decade in English Renaissance Cultural history' (p. 249).

compiling glossaries, the one of the Indians, the other of his companions in Eastcheap. Both will later use the knowledge this gives them to control and rule their one-time companions. Greenblatt is quite aware of his novelty: 'it may be objected that there is something slightly absurd in likening such moments [Hal's declarations of purpose] to aspects of Harriot's text'.[64]

As a rationale, Greenblatt brings forward the New Historicist argument concerning the endlessly connected nature of culture. Yet a strange thing begins now to happen. Harriot's diary continually recedes in importance, eventually becoming little more than a literary gloss on the Shakespearian text. This movement from the shock of new material to the focus on a standard text, is common enough to be a scheme of Greenblatt's writing. The canonical text dominates, and Greenblatt is willing to say why. In *The History of Henry IV*, 'The balance is almost perfect, as if Shakespeare had somehow reached through in *1 Henry IV* to the very centre of the system of opposed and interlocking forces that held Tudor society together.'[65] The reason why Shakespeare is still the king of the canon then, is that he is the privileged cultural key. This sense of revelation cuts wholly against the declared theoretical thrust of New Historicism. The text of genius becomes somehow able to give the critic access to the real; as Lentricchia notes, this is the same wholly anomalous humanist impulse that was seen in Taine.[66] It is hard to imagine anything more conservative. Indeed, Greenblatt's account may be seen to out-Taine Taine; for, in Greenblatt's world picture there is no lock, no culture that exists either to be explained by the text or to explain the text. The play is the culture, and Shakespeare's play is the most perfect expression of that—both lock and key.

Harriot's diary fades in importance because its only purpose is to illustrate an aspect of Shakespeare's achievement, to show his genius. By invoking Geertz's concept of 'thick' reading, as Greenblatt had already done in *Renaissance Self-Fashioning*, all that is important in Elizabethan culture can be reached through the Shakespearian master text. The miracle then becomes how Shakespeare was able to do this; in this case how he understood the strategies by which political authority sought to impose itself on the Algonquian Indians:

> Shakespeare evidently grasped such strategies not by brooding on the impact of English culture on far-off Virginia but by looking intently at the world immediately around him, by contemplating the queen and her powerful friends and enemies, and by reading imaginatively the great English chroniclers.[67]

This would not, it strikes me, be out of place in the criticism of Dowden or Quiller-Couch. At this central point in his critical practice, Greenblatt merges

[64] Greenblatt, *Shakespearean Negotiations*, 45.

[65] Ibid. 47.

[66] Lentricchia, 'Foucault's Legacy—A New Historicism?', in Veeser (ed.), *The New Historicism*, 231–42 (233).

[67] Greenblatt, *Shakespearean Negotiations*, 40.

with old historicism and traditional humanist criticism. Some protest, of course. James Holstun, as part of his 'Ranting at the New Historicism', notes how it is with this notion of a cultural key that New Historicists generally tend to merge with the Tillyard trope: 'Even though we have replaced an "order model" of the Elizabethan world picture with a "power model", each canonical cultural artifact remains a cultural synecdoche.'[68]

Yet the new New Historicist kingdom does not have all the old kings; one absence is remarkable. For, given the centrality of the Renaissance and its drama to New Historicism; and given the centrality to Renaissance drama of Shakespearian drama; and seeing that the centrality of all three of these categories is due to the critical insights they offer to the question of 'Who's there?'—where is *Hamlet*, the Prince and the play? *Hamlet*, whose opening question also began the drama of New Historicism, as it begins the drama of ideology? *Hamlet*, the most famous of all whodunnits? This absence from the most influential New Historicist works is all the more remarkable since not only is *Hamlet* a drama intimately bound up with many aspects of the question of identity, but, as Part II argues, *Hamlet* has been the text through which literary, and to some extent cultural, notions of subjectivity have been defined in the following three centuries. *Hamlet*, then, plays the ghost in New Historicism's drama, but it is a ghost to which New Historicism has not spoken.

> *Mar.* Thou art a Scholler; speake to it *Horatio.*
> *Barn.* Lookes it not like the King? Marke it *Horatio*
> (I. I. 40–I)

New Historicists, although they have not questioned *Hamlet*, have asked and answered 'Who's there?' of other works. The work of their paramount 'Scholler', Stephen Greenblatt, is representative. Greenblatt's *Renaissance Self-Fashioning* is an impressive work—thoughtful, alive to the dialectical nature of the questions with which it is concerned, constantly returning to the particular examples of its argument, whether those are from life or art, and full of interest. Yet the way in which it achieves its answer of 'nobody' to 'Who's there?' is less satisfactory.

'My subject', Greenblatt begins, 'is *self-fashioning* from More to Shakespeare; my starting point is quite simply that in sixteenth-century England there were both selves and a sense they could be fashioned' (p. I). While such fashioning has always occurred, Greenblatt argues, he focuses on this period as it is one in which critics have long asserted that 'there appears to be an increased self-consciousness about the fashioning of human identity as a manipulable, artful process' (p. 2). It is this thesis that Greenblatt sets out to examine. He set out earnestly wishing to confirm the thesis since, as he tells us in his epilogue, he saw the 'power and freedom' that self-fashioning implied, the sense of agency it accorded to the 'I', 'as an important element in my own sense of myself'

[68] James Holstun, 'Ranting at the New Historicism', *ELR* 19 (1989), 189–225 (203).

(p. 256). Indeed, 'in our culture to abandon self-fashioning is to abandon the craving for freedom, and to let go of one's stubborn hold upon selfhood, even selfhood conceived of as a fiction, is to die' (p. 257). Sadly, by the end of his research, 'the human subject itself began to seem remarkably unfree, the ideological product of relations of power in a particular society' (p. 256). Greenblatt could find no agency, only the answer 'nobody' or 'everything'.

Given the account New Historicists provide of their founding theories, this conclusion is expected. The occurrence of 'power' alerts us to the presence of Foucault, the description of the human subject as an 'ideological product' to Althusser and revised Marxism. Autonomy and agency may be expected to dissolve away. This dissolution is facilitated by the terms of Greenblatt's investigation. They are surprisingly fluid: in the introduction, 'selves' being 'fashioned' becomes the equivalent of the 'fashioning of human identity' which, by the epilogue, becomes the equivalent of 'the human subject itself'. This suggests that there are no worthwhile distinctions to be made between 'self', 'identity', and the 'human subject'; as with Greenblatt's sense of culture, every part of the 'human subject' is interrelated and equal. Identity seems to be an undifferentiated whole, existing on one level, and capable of analysis through any one point. The idea of distinct parts of identity, of an anatomy of identity, is rejected.

This conflation is central to *Renaissance Self-Fashioning* and goes hand in hand with a rather unusual use of particular terms. For instance, in the introduction Greenblatt suggests that fashioning of selves is, 'The achievement of . . . a distinctive personality, a characteristic address to the world, a consistent mode of perceiving and behaving.' (p. 2) This precise-sounding list uses terms that are large in two ways. First, the concepts are complicated; what are 'personality', perception, and behaviour? Second, the qualifications are rigorous; 'distinctive', 'characteristic', and 'consistent'. The first group allows Greenblatt to focus on almost anything within a subject-person's or a dramatic-person's life, and so move outwards to identity; the second to disqualify, should he want to, any of the terms from being achieved. And given the conflation of this set of terms, central to the question of 'Who's there?', once one term fails, all fail. What is quickly clear within *Renaissance Self-Fashioning*, then, is that though it may be about the fashioning of selves, in the very broad sense of a subject-person or identity as a whole, it is not about the fashioning of self. Quite what 'self' is, has been and remains a matter of intense debate.[69] However, many definitions see it as an area within, or a subset of, identity. In *Renaissance Self-Fashioning*, Greenblatt repeatedly subsumes self to identity or even to human nature, insisting that there is only an undifferentiated whole. Once self-fashioning is taken to be the fashioning of identity or of human nature, it is seen always to be compromised, a product, and never to be fashioned by oneself.

[69] This book does not propose an answer, but borrows a terminology with which to describe the variety of answers. For the discussion of the meanings of 'self', see Ch. 6.

How could it be otherwise? For who would, who indeed has ever suggested that identity can be purely fashioned by oneself? Identity relies on too many givens: appearance, occupation, upbringing, and so on. Even Coriolanus, who is not much given to qualifications, recognizes the theoretical nature of pure agency; he will stand before his family, '*As if* a man were Author of himself, & knew no other kin' (my emphasis; 5. 3. 36–7). Such a theoretical stance, a belief in pure agency, cannot last the scene. The un-self-fashioned nature of identity depresses Greenblatt, and the movement from hope of self-fashioning to distress at its absence, is present throughout *Renaissance Self-Fashioning*. Each chapter begins in light but ends in darkness; More executed on a scaffold; Tyndale burnt on the stake; Wyatt betrayed and under the scourge of royal discipline; Spenser yoked to a colonialism of language in the service of his queen; Marlowe destroying himself in the pursuit of insatiable desire; and, in *The tragedy of Othello, the Moor of Venice*, Shakespeare's failure to produce more than an erotic fantasy of escape from power. (Though we might remember that Shakespeare himself becomes reasonably wealthy and relatively powerful.)

The use of this particular terminology, then, gives rise to an absolute choice: either there is pure agency, total self-fashioning, or there is none. Greenblatt opts for the latter. His description of how this agency-less identity is produced has already been seen. It is given at the end of the introduction to *Renaissance Self-Fashioning*:

> We may say that self-fashioning occurs at the point of encounter between an authority and an alien, that what is produced in this encounter partakes of both the authority and the alien that is marked for attack, and hence that any achieved identity always contains within itself the signs of its own subversion or loss. (p. 9)

For all that Greenblatt talks of the complex nature of human beings, the theory of personality and identity which is found in *Renaissance Self-Fashioning* appears simple; identity is the product of 'an authority and an alien'. Identity, whether that of a fictional or real person, whether produced in the Renaissance or in the present, is always and everywhere expressive of the external factors which created it, and into which it always threatens to break down; the answer to 'Who's there' is always either 'nobody' or 'everything'.[70] This conclusion, Greenblatt tells us, upsets him deeply. He tells a story of a father who sat next to him on a plane, distraught at the thought of a coming visit he would pay to his dying son. The father, worried whether he will be able to understand his now speechless son, asks Greenblatt to mouth 'I want to die', and Greenblatt regretfully finds that he cannot. That he could not testifies, Greenblatt argues,

[70] As Howard points out in 'The New Historicism', this theory of personality shows the influence of 'Lacan's neo-Freudian psychology with its assumption . . . of a provisional and contradictory self which is the product of discourse' (p. 37). Greenblatt only mentions Lacan once by name towards the end of *Renaissance Self-Fashioning*; however, Holbein's 'The Ambassadors', which Greenblatt uses as his cover, is a picture which features famously within Lacan's work. See Vickers, *Appropriating Shakespeare*, 307.

'to my overwhelming need to sustain the illusion that I am the principal maker of my own identity' (p. 257).[71] Yet Greenblatt need not have become so upset. No one is going to be 'the principal maker' of their identity; far more likely is the possibility, abandoned in Greenblatt's conflation of terms, that they might be the maker of an aspect of their identity, an area indicated by a label such as 'self'. This is the argument which is pursued in Part III.

Hora. Most like: It harrowes me with fear & wonder
(I. I. 42)

Given Greenblatt's and New Historicists' interest in the fashioning of identity, the absence of a significant consideration of *Hamlet* from his work and from that of New Historicists more generally becomes not only a question of 'why?' but 'how?' How did Greenblatt and other New Historicists fail to begin by questioning the Ghost that stalked across the opening scene of their drama? In offering answers to the questions of 'why?' and 'how?', this second chapter closes the discussion of New Historicism with its own definition of the critical movement, particularly as that movement is exemplified in Greenblatt's criticism.[72] 'Resonance and Wonder', the last essay in *Learning to Curse*, is an obvious place in which to look for answers to the related questions of 'why?' and of 'how?' Its subject is Greenblatt's understanding of what New Historicism is, has been, and ought to be, this last being related to and dependent on what Greenblatt believes art to be. The essays of *Learning to Curse* also chart, as Greenblatt puts it in the introduction, 'The Trajectory' (p. 1) of his critical practice from 1976 to 1990.

Greenblatt begins the article as his readers have come to expect, with an anecdotal story: 'In a small glass case in the library of Christ Church, Oxford, there is a round, broad-brimmed cardinal's hat; a note card identifies it as having belonged to Cardinal Wolsey' (p. 161). This anecdote is offered as an illustrative example of the historical and theoretical interests of New Historicism. New Historicism is fascinated by 'The peregrinations of Wolsey's hat' that 'suggest that cultural artifacts do not stay still, that they exist in time, and that they are bound up with personal and institutional conflict, negotiations, and appropriations'. This scheme of cultural production Greenblatt rapidly traces, by retelling the somewhat tortuous route by which the hat arrived at Christ Church. It was sent off alone into the world, Greenblatt says, by 'the ominous form of Henry VIII', who 'cut off [Christ Church] from its original

[71] Greenblatt might have pointed out, as Charles Taylor has done, that the Western concept of human rights depends on the idea, fictional or not, that the subject-person is in some degree separate from society. (If Cultural Materialists wish to dispose of the ideology of the individual, they will also dispose of the rationale on which human rights are based.) See Charles Taylor, *Sources of the Self: The Making of Modern Identity* (Cambridge: Cambridge University Press, 1989), 11–12.

[72] The section which follows is indebted to Anne Barton's 'Perils of Historicism', a review of *Learning to Curse*, in *The New York Review of Books*, 28 Mar. 1991, 51–4.

benefactor', Cardinal Wolsey (1472/3–1530). This kingly action prevented any direct bequest:

> Instead, as the note informs us, after it had passed through the hands of various owners—including Bishop Burnet, Burnet's son, Burnet's son's housekeeper, the Dowager Countess of Albemarle's butler, the countess herself, and Horace Walpole—the hat was acquired for Christ Church in the nineteenth century, purchased, we are told, for the sum of sixty-three pounds, from the daughter of the actor Charles Kean. Kean is said to have worn the hat when he played Wolsey in Shakespeare's Henry VIII. (p. 161)

There are several problems with this account. The first is that it is not certain that the hat was Wolsey's. A visitor to the upper floor of the library at Christ Church finds a more modest note card than Greenblatt suggests. It reads:

> This hat was found in the Great Wardrobe by Bishop Burnet (d.1715) when Clerk of the Closet. . . . At the Strawberry Hill sale (1842), the catalogue of which described the hat as Wolsey's, it was bought for £21.

The hat may have been Wolsey's hat—it would clearly be pleasantly apposite for Christ Church if it was, for Wolsey's cardinal's hat is a prominent part of the College's arms—but as the card suggests, and as Dr J. F. A. Mason, the librarian of Christ Church and the compiler of the note card some twenty to thirty years ago, happily admits, it may not be.[73] It would be satisfying to be sure of the hat's provenance, but certainty is, here, elusive. The catalogue's attribution has more authority than might be expected since it was based on Horace Walpole's own sale catalogue. The auction was an amazing event. Walpole, helped by two others, had built Strawberry Hill over a period of forty-five years in a gradually evolving English Gothic style. The design of the house was a kind of synthesis; details from cathedrals and tombs, for instance, were merged in the design of chimney pieces. Walpole had crammed it with paintings, pictures, and objects from the past until, in Thomas Macaulay's words, 'every apartment' had become 'a museum; every piece of furniture a curiosity'.[74] Macaulay singled out as particularly interesting 'Queen Mary's comb, Wolsey's red hat, the pipe which Van Tromp smoked during his last sea fight, and the spur King William struck into the flank of Sorrel'. Like relics these evoked visions, and 'Wolsey's red hat' was particularly evocative; W. Harrison Ainsworth, who was given the task of describing Strawberry Hill in the 'Prefatory Remarks' of the catalogue, thought it probably 'the chiefest amongst this class of relics'.[75]

73 Dr J. F. A. Mason, in private conversation, 16 Feb. 1993.

74 Thomas Macaulay, *Edinburgh Review*, Oct. 1833. Quoted in Wilmarth Sheldon Lewis, *Horace Walpole* (London: Rupert Hart-Davis, 1961), 127.

75 *A Catalogue of the Contents of Strawberry Hill* (London: Smith and Robins, 1842), p. xv. Further references to this catalogue are given after quotations in the text.

The entire collection was to be sold, and as the auctioneer, Mr George Robins, was well aware, 'An object is prized, not only from its intrinsic value but from its association with remarkable events or illustrious names' (p. viii). It was just such associations that Strawberry Hill had made concrete, intensified, and deepened, as Walpole intended. Wolsey's hat was kept in the Holbein room, along with an 'exquisitely carved head of Henry the Eighth' said to be by Holbein (p. xv). Placing these two objects together, the master and servant once more reunited, created a far greater impact, or 'resonance' in Greenblatt's terms, than if they had remained apart. In fact Walpole may be said to have collected on the principle of resonance, a principle which governed many of his interests. W. Sheldon Lewis, in his biography of Walpole, notes how fond he was 'of recording anecdotes, pointing out family relationships, and adding odd circumstances' in the books he read.[76]

Robins, 'the King of Puffery',[77] had declared in his 'Prefatory Remarks' that the auction would be a 'Herculean undertaking . . . far exceeding in interest and importance all that has preceded it in the chronicles of auctions'.[78] Remarkably, this turned out to be a reasonable description. The auction took twenty-four days, not including the later sale of the library, which took another ten days. It generated great interest, being 'perhaps the most written about auction ever held in England'.[79] Much of this writing questioned the importance of the objects in Walpole's house, for the same relics which could evoke visions could also seem ridiculous, items of sentimental tat. 'You would laugh,' Macaulay had confided, 'if you saw in the midst of what trumpery I am writing' (p. 127). Parodies of the catalogue appeared, offering objects such as 'the bridge of the fiddle on which Nero played while Rome was burning' (p. 133). *The Times* scorned Walpole's collection, while the *Athenaeum* defended it.

Robins was presumably gratified by the interest. The sale was an enormous success, fetching what many considered the absurdly high price of £33,000. Lot 73, described on p. 175 as

A MOST INTERESTING AND VALUABLE RELIC THE RED HAT OF CARDINAL WOLSEY, FOUND IN THE GREAT WARDROBE, BY BISHOP BURNET, WHEN CLERK OF THE CLOSET; FROM HIS SON THE JUDGE, IT CAME TO THE COUNTESS DOWAGER OF ALBEMARLE, WHO PRESENTED IT TO HORACE WALPOLE

was sold on the seventeenth day, Friday 13 May, to Charles Kean, the actor, for £21. The description that Kean read was almost exactly that made as a manuscript note by Walpole in his copy of his own *Description of Strawberry Hill.* All that was missing was the route from Burnet's son to the Countess Dowager.

76 Lewis, *Horace Walpole*, 124.

77 Ibid. 132.

78 *A Catalogue*, 5.

79 Lewis, *Horace Walpole*, 132. Further references to this biography are given after quotations in the text.

Judge Burnet, Walpole writes, left the hat 'to his housekeeper, who gave it to the butler of Lady Anne Lennox, first Countess Dowager of Albemarle; he gave it to his Lady, and she to Mr Walpole in 1776'.[80] Perhaps Robins felt housekeepers and butlers detracted from the value of other 'illustrious names', and so hid them.

The text of the original letter from the Countess of Albemarle giving the hat to Walpole has been preserved, through being transcribed by Thomas Kirgate into his copy of the *Description of Strawberry Hill.* The letter adds the details that Bishop Burnet 'took it *or stole it* out of the Wardrobe' while Clerk of the Closet 'to Queen Anne', and that the butler's name was Gerrard.[81] I have been unable to find any mention of the hat in the writings of Bishop Burnet, but if Burnet did find it, this would still not prove that the hat was Wolsey's.[82] Wolsey's was not the only cardinal's hat, and there is no particular reason to imagine that it would end up in the King's possession. Unlike his successor, Thomas More, Wolsey was not put in the Tower, executed, and his goods confiscated as Greenblatt's talk of Henry VIII as the 'ominous form', which 'cut off [Christ Church] from its original benefactor' might suggest. Wolsey, when disgraced in October 1529, had been allowed to leave the court and keep his archbishopric of York and a pension of 1,000 marks from the see of Winchester, as well as being given about £3,000 in ready money.[83] His position at York meant that he was still one of the leading representatives of the Crown in the north of England.[84] Moreover, Henry sent messages, accompanied by his personal ring (the guarantee that the message was from the King) to reassure Wolsey that his remarkably soft fall from grace was temporary.[85] When Wolsey was arrested in 1530 on a charge of treason, he was allowed to make the journey to London at his own pace and with considerable dignity. He never arrived at the capital; taken ill on the journey, he died at Leicester Abbey, and was buried the next morning. According to George Cavendish, his gentleman usher, there was placed in his coffin 'all suche vestures & ornamentes as he was professed in whan he was consecrated bysshope & Archebysshope/ As myter crosseer ryng & palle w^{t} all other thynges appurtenaunt to his profession'.[86] Was his hat one of those 'other things'? Wolsey certainly cherished it. One of the charges

[80] *The Yale Edition of Horace Walpole's Correspondence*, ed. W. S. Lewis and John Riely, 48 vols. (Oxford: Oxford University Press, 1937–83), xli. 333.

[81] Ibid. xli. 332.

[82] George Burnet, *Bishop Burnet's History of His Own Time*, 2 vols. (London: T. Ward, 1724–34).

[83] See Peter Gwyn, *The King's Cardinal: The Rise and Fall of Thomas Wolsey* (London: Barrie & Jenkins, 1990), 612.

[84] Ibid. 617.

[85] E. W. Ives, 'The Fall of Wolsey', in S. J. Gunn and P. G. Lindley (eds.), *Cardinal Wolsey: Church, State and Art* (Cambridge: Cambridge University Press, 1991), 286–315 (287). The softness of Wolsey's fall has made it a subject of debate; Ives suggests that Henry was acting under the influence of Anne Boleyn, around whose dislike of Wolsey factional interests had cohered.

[86] George Cavendish, *The Life and Death of Cardinal Wolsey*, ed. Richard S. Sylvester (London: EETS, 1959), 182.

against him in 1529 was that the public triumph he organized to celebrate the arrival of his cardinal's hat in London (a celebration Cavendish likens to the coronation of a prince), 'was a prodigal and wasteful expense', and 'a token of vainglory'.[87]

Negative propositions are far harder to demonstrate than positive ones, and it may never be possible to establish either that Burnet never had the hat or that the hat in the Wardrobe was not Wolsey's. At present, the Countess Dowager of Albemarle, or her butler, Gerrard, is our authority for the hat's peregrinations. Walpole regarded the Countess in 1755 as 'the most meritorious wife' of a spendthrift husband.[88] Lady Mary Coke, in her journal on 20 June 1773, described her as 'that old foolish woman'.[89] Either way, it must remain a possibility, if not a strong one, that the hat in Christ Church really is Wolsey's. Only in a very loose sense, it would seem, could it be said that the note card 'identifies' the hat 'as having belonged to Cardinal Wolsey'. Greenblatt appears to be taking the qualifications, particularities, and uncertainties of history a little too lightly.

Further discrepancies between the note card and Greenblatt's history are pointed out in Anne Barton's review of *Learning to Curse*:

> The elegance with which Greenblatt accommodates Wolsey's hat to a story about how the Reformation tried to dismantle the 'histrionic apparatus of Catholicism' by selling off papist vestments to the professional players makes one almost regret having to disturb it with the specificities of Burnet and his son's housekeeper, Horace Walpole, Kean, and Mrs. Logie.[90]

[87] Quoted in John Guy, *Tudor England* (Oxford: Oxford University Press, 1988), 89. The history of Wolsey's cardinal's hat is fascinating. The hat's importance extends beyond its symbolic value as the sign of Wolsey's papal powers. Wolsey wove the hat through his schemes and ambitions—the hat came to express who and what Wolsey was about. This can be seen particularly in the way in which he put its symbolic value into circulation. He had it carved in his houses, depicted in manuscripts and stained-glass windows, engraved on gold bowls, and sculpted for his intended tomb. The hat, in fact, functioned as an icon rather like the Tudor rose—a dangerous similarity, which involved Wolsey in a constant play of negotiation and exchange with the King over the appropriations he had himself made from others. In the end, the negotiation was unsustainable. When the clock tower at Hampton Court was restored in 1845, Wolsey's arms were seen to have been replaced by the King's, and the cardinal's hat was covered by a crown worked in wrought iron. This history, demonstrating the visual nature of Tudor power and the politics of appearance, can be followed in Gunn and Lindley (eds.), *Cardinal Wolsey*. See particularly Hilary Wayment, 'Wolsey and stained glass', pp. 116–30; Philippa Glanville, 'Cardinal Wolsey and the goldsmiths', pp. 131–48; P. G. Lindley, 'Playing check-mate with royal majesty? Wolsey's patronage of Italian Renaissance sculpture', pp. 261–85. The detail concerning Hampton Court is given on p. 281. Cardinals' hats were general currency in the Elizabethan period: e.g. the resignation of one is mentioned in John Webster's *The Tragedy of the Duchess of Malfi* (1613–14) at 3. 4. 3; Wolsey is charged with having the hat struck 'on the King's coin' in Shakespeare's *All is True* (*Henry VIII*) at 3. 2. 325. There was even a brothel, the lease of which was owned by the Bishop of Winchester, called 'The Cardinal's Hat'. See E. J. Burford, *Bawds and Lodgings* (London: Peter Owen, 1976).

[88] *Correspondence*, xx. 459.

[89] Ibid. xxxi. 172.

[90] Barton, 'Perils of Historicism', 51. Further references to this review are given after quotations in the text. In the rest of the section, I make clear which text of 'Resonance and Wonder' is being used.

The peculiarity of this is that Greenblatt has mentioned these 'specificities', as seen above. What soon becomes clear, thanks to the accuracy of Barton's quotation, is that the hardback version of 'Resonance and Wonder' (1990), the version Barton reviewed, is different—in its first page and endnotes—from the paperback version (1992) that was quoted from above. Here are the opening lines as Barton read them in the hardback version:

In a small glass case in the library of Christ Church, Oxford, there is a round, red priest's hat; a note card identifies it as having belonged to Cardinal Wolsey. . . . The hat was acquired for Christ Church in the eighteenth century, purchased, we are told, from a company of players. If this miniature history of an artifact is too vague to be of much consequence—I do not know the name of the company of players, or the circumstances in which they acquired their curious stage property, or whether it was ever used, for example, by an actor playing Wolsey in Shakespeare's *Henry VIII*, or when it was placed under glass, or even whether it was anything but a clever fraud—it nonetheless evokes a vision of cultural production that I find compelling. (p. 161)

Here they are as they appear in the paperback version:

In a small glass case in the library of Christ Church, Oxford, there is a round, broad-brimmed cardinal's hat; a note card identifies it as having belonged to Cardinal Wolsey. . . . After it had passed through the hands of various owners—including Bishop Burnet, Burnet's son, Burnet's son's housekeeper, the Dowager Countess of Albemarle's butler, the countess herself, and Horace Walpole—the hat was acquired for Christ Church in the nineteenth century, purchased, we are told, for the sum of sixty-three pounds, from the daughter of the actor Charles Kean. Kean is said to have worn the hat when he played Wolsey in Shakespeare's *Henry VIII*. If this miniature history of an artifact is too slight to be of much consequence, it nonetheless evokes a vision of cultural production that I find compelling. (p. 161)

Greenblatt has corrected his account, and has done so, it would seem, by consulting Barton's review. One cannot be sure of this, for the relevant acknowledgement, added in the paperback to the hardback's first endnote, does not mention the review itself; instead Barton is thanked 'for correcting my description of the hat in Christ Church and for transcribing the note card that details its provenance'. (This is, in itself, a little confusing, for what must be meant is that Barton is thanked for her correction of the description of the hat and its provenance.)[91]

[91] At this point I would like to repeat an apology made to Professor Greenblatt in *Essays in Criticism*. In the July 1988 issue, a correction to an earlier article of mine, 'The Man who Mistook his Hat: Stephen Greenblatt and the Anecdote', was published. Greenblatt had rightly pointed out to the journal's editors that my article did not acknowledge his acknowledgement of Barton, and so misled readers. This was a serious error, and I have tried to ensure that the present argument is free of any further errors. What I hope will also be quite clear is that my argument—here as I intended it to be in the article—is not substantially concerned with issues of direct acknowledgement. The argument is rather concerned with the selective use within 'Resonance and Wonder' of the more detailed history pointed out by Barton in her review; with, that is, Greenblatt's response to Barton. For this reason I trace that use below, as I did in the article.

However, although Greenblatt thanks Barton, he clearly does not believe, as Barton did, that the 'historical specificities' she points out would 'disturb' the 'elegance with which [he] accommodates Wolsey's hat to a story about how the Reformation tried to dismantle the "histrionic apparatus of Catholicism"'. In fact, it would seem that Barton's corrections are of factual import only; her specificities are easily embedded within Greenblatt's argument, proof that she has missed the point. Yet this is made possible by the paperback version's omission of two of the details that Barton included. One is the note card's statement that the hat was described as Wolsey's 'at the Strawberry Hill sale'. This allows Greenblatt's claim that the note card 'identifies' the hat as 'having belonged to Cardinal Wolsey' to stand uncontested.[92] Greenblatt's second omission from Barton's account is the fact that 'the hat was found in the Great Wardrobe by Bishop Burnet (who died in 1715) when he was Clerk of the Closet'.[93] This historical detail concerning the hat's origin renders very unlikely Greenblatt's argument that the hat was sold off to the theatre as part of the Reformation's dismantling of 'the histrionic apparatus of Catholicism'.[94] Unless, that is, we are to assume that it was bought back by the government. In leaving out this detail, Greenblatt has retained his argument's plausibility by absorbing Barton's historical details, her list of the hat's owners, within it: 'as the note informs us, after it had passed through the hands of various owners—including Bishop Burnet, Burnet's son', etc. (p. 161). That 'including' allows the suggestion of owners before Burnet. Into this space of chronological vagueness (all the specific dates given by Barton and the note card are omitted, though the date of the hat's acquisition by Christ Church is corrected from the eighteenth century to the nineteenth), Greenblatt introduces the historical fact that some of the 'gorgeous properties' of Catholicism were sold in the Reformation to theatrical companies, who acquired 'the tarnished but still potent charisma that clung to the old vestments' (p. 162). Then, through the logic of language, he makes this piece of history a piece of the hat's history; the following sentence begins, 'By the time Wolsey's hat reached the library at Christ Church, its charisma must have been largely exhausted' (p. 162). The same charisma, it is presumed, as that which 'clung to the [other] old vestments' that had been sold off.

The hat can thus remain one of the relics that 'enable us to glimpse the social process through which objects, gestures, rituals and phrases are fashioned and moved from one zone of display to another' (p. 162). Indeed, the hat becomes such a relic even more definitely, since Greenblatt, now backed up by Barton's 'specificities', feels able to do without his former admission that the hat might be nothing 'but a clever fraud' (p. 161). The importance of these relics lies in the

[92] Greenblatt, *Learning*, 161–2.

[93] Barton, 'Perils of Historicism', 51.

[94] Greenblatt, *Learning*, 162. Further references to this book are given after quotations in the text.

fact they 'reveal something critically important about the *textual* relics with which my profession is obsessed' (p. 162), which is that

> The display cases with which I am most involved—books—characteristically conceal this [social] process, so that we have a misleading impression of fixity and little sense of the historical transactions through which the great texts we study have been fashioned. (pp. 162–3)

Barton is perhaps too severe when she talks of Greenblatt's 'suppressing or reinventing what the Christ Church note card actually says',[95] for it would seem unlikely that Greenblatt's inaccuracies were deliberate, given the visionary quality of his subsequent musings in the hardback on the hat's provenance; it is hard to believe that Greenblatt is acting deliberately when he tells us that he does not 'know the name of the company of players or the circumstances in which they acquired their curious stage property, or whether it was ever used, for example, by an actor playing Wolsey in Shakespeare's *Henry VIII*' (p. 161). (The note card states that the hat 'was bought for £21 by Charles Kean the actor, who is said to have worn it more than once when playing Wolsey in *Henry VIII.*') Memory is selective, and errors are easily made.[96] Yet such selectivity does seem to colour Greenblatt's treatment of Barton's review and its arguments; though again, it may simply be that Greenblatt does not consider historical specificities, or Barton's arguments, as of any great importance.

While these are only details, and while one can never be sure of the intentions of others, such unfortunate omissions of history's difference, and of another's voice, rob Greenblatt of the moral authority he admired in Raymond Williams. For the Greenblatt of *Learning to Curse* seems less concerned than he wishes to be to do justice to the positions of others. Perhaps the clearest example of this comes in the paperback's revisions to the introduction to *Learning to Curse*—revisions again made in response to Barton's review. The introduction, quite short and at times intimately personal, culminates with a section entitled 'Fiction and Reality'. In this, Greenblatt voices his worries over some of the effects of recent literary theorizing, and he stresses the need never to lose sight of the reality of pain for those who suffer, insisting on the final inadequacy of the 'post-structuralist confounding of fiction and non-fiction' (p. 15).

Greenblatt takes as his text the horrific torture and murder of a Chinese goldsmith by Edmund Scott and other Englishmen, as described in Scott's *Exact Discourse of the Subtilties, Fashions, Pollicies, Religion, and Ceremonies of the East Indians* (1606). Sir William Foster praises Scott and the other Englishmen in his introduction to the Hakluyt Society's edition, published in 1943, and, as Greenblatt says, 'makes no direct comment' on their treatment of the Chinese goldsmith. This outrages Greenblatt: 'the moral stupidity of this drivel obviously

[95] Barton, 'Perils of Historicism', 51.

[96] See n. 90 above.

reflects the blind patriotism of a nation besieged' (p. 12). Indeed, Greenblatt wonders if such silences do not show us 'collaborating with Scott and with all the others like him' in crimes against humanity (p. 13). The weight of the charge is immense, and yet Greenblatt's treatment of Foster and Scott might itself be seen to be marked by silences; as Barton points out, Greenblatt's charge against Foster 'seems somewhat disingenuous, given that the editor does in fact deplore "these barbarous proceedings" in a note appended to the passage itself'.[97] Strictly speaking, Greenblatt is quite correct; there is 'no direct comment', and one may feel that Foster had an obligation to make direct comment. Equally, however, Barton's sense of the misleading nature of Greenblatt's formulation may seem just, and be seen to be evidence of his 'distortion of the evidence in order to convict' (p. 52). Barton goes on to point out that Greenblatt's description of the historical context to Scott's actions is similarly misleading; where Greenblatt talks in general terms of commercial rivalry, fear of fire and theft, and hatred of the natives, Barton allows us to hear Scott's voice more clearly, describing a situation of mental and physical siege that drove some of the Englishmen insane through lack of sleep and fear. More importantly, Barton points out that Greenblatt, following Foster, omits a key clause from the beginning of Scott's description of the torture: 'Wherefore, because of his sullennesse, *and that it was hee that fired us*, I thought I would burne him now a little.' As Barton points out, the omitted clause (here in italics) does not justify Scott; but it transforms our reading of the text and allows a fuller understanding of his act.

As with the errors in Greenblatt's account of the cardinal's hat, Barton may be being too harsh on Greenblatt when she sees this as intentional distortion; yet, as with the hat, Greenblatt's response to Barton in the paperback version lends some weight to Barton's conclusions. In the paperback edition, Greenblatt's condemnation of Foster is neither moderated, nor Foster's footnote mentioned; 'no direct comment' still remains, along with the comments on 'moral stupidity' and the implicit charge of crimes against humanity. Similarly, beyond the recognition that the Chinese were not natives in Java, no change is made to give a greater sense of the desperation of the Englishmen's situation. Even the omitted clause remains missing from the body of the text, to be mentioned in an addition to the hardback's fourth endnote:

> As Anne Barton has pointed out in a review of my book (*New York Review of Books* 38 p. 54), the Hakluyt Society editor omits from the opening sentence of this passage a phrase that emphasizes the 'horrible symmetry' of the torture: 'Wherefore, because of his sullennesse, *and that it was hee that fired us*, I thought I would burne him now a little . . .' (italics added). (p. 15)

Barton's review is mentioned here, yet neither is there any sense given of Barton's argument with Greenblatt, nor is there any sense of the resistance of

[97] Barton, 'Perils of Historicism', 51.

the historical evidence to Greenblatt's argument; once again, Barton appears more in the role of amanuensis than equal or critic, transcribing note cards and doing helpful research in the library. The mention of 'horrible symmetry', meanwhile, will remain opaque to many of Greenblatt's readers, given as it is without contextualization.

There are many possible arguments to explain why Greenblatt refuses to mention Foster's footnote, why he does not take account of the omitted clause in the body of the text, and why he makes no mention of Barton's disagreements. Yet it is hard to imagine how they could be made in terms that would satisfy Greenblatt, after having read Greenblatt's declaration of the criterion by which he wishes his own and New Historicist practice to be judged. 'If there is any value to what has become known as "new historicism",' Greenblatt writes, 'it must be here, in an intensified willingness to read all of the textual traces of the past with the attention traditionally conferred only on literary texts' (p. 14). Coming after the treatment of Foster, Scott, and Barton, the 'all' is problematic, while 'intensified willingness' is a poor description of Greenblatt's hardback practice, and an even poorer description of his paperback revisions. In the paperback edition, both historical specificities and the voices and arguments of others lose out to the previously existing structure of Greenblatt's argument. This seems to go beyond the natural and unavoidable tendency to simplify the accounts of others.

The dominance of Greenblatt's argument, and its willingness to shape the past, whether by partial inclusion or exclusion, is paralleled in Greenblatt's sense of what a work of art is. A work of art has two qualities for Greenblatt; one is resonance, by which is meant 'the power of the object displayed to reach out beyond its formal boundaries to a larger world, to evoke in the viewer the complex, dynamic cultural forces from which it has emerged'.[98] Greenblatt is worried that New Historicism, with its contextualizing drive, has tended to concentrate overmuch on resonant aspects of objects. In that sense it has created literary museums rather like Horace Walpole's Strawberry Hill, where the trivial sits by the great, and assumes equal importance because of the connections it demonstrates. In refusing to consider the text in any kind of isolation, New Historicism has mislaid it in the web of connections which it has traced between the text and its culture. To counter this tendency, Greenblatt stresses the work of art's other quality, that of generating 'wonder'. He defines this as 'the power of the object displayed to stop the viewer in his tracks, to convey an arresting sense of uniqueness, to evoke an exalted attention' (p. 170), and as 'the art work's capacity to generate in the spectator surprise, delight, admiration and intimations of genius' (p. 180). To clarify these terms further he uses as an explanatory analogue two alternative practices of museums: you can display great works of art either wondrously—on their own, often in mystical,

[98] Greenblatt, *Learning*, 170. Further references to this book are given after quotations in the text.

isolating pools of white light—or resonantly, in and among contemporary, lesser works, so that a sense of the relationships with their artistic community is gained, at the expense of their individual impact.

At first Greenblatt's worry and his suggested remedy may seem unobjectionable, but his definition of the art work prepares it for the subservience his argument will enforce from it. Putting aside his understanding of 'resonance', his sense of 'wonder' lacks any sense of the challenge of works of art. They are generators of pleasure and amazement only; he traces wonder's descent from the cult of the marvellous. Works of art—through the analogy with paintings—also appear relatively static; they are there to be viewed, appreciated, and explained by the magisterial critic; the critic is not there to answer to the objects. He decides where the works of art are to be placed or hung; it is fully his decision. Yet is it helpful to compare texts with pictures in a museum? Texts are far more talkative (particularly so when compared with Greenblatt's especially static pictures) and combative.

Greenblatt's sense of a static, passive wonder, waiting to be explained, takes any sense of resistance away from the work of art. What his definition of wonder lacks is the sense of the challenge and fearfulness of texts. Such a sense is only admitted, uncommented on, in his concluding quotation from Albertus Magnus' (*c.*1200–80) *Commentary on the Metaphysics of Aristotle*:

> wonder is defined as a constriction and suspension of the heart caused by amazement at the sensible appearance of something so portentous, great, and unusual, that the heart suffers a systole. Hence wonder is something like fear in its effect on the heart. This effect of wonder, then, this constriction and systole of the heart, spring from an unfulfilled but felt desire to know the cause of that which appears portentous and unusual.[99]

Wonder can terrify the viewer half to death; it is a kind of artistic cardiac arrest, and like any brush with death, tends to provoke its victim to examine himself or herself. Greenblatt, however, never appears similarly frightened in his practice, though he often talks about his worries in asides. One who is frightened, one who is absolutely and immediately struck with the sense of the fearfulness and communicativeness of wonder, is Horatio; the Ghost 'harrowes' Horatio not with 'resonance and wonder', but 'with fear & wonder', and afterwards he realizes that it 'boades some strange erruption to our State' (I. I. 69). Horatio's reaction is, perhaps, the better model for the critic; while the Ghost itself, 'the sensible appearance of something so portentous, great and unusual', might be seen as Albertus Magnus' wonder (spiritually) bodied forth.

Greenblatt's New Historicism, however, is more than the imperialism of argument. It was tentatively suggested above that New Historicism might profitably be seen as a phase in the history of rhetoric. New Historicism can, in

[99] Greenblatt quotes from J. V. Cunningham, *Woe or Wonder: The Emotional Effect of Shakespearean Tragedy* (Denver: Alan Swallow, 1960; orig. edn. 1951), 82.

fact, be seen as a style of argument; the movement may be described through the use of an enchiridion, manual, or 'Art of Rhetoric'. To begin with what is usually the second part of such manuals, New Historicism proclaims its identity through the particularly heavy use of certain figures of speech. On the most local level, this is built up from the vocabulary employed. Certain literary-critical terms must not be used, such as allusion, symbolism, allegory, and mimesis; any term, in fact, that might carry the suggestion of discrete foregrounds and backgrounds to texts. In their place should be used such terms as negotiation, circulation, and exchange, terms that suggest the interconnectedness of culture. Moving on to schemes, one particularly favoured is chiasmus, as in Montrose's slogan, 'The Historicity of Texts and the Textuality of History'.[100] The prevalence of chiasmus reflects New Historicism's concern to insist on the circularity of cultural relationships. Another scheme much used is metanoia, which George Puttenham defines (with his usual playful wit) in *The Arte of English Poesie* (1589):

> Otherwhiles we speake and be sorry for it, as if we had not wel spoken, so that we seeme to call in our word againe, and to put in another fitter for the purpose [. . . for example, I,] singing in honor of the mayden Queen, meaning to praise her for her greatnesse of courage, ouershooting my selfe, called it first by the name of pride: then fearing least fault might be found with that terme, by & by turned this word pride to praise: resembling her Maiesty to the Lion.[101]

Metanoia is usually employed in the introduction to New Historicist articles; it is part of New Historicist belief in the need to be methodologically self-conscious, and more specifically reflects the attempt both to abandon the violence of boundaries and categories, and to avoid being placed (co-opted would be their preferred term) within any such categories. So, for example, when Joel Fineman discusses New Historicism as a term:

> however unreflectingly or naively this oxymoron may initially have been intended, and whatever it was the old and unreformed 'Historicism' of the New Historicism may have been supposed to have been before its supplanting renovation—this oxymoron is witness to or earnest of an impulse to discover or to disclose some wrinkling and historicizing interruption.[102]

The problem with this tendency, as Stanley Fish points out in parodic style, is that 'you cannot live the radical or indeterminate or provisional or textualist life'.[103] Action or critical judgement is dependent on the crudity of categories

[100] Montrose, 'Renaissance Literary Studies', 8. Quoted in Greenblatt, *Learning*, 170.

[101] George Puttenham, *The Arte of English Poesie* (Menston: Scholar Press, 1968; first pub. 1589), 179–80. Puttenham's work had probably been circulating in manuscript for some twenty years before publication.

[102] Fineman, 'The History of the Anecdote', 60.

[103] Stanley Fish, 'Commentary: The Young and the Restless', in Veeser (ed.), *The New Historicism*, 303–16 (311).

and the abandonment of self-observing self-consciousness, and hence metanoia is usually not employed after the introduction.[104]

In terms of figures of thought, the Tillyard trope, which has already been mentioned, is a specialized example of New Historicists' use of metaphor. More standard is the profound reliance of their critical procedure on the particular metaphorical usage of metonymy. Often, New Historicism's critical procedure is said to be synecdochic. However, this is, in respect of New Historicists' critical explanation of the primary, 'wondrous' text, incorrect. What is synecdochic is the procedure of Cultural Materialists; Cultural Materialists will typically concentrate on some aspect of culture that is marginalized within the text that is being studied, such as the witches in *Macbeth*, and begin to contextualize the play from this point, thus giving themselves criteria of relevance. New Historicists, by contrast, contextualize a play by placing it next to an aspect of culture—often to be used synecdochically to stand for all culture—which it will argue it should be closely associated with, even though there is no literal connection. An example of this would be Greenblatt's use of the Reverend Francis Wayland's 1831 account of how he made his 15-month-old son obedient by starving him, as a parallel to Lear's relationship to Cordelia. The aim of New Historicists is to create metonymic metaphors for texts. In so doing, they need only the barest criteria of relevance and none of coverage.

This brings us back to what is usually the first part of an Art of Rhetoric, the discussion of 'inventio' and 'dispositio'—the finding of arguments and the arrangements of those arguments into a structured discourse. 'Inventio' ceases to be a problem for New Historicists, because of their metonymic procedures; once criteria of relevance have been removed, everything becomes relevant. For a critical profession that measures success in terms of publication this is immensely attractive. 'Dispositio' has tended to be fourfold. Typically the article or chapter begins with an anecdote, goes on to an 'amplificatio' of the cultural resonances the anecdote sets off, turns to the primary text, then argues for the metonymic relationship between the two texts, and concludes with a moralizing ending. Greenblatt's 'Invisible Bullets', discussed above, is a good example of this structure. By the time of *Learning to Curse*, however, Greenblatt's 'dispositio' has tended to become a sequence of anecdotes, interwoven with a sequence of moral conclusions.[105]

[104] This is not the case with the quotation from Fineman. However, as Fineman never gets to his main subject which was, as declared in his opening paragraph, to examine the use of the anecdote in Greenblatt's 'Fiction and Friction', the entire article may be considered introductory. The quotation comes, in fact, from a footnote—footnotes making up slightly under half the article's length. Fineman's appending of the argument is done in a partly humorous vein. See Veeser (ed.), *The New Historicism*, 49–76. Greenblatt, by contrast, very rarely uses metanoia, and has for a New Historicist little interest in self-consciousness; as he says in 'Resonance and Wonder' while commenting on the practices of others, 'I am certainly not opposed to methodological self-consciousness, but I am less inclined to see overtness—an explicit articulation of one's values and methods—as inherently necessary or virtuous.' Greenblatt, *Learning*, 167.

[105] See e.g. 'Learning to Curse: Aspects of Linguistic Colonialism in the Sixteenth Century',

Anecdotes, in fact, lie at the heart of New Historicism, as metonymic vehicle controlling the critical practice, enabling 'inventio', and shaping 'dispositio'. One reason for this is that anecdotes create the effect of newness; Lear seen through the Reverend Wayland's disciplining of his son has not been written about before. Such a rhetorical explanation seems reinforced by the now you see it, now you don't qualities of the cardinal's hat; in two versions of 'Resonance and Wonder', the cardinal's hat does not appear at all.[106] Joel Fineman, in 'The History of the Anecdote: Fiction and Fiction', argues that the anecdote lies at the centre not only of New Historicist practice, but, 'in significant ways, determines the practice of historiography'.[107] The anecdote is so important to historiography and New Historicism as it 'is the literary form or genre that uniquely refers to the real' (p. 56). Fineman's 'uniquely' is unsubstantiated and its meaning difficult.[108] What he would seem to be arguing is that the anecdote makes plain the interplay between literature and reality, which interplay was one of the central concerns of New Historicism. Moreover, the anecdote makes clear that this interplay is not in any way simply causal, but rather complicatedly contingent. In a later definition, Fineman argues that it is 'the literary form that uniquely *lets history happen*' by producing 'the effect of the real, the occurrence of contingency' (p. 61). This 'effect' and 'occurrence' seems to be gained by the anecdote's inability to contain all of the reality it refers to (though this would seem to apply to language as a whole). It is contingent, not autonomous. Thus the anecdote disrupts any simple teleological view of history: 'its narration both comprises and refracts the narration it reports' (p. 61).

Greenblatt uses this account of Fineman's to explain his own practice; Greenblatt describes Fineman's account as having 'brilliantly explored the

or 'The Cultivation of Anxiety: King Lear and His Heirs', in *Learning*, 16–39 and 80–98 respectively.

[106] Greenblatt, 'Resonance and Wonder', in *Bulletin of the American Academy of Arts and Sciences*, 43 (1990), 11–34 and Peter Collier and Helga Geyer-Ryan (eds.), *Literary Theory Today* (Oxford: Polity Press, 1990), 74–90 (77).

[107] Fineman, 'The History of the Anecdote', 50. Further references to this article are given after quotations in the text.

[108] This uniqueness is particularly difficult when Fineman argues that New Historicism's name is justified by its own anecdotal qualities. To quote the passage from which the example of metonoia was drawn: 'the cheery enthusiasm with which the New Historicism, as a catchy term or phrase, proposes to introduce a novelty or an innovation, something "New," into the closed and closing historiography of successive innovation, "Historicism"—however unreflectingly or naively this oxymoron may initially have been intended, and whatever it was the old and unreformed "Historicism" of the New Historicism may have been supposed to have been before its supplanting renovation—this oxymoron is witness to or earnest of an impulse to discover or to disclose some wrinkling and historicizing interruption, a breaking and a *realizing* interjection, within the encyclopaedically enclosed circle of Hegelian historical self-reflection. . . As a title, the New Historicism strives to perform and thereby to enable the project it effectively entitles, and thus to earn thereby its access to the real through the excess of its name.' Fineman, 'The History of the Anecdote', 60.

theoretical implication of new historicism's characteristic use of anecdotes'.[109] Yet, though erudite, Fineman's argument is very hard to grasp, particularly in its claim that the anecdote, as used by New Historicism, has underpinned the development of historiography. In a footnote, Fineman applies his theoretical arguments to Greenblatt's 'Fiction and Friction', and it becomes clear that the use of the anecdote short-circuits any need for chronology:

> It should also be noted that, given the predeterminative force of these literary exigences [the forces of language]—i.e., that they precede Shakespeare, the gynecologists, and Stephen Greenblatt—objections to Greenblatt's essay . . . which complain that the gynecological texts Greenblatt cites are posterior to the Shakespearian texts they are supposed to influence, rather completely miss the point.[110]

Little traditional historiography uses anecdotes in this way. In fact, Fineman's attempt to justify New Historicism's use of anecdotes through an argument based on historiographic tradition seems less plausible than Hayden White's account of New Historicist historiography. White, noting New Historicism's lack of traditional historical criteria such as relevance and coverage, argues that this lack of concern with causal relationships is a function of what is truly new about New Historicist practice. For New Historicists concentrate on the poetic, in the sense of creative, aspects of history, aspects which themselves elude historical frameworks. These aspects 'can be said to resemble poetic speech which, even though it may contravene the rules of both grammar and logic, not only *has* meaning, but also always implicitly challenges the canonical rules of linguistic expression prevailing at the time of its utterance'.[111] These aspects, of course, bring us back to the anecdote, for that is the main form in which they are brought into New Historicist writing. New Historicism, then, is a rather poetic prose style.

Anecdotes have several other advantages that Fineman does not mention. Their small narrative size makes them easily manipulated by a master narrative, and they create no great expectation of accuracy. Moreover, in presenting literary and other texts anecdotally as New Historicists have tended increasingly to do, the internal resonances within texts, another area of potential resistance to the critic's argument, are effectively silenced. Anecdotes are, in fact, what all objects of art tend to become when subjected to Greenblatt's definition of wonder. There is also another reason why anecdotes lie at the heart of New Historicism. Anecdotes are stories that have usually been gathered up in the course of life, whether through reading or living, and thus have a personal aspect. This cannot be missed when Greenblatt, for instance, tells about his meetings with a man on a plane, or his experiences when a child,

[109] Greenblatt, *Learning*, 5.

[110] Fineman, 'The History of the Anecdote', 75. Greenblatt's 'Fiction and Friction' is in *Shakespearean Negotiations*, 66–93.

[111] Hayden White, 'New Historicism: A Comment', in Veeser (ed.), *The New Historicism*, 293–302 (301).

or his difficulties in Cambridge. It is also true of historical anecdotes; they not only illuminate the story they are chosen to illuminate, but also define the person who chose to tell them. This personalizing of the critical voice is supposedly part of New Historicism's challenging of 'the norm of disembodied objectivity to which humanists have increasingly aspired'.[112]

Greenblatt has developed this aspect of the anecdote further than any other critic. New Historicism's style of rhetoric becomes, for Greenblatt, an attenuated form of confessional autobiography. He tells, among other things, of his love of the *Arabian Nights*, and how on his first night in Bali he walked by moonlight on narrow paths through silent rice paddies glittering with fireflies. As he says in the introduction to *Learning to Curse*, the essays reflect his 'will to tell stories, critical stories or stories told as a form of criticism'.[113] And telling stories is part of the creation of one's identity: 'My earliest recollections of "having an identity" or "being a self" are bound up with story-telling.'[114] Another reason for the dominance of Greenblatt's argument over his examples is, then, that his stories are his own identity. Yet, if New Historicism is a development of the rhetorical movement, as I suggest it is, it would be unlikely that Greenblatt's practice here was unique. It is not. Fineman suggests in passing that New Historicism's criticism is in fact a reborn literary form, and one that is particularly humanist: '(and here I will just assert that it is the prosaic and considerable achievement of the new historicism to have reinvented for our time the essay form invented by Francis Bacon in the Renaissance).'[115]

Montaigne provides a more illuminating parallel with Greenblatt. For both writers, their essays form an autobiography made up from the various pictures of their mind given as they consider the relationships between cultures, a consideration often initiated by their telling of an anecdote.[116] What distinguishes the two is Montaigne's far greater willingness to be surprised, which is in part his ability to grant difference to what he studies—an ability which is related to his willingness to fear. This extended even to his sense of himself; as Charles Taylor notes in his *Sources of the Self*, when Montaigne 'sat down to write and turned to himself, he experienced a terrifying inner instability', an instability which changed the way in which he thought about himself.[117] Greenblatt has less fear; when he sits down to write his essays, his identity seems not to be at question; he seems rather to assert its dominance and moral authority. This is to judge Greenblatt's work morally, but that, in his later writing, is how it asks to be judged.

[112] Veeser, *The New Historicism*, p. ix. It also tends to make of any counter-argument an *ad hominem* argument.

[113] Greenblatt, *Learning*, 5.

[114] Ibid. 6.

[115] Fineman, 'The History of the Anecdote', 64.

[116] See e.g. the discussion of Montaigne's 'On Cannibals' in Ch. 1 above. The essay starts with an anecdote about King Pyrrhus.

[117] Taylor, *Sources of the Self*, 178.

3
Something More Than Fantasy

Barn. It would be spoke too.
Mar. Question it *Horatio.*

(I. I. 45)

PART I opened with the proposition that questions of identification and subjectivity were central to New Historicism and Cultural Materialism, and also to *Hamlet.* Barnardo's opening challenge—'Who's there?'—was a fitting opening line for the dramas of both critical movements. New Historicists, given their self-definitions and critical practice, were seen to have many reasons to focus on *Hamlet* as a key text to substantiate their arguments regarding notions of subjectivity. Yet *Hamlet* was an absent presence, often sensed but rarely seen; the play was described as the ghost that walked across the New Historicist stage, representing as it did both an unacknowledged past and a critical task that remained deferred in the present.

Cultural Materialists, by contrast, recognize that, given their concerns over subjectivity, it is *Hamlet* that 'would be spoke to'. What is more, Cultural Materialists question this play directly and repeatedly; *Hamlet* becomes what it always promised to be within New Historicism—a central text. Walter Cohen, in an article that provides one of the best overviews of Cultural Materialist criticism, notes that it is *Hamlet* which has been the site of 'especially stimulating work'.[1] Indeed, explaining the presence of *Hamlet* at the centre of Cultural Materialist criticism is a particularly profitable way of distinguishing that critical movement from New Historicism—at least in respect to those movements' discussions of the issue of subjectivity. In examining this presence, this chapter focuses predominantly on areas which distinguish the two movements. This might give the impression that there are simple, clear-cut divisions between the two critical movements, but this is not so. They are deeply interrelated, though often antagonistic to each other—kin though less than kind.

In Cultural Materialists' questions concerning subjectivity, their kinship with New Historicists is immediately striking. The dramatis personae of the critical drama are the same. E. M. W. Tillyard, old historicism, and the ahistorical tendencies of literary structuralism, literary formalism, and New

[1] Walter Cohen, 'Political Criticism of Shakespeare', in Jean E. Howard and Marion F. O'Connor (eds.) *Shakespeare Reproduced: The Text in History and Ideology* (Methuen: New York and London, 1987), 18–46 (24).

Criticism again appear as the enemies, and do so for many of the same reasons. As friends and parents are met again the French 'new philosophers', Michel Foucault, Jacques Lacan, and Jacques Derrida; social historians such as Lawrence Stone; Marxist historians such as Christopher Hill; various anthropologists; and some structuralist theories, prominent among which are forms of the Whorf–Sapir hypothesis.

Many beliefs are held in common; as the choice of dramatis personae suggests, Cultural Materialists share the New Historicist conviction of the need for and benefits of an interdisciplinary approach.[2] The setting or stage for the battle for the critical kingdom is also identical; Cultural Materialists recognize that their movement has taken shape particularly among critics of English Renaissance literature, and, more specifically still, has concentrated its attention on Shakespeare.[3] And the acknowledged starting-point is once again the nature of subjectivity. Indeed, Cultural Materialists claim that the question of subjectivity is central to any academic study of English. In Jonathan Dollimore's words, 'No issue is more central to English studies as it has been historically constituted than this question of subjectivity.'[4]

Yet the Cultural Materialist drama concerning subjectivity, though opening with the same cast, scene, and question, develops quite differently from that of the New Historicists. This is the result of another affinity; Cultural Materialists, like New Historicists, indulge in an imperialism of choice; their friends are never allowed to stand whole, but are represented by aspects of their positions and works, and specifically those aspects which serve the dominant, Cultural Materialist narrative. In examining what distinguishes this Cultural Materialist drama, the differences between the two critical movements are divided into two kinds: general differences of outlook and belief; and particular differences demonstrated by the presence and treatment of *Hamlet* by Cultural Materialists.

[2] See Jonathan Dollimore's 'Critical Developments' in Wells (ed.), *Shakespeare: A Bibliographical Guide*, 405–25. Dollimore argues that one of the benefits of this approach is the 'tension between incompatible methodologies' that is produced. This incompatibility manages to become 'a source of insight rather than confusion' (413).

[3] For summaries of Cultural Materialism which demonstrate aspects of this cast, stage, and issue, see: Catherine Belsey, 'Introduction: Reading the Past', in her *Subject of Tragedy*, 1–10; Cohen, 'Political Criticism of Shakespeare', and Don E. Wayne, 'Power, Politics, and the Shakespearean Text: Recent Criticism in England and the United States', in Howard and O'Connor (eds.) *Shakespeare Reproduced*, 18–46 and 47–67; Dollimore, 'Critical Developments', 405–25; Jonathan Dollimore's and Alan Sinfield's 'Foreword' to *Political Shakespeare: New Essays in Cultural Materialism* (Manchester: Manchester University Press, 1985), 2–17: John Drakakis's 'Introduction' to *Alternative Shakespeares* (London: Methuen, 1985), 1–25; Richard Wilson's 'Introduction' to Wilson and Dutton (eds.) *New Historicism and Renaissance Drama*, 1–18. David Norbrook's 'Introduction' to *Poetry and Politics* belongs in this group; Norbrook, however, is scholarly and historical in a way that distinguishes him from Cultural Materialists. See Norbrook, *Poetry and Politics*, 1–17.

[4] Jonathan Dollimore, *Radical Tragedy: Religion, Ideology and Power in the Drama of Shakespeare and his Contemporaries* (Brighton: Harvester, 1984), 249.

There are three general differences: one predominantly of belief, another of interest, and a third of attitude. The first of these differences was discussed at the end of Chapter 1. This was the Cultural Materialists' political belief, itself a product of their definition of ideology. Cultural Materialists' sense of ideology was seen to be that of a more traditional Marxism than that employed by New Historicists. Cultural Materialists believe, to a greater or lesser extent, that by exposing the contradictions in a culture (which it is ideology's function to conceal), ideology, and so the culture which relies upon it, will be overturned. Literary criticism can, then, have a great effect; it has the potential to change not only the literary-critical state, but also the state the critic lives in. As Jonathan Dollimore puts it, the critic is involved in a 'process of cultural struggle and change in which real power is at stake'.[5] This belief gives Cultural Materialist criticism a tone of political, almost social, mission and a sense of group purpose. This sense of group purpose, far less prominent in New Historicism, is seen particularly in the way in which straightforward, moralistic comments from prominent Cultural Materialists are tirelessly quoted by less well-known members: for instance, Richard Wilson, in his introduction to *New Historicism and Renaissance Drama*, quotes Jonathan Dollimore's formulation of 'the task' of the literary critic in *Political Shakespeare*: '[The] ruling culture does not define the whole of culture . . . and it is the task of the oppositional critic to re-read culture so as to amplify the voices of the ruled, exploited, oppressed and excluded.'[6]

The second fundamental difference is one of interest. Cultural Materialists focus particularly on usage, that is on the way in which texts have been deployed by the ruling culture, or more specifically by the critics who have served the ruling culture, to justify its ideology. Traditional literary criticism, a phrase which Cultural Materialists, like New Historicists, employ to describe criticism prior to their own, has used literary texts (so it is said) to silence those voices of the ruled, exploited, oppressed, and excluded. This focus on usage has led Cultural Materialists to produce studies of the ways in which texts have been 'appropriated', 'reproduced', or used as a form of modern 'myth', often in the service of the British nation-state's imperial designs. Unlike New Historicists, Cultural Materialists are thus clear as to why they have focused on Shakespeare's texts and plays; Shakespeare's works, they argue, have been used particularly frequently and powerfully. Alan Sinfield, in his recent *Faultlines: Cultural Materialism and the Politics of Dissident Reading*, a book which draws on much of the best Cultural Materialist criticism of the 1980s, provides a typical statement of this view: 'What we make of Shakespeare is important politically because it affects what he makes of us. It is, we may say, a theatre of war.'[7] Indeed, it has often been a weapon in literal wars, because, 'for

[5] Dollimore, 'Critical Developments', 405.
[6] Wilson, 'Introduction', 15.
[7] Alan Sinfield, *Faultlines: Cultural Materialism and the Politics of Dissident Reading* (Oxford: Clarendon Press, 1992), 26.

centuries', Shakespeare has 'been a key imperial site where ideology is produced'.[8] Not only has Cultural Materialism a political mission, but it is one in which the stakes are high.

This focus on political usage has many effects. E. M. W. Tillyard is frequently invoked by Cultural Materialists, as has been said. Yet, though he is still a key representative of a traditional criticism, he is not used, as he was by New Historicism, to represent all of that criticism and so to banish the past; there is less of a Tillyard trope. Instead, often alongside Laurence Olivier's production of *The Life of Henry the Fifth*, Tillyard is seen to demonstrate a particular moment in an Anglo-American critical tradition which has been intent on stressing the values of order and the ruling culture.[9] That is, he is seen as part of an evolving critical history.

As this suggests, this history is predominantly a vertical, evolutionary, and diachronic history, as opposed to the New Historicists' more horizontal, synchronic history, which aims to show the contingencies of texts. Cultural Materialist histories are those of broad intellectual sweeps, to which—in a manner which distinguishes them very sharply from New Historicists—the detail of history is often subsumed within the demands of an evolutionary outline. Don E. Wayne sees this as the defining difference between British Cultural Materialists and American New Historicists: 'We Americans tend to be meticulous readers and diligent historiographers. . . . By contrast, the British are relatively freewheeling in the way they range from Shakespeare's time to our own and back again.'[10] In the light of aspects of New Historicists' use of history, Wayne's distinction may seem open to challenge; it is, however, valid. Sinfield provides an explanation for this: 'The reason for the quality of new historicists' work is that they really believe in literary research, whereas cultural materialists are beset by the question of what it is all for.'[11] Yet Sinfield's contention, that Cultural Materialists are uncertain of 'what it is all for', rather obscures the issue. Cultural Materialists freewheel back and forward through history, not from some existential angst, but because they seek to write the histories that advance their political mission.

Cultural Materialists' histories (those that concern Shakespeare), aim basically to show how, through the ages, Shakespeare has been 'appropriated' by critics and nation-states in order to oppress cultures, subcultures, and persons. One result of this is surprisingly traditional; the Shakespearian texts are vindicated from responsibility for the ways in which they have been used, and so are recuperated to support Cultural Materialism's radical political goals. Shakespeare yet again turns out to be, or is to be made into, an enlightened politically correct author, on our side whatever that side may be.[12] Given

[8] Ibid. 28.

[9] See e.g. Dollimore, *Radical Tragedy*, ch. 1, 'Literary Criticism: Order versus History', 5–8.

[10] Wayne, 'Power, Politics, and the Shakespearean Text', 52.

[11] Sinfield, *Faultlines*, 8.

[12] Greenblatt's willingness to propose that plays, such as the Henriad, are not politically correct is a telling contrast.

this sense of a political and social mission, as well as the recognition of the substantial and pernicious influence which Shakespeare's works have had, it is not surprising that Cultural Materialists have a profoundly different attitude to literature from New Historicists. Where Greenblatt's approach was seen to be one which concentrated on wonder, and relegated fear, the Cultural Materialist approach might be said to be one of all fear, and no wonder. Their criticism is marked throughout by an utter earnestness.

Catherine Belsey, in an article entitled 'Literature, History, Politics', makes this dismissal of wonder plain. From the beginning of her article, it is clear that the political mission dominates the literary work or experience. For instance, Belsey discusses the way in which the 'enterprise' of producing 'a political history from the raw material of literary texts' should be conducted. A little further on she is more specific: 'Literary value becomes irrelevant: political assassination is problematised in Pickering's play, *Horestes* (1567) as well as [it is] in Hamlet.'[13] Whether or not this is accepted, the dismissal of wonder is a mistake in terms of the Cultural Materialist mission. To appreciate why this is a mistake, what must be understood are the ways in which Cultural Materialists seek to let the voices silenced by ruling cultures once again speak out.

Cultural Materialists reject the notion that their readings of texts are simply more readings, all readings being of equal validity. This might seem a little strange; a major conclusion of Cultural Materialists' histories of usage is the demonstration that meaning does not reside in the text which is the object of study, but is rather produced by the ways in which the text is inserted into a culturally specific context. How, then, may one reading be preferred above another? This is an important question for a political and socially concerned criticism; as Francis Barker and Peter Hulme recognize, if the text is, 'wholly dissolved into an indeterminate miscellany of inscriptions, then how could any confrontation between different but contemporaneous inscriptions take place?' Barker's and Hulme's way out of this impasse is to chop logic and simply appeal to their goal. 'Struggle', they say, 'can only occur if two positions attempt to occupy the same space', and, as they wish to struggle against the *status quo*, they must therefore insist that their reading replace previous readings, just as if those previous readings were incorrect. For readings which are content 'to be seen as alternative [to other readings] condemn themselves to mere irrelevance'.[14] Concepts of pluralism are seen as another form of repressive tolerance, a way by which readings which challenge the *status quo* can be absorbed by the dominant culture.

Though Belsey leaves the *de facto* nature of this aggressive attitude implicit, her article supports it. She makes clear that she not only sets aside criteria of

[13] Catherine Belsey, 'Literature, History, Politics', in Wilson and Dutton (eds.), *New Historicism*, 33–44 (43). Originally printed in *Literature and History*, 9 (1983), 17–26.

[14] Francis Barker and Peter Hulme, 'Nymphs and Reapers Heavily Vanish: The Discursive Con-texts of *The Tempest*', in Drakakis (ed.), *Alternative Shakespeares* 191–205 (193).

wonder, but also that diminished version of truth, 'accuracy'. Her reason for preferring the political history produced by her enterprise is one of personal belief: 'The claim is not that such a history, or such a reading of literary texts, is more accurate, but only that it is more radical.'[15] That is, Belsey's history is admittedly partisan—'No less partial, it produces the past'—but is preferable because it supports the Cultural Materialist political mission, which is 'radical' in the sense that it seeks the change she wants (p. 44). Cultural Materialists seek to dominate critical discourse, actively attacking any opinions that do not agree with their own. And the criteria under which they do this is their own, sincere, conviction that they are correct.

As these quotations from these three critics show, the text itself is of minor consequence, and it is sometimes hard to see why there is any necessity for texts at all—let alone 'wonder'—in Cultural Materialist criticism, beyond the fact that texts have in the past been put to use by the ruling culture. What is most remarkable about Belsey's article is that it turns out to be a conservative defence of the use of literary texts against the Materialist project at its height. 'The effect of this project', is, as Belsey summarizes it, to

> decentre literary criticism, to displace 'the text', the 'primary material', from its authoritative position at the heart of the syllabus, to dislodge the belief in the close reading of the text as the critic's essential and indispensable skill. Quite whether we can afford to dispose of the literary text altogether is not usually made clear, but it seems implicit in the project that we can do without it for most of the time. What is to be read closely is criticism, official reports on the teaching of English, examination papers, and all the other discursive displays of institutional power. (p. 40)

Belsey thinks this goes too far. She argues that the text should still be studied, arguing that a play such as *The Tragedy of Macbeth* is of value as it displays particularly well the competition between an age's discourses. This is not to claim much for the value of literature, but Belsey senses that within her peer group she is on dangerous ground: 'To say this is not, I hope, to privilege literature (and certainly not Literature) but only to allow it a certain specificity which identifies its use-value in the construction of the history of the present' (p. 42).

Cultural Materialism's explicit dismissal of aesthetic criteria is a blunder because it works in several ways to reduce Cultural Materialists' chances of dominating critical discourse and so fulfilling their mission. The dismissal of wonder, for instance, immediately alienates a large body of literary critics, who generally enjoy and place importance on the literary or wondrous qualities of literature. Greenblatt's avowal of wonder, by comparison, is a remarkably positive rhetorical move. For instance, Frank Kermode, in 'The High Cost of New Historicism', a review which deplores the de-aestheticizing tendencies of New Historicism, singles out Greenblatt for praise because of his insistence on the

[15] Belsey, 'Literature', 44. Further references to this article are given after the quotations in the text.

importance of wonder. Indeed, Kermode praises Greenblatt even though he is aware that Greenblatt's critical practice rarely demonstrates such an insistence.[16] The dismissal of wonder is also reflected in Cultural Materialists' style; seeing no point in literary value, most do not concern themselves with writing engagingly; they are unlike New Historicists in this. Instead, perhaps because of their (near-religious) sense of mission and concomitant sense of being right, they seem to believe, rather naïvely, that their 'truths' only need to be uttered to persuade. Finally, this dismissal of wonder also damages the content of their literary and political criticism. For it leads them to ignore the profound point that beauty (by which I mean that which is considered beautiful) is intrinsically bound up with power and usage. Bluntly put, beauty is more truthful, in the sense of powerful, than coarse plainness. To return to Belsey's example, *Horestes* does not 'problematise' political assassination 'as well as' *Hamlet*, because *Horestes* does not have the aesthetic qualities which make others wish to appropriate it. *Horestes* has little useful power, while *Hamlet* has a great deal; *Hamlet*'s use-value is far greater than that of *Horestes*, specifically because of its aesthetic qualities.

For these reasons, the Cultural Materialist discussion of subjectivity, of the issues centred on the question of 'Who's there?', is overshadowed by the New Historicist discussion. This is in a non-literary sense unfair; for Cultural Materialists are often more thorough and theoretically coherent in their discussion of subjectivity than New Historicists, and are certainly so concerning *Hamlet*. But New Historicists, with their anecdotes and sense of personal biography, tell the best stories and so have the largest audience. Whereas Cultural Materialists, with their constant moral earnestness, their labouring of their truths, are rather dull.

New Historicism, it has been argued, has affinities with sixteenth-century humanism, and may be seen as a phase in the history of rhetoric, a style of argument. Cultural Materialism may usefully be regarded as a more scholastic movement, deeply antagonistic to the humanist insistence on the pre-eminence of eloquence to every discipline. Instead Cultural Materialists try to inspire by communicating their own sense of converted zeal; the format of Cultural Materialist articles and books is distinctly religious. A work will begin with an example which demonstrates an aspect of social oppression, move on to expose the ways in which the oppression has been sustained, next give its own rules for correct living (which are also rules for the overthrow of oppression), and finally end with a picture of the Utopian vision that will follow if the reader complies with those rules. Exodus provides the archetypal pattern.

[16] Frank Kermode, 'The High Cost of New Historicism', in *NYRB*, 19 June 1992, 43–6. By 1998, Kermode rather lost his patience, seeing in the Cambridge Studies in Renaissance Literature and Culture a critical grouping based around a shared sexual agenda, and deploring the 'unashamed employment of a repellent professional jargon' of the series. Frank Kermode, 'Toe-lining', *London Review of Books*, 22 Jan. 1998, 9–10 (9).

Alan Sinfield's *Faultlines* provides a recent example, both within its chapters and as a whole. The first chapter begins with a discussion of the use of Shakespeare in a Royal Ordnance advert, and so within imperialism. Next, the ways in which the dominant ideology has used Shakespeare are discussed. Then a method for stopping Shakespeare being so used is outlined, specifically in relation to *Julius Caesar*. This Sinfield calls, following Jonathan Dollimore, 'creative vandalism'.[17] (Cultural Materialism's earnestness is never more apparent than in its jokes.) This is a term for a critical approach which releases the reader from 'the demand of literary criticism that lines that seem to resist your reading must somehow be incorporated or explained away'.[18] (Given this belief, which is at least stated explicitly, it is not surprising that Sinfield often mis-states in a *Learning to Curse* manner—though Sinfield, unlike Greenblatt, is unlikely to recognize a need for accuracy concerning historical or textual specificities. Eric Griffiths' accusation that he is clearly shaping *The Tragedy of Othello, The Moor of Venice* to his own political ends by discussing Othello as a 'black' and not a 'Moor' will not worry Sinfield at all.[19]) Sinfield replaces this standard critical demand by a goal, with the same chop-logic seen previously in Barker and Hulme, and Belsey: 'My aim is simply this: to check the tendency of *Julius Caesar* to add Shakespearian authority to reactionary discourses.'[20] If this practice is followed, then the reader/critic will be able to change the state: as Sinfield concludes, 'In the long term, the emperors could not keep out the Vandals' (p. 28). (The Vandals are to be preferred, presumably as they are seen to proffer solidarity with Sinfield's view of the common person.) A fuller vision of the Utopia that will follow upon the rejection of the ruling culture's imperialisms is given at the end of the book, a vision which centres upon the laudable aim of enabling subcultures, if not to conquer oppression, then to maintain their own dignity (p. 299).

Given Cultural Materialists' religio-political mission to change society, it is not surprising that the chief complaint they level at New Historicists is their use of an entrapment model of power, derived from Foucault. Indeed, they are infuriated by the New Historicist argument that a ruling culture is not only able to contain subversion, but also to use subversion to sustain itself; Cultural Materialists often describe this argument in terms of despair.[21] Despair is, of course, the ultimate sin, and Cultural Materialists find such an attitude outrageous. Richard Wilson, in his introduction to *New Historicism and Renaissance Drama*, points out the dangers of this despair in stark terms through a comparison of French New Philosophy to New Historicism:

[17] Sinfield, *Faultlines*, 22.

[18] Ibid. 16.

[19] Eric Griffiths, 'To Care & Not to Care', *TLS* 28 May 1993, 13–14 (13).

[20] Sinfield, *Faultlines*, 21. Further references to this book are given after the quotations in the text.

[21] This movement from the containment of subversion to its use can be seen e.g. within Greenblatt's work. Where *Renaissance Self-Fashioning* explored the containment of subversion, *Shakespearean Negotiations* considered the ruling culture's use of subversion to reproduce its own power.

Like New Historicism, New Philosophy was politically diffuse, with leftist and conservative tendencies, but it was characterized by an unexamined hypostatisation of power that made it liable to be coopted to the libertarianism of the New Right.[22]

Wilson constantly brings this danger into view; New Historicism is guilty of 'fetishising power' and 'essentialis[ing] capitalism' (p. 10), so mirroring the 'Reaganomics' of the early 1980s (p. 9). New Historicism aestheticized history, in a way reminiscent of Nietzsche or, more directly, of Burkhardt's 'idea of "the state as a work of art"' (p. 11). New Historicists, in Wilson's account, become the paranoid defeatists unwittingly playing into the hands of the fascists. Cultural Materialists are the cavalry, riding over the hill.

Yet the hope that Cultural Materialists insist on in contrast to New Historicists is itself rather desperate. One argument is that *all* plays are 'subversive' or 'dissident', simply because no author or director or censor is able fully to control all the meanings that an audience may find in a play. Another is that ideology, in having constantly to reproduce itself, is bound in the end to reproduce itself incorrectly; the analogy here would be with the reproduction of cells within the human body, a reproduction that is more likely to fail or misfunction with age, so leading to death or cancer and then death.[23] Summarily put, to Greenblatt's quotation from Kafka, 'There is subversion, no end of subversion, only not for us',[24] Cultural Materialists would want to respond with Yeats's, 'Things fall apart; the centre cannot hold'.[25] This cannot be denied, but, in the end, it is a rather shaky belief on which to base one's hope of success.

Hor. What art thou that vsurp'st this time of night,
Together with that Faire and Warlike forme
In which the Maiesty of buried Denmarke
Did sometimes march.

(1. 1. 44–7)

Unconcerned with delights, focused specifically on the utility of texts, driven by political goals, with a quasi-religious, scholastic tone, Cultural Materialists ask 'What art thou?' They ask the question to substantiate their political mission; that is, to answer the related question of 'How does what we are demonstrate that there is "subversion, no end of subversion", and especially for us?' In this way, 'What art thou?' becomes the question that is not only central to Cultural Materialism, but also distinguishes it from what it perceives to be the political incorrectness of New Historicists. And as Cultural Materialists ask this question, *Hamlet* moves centre stage.

[22] Wilson, 'Introduction', 4. Further references to this introduction are given after the quotations in the text.

[23] See Sinfield, *Faultlines*, 41.

[24] Greenblatt, *Shakespearean Negotiations*, 39.

[25] The line comes from Yeats's 'The Second Coming', published as part of *Michael Robartes and the Dancer* (1921).

This move needs explanation; the argument has so far only given reasons why Shakespeare's works should be centre stage within the Cultural Materialist drama. *Hamlet* moves centre stage within those works as it is seen to confirm Cultural Materialists' evolutionary histories of subjectivity; *Hamlet* is seen to demonstrate the Renaissance answer to 'What art thou?' which proves that subversion is for us. *Hamlet*'s use in this role (within Cultural Materialism) was established by Francis Barker's *The Tremulous Private Body: Essays in Subjection* (1984) and substantiated by two other influential books: indirectly by Jonathan Dollimore's *Radical Tragedy* of the same year, and directly by Catherine Belsey's *The Subject of Tragedy* in 1985. All these books were concerned to give an evolutionary history of what it has been to be a subject. They each focused on a different aspect of that history, but developed a historical overview that was recognizably similar. They produced, in fact, the Cultural Materialist paradigm of English Renaissance subjectivity.

To try to convey the profound similarities of these three books, similarities which increased the books' impact within Cultural Materialist and English Renaissance studies generally, their accounts are here interwoven. Barker's account of the history of subjectivity is given most attention, as it establishes *Hamlet*'s pivotal importance within that history. Belsey is brought in to elucidate Barker's dense argument, and so also to demonstrate how close is her historical scheme to Barker's, and how reliant her historical argument is (as she acknowledges) upon his arguments concerning *Hamlet*.[26] Dollimore is mentioned in parallel with these two, for though his historical account is quite distinct from theirs in many ways, in effect its conclusions concerning the history of Renaissance subjectivity are identical.

Barker, in *The Tremulous Private Body*, sets out to add to an evolutionary history of Renaissance subjectivity by focusing on 'the political history of the body', that is the changing ways in which the body was socially constructed during a period centred upon the seventeenth century.[27] So doing, he takes as his inspiration and authority the work of Michel Foucault, work which has provided the master narrative for Cultural Materialists' view of subjectivity.[28] In the light of the Cultural Materialist antagonism to New Historicists' Foucauldian model of power, this might be surprising. However, Barker and Cultural Materialists ignore the Foucauldian model of power as best they can, as they extract from his works a historical framework of the evolution of subjectivity. In particular they concentrate on the Foucault of *Madness and Civilisation* (1961), *Discipline and Punish: The Birth of the Prison* (1975), and *The History*

[26] *The Subject of Tragedy* is in two halves. The first deals with the construction of 'Man' in Renaissance drama, and the second compares this with the dramatic representation of women in the same period. Belsey's dependence on Barker does not extend to the second half of her book.

[27] Barker, *The Tremulous Private Body: Essays in Subjection* (London: Methuen, 1984), 14. The relevant passages on *Hamlet* (pp. 19–40) are quoted from 'Hamlet's Unfulfilled Interiority' in Wilson and Dutton (eds.), *New Historicism*, 157–66.

[28] Barker, *The Tremulous Private Body*, 12.

of Sexuality: An Introduction, volume i (1976). This framework has been given the status of unquestioned authority and has had a profound and determining impact on their own history. Wilson, in his introduction to *New Historicism and Renaissance Drama*, describes Foucault's 'account of the genesis of our subjectivity', as 'So compelling . . . that even a Marxist critic, such as Louis Montrose, found it hard to resist'.[29]

Foucault's account of the genesis of 'our subjectivity' develops through the three works as he concentrates on its different aspects. Central to it, and to Cultural Materialists' use of Foucault, is Foucault's concentration on the classical age (a loose term, equivalent in its looseness, though not in its connotations, to the Enlightenment) as a period of transition, out of which emerges 'our subjectivity' and its concomitant, modern Western industrialized society. These links—that between the subject and society, and that between the subjectivity which emerged in the classical age and our own subjectivity—are vital to Cultural Materialism. They are most memorably expressed, within Foucault's works, in *Discipline and Punish*, whose subtitle could be rephrased from *The Birth of the Prison* to 'The Birth of the Soul'.[30]

Discipline and Punish begins with a striking juxtaposition. First comes a long and terrible description of 'Damiens the regicide['s]' public execution in 1757 at the Place de Grève in Paris.[31] (Foucault gives no further details of the crime. Robert Damiens had stabbed Louis XV as the King was entering his carriage, inflicting only a slight wound.) Damiens's right hand, the hand which held the knife, was covered in sulphur and burnt, his flesh was torn with red-hot pincers, and then he was torn apart (after many attempts) by horses.[32] This description is followed by a timetable of some 'Eighty years later', detailing the expected daily regime of the inmates of 'the House of young prisoners at Paris' (p. 6)—what time they would get up, how long they would work, when they would eat, and so on. Foucault uses this juxtaposition of execution and timetable to draw attention to the move that has taken place away from spectacular (in the visual and extraordinary senses of that word) and corporal techniques of punishment, that is, punishments of the body, and towards punishments aimed at correcting the will, the thoughts, the inclinations—punishments aimed, that is, at correcting the soul.

Foucault's argument is that the new techniques of punishment—of which

[29] Wilson, 'Introduction', 8. Wilson suggests that Foucault is particularly inimical to Marxists because Foucault argues that the human subject is circumscribed by power acting not through economic relations but through systems of signification.

[30] As Foucault suggests: 'This book is intended as a correlative history of the modern soul', p. 23.

[31] Foucault, *Discipline and Punish*, 3. Further references to this book are given after quotations in the text.

[32] In *Learning to Curse*, Greenblatt rightly worries over a tendency within recent criticism to dwell on scenes of torture (a tendency that is perhaps under the influence of Foucault). This leads on to Greenblatt's insistence on the critic's obligation to attend to all the textual traces of the past, discussed in Ch. 2.

the disciplinary timetable is representative—create the modern soul, which replaces the soul created by Christianity:

It would be wrong to say that the soul is an illusion, or an ideological effect. On the contrary, it exists, it has a reality, it is produced permanently around, on, within the body by the functioning of a power that is exercised on those punished. (p. 29)

This soul becomes, then, the point of application of punitive power on the individual. On or in this point, which is non-corporal but real in its effects on the person, Foucault argues that, 'various concepts have been constructed and domains of analysis carved out'. These include, '[the] psyche, subjectivity, personality, consciousness' (p. 29). As this list of concepts suggests, the area of reference has traditionally been thought to be particularly the person's own. Foucault's argument reverses that traditional view, while maintaining (from the Christian tradition in this case) the central importance of 'the soul' in animating man; 'A "soul" inhabits him [modern man] and brings him to existence' (p. 30). For Foucault, then, power creates the soul which creates man; moreover, as this power is punitive, designed to control, repress, and crush, the soul becomes 'the prison of the body' (p. 30). Indeed, this soul was born in prison, or out of the individualizing techniques developed there. Damiens was torn apart in hours; we are incarcerated for life. 'Is there a diminution of [punitive] intensity?' (p. 16) Foucault is not sure.

This bleak picture of subjectivity, and of the modern Western state which both produces and is produced by it, is central to Foucault's other works mentioned above. They all have as their basic tenet the argument that modern man is produced by power, which creates him as a captive object of various fields of knowledge.[33] All these books see this production as being the result of the technologies of power which emerge and become dominant towards the end of the eighteenth century (there is some chronological slippage within the books). Foucault's answer to 'Who's there?', then, is a particularly bleak form of 'no one' or 'everything'. It is this bleak picture of 'our subjectivity', with its causal relationship to the modern state, and this chronological scheme that Barker and Cultural Materialists adopt. It suits their political mission in two ways: temperamentally, with its sense that we are all victims horribly and endlessly punished by an unjust state, it matches their sense of present oppression; historically, with its tracing of modern man emerging towards the end of the eighteenth century, it offers support for their argument that the individual, on which the bourgeois state is founded, cannot be found before 1660.[34]

Before examining how *Hamlet* comes centre stage, there is another objection

[33] For a (in the end) hostile discussion of Foucault's conception of subjectivity in relation to other forms of political critique, and in particular those centred on the Frankfurt School, see Peter Dews, *Logics of Disintegration: Post-Structuralist Thought and the Claims of Critical Theory* (London: Verso, 1987), 144–77.

[34] Though Foucault's dating of the emergence of 'modern man' at the end of the 18th c. is troublesome to the argument that the individual is the linchpin of the bourgeois state.

that needs to be made to Barker's and Cultural Materialists' use of Foucault. Another objection, because the objections already mentioned with respect to the New Historicist use of Foucault could equally well be applied to the Cultural Materialist use of Foucault. Primarily these were historical and centred on the inappropriateness of applying debatable conclusions about the history of France to illuminate English history, a practice Foucault discouraged.[35] There were also theoretical objections, one such—concerning Foucault's account of subjectivity—being the way in which although Foucault is concerned to write a 'political anatomy of the body', the body is oddly incorporeal within his narrative; its wants and physical desires rarely appear, even in *The History of Sexuality*.[36] But there is a further, and more profound, objection to Cultural Materialists' (and New Historicists') use of Foucault; that objection is that they ignore, or are not aware of, the final and vital phase of Foucault's work on subjectivity before his death in 1984.

This phase can be seen in the posthumously published *Technologies of the Self: A Seminar with Michel Foucault.* As the subtitle suggests, this is not a work of Foucault's (though the title was that suggested by Foucault for a book he intended to write on the work of his last years). Perhaps because of this, *Technologies of the Self* has been given little attention. It is made up of transcripts

[35] In a footnote to the first part of *Discipline and Punish* Foucault states: 'I shall study the birth of the prison only in the French penal system. Differences in historical developments and institutions would make detailed comparative examination too burdensome and any attempt to describe the phenomenon as a whole too schematic' (p. 309). However, Foucault elsewhere feels free to link English and French practices, most importantly when he uses Bentham's panopticon as the central descriptive analogy of the new techniques of power that were developed within prisons and other institutions (what he terms the 'carceral' system). He also occasionally refers specifically to the Elizabethan age itself, or rather does so through Shakespeare. This is typical of his tendency to use a fictional text to characterize a historical period. Indeed, it is often difficult to know the status of the evidence that Foucault presents; whether, for instance, a quoted passage is purely theoretical writing concerning a subject or whether it guided and shaped an actual practice; for example, the reader cannot be sure if the timetable quoted at the beginning of *Discipline and Punish* was the actual timetable used in 'the House of young prisoners in Paris' (p. 6), or one simply drawn up for 'the House' as a suggested regime. When Foucault does refer to Elizabethan or Shakespearian England it also raises questions immediately about the depth of his knowledge of either. In describing the new system of punitive power, he contrasts it with the old: 'The Shakespearean age when sovereignty confronted abomination in a single character had gone: the everyday melodrama of police power and of the complicities that crime formed with power was soon to begin' (p. 282). As a description of Shakespeare's plays, or the period Shakespeare lived within, this is unhelpful; within the plays sovereignty can only rarely be argued to confront abomination in a single character, and in such cases, for instance in *Macbeth*, sovereign power is complicit with crime. Foucault's description has less relevance to Shakespeare's Roman plays e.g. *The Tragedy of Coriolanus*, where competing power-groups struggle to retain their ability to wield power by manipulating the aspirations of the common populace.

[36] Foucault was aware of both these historical and theoretical objections; e.g. in *The History of Sexuality* he writes, 'People are going to say that I am dealing in a historicism which is more careless than radical . . . and that I speak of sexuality as if sex did not exist.' Michel Foucault, *The History of Sexuality: An Introduction*, trans. Robert Hurley (Harmondsworth: Penguin, 1990; first pub. as *La Volonté de savoir*, Paris: Editions Gallimard, 1976), 150–1. For Foucault's answer to these charges the pages following on from this quotation should be consulted.

of the lectures and interview that Foucault gave at the University of Vermont in 1982, along with related papers presented by other academics. In these, it emerges that Foucault had begun to consider another aspect of the history of subjectivity. In the lectures, Foucault describes the course of his work over the last twenty-five years as the exploration of the ways in which humans develop knowledge about themselves. He names four 'technologies' which allow this development of knowledge, listing as the two which his work has considered,

> (3) technologies of power, which determine the conduct of individuals and submit them to certain ends or domination, an objectivizing of the subject; (4) technologies of the self, which permit individuals to effect by their own means or with the help of others a certain number of operations on their own bodies and souls, thoughts, conduct, and way of being.[37]

His work, he acknowledges, has predominantly focused on the 'third' technology, and it is to the 'fourth' that he now wants to turn:

> Perhaps I've insisted too much on the technology of domination and power. I am more and more interested in the interaction between oneself and others and in the technologies of individual domination, the history of how an individual acts upon himself, in the technology of self. (p. 19)

Foucault recognizes, then, that subjectivity is not the same as subjection. Technologies of power (the central interest of his earlier books mentioned above) are one aspect of the history of subjectivity, and so one aspect of the sense of self—and the one on which Foucault's books have predominantly focused. Foucault's new focus is not on 'the self' as an externally produced product, but on 'the self' as an internally produced product of oneself. In the terms of this book's discussion, he is leaving behind the structuralist Whorf–Sapir hypothesis, and examining the subject in a way which is moving closer to Piaget and social constructivism.

This is a momentous change within Foucault's writing, and as he begins to trace this other aspect of the genealogy of subjectivity, it becomes clear that it has very much older origins than the eighteenth century. 'The self', as 'something to write about, a theme or object (subject) of writing activity', is seen to be: 'not a modern trait born of the Reformation or of romanticism [. . . but] one of the most ancient Western traditions. It was well established and deeply rooted when Augustine started his *Confessions*' (p. 27). What emerges in Foucault's lectures, in fact, is an account of the history of subjectivity which reinstates many of the figures traditionally important to the Western account of the history of subjectivity; Foucault begins with the writings of Plato and the Stoics, and goes on through Seneca to the fourth- and fifth-century Christian writers.[38]

37 *Technologies of the Self: A Seminar with Michel Foucault*, ed. Luther H. Martin, Huck Gutman, and Patrick H. Hutton (London: Tavistock, 1988), 18. Further references to this work are given after quotations in the text.

38 However, Foucault argues that 'take care of yourself' was a prior and more fundamental principle in Greek thought than 'know thyself'. See *Technologies of the Self*, 19ff.

Indeed, as the editors' introduction puts it, Foucault 'located the roots of the modern concept of self' in these writers (p. 4). Within this other tradition, then, the answer to 'Who's there?' is not 'no one' or 'every one' or even 'power', but versions of 'I am'. I say 'versions', because the ways in which subjects constitute themselves have changed over time. What remains constant, however, is the fact that they are self-fashioning products.

The existence of this 'technology of the self', as Foucault puts it, in a line that can be traced from Plato, through the Renaissance, and to the present day, cuts both theoretically and historically against the central thrust of Cultural Materialism and New Historicism—that the person is a produced product. Moreover, it upsets Cultural Materialists' historical scheme; the bourgeois, or in Foucault's terms, disciplined individual may arrive after 1660, but concepts of self-constituting interiority pre-date that arrival by a thousand years or more. Shakespeare, according to Foucault, would be able to draw on a long tradition of 'writing about the self'. This is not to say that Foucault's later work automatically invalidates Cultural Materialists' (or New Historicists') arguments—Foucault's analysis may be incorrect—but it does withdraw Foucault's authority from their positions. It is this late aspect of Foucault's work, his work on the tradition of a self-constituting self, that Part III develops in relation to *Hamlet*.

Barker and Cultural Materialists, then, have used only Foucault's bleak picture of subjectivity, often in conjunction with the traditional Marxist interpretation of the English Revolution, to underpin their evolutionary scheme of the history of subjectivity.[39] Barker's argument is that there have been two different worlds since the Middle Ages, the pre-bourgeois and, after 1660, the bourgeois, distinguished by its imposition on its subjects of Foucault's disciplined, imprisoning soul, which Barker terms 'essential subjectivity'.[40] Belsey explains this large-scale division in (relatively) greater detail; she describes the post-1660 world as that of 'liberal humanism', using that term to denote 'the ruling assumptions, values and meanings of the modern epoch. Liberal humanism, laying claim to be both natural and universal, was produced in the interests of the bourgeois class which came to power in the second half of the seventeenth century.'[41] She is aware (more so than Barker) that 'There are, or course, dangers in collapsing the historical specificities and the ideological differences of three centuries into a single term',[42] but she pays no significant attention to them. Dollimore, by contrast, is more cautious and his historical scheme more complex, drawing on the work of Raymond Williams.[43] His scheme posits three periods, one which precedes the English Renaissance, then the Renaissance, and finally the post-1660 world. However, although he has two divisions within his scheme, he maintains a division

39 Both Barker and Belsey use this traditional Marxist history.

40 Barker, in Wilson and Dutton (eds.), *New Historicism*, 164.

41 Belsey, *The Subject of Tragedy*, 7. 42 Ibid. 7. 43 See Dollimore, *Radical Tragedy*, 158.

similar to that proposed by Barker and Belsey between the English Renaissance and the post-1660 world. His term for the subjectivity which defines the post-1660 world is 'essentialist humanism'.

Barker's literary evidence for this sea-change is Samuel Pepys's *Diary* (1668). Barker takes the *Diary* as evidence that the interlinked bourgeois individual and state have arrived, hard on the heels of the 'grand historical process' that produced the English Revolution.[44] For Barker, the *Diary* is 'one of the first of the autobiographies in that tradition of subject centred discourse which, as we shall see, Descartes began' (p. 10). Barker takes this 'inner history' as proof that the incarcerated and disciplined subject (which Foucault described as being produced by the technologies of power at the end of the eighteenth century) is already, in an early form, present (p. 10).

He contrasts this with pre-bourgeois (pre-1660) subjects, who exist in a quite different world in which the body is still both visible and the object of punishment. For them, such inner histories would not be possible, since

> Pre-bourgeois subjection does not properly involve subjectivity at all, but a condition of dependent membership in which place and articulation are defined not by an interiorized self-recognition . . . but by incorporation in the body politic which is the king's body in its social form. (p. 31)

Before 1660, that is, people were given a sense of themselves through their placement in a stable social network; they knew their place and so themselves. They were in no sense self-constituting; they were possessed of no sense of an inner world which was in some way separate from the social body which both constituted, and was constituted, by them. Barker's picture of this 'pre-bourgeois' world depends on a picture of the medieval age even more stable and homogeneous than that of the New Historicists.

What, then, is the bourgeois subjection that takes over from the earlier conception of subjectivity? 'Essential subjectivity' is 'the myth by which the autonomous individual is made the undetermined unit of being, in contrast to an inert social world'.[45] Throughout Cultural Materialism, it is this myth of absolute autonomy, or free will, or self-unity, as it is posited as the essential attribute of being human, that is argued to define bourgeois subjectivity. So Belsey describes the myth: 'Liberal humanism proposes that the subject is the free, unconstrained author of meaning and action, the origin, of history. [He or she is] Unified, knowing and autonomous.'[46] And Dollimore describes the myth as: 'the idea of the autonomous, unified self-generating subject postulated by essentialist humanism.'[47]

[44] Barker, *The Tremulous Private Body*, 9. Further references to this book are given after quotations in the text.

[45] Barker, in Wilson and Dutton (eds.), *New Historicism*, 164–5.

[46] Belsey, *Subject of Tragedy*, 8.

[47] Dollimore, *Radical Tragedy*, 155. Further references to this work are given after quotations in the text.

Autonomy, above all, is taken to define the post-1660 myth. This becomes clearest in Dollimore's account. For his first stage, that prior to the English Renaissance, was defined by a subjectivity reliant on 'Christian essentialism', which saw the person as given unity and essence by a 'metaphysically derivative' soul (p. 155). Dollimore's account thus has the great advantage over Barker's (and Belsey's) that it does not argue that inner histories do not exist before 1660. Indeed, Dollimore traces the standard figures of the traditional history, starting, where Foucault left off, with Augustine, and looking at (among others) Aquinas, Pico, Castiglione, and Montaigne. Dollimore argues instead that those inner histories undergo a profound transformation at around 1660, a transformation which gives cultural primacy to the myth of autonomy, a concept disallowed by Christian essentialism. (The in-between stage of the English Renaissance Dollimore describes as having a subjectivity of 'anarchic egotism' (p. 158).)

The Cultural Materialists' argument, then, is that there are at least two radically different subjectivities, and so worlds—one pre- and the other post-1660.[48] This, Barker argues, is unpalatable to traditional criticism, which wants to believe that subjectivity has always taken the form of 'essential subjectivity' for the simple reason that this makes political rebellion against such a subjectivity, and the state with which it is concomitant, pointless. Why rebel against the natural, unchanging order of things?[49] Clearly, literary proof of the absence of the post-1660 subjectivity in the pre-1660 world is needed. For Barker it was the 'inner histories', such as Pepys's *Diary*, which demonstrated the post-1660 myth of autonomy as they 'distance[d] the external world', concentrating on the subject's inner world, 'in order to construct subjectivity as the (imaginary) property of inner selfhood'.[50] Therefore, for literary proof he looked to demonstrate that there were no such inner histories significantly before that date.

> *Barn.* How now *Horatio*? You tremble & look pale:
> Is not this something more then Fantasie?
>
> (I. I. 51–2)

At this point *Hamlet* moves centre stage; it assumes central importance within Cultural Materialism as the proving ground of the movement's history of subjectivity, and so of the movement's political project. For Barker recognizes, rightly, that 'successive generations of criticism' (p. 164) have seen the emer-

[48] Barker occasionally suggests that the historical picture is more complex; this suggestion is, however, gestural.

[49] For Belsey's account of this stage of the argument, see *Subject of Tragedy*, 8. Cultural Materialists give other reasons for their dislike of essential subjectivity; it is argued to efface the historical conditions under which men and women lived and to allow a culturally specific notion of what it is to be human to be used as a universal norm, so excluding and relegating other conceptions—with often horrific consequences. See Dollimore, *Radical Tragedy*, 258.

[50] Barker, in Wilson and Dutton (eds.), *New Historicism*, 159. Further references to this book are given after quotations in the text.

gence of modern man, or rather man with a sense of self that is recognizably modern, in *Hamlet.*[51] Crucial to that has been the sense that Prince Hamlet, in contra-distinction to his surrounding world, has a complex and sustained sense of interiority. Barker's argument, however, is that the critics, in finding Prince Hamlet to have such an inner history, have misrepresented *Hamlet.* Their motive in doing so, Barker argues, was to remake the Elizabethan and Jacobean age, and so its subjects, 'in the eternal image of the bourgeois world'—to create a fantasy of fulfilment (p. 164). Barker plays a cynical, unshaken Horatio; his argument is that the Prince's interiority is nothing more than fantasy.

To disprove the traditional view, Barker discusses a passage which has often been used as evidence that Prince Hamlet has an inner history. This is the speech beginning at I. 2. 76, 'Seemes, Madam? Nay, it is: I know not Seemes', in which Hamlet states to his mother that whatever can be seen (or represented) cannot 'denote me truly'. It concludes, 'But I haue that Within, which passeth show; | These, but the Trappings, and the Suites of woe' (I. 2. 85–6). Barker agrees that Hamlet here 'asserts against the devices of the world an essential interiority', and in doing so 'a separation has already opened up between the inner reality of the subject, living itself, as "that within that passes show", and an inauthentic exterior' (p. 162). Yet this separation, or gap, remains only that—a vacant space. Hamlet does not tell us what he does have within that 'passeth show'. Barker argues from this that Hamlet has no developed sense of inner self, but rather his 'interiority remains, in *Hamlet*, gestural . . . At the centre of Hamlet, in the interior of his mystery, there is, in short, nothing' (pp. 163–4).

This 'nothing', once again the answer to 'Who's there?', validates Cultural Materialists' history of subjectivity, maintaining the pre- and post-1660 divide. The interiority of Young Hamlet is nothing more than fantasy; the fantasy of generations of 'traditional' critics, who—Barker argues—have filled this vacant gap within the Prince with their own anachronistic and multitudinous versions of the essentialist subjectivity they desired to find. 'The startling effect' of this, 'has been to reproduce the text as the great tragedy of . . . *bourgeois* culture' (p. 164). In fact *Hamlet*, by demonstrating that there is more than one form of subjectivity, enables Cultural Materialism's political mission; it is the great tragedy of materialist criticism. At this point, 'truth' arrives strangely. *Hamlet*'s inability to present 'essential subjectivity', which had been seen to be a function of its pre-1660 composition, is now seen to express the truth that essential subjectivity cannot exist. The play 'dramatize[s] its impossibility' (p. 164). So doing, the text, Barker declares, 'scandalously reveals the emptiness at the heart of that bourgeois trope' (p. 164). Thus *Hamlet* becomes a gospel of hope to those (all of us) who must still 'pay some of the price for what was done to us in the seventeenth-century'. For the fantasy of subjectivity which was then

[51] The emergence of this critical tradition is traced in Part II.

imposed on us was particularly sick; since then we have all been, Barker argues, guilt-ridden, schizoid, like Pepys 'quite mad' as we attempt to efface the visible nature of our body from our subjectivity.[52] The vision of truth that *Hamlet* offers gives us the chance to be whole again.

Barker's argument that Hamlet's interiority is gestural has been influential. Belsey, for instance, uses it as the keystone within her own wider-ranging discussion of the representation of subjectivity on the English Renaissance stage:

> The classic case is, of course, Hamlet. Francis Barker has written of Hamlet's assertion of an authentic inner reality . . . this essence, the heart of Hamlet's mystery, has been the quarry not only of Rosencrantz and Guildenstern, agents of the king's surveillance, but of liberal-humanist criticism of the nineteenth and twentieth centuries. . . . The quest is, of course, endless, because the object of it is not there. As Barker goes on to argue, 'this interiority remains, in *Hamlet*, gestural . . . At the centre of Hamlet, in the interior of his mystery, there is, in short, nothing.'[53]

The impact of Barker's scheme can be gauged from the way in which Terry Eagleton, in *William Shakespeare*, a general introduction to Shakespeare which is not specifically a Cultural Materialist work, uses it as if it were a commonplace.[54]

Yet Barker's argument, for all the large claims that ride upon it, is built upon a short and cursory discussion of one passage of *Hamlet*. Barker uses a historical argument to underpin his interpretation of the text; there is no textual evidence of interiority—and so no need for textual analysis—he argues, because the bourgeois 'myth' of essential subjectivity does not yet exist, and will not do so until 1660. Barker's argument here is unsatisfactory. It is circular, using the historical scheme the textual evidence was meant to prove in order to determine the interpretation of the text. Thus it reduces the text to the level of illustration of a pre-existing argument, which in this case is the Cultural Materialist political project.

This use of history as the background context through which to control the textual foreground is typical of Cultural Materialism, and is another factor differentiating it from New Historicism. This goes against the movement's statements of theoretical beliefs, but is an inescapable feature of Cultural Materialists' retention of the concept—vital to their political mission—of strong causality. By retaining such a background-history–foreground-text divide, it is hard to see how Cultural Materialism's practice of history differs from the nineteenth-century positivistic history of ideas. Ironically, given their dislike of Tillyard, Cultural Materialists seem to out-Tillyard the supposed-Tillyard of *The Elizabethan World Picture*, and run into all the objections that

[52] Barker, *The Tremulous Private Body*, 68.
[53] Belsey, *Subject of Tragedy*, 41.
[54] Terry Eagleton, *William Shakespeare* (Oxford: Basil Blackwell, 1986), 74–5.

New Historicists made against such a literary history. Only now the Cultural Materialists' aim is not to explain what was thought, but instead the far more ambitious task of defining what it was possible to think. As Belsey, with remarkable equanimity, puts it: 'The project is to construct a history of the meanings which delimit at a specific moment what it is possible to say, to understand, and consequently to be.'[55] Cultural Materialist history, then, is a history of 'non-ideas of the time'.[56]

This is not only an impossibly ambitious task but an impossible one. A negatively defining normative scheme, such as Belsey suggests, would seem unsuited to deal with works of art that are in various ways innovatory, often themselves creating new meanings. Moreover, to begin to be plausible it requires a *complete* knowledge of the historical period. Cultural Materialists, by contrast, have little concern—as has been seen—even for the concept of historical accuracy. Their histories are overbroad and their assumptions large, more than justifying Wayne's description of their historical practice as 'relatively freewheeling'. Other large-scale objections could be raised to Cultural Materialists' histories of subjectivity. Why, for instance, has there been so little attention to the different conceptions of subjectivity between different genres? Why has Jacobean tragedy been seen to be representative of Renaissance subjectivity? Clearly, the dramatic persons in a Jacobean tragedy are less likely to demonstrate a viable agency, to shape their lives in any but a destructive way, than those in an Elizabethan comedy.

Similarly, objections can be raised on a smaller scale. The terminology in which Cultural Materialists discuss subjectivity is both overbroad and narrow, in a manner akin to Greenblatt's criteria in *Renaissance Self-Fashioning*. This is seen more clearly in Belsey's and Dollimore's accounts, as Barker generally avoids most matters of detail. Like Greenblatt, Belsey and Dollimore collapse terms such as 'the self', 'the human subject', and 'identity' into one another. For example, Belsey asserts: 'The human subject, the self, is the central figure in the drama which is liberal humanism.'[57] In fact, Dollimore and Belsey collapse the terms outward, so 'the self', whatever that may be, comes to be the equivalent of identity. Thus, when they come to look for an autonomous inner self—autonomy was taken, as has been seen, to be the defining quality of the post-1660 sense of inner subjectivity—they do not find it, for as they rightly argue, no one's identity is purely self-generated. By collapsing these terms, Belsey and Dollimore dismiss the possibility of considering whether there are component areas within general identity, some of which might demonstrate a significantly higher degree of self-constituting agency than that possessed by overall identity.

[55] Belsey, *Subject of Tragedy*, p. x.

[56] This is Richard Levin's phrase, from his 'Unthinkable Thoughts in the New Historicizing of English Renaissance Drama', *New Literary History*, No. 3, Spring 1990, 433–48.

[57] Belsey, *Subject of Tragedy*, p. ix.

The argument is then made that as there is no inner sense of self during the English Renaissance, the concepts that are founded on it, such as interiority, the individual, and character, do not exist. How, then, is *Hamlet* to be read? Belsey argues that it is best considered within the morality-play tradition. The Prince's soliloquies, are 'traversed by the voices of a succession of morality fragments, wrath and reason, patience and resolution. In none of them is it possible to locate the true, the essential Hamlet.'[58] Dollimore suggests that the Prince should be treated as a Brechtian hero, in Walter Benjamin's words, 'like an empty stage on which the contradictions of our society are acted out'.[59]

The presence of such objections as those described above makes it tempting to dismiss Barker's and Cultural Materialists' arguments concerning *Hamlet.* This is, to an extent, what a second generation of Cultural Materialist critics is tending to do. As I have said, Alan Sinfield's *Faultlines* draws on much of the first decade of Cultural Materialist work. In his third chapter, 'When is a character not a character?', he examines Cultural Materialism's discussion of subjectivity. He argues that Barker and Belsey dismiss interiority too easily, and that Belsey is 'slightly too insistent on banishing agency and meaning from the dramatis personae of early modern plays'.[60] To him it seems that 'it should be possible to probe further into the relations between subjectivity and character' (pp. 60–1). Sinfield uses Joel Fineman's argument that Shakespeare's *Sonnets* created the literary effect of a 'deep personal interiority' by having the sonnet's poetic persona experience 'himself *as* his difference from himself' (p. 59).[61] Sinfield argues that *Hamlet*, the Prince and the play, does not, as Barker maintains, lack subjectivity, but produces 'subjectivity effects all the time' (p. 65). In fact, the play's superfluity of such subjectivity is what has allowed so many different interpretations. Yet, in the end, it is hard to see how such 'subjectivity effects' do probe further into the relations between subjectivity and character. For Sinfield's later discussion of Young Hamlet, in chapter 9, 'Tragedy, God and Writing: *Hamlet*, *Faustus*, *Tamburlaine*' seems to follow Dollimore's Brechtian approach to subjectivity: Sinfield's aim is, 'to locate Hamlet at the intersection point of Senecan and Calvinist discourses' (p. 227).

What is remarkable about Barker's argument concerning *Hamlet*, particularly in the light of the many temptations to dismiss it, is how hard it is to refute. For direct evidence of Prince Hamlet's interiority (with which to refute Barker's charge of interiority's gestural, fantasy-like nature), proves hard to find. One reason, already mentioned, is that the modern critical vocabulary in which subjectivity is described is not available to Shakespeare; words such as character, individual, self, personality, let alone words such as interiority,

[58] Ibid. 42.

[59] Dollimore, *Radical Tragedy*, 153.

[60] Sinfield, *Faultlines*, 60. Further references to this work are given after quotations in the text.

[61] Sinfield quotes from Joel Fineman, *Shakespeare's Perjured Eye: The Invention of Poetic Subjectivity in the Sonnets* (Berkeley: University of California Press, 1986).

do not have those meanings which are at present bound inextricably to inner senses of subjectivity. To repudiate Barker and the Cultural Materialist argument, then, the verbal text must be shown to express meanings which, in terms of the absence of the relevant modern vocabulary of interiority, might be thought inexpressible. This is attempted in Part III. Before that, however, Part II turns to the early days of Shakespearian criticism, and it becomes clear how well Cultural Materialists have chosen their point of attack. For the ability to create an area of inner self is the ability through which literary critics first claim greatness for Shakespeare; historically, this ability to create this inner area is central to the critical evaluation of Shakespeare. Moreover, while this area is of pivotal importance within literary-critical debates, in describing it the critical commentary becomes vague, abandoning descriptive analysis. Part II, then, makes clear the critical importance of 'that Within'.

Part II

4
Fools of Nature

Mar. Tell me he that knowes
Why this same strict and most obseruant Watch,
So nightly toyles the subiect of the Land.

(I. I. 69–71)

ONE bibliography of *Hamlet* criticism from 1877 to 1935 records 2,167 books and articles.[1] More recently, the Modern Language Association recorded 1,200 books concerning *Hamlet* published between 1960 and 1990, 700 after 1975.[2] And this represents only a small measure of the play's presence in the world. *Hamlet in the 1950s* finds, in that decade, 1,115 books, articles, notes, dissertations, summaries, adaptations, recordings, reviews of productions, and works directly indebted to *Hamlet. Hamlet in the 1960s* finds more than double that number.[3] Already by the end of the nineteenth century, Oscar Wilde was suggesting it was time to stop considering the issue of the Prince's madness in favour of a more pressing concern—'a discussion as to whether the commentators on *Hamlet* are mad, or only pretending to be'.[4]

Literary critics have toiled through many nights, producing vast amounts of criticism, in their strict and most observant watch over *Hamlet.* Yet, typically, the conclusion of all this labour is that there is not only no conclusion, but also no consensus. Henry Mackenzie, writing in the *Mirror* in 1780, suggested that, 'No author, perhaps, ever existed of whom opinion has been so various as *Shakespeare* . . . Of all the characters of *Shakespeare* that of *Hamlet* has been generally thought the most difficult to be reduced to any fixed or settled principle.'[5] Mackenzie aimed to provide such a principle for the Prince and the play; he did not convince his successors. Two hundred years later, Graham Bradshaw was expressing a similar sense of a lack of consensus to Mackenzie's, but with

[1] A. A. Raven, *A 'Hamlet' Bibliography and Reference Guide, 1877–1935* (Chicago: University of Chicago Press, 1936). Quoted in Graham Bradshaw, *Shakespeare's Scepticism* (Brighton: Harvester Press, 1987), 95.

[2] Quoted in David Daniell, '*Hamlet*', in Wells (ed.), *Shakespeare: A Bibliographical Guide*, 201–21 (201).

[3] Randal F. Robinson, *'Hamlet' in the 1950s: An Annotated Bibliography* (New York: Garland, 1984). Julia Dietrich, *'Hamlet' in the 1960s: An Annotated Bibliography* (New York: Garland, 1992). Dietrich lists 2,487 items.

[4] Oscar Wilde to Robert Ross in 1889. Quoted in Richard Ellmann, *Oscar Wilde* (London: Hamish Hamilton, 1987), 282.

[5] Henry Mackenzie, quoted in Brian Vickers (ed.), *Shakespeare: The Critical Heritage*, 6 vols. (London: RKP, 1974–81), vi. 272–3 (first pub. in the *Mirror*, 17 Apr. 1780).

more vigour: 'In the case of *Hamlet* the staggering proliferation of conflicting, utterly incompatible readings makes it desperately hard even to agree on what the critically relevant *questions* are.'[6] This lack of consensus has become known as 'the *Hamlet* Problem', which in turn has become its own problem. 'The problem of the Problem', William Empson argued in 1953, is that it took critics almost two hundred years to realize that they were failing to achieve any meaningful areas of consensus concerning the play: 'What is peculiar is that he [Hamlet] does not seem to have become one [a problem] until the end of the eighteenth century; even Dr. Johnson, who had a strong grasp of natural human difficulties, writes about Hamlet as if there was no problem at all.'[7] 'The *Hamlet* Problem' functions a little like the Tillyard trope; though it does not banish the literary-critical past, it tends to discount it. By denying the body of commentary on *Hamlet* any meaningful consensus, 'the Problem' robs the commentary of weight, picturing it as a formless mass of insights and arguments, lacking any clear critical voices. The critic is, to a degree, freed from the constraints of the past.

Part II of this book introduces the critical drama of those first two hundred years of *Hamlet* criticism, the drama which 'the Problem' plays down, New Historicists banish, and Cultural Materialists attack.[8] In staging the drama, this Part tries to listen carefully to the past and suggests that 'the Problem' overstates its case. For there is an area of consensus within the critical commentary on the play, and it is this area that Part II focuses on, developing an observation made by A. P. Rossiter in a lecture on *Hamlet*:

> Though nineteenth- and twentieth- century commentators differ stupendously, there is a consensus that there is something very 'personal' or 'subjective' in the play.[9]

[6] Bradshaw, *Shakespeare's Scepticism*, 95–6.

[7] W. Empson, '*Hamlet*', in David B. Pirie (ed.), *Essays on Shakespeare* (Cambridge: Cambridge University Press, 1986), 79–136 (80). This is a substantially revised and expanded version of '*Hamlet* When New', first pub. in *Sewanee Review*, 61 (1953), 15–42 and 185–205.

[8] The following collections of criticism have been drawn on: J. Munro (ed.) *The Shakespeare Allusion-Book: A Collection of Allusions to Shakespeare from 1591 to 1700*, 2 vols. (London: Oxford University Press, 1932); Vickers (ed.), *Shakespeare: The Critical Heritage*; D. Nichol Smith (ed.), *Eighteenth Century Essays on Shakespeare* (2nd edn.; Oxford: Clarendon Press, 1963); C. C. H. Williamson (ed.), *Readings on the Character of Hamlet; 1661–1947* (New York: Gordian Press, 1972; first pub. 1950); Laurie Lanzan Harris, *Shakespearean Criticism: Excerpts from the Criticism of William Shakespeare's Plays and Poetry from the First Published Appraisals to Current Evaluations*, 7 vols. (Detroit, Mich.: Gale, 1984–), vol. i. For convenience, quotations have been taken, wherever possible, from Vickers.

The following articles, though sometimes inaccurate in their histories of *Hamlet* criticism (understandable before the arrival of Vickers's collection of criticism), have been generally helpful: G. K. Hunter, '*Hamlet* Criticism', *The Critical Quarterly*, 1 (1959), 27–32 (the argument that *Hamlet*'s ascendancy was the result of Romanticism is no longer plausible); Harold Jenkins, '*Hamlet* Then Till Now', *SS* 18 (1965), 34–45 (the stage history is misleading and the arrival of consistency as a criterion by which to judge Shakespeare's 'characters' misdated); T. J. B. Spencer, 'The Decline of Hamlet', *Stratford Upon Avon Studies*, 5 (1963), 185–99 (the pre-1800 history of criticism is rather tendentious).

[9] A. P. Rossiter, *Angel with Horns: Fifteen Lectures on Shakespeare*, ed. Graham Storey (Harlow: Longman, 1989; first pub. 1961), 171.

This consensus, it is argued, is audible before the nineteenth century. However, the presence of consensus does not rule out debate. Sixteenth- and seventeenth-century commentators, when faced with Marcellus' questioning of the reason for their watch, would reply that their interest springs from the 'something very "personal" or "subjective" in the play'. Yet some would see that 'something' as a reason for censuring Shakespeare, while others would see it increasingly as Shakespeare's greatest achievement. Hamlet the Prince and *Hamlet* the play were a problem within literary criticism long before 1800; the 'problem of the Problem', like 'the Problem', overstates its case.

This area of consensus was a consensus over the answer to the question of 'Who's there?' Asking 'Who's there?' of Shakespeare and particularly of *Hamlet*, it was argued—with increasing frequency through these two centuries—provided a distinctive answer that could not be found in other playwrights. Shakespeare's answer relied on his ability to create 'that Within' the Prince, an area that was seen to generate a 'very "personal" and "subjective" quality'. This area became one of the central marks of his difference and distinction from other dramatists. To some it was Shakespeare's glory, to others his great weakness. Yet what was this answer, this area—how was it constituted? Answers to the question were bound up with notions of 'character'; 'character' was the area that made Shakespeare's dramatic persons different—for the better or for the worse—from other dramatists', and that, similarly, distinguished his plays. The debates over this answer and area were to an extent semantic debates over the meaning of 'character'; during this period the term gradually developed a more inward and interior range of meanings. However, although it becomes central to criticism of *Hamlet*, and also of Shakespeare, the answer to 'Who's there?' always remains finally vague; Rossiter's inverted commas—'something very "personal" or "subjective"'—have a long tradition behind them. Typically, at the moment that Shakespeare's ability to create this area is asserted, the critic tends to relapse into statements of wonder, as if the play and Prince had made them 'fooles of Nature . . . With thoughts beyond the reaches of our Soules' (I. 4. 35, 37).[10]

> *Hor.* and this (I take it)
> Is the maine Motiue of our Preparations,
> The Sourse of this our Watch.
> (I. I. 103–5)

This chapter turns, then, to 'the Sourse of this our Watch', looking at the beginnings of the critical drama up to 1801. It brings onto its stage criticism both of *Hamlet* and of Shakespeare in general. This is partly because, in the seventeenth century, criticism of *Hamlet* is scarce, and partly to substantiate the

[10] For ease of reading the Folio text has been amended; the Folio reads, 'fooles of Nature . . . With thoughts beyond *thee;* reaches of our Soules'.

argument that Shakespearian and *Hamlet* criticism grew up together, united by their answer to 'Who's there?'

The period to 1801 can be divided into a number of kinds of critical practice. The first begins with references contemporary with Shakespeare and stretches up to the Restoration. It consists of criticism primarily of Shakespeare the poet and playwright (as opposed, for example, to criticism of particular poems and plays). After Greene's initial deathbed attack on the, 'upstart Crow, beautified with our feathers . . . in his owne conceit the onely Shake-scene in a countrie',[11] almost all references consist of general praise of a successful peer, first as a poet and then also as a playwright. Often this praise is particularly of Shakespeare's eloquence; he tends to be 'honie-tong'd Shakespeare'.[12] A more concrete demonstration of the esteem in which Shakespeare was held is seen in the false attribution of plays and poems to him by unscrupulous printers and piratical publications of his plays, both of which are evidence of his market value.[13] Yet although many commentators are certain of his immortality, particularly after his death,[14] the lavish praise that they offer does not mark Shakespeare as pre-eminent among his peers. Often, Shakespeare is praised as one of a group of writers, adduced to prove that the vernacular has been vindicated.[15] So, for example, Francis Meres, in his commonplace book *Palladis Tamia, Wit's Treasury* (1598), heaps effusive praise on Shakespeare, stating, among other assertions, that if the Muses spoke English, they would choose to speak Shakespeare's 'fine filed phrase'.[16] Yet Shakespeare is only one of 125 English writers, painters, and musicians that Meres praises, and it is Drayton who is mentioned most frequently.[17]

[11] Robert Greene, *Green's Groats-Worth of Wit; bought with a million of Repentaunce* (1592); quoted in Munro, *The Shakespeare Allusion-Book*, i. 2.

[12] See Francis Meres, *Palladis Tamia, Wit's Treasury* (1598); Richard Barnfield, 'Poems in Divers humours' (1598); John Weever, 'Ad Gulielmum Shakespeare' in *Epigrammes* (1599); and Thomas Heywood, 'The Hierarchie of the Blessed Angells' (1635); quoted in Munro, *The Shakespeare Allusion-Book* i. 24, 46, 51, and 393 respectively.

[13] So e.g. there are *The Lamentable Tragedie of Locrine* 'By W.S.' in 1595, *The Passionate Pilgrim* 'By W. Shakespeare' in 1599 (in which only five of the twenty poems—all probably published without consent—were by Shakespeare), *The true Chronicle History . . . of Thomas Lord Cromwell* 'Written by W.S.' 1602, *The London Prodigall* 'By William Shakespeare' in 1605, *The Puritaine* 'Written by W.S.' 1607, *A Yorkshire Tragedy* 'Written by W. Shakspeare' in 1608, *The . . . troublesome Raigne of John King of England* 'Written by W. Sh.' in 1611. All quoted in Munro, *The Shakespeare Allusion-Book*, i. 21, 62, 104, 147, 166, 186 and 226 respectively. Honigmann takes the six 'agreed' and eleven possible 'bad' quartos as his evidence for piratical publication, arguing that no other dramatist was honoured to anywhere near such an extent. See E. Honigmann, *Shakespeare's Impact on his Contemporaries* (London: Macmillan, 1982), 46.

[14] See the prefatory poems by Ben Jonson, Hugh Holland, Leonard Digges, and James Mabbe in the First Folio (1623); and those by John Milton, an anonymous poet, and 'I.C.S.' prefatory to the second edition of 1632; quoted in Munro, *The Shakespeare Allusion-Book*, i. 307, 317, 318, 319, 342, 363 and 366 respectively.

[15] Early and later examples are Meres's *Palladis Tamia* and William Basse's elegy 'On Mr. Wm. Shakespeare' (1622); quoted in Munro, *The Shakespeare Allusion-Book*, i. 46 and 286 respectively.

[16] Ibid. i. 46.

[17] See S. Schoenbaum, *Shakespeare's Lives* (Oxford: Clarendon Press, 1991), 25–9. Honigmann,

Jonson is the exception to this picture of general praise. Though scattered, his comments up to the publication of the First Folio (1623) represent a coherent criticism of Shakespeare's dramatic practice, founded on the argument that Shakespeare deviated from the requirements of nature, truth, and art.[18] In the prefatory poem Jonson wrote for the First Folio, his attitude changed, perhaps because he was able to read Shakespeare's work as a reasonable whole for the first time.[19] Shakespeare is now praised both for his truth to nature and his art, and is seen as exceptional within his time and all time. The seriousness present in Jonson's criticism is absent elsewhere; from the publication of the First Folio until the 1640s, Shakespeare is referred to in terms of a general and sustained panegyric.

Throughout this period, there are remarkably few written comments concerning *Hamlet.* Gabriel Harvey, probably in 1600, calls it a play 'to please the wiser sort';[20] then four years later Anthony Scoloker describes a play that 'should please all, like Prince *Hamlet*' (p. 133).[21] These comments are typical in their generality. In terms of allusions and imitations incorporated into other writers' works *Hamlet* made a huge and immediate impact (though the picture is complicated by the fact that some allusions may be to the *Ur-Hamlet*). Chambers calculated that of the four most 'borrowed' from plays of Shakespeare—the other three plays being *The Most Excellent and Lamentable Tragedy of Romeo and Juliet*, *The Tragedy of King Richard the Third* and 'the Falstaff pieces'—*Hamlet* accounted for 43 per cent of the borrowings.[22] D. G. McGinn puts a

however, argues that Francis Meres's and others' classical comparison show a sense of perceived uniqueness concerning Shakespeare; see his *Shakespeare's Impact*, 39–40.

[18] See Jonson's 'Prologue' to *Every Man In His Humour* (1598); the prefatory epistle 'To the Reader' of *The Alchemist* (1610); 'The Induction' to *Bartholomew Fair* (1614) (esp. ll. 128–35); and 'De Shakespeare nostrat', in *Timber: or Discoveries* (first pub. 1640), which finds Shakespeare's virtues in excess of his faults (ll. 803–28). Jonson's criticism also continues after 1623; see his 'Ode to Himself' (1631) where he attacks Shakespeare's and George Wilkins's *Pericles Prince of Tyre* (1607/8). The 'Ode', however, is criticism of a different nature; it was written as a response to the failure of *The New Inn; or, The Light Heart* (1629), a play in which Jonson celebrates and pays homage to Shakespearian comedy and tragicomedy by using many of its central dynamics. (See Anne Barton, 'The New Inn' in *Ben Jonson, Dramatist* (Cambridge: Cambridge University Press, 1984), 258–85.) Jonson, by this time, is not attacking Shakespeare for his deviation from neo-classical principles of art; indeed as some of the responses to his 'Ode' pointed out, *The New Inn* out-Periclesed *Pericles* in breaking the bounds of decorum. (See Owen Felltham's 'An Answer to the Ode of Come Leave the Loathed Stage, &c.', ll. 21–30; repr. in *The New Inn*, ed. Michael Hattaway (Manchester: Manchester University Press, 1984), 216–17.) Jonson's 'Ode', then, is better read as an expression of resentment at perceived injustice than as part of his critique of Shakespearian drama.

[19] For a discussion of Jonson's criticism, and the impact of the First Folio, see Honigmann, *Shakespeare's Impact*, 93–103.

[20] Harvey made his comment as a manuscript note in Speght's *Chaucer.* Quoted in Munro, *The Shakespeare Allusion-Book*, i. 56. Further references to this work are given after quotations in the text.

[21] Scoloker's comment comes from a 'spoof epistle'. See Honigmann, *Shakespeare's Impact*, 18.

[22] E. K. Chambers, 'Preface, in Munro, *The Shakespeare Allusion-Book*, p. lix.

number to these 'echoes' of *Hamlet*, finding around 500 by 1642.[23] Paul Conklin, using these as evidence, argues for a Jacobean prince,

> Who was an eloquent talker whose dramatic picturesqueness, liveliness and human quality made him the foremost character on the Elizabethan stage. He was, in addition, a malcontent avenger whose bitter and cynical words were stamped indelibly upon the memory of at least the first thirty years of the century.[24]

The allusions and imitations, however, provide fragmentary evidence, and Conklin's account is occasionally too willing to unify them by such declarations as, 'these bits too, if interpreted imaginatively . . .'.[25] Another line of commentary can be found in the plays that *Hamlet* begat; as David L. Frost argues, *Hamlet* gave the revenge tragedy a new lease of life, spurring Cyril Tourneur, George Chapman, and perhaps Thomas Middleton to write their own.[26] Yet these plays, reacting to Shakespeare's tragedy, expressed a different attitude to and vision of the tragedy of revenge. Again, the evidence for a commentary on *Hamlet* is fragmentary. All that is certain is that *Hamlet*, like Shakespeare, had an established reputation[27] in the years leading up to the Restoration, and its Prince had quickly become famous.

Up to this time, then, no consensus over a 'subjective' or 'personal' quality peculiar to Shakespeare or *Hamlet* can be found in critical writing. However, there may be the suggestion of such a quality within the visual arts.[28] Van Dyck's portrait of Sir John Suckling (1638) shows him staring off into the distance, meditating presumably on the book which lies open on the rock beside him. The book, the viewer is informed by a slip, is a Folio edition of the works of 'SHAKESPEARE'. It lies open at 'HAMLET', and cut into the rock is the Latin tag, 'NE TE QUAESIVERIS EXTRA'—'do not seek outside yourself'.

Malcolm Rogers, in an article interpreting this portrait, notes that this is the first painting to show a vernacular non-religious book not written by the sitter.[29] The book's presence is interesting in itself; clearly it has a great deal of

[23] Donald J. McGinn, *Shakespeare's Influence on the Drama of his Age Studied in 'Hamlet'* (New Brunswick: Rutgers University Press, 1938), 123.

[24] Paul S. Conklin, *A History of 'Hamlet' Criticism 1601–1821* (New York: Humanities Press, 1968), 35.

[25] Ibid. 20.

[26] D. L. Frost, *The School of Shakespeare* (Cambridge: Cambridge University Press, 1968), 167–208; quoted in *Hamlet*, ed. G. R. Hibbard (Oxford: Oxford University Press, 1987), 16. See Middleton's or Tourneur's *The Revenger's Tragedy* (1606), Tourneur's *The Atheist's Tragedy* (1609), and Chapman's *The Revenge of Bussy D'Ambois* (1610).

[27] Also testament to the play's popularity is the piracy that the first Quarto may represent, and both versions of the elegy to Burbage. The latter, where it concerns the actor's connection with Shakespeare, dwells most on Burbage's playing of 'young Hamlett', describing (and so providing authority to the first Quarto's direction) his spectacular vaults into the grave. Quoted in Munro, *The Shakespeare Allusion-Book*, 272.

[28] I was directed to Van Dyck's portrait of Suckling by Dr James Knowles.

[29] Malcolm Rogers, 'The Meaning of Van Dyck's Portrait of Sir John Suckling', *Burlington Magazine*, 120 (1978), 741–5.

cultural authority even at this early date. Rogers argues that the book is to be understood by reference to a controversy between the Ancients and the Moderns: respectively, the lovers of Jonson and of Shakespeare. Rogers recontextualizes the Latin tag; he gives to the line the meaning it has within Persius' (AD 34–62) *First Satire*—'be content with your own opinion'. Having ascribed this meaning to the line, Rogers sees the portrait as an exhortation to (and presumably declaration by) Suckling: Suckling must be content with his own opinion, ignoring the critics of his plays, refusing to trace out a path of servile classicism, and so maintaining his love of Shakespeare.

Rogers concentrates, then, on the presence of the works of Shakespeare.[30] What his interpretation plays down is the presence of *Hamlet*. The portrait, with its open pages, asks us to associate Suckling not with Shakespeare in general but with Prince Hamlet in particular. The presence of *Hamlet* is a statement expressive of personality; *Hamlet* (and to a lesser extent the Folio edition of Shakespeare's works), is the first non-religious book that can express a personality other than that of its author. *Hamlet*, in fact, structures the portrait's composition; Suckling's stance invokes the Prince, meditating over an open book. The living person is being explored through the dramatic person.

There is no need to restrict the meaning of the Latin tag by insisting that it has only the (dominant) meaning that it had in Persius' *First Satire*; the tag is full of meaning in its new context, as the 'rock' which supports *Hamlet*. Is 'do not see outside yourself' to be taken as the motto to be carried away from *Hamlet*? Or is it a summary of the temptation to which the Prince saw himself succumbing, with shameful effect on his personal integrity? Suckling's meditative pose would suggest that it is just the undecidability of *Hamlet* and the Prince's attitude that is being dwelt on; in other words that the identification which the portrait suggests is an identification with the questions of identity and identification, as opposed to any answers.

'Do not see outside yourself' is, of course, a paradoxical injunction for a portrait, committed as it must be to depicting the sitter's outward gaze. Yet this portrait seeks to turn that gaze back upon the sitter, as Suckling's looks away from the sitter, and then—through the Latin tag and the play that occupy his thoughts—inside himself. Van Dyck's portrait realizes in visual terms an analysis of *Hamlet* that sees it not only as possessing a particularly '"subjective" and "personal" quality', but also as acting as a model through which to examine and construct living personality. Literary criticism of that time, lacking as it does the modern vocabulary of interiority, cannot directly express such an analysis, which will only be fully expressed by Hazlitt, almost two hundred years later.

*

[30] Rogers's analysis is more suitable to Thomas Gainsborough's portrait of David Garrick (1769), where Garrick leans on a bust of Shakespeare. Repr. in Jonathan Bate, *Shakespearean Constitutions: Politics, Theatre, Criticism 1730–1830* (Oxford: Clarendon Press, 1989), pl. 2 (p. 18).

With the return of Charles II and his court from France, discordant voices broke up the general panegyric directed towards Shakespeare. John Evelyn, writing in his diary on 26 November 1661, is typical: 'I saw *Hamlet* Prince of Denmark played: but now the old playe began to disgust this refined age: since his Majestie being so long abroad.'[31] With the King and court's return, neo-classic criteria of literary worth had become dominant. 'Neo-classic' has no single definition; in this context, it refers to the conception of literature as an art, which must be perfected by study, and should follow classical precedent, decorum, and the relevant rules of drama, such as the three unities. In this context, the worth of Shakespeare and of *Hamlet* was no longer certain.

Margaret Cavendish, the Duchess of Newcastle, like Evelyn and the King, had herself spent many years abroad, first as the Maid of Honour to Henrietta Maria, and then as the wife of William Cavendish, a man disliked intensely by the Commonwealth government. Unlike Evelyn, she was a defender of Shakespeare. A year after Evelyn saw *Hamlet*, she wrote a letter in answer to a friend's report of a man who had 'dispraise[d]' Shakespeare's plays since 'they were made up onely with Clowns, Fools, Watchmen, and the like'.[32] After having pointed out that it takes equal or greater 'wit' to express the 'Ignorance of clowns, and the Simplicity of Naturals' as it does to express the 'Course of Life, of Kings and Princes' (i. 42), Cavendish declares:

> *Shakespeare* did not want Wit, to Express to the Life all Sorts of Persons, of what Quality, Profession, Degree, Breeding, or Birth soever; nor did he want Wit to Express the Divers, and Different Humours, or Natures, or Several Passions in Mankind; and so Well he hath Express'd in his Playes all Sorts of Persons, as one would think he had been Transformed into every one of those Persons he hath Described. (i. 43)

Where previous criticism, with the exception of Jonson, dwelt on the playwright, here the focus is upon the playwright's achievement and method. In particular, Cavendish focuses on the achievement of the expression 'to the Life [of] all Sorts of Persons', and on the method that underlies that achievement, Shakespeare's ability to be 'Transformed into every one of those Persons he hath Described'.

Cavendish's choice of this achievement and method as the area from which to begin a defence of Shakespeare anticipates the critical debate for the next century and a half. Shakespeare's ability 'to Express to the Life' is constantly taken to be one of the best 'proofs' of his 'genius'; the answer to 'Who's there?', from those defending Shakespeare, is a variation on the answer of 'a distinct person', 'someone, and no other'. Similarly, Shakespeare's ability to be 'Transformed' is often advanced as the explanation for this achievement; the

[31] *The Diary of John Evelyn*, ed. E. S. de Beer (London: 1959; first pub. 1818), 431; quoted in Vickers (ed.), *Shakespeare*, i. 4.

[32] Letter 113, from *CCXI Sociable Letters, written by the Thrice Noble, Illustrious, and Excellent Princess, The Lady Marchioness of Newcastle* (1664), 224–8; quoted in Vickers (ed.), *Shakespeare*, i. 42. Further references to this book are given after quotations in the text.

dramatic persons, though written by the same playwright, all stand apart from him. But how precisely is this accomplished—how can it be seen? Cavendish's explanation is not descriptive; it relies on equating Shakespeare with the mythical figure of Proteus, the sea-god in Homer's *Odyssey*, who knew everything and could change into any shape he wanted. Shakespeare's achievement becomes wondrous, god-like, divine. Cavendish discusses his persons as if they were living persons; there seems to be no recognizable difference between Shakespeare's dramatic persons and living people. Indeed, Shakespeare's achievement becomes both representative of human nature at its height, and also to be identified with language itself. Proteus, during the Renaissance, had become a symbol both of man's nature—his ability to learn and shape himself, to rise and fall—and of language's creative and expressive powers.[33]

Cavendish's letter anticipates the subsequent critical debate in other ways. It is a defence, generated by another's attack, and its aim is frankly evaluative. Moreover, although this attack seems likely to have been produced by the application of neo-classical principles to Shakespearian drama—neo-classicists often insisting that such persons as 'Clowns, Fools, and Watchmen' should neither feature in tragedy nor be mixed in any genre with persons of a higher class—the defence remains within the governing assumptions of neo-classical theory. For though Cavendish praises Shakespeare's ability to 'Express to the Life all Sorts of Persons', she does so because this variety maintains a neo-classical principle concerning dramatic persons, that they should act in conformity with their social position and social type. She praises Shakespeare's accurate delineation of, 'The *Subtilty* of Knaves, the *Ignorance* of Clowns, and the *Simplicity* of Naturals, or the *Craft* of Feigned Fools' (my emphasis).[34] Her argument with the detractor of Shakespeare is not an argument with his use of neo-classical principles, but rather that he has given priority to the incorrect neo-classical principle.

Finally Cavendish's letter demonstrates the absence of a modern vocabulary of interiority, and its assumptions: she uses 'person' where 'character' would be expected, and she suggests that persons can be depicted through the requisite attribution of standard traits and passions. Her account of dramatic persons seems to lack that sense of a distinctive whole that has become associated with the word 'character'. Though she talks of a Fool's 'Humour, Expressions, Phrases, Garbs, Manners, Actions, Words, and Course of Life' (i. 42), these categories are distinct and divisible from one another. They produce a Fool, instead of a particular fool. Cavendish, then, displays in embryo Rossiter's sense of 'something very "personal" or "subjective"', but she takes this to be typical of Shakespeare's dramatic works as a whole. 'Who's there?' is asked of Shakespeare's works and that question is accorded a central place in an

33 For further details see Ch. 7, pp. 222–3.

34 Quoted in Vickers (ed.), *Shakespeare*, i. 42. Further references to this book are given after quotations in the text.

evaluation of Shakespeare; yet the answer given to that question remains vague; Rossiter's inverted commas are already in place.

With Thomas Rymer's *The Tragedies of the Last Age Consider'd and Examined by the Practice of the Ancients, and by the Common Sense of all Ages*, published in 1677, the neo-classical detractor is given a more formal voice. Rymer has a low opinion of 'the Last Age'. His attack is levelled particularly at the plots of Elizabethan and Jacobean tragedies:

> I have chiefly consider'd the *Fable* or *Plot*, which all conclude to be the *Soul* of a *Tragedy*; which, with the *Ancients*, is always found to be a *reasonable Soul*; but *with us*, for the most part, a *brutish*, and often worse than *brutish*. (i. 186)

This charge is not made specifically against Shakespeare, but he is damned along with his contemporaries. Rymer goes on to attack what he sees as subsidiary areas of dramaturgy, one of which is the area from which Cavendish had defended Shakespeare—the depiction of persons. The writers of 'the Last Age', for Rymer, were culpable because they did not understand what such depiction should involve:

> We are to presume the greatest vertues, where we find the highest of rewards; and though it is not necessary that all *Heroes* should be Kings, yet undoubtedly all crown'd heads by *Poetical right* are *Heroes*. This Character is a flower, a prerogative, so certain, so inseparably annex'd to the *Crown*, as by no Poet, no *Parliament* of Poets, ever to be invaded. (i. 191)

Rymer's criticism is driven by a political agenda; particularly in its deep desire, presented as an assertion, that monarchy has a 'character', given by '*Poetical right*', which cannot be taken from it, even by a '*Parliament* of Poets'. Rymer's assertion asks to be read in the context of Charles I's assertion of the divine right of kings at his trial, and Parliament's rejection of that theory and subsequent execution of the King. Literature, in Rymer's criticism, is involved in those events. On the one hand, it seems to offer a place of safety, where the king's rights cannot be 'invaded' without being bad literature; on the other hand, there is the suggestion that, should a poet deny this character to a king, it is a form of literary regicide, making possible literal regicide.

A remarkable political burden is being placed on the notion of 'character', and the political motives of neo-classicism are glimpsed. Rymer is casting the Elizabethan and Jacobean drama as a dangerous theatre of ideological insurrection. Once again, 'Who's there?' is the founding question in this critical appraisal of that drama, and the judgement depends on how satisfactorily that drama understands the answer of 'a character'. Rymer uses 'character', but 'character' is here synonymous with Cavendish's 'person'. A 'character', for Rymer, is something which lacks individuality; it defines only a class. It must be easily recognizable; kings must clearly be heroes, that is their inalienable right. It must be true to tradition and true to type; 'all crown'd heads' share this character. Finally, as a concomitant of the previous qualities, it must be consistent.[35] Underlying this conception is another of the central assumptions of neo-classicism (though not, *pace* New Historicists and Cultural Materialists, of the Renaissance or of Renaissance drama): that human nature is constant. Rymer replies to those that urge that 'Athens' is in some way different from 'London':

> Certain it is, that *Nature* is the same, and *Man* is the same; he *loves*, *grieves*, *hates*, *envies*, has the same *affections* and *passions* in both places, and the same *springs* that give them *motion*.[36]

This definition of character and its assumption did not strike the age as remarkable. Indeed, it was influential, shaping the redactions of Shakespeare's plays that began to hold sway on the stage. Nahum Tate, for instance, quotes Rymer to justify his dignifying of the King in his 1680 version of *Richard II* (i. 321). As Tate's need to adapt suggests, this definition of 'character' was not felt to sit easily with Shakespeare's practice. Shakespeare's ability to create 'character' was, increasingly, seen as a disability. Critics subsequent to Rymer often cited Claudius in *Hamlet* as their evidence.[37]

John Dryden, on the blank leaves at the beginning and end of the copy of *The Tragedies of the Last Age* which Rymer had sent him, made preparatory notes for a defence.[38] In the notes, Dryden begins by denying the importance of plot, pointing out that Aristotle dealt with this first not 'quoad dignitatem, sed quoad fundamentum' (i. 197)—not because of its essential worth, but because it was the foundation on which the play was built. Dryden then argued that other areas must be given greater weight to produce a proper evaluation, one of which is the depiction of dramatic persons: 'For the Characters, they are neither so many nor so various in *Sophocles* and *Euripedes*, as in *Shakespeare* and *Fletcher*' (i. 200). To Dryden, as to Cavendish, 'character' was an area from which to begin a defence of Shakespeare, an area in which Shakespeare and Fletcher outshone the ancients.

Two years later, in 1679, Dryden enters into a more formal dialogue with Rymer, in his Preface to *Troilus and Cressida*. He admits Rymer's charges against Elizabethan and Jacobean plots (i. 259), choosing to contest Rymer's overall judgement of the Last Age on the ground of 'character'. In choosing this area, Dryden is defending Shakespeare in particular: 'Tis one of the excellencies of *Shakespeare*, that the manners of his persons are generally apparent . . . no man ever drew so many characters, or generally distinguished 'em better

35 These are the four neo-classic rules of character, as defined by John Bligh, 'Shakespearean Character Study to 1800', *SS* 37 (1984), 141–53.

36 Vickers (ed.), *Shakespeare*, i. 187. Further references to this book are given after quotations in the text.

37 For an example demonstrating the longevity of this tendency, see William Guthrie in *Critical Review*, 20 (1765), 321–32; quoted in Vickers (ed.), *Shakespeare*, v. 211.

38 First pub. in 1711 as part of the preface to Jacob Tonson's edition of Beaumont and Fletcher; quoted in Vickers (ed.), *Shakespeare*, i. 196–203.

from one another, excepting only *Jonson*' (i. 260). Rymer, Dryden argues, has not correctly understood the notion of 'character':

A character, or that which distinguishes one man from all others, cannot be suppos'd to consist of one particular Virtue, or Vice, or passion only; but 'tis a composition of qualities which are not contrary to one another in the same person: thus the same man may be liberal and valiant, but not liberal and covetous. (i. 257–8)

This definition of 'character' is more flexible and complex than Rymer's vigorous assertion that 'all crown'd heads by *Poetical right* are *Heroes*'. 'Character' is a 'composition of qualities', and does distinguish one man from another, though still in external terms; the virtues, vices, and passions provide an alphabet from which a particular name is written. Yet this definition of character, if allowing for a more complex mix of qualities, still insists that they be complementary and not 'contrary to one another in the same person'. Dryden does not seek to overturn Rymer's approach, but to modify Rymer's terms. Dryden's poet, when he 'has given the Dignity of a King to one of his persons', must ensure that, 'in all his actions and speeches, that person must discover Majesty, Magnanimity, and jealousy of power' (i. 257). The neo-classical insistence on consistency is thoroughly maintained.

Dryden's definition of 'character', in its insistence on consistency, is poorly suited—as Rymer later pointed out—for evaluating the plays of Shakespeare. It more usefully describes the dramatic persons of Restoration redactions of Shakespeare, partly because it influenced and was influenced by their composition. Very generally, the redactions tend both to be emotionally more simple, concentrating not on individual experience but rather on the social patterns of human relationships, and politically more pointed.[39] Dryden's defence is only able to praise Shakespeare by maintaining a very general discussion of Shakespeare's works.

This inappropriateness of Dryden's definition of 'character' is partly the result of the self-generating nature of the critical debate; defence replies to attack, without returning to the text. That resistance to returning to the text is partly due to a dislike of the language of Shakespeare and his age. Dryden is expressing a commonplace of the period when he states:

Yet it must be allow'd to the present Age, that the tongue in general is so much refin'd since *Shakespeare's* time, that many of his words, and more of his Phrases, are scarce intelligible. And of those which we understand some are ungrammatical, others coarse; and his whole stile is so pester'd with Figurative expressions, that it is as affected as it is obscure.[40]

[39] See Christopher Spencer, 'Introduction', *Five Restoration Adaptations of Shakespeare* (Urbana, Ill.: University of Illinois Press, 1965), 1–32 (7–14) and Michael Dobson, *The Making of the National Poet: Shakespeare, Adaptation and Authorship, 1660–1769* (Oxford: Clarendon Press, 1992). Dobson's account, which traces the political engagements of the Restoration adaptations with subtlety and clarity, supersedes Spencer's account.

[40] Quoted in Vickers (ed.), *Shakespeare*, i. 250. Further references to this book are given after quotations in the text.

The dislike of the pestering 'figurative expressions' constantly recurs, often far more stridently. Shakespeare's poems and particularly his *Sonnets*, which had once won him the title of 'honie-tong'd', fell out of favour remarkably quickly after the Restoration, and did not return to it until after the eighteenth century. Editions of his works, such as Samuel Johnson's and George Steevens's, omitted the *Sonnets*, the latter giving as his reason in his 1793 edition, 'because the strongest act of Parliament that could be framed would fail to compel readers into their service'.[41] Brian Vickers's assertion that Edward Capell's was the only voice arguing in their favour in the eighteenth century is quite plausible (vi. 41). The critical debate, for this reason, was more theoretically than textually based.

Dryden, then, reproduces the pattern noted in Cavendish: first, Dryden's defence of Shakespeare is generated by an attack, and both attack and defence are evaluative; secondly, his defence is based upon Shakespeare's ability to create 'character', and his definition makes no distinction between dramatic and living persons; finally, his defence stays within neo-classical assumptions. Dryden also adds two refinements to this pattern, which will be developed by subsequent critics: first, Shakespeare's ability to express to the life is now seen as marking him out as excellent within his age,[42] an age itself marked by the excellence of such expression; secondly, Dryden's theoretical quarrel, his readjustment of neo-classical priorities, is advanced through a definition of 'character'. The battle over Shakespeare's relative worth is, in part, a semantic battle over 'character' (the *OED* sense 17a of 'character' credits Dryden and Rymer with developing the literary-critical meaning of the word). Dryden, like Cavendish, insists on the quality of Shakespeare's answer to 'Who's there?', a quality he too sees as being bound up with the creation of distinct dramatic persons.

The general nature and fragility of Dryden's praise was not wasted on Rymer. In 1693 he published his *A Short View of Tragedy, Its Original Excellency, and Corruption*, and in it launched a vitriolic and far more precise attack on Shakespeare by way of an account of *Othello*. In his doing so another kind of critical practice can be seen beginning, as Shakespearian criticism starts to consider not only the dramatist and the dramatist's method, but also particular plays. Rymer picked *Othello* because, he argued, it was said to be the greatest of 'all the Tragedies acted on our English Stage' (ii. 26). Again Rymer opens with an attack on the plotting, arguing that Shakespeare's alterations of Cinthio's plot are all made for the worse. Then he turns to the depiction of character,

[41] In *The Plays of William Shakespeare. In Fifteen Volumes . . . The Fourth Edition*; quoted in Vickers (ed.), *Shakespeare*, vi. 576.

[42] Others were happy to assert Shakespeare's supremacy. See the anonymous translator's preface to Scudery's *Amaryllis to Tityrus* (1681): 'and for maintaining of the Characters of the persons, I think none ever exceeded him [Shakespeare]'. Quoted in Vickers (ed.), *Shakespeare*, i. 14.

denying that any cause for a higher estimation of Shakespeare can be found there. Iago in particular is 'most intolerable', because:

Shakespeare knew his Character was inconsistent. In this very Play he pronounces,
If thou dost deliver more or less than Truth,
Thou are no Souldier—
This he knew, but to entertain the Audience with something new and surprising, against common sense and Nature, he would pass upon us a close, dissembling, false, insinuating rascal instead of an open-hearted, frank, plain-dealing Souldier, a character constantly worn by them for some thousands of years in the World. (ii. 30)

Rymer, in his attack, implicitly cedes that plot is not the sole criterion of evaluation, as he attacks Shakespeare's creation of dramatic persons. But he only admits the importance of 'Character' in order to point to the inconsistency, and so for him the unnaturalness and immorality, of Shakespeare's 'characters'. Later in the *View*, Rymer formulates his charge more colourfully, describing it as, '*Shakespeare's* own blundering Maggot of self-contradiction' (ii. 56). The lack of consistency is maggot-like in eating away and rendering corrupt all that surrounds it.

Answering this charge of inconsistency is an important and difficult task for the critics writing in defence of Shakespeare during the next century, remaining as they do within a neo-classical approach. It cannot be done within Dryden's definition of character. Dryden seems to acknowledge this in a letter where he indulges simply in personal attack of Rymer, calling him one of a 'sort of Insects . . . who manifestly aim at the destruction of our Poetical Church and State'.[43] (So doing, he draws, as had Rymer, on the political context to their theoretical debates.) Rymer's charge remains uncontested, perhaps since, in Dryden's own terms, Rymer is correct.[44] Charles Gildon, though he had written a defence of Shakespeare from Rymer's charges, admitted this in his *The Laws of Poetry Explain'd and Illustrated* (1721):[45]

Tho' Mr. Dryden owns that all or most of the faults Mr. *Rymer* has found are just, yet he adds this odd reflection . . . *And yet . . . Who minds the Critic and who admires* Shakespeare *less*? . . . Which I take to be a greater proof of the folly and abandon'd taste of the town than of any imperfections in the critic. (ii. 369)

Indeed, Rymer's antagonism was at one with the times; according to Brian Vickers, from around 1690 up to the 1730s Shakespeare was more attacked than praised (ii. 1).

[43] From the Epistle affixed to *Examen Poeticum: Being the Third Part of Miscellany Poems* (1693); quoted in Vickers (ed.), *Shakespeare*, ii. 62.

[44] For a discussion of other critics who wanted to disagree with Rymer but found themselves embarrassingly unable to muster a defence because of their neo-classical beliefs, see Vickers (ed.), *Shakespeare*, ii. 3.

[45] Gildon's essay in defence of Shakespeare was 'Some Reflections on Mr. *Rymer's Short View of Tragedy* and an Attempt at a Vindication of *Shakespeare*, in an Essay directed to *John Dryden* Esq.' (1694); quoted in Vickers (ed.), *Shakespeare*, ii. 63–85.

Yet Alexander Pope, prefacing his edition of *The Works of Shakespeare* in 1725, writes with a remarkable confidence of tone concerning Shakespeare's worth. Setting out to mention 'his principal and characteristic Excellencies' (ii. 403), he mentions first his originality and then his ability to create dramatic persons:

> His *Characters* are so much Nature her self that 'tis a sort of injury to call them by so distant a name as Copies of her. Those of other Poets have a constant resemblance, which shews that they receiv'd them from one another and were but multiplyers of the same image . . . But every single character in *Shakespeare* is as much an Individual as those in Life itself; it is impossible to find any two alike . . . To this life and variety of Character we must add the wonderful Preservation of it. (ii. 404)

Pope here combines the praise of Cavendish and Dryden (as well as that of others, here unmentioned).[46] As in Cavendish's argument, there is the sense that there is something remarkable about Shakespeare's ability to create 'character', something—in Pope's terms—unliterary, coming straight from nature instead of literary tradition. The dramatic persons have such a 'very "personal" and "subjective" quality' that they seem natural and original; Shakespeare, again, is seen to create 'characters' that are, as they are discussed, indistinguishable from living beings. Pope places this sense of Shakespeare's near divinity firmly within Dryden's praise of Shakespeare's neo-classicism; alongside this 'life and variety of Character' must be added 'the wonderful Preservation of it'. Pope adds to Cavendish's and Dryden's praise by bringing in the term, 'individual'. 'Individual' was not an obviously positive term at this time; indeed within neo-classical theory it had negative associations. James Drake had earlier pointed out, in answer to Jeremy Collier's attack on the English stage (itself inspired by Rymer), that in plays 'characters' must not be '*Individuals*' because the audience could neither profit nor divert themselves with people 'of so narrow a Compass'; such people would be 'probably unknown to the greatest part' of them.[47] Pope, however, here uses 'individual' as the particular mark of excellence of Shakespeare's 'characters'.

Yet Pope's definition of 'individual' goes no further than the assertion of difference. It is Shakespeare's ability to distinguish between his dramatic persons that is stressed, not the creation of inner worlds. Again, the suggestion is that the 'individual' is so because of a unique combination of common elements—of vices, virtues, and passions. In a manner akin to Cavendish and Dryden, Pope is able to label the particular area that, he believes, marks out Shakespeare's achievement, yet he does not offer any useful description of how

[46] This is an interpretive not exhaustive critical history; there are very many unmentioned praisers and detractors whose commentary lies alongside and perhaps behind those mentioned. See particularly Charles Gildon, in his *An Essay on the Art, Rise and Progress of the Stage in Greece, Rome and England* of 1710, whom Pope seems at times almost to duplicate; quoted in Vickers (ed.), *Shakespeare*, ii. 216–62 (225). Further references to this book are given after quotations in the text.

[47] In *The Antient and Modern Stages survey'd* (1699); quoted in Vickers (ed.), *Shakespeare*, ii. 97. The work of Collier was *A Short View of the Immorality, and Profaneness of the English Stage* (1698); quoted in Vickers (ed.), *Shakespeare*, ii. 87–8.

or from what that area is created. His suggestion is simply that Shakespeare's 'characters' somehow provide unmediated access to 'Nature her self'. Rymer's criticisms, then, remain unanswered.[48] Pope's confident tone is the result not of a rebuttal of Rymer, but rather of an ability to ignore him. Pope's answer to 'Who's there?'—'an individual'—remains vague; quite what that individuality is founded on, or how it is distinguished from the persons of other dramatists, remains unclear.

Hor. The cheefe head
Of this post-hast, and Romage in the Land.
(I. I. 104–5)

Pope's confidence is matched by Shakespeare's increasing stature outside the domain of formal literary criticism. In part, this was a product of Shakespeare's constant theatrical presence and success. When the theatres had reopened after the Restoration, theatre-managers put on 'old' plays—perhaps because of the fund of available, well-wrought, and previously successful plays, a situation which did not apply at the first opening of the theatres in 1567.[49] There were relatively few new plays, the professional status of playwright not being recognized by contract until 1669.[50] In this way Shakespeare's plays kept a constant presence on the stage, even if they were not the most performed or intellectually preferred—Beaumont and Fletcher's plays claiming the former and Jonson's the latter honour.[51]

The continued performance of Shakespeare's plays bred a theatrical literary criticism, a criticism concerning and reflecting primarily the plays which were performed to acclaim. *Hamlet* was one of these, having continued to be successful in the theatre after the Restoration. Sir William Davenant's company, having been granted in 1660 the exclusive right to perform the play, drew on it for their third production at the newly opened theatre in Lincoln's Inn Fields in 1662. According to John Downes, their book-keeper, 'No succeeding tragedy for several years got more reputation or money to the company than this'.[52] Yet *Hamlet* was not the most performed of Shakespeare's plays at this

[48] Pope had a good deal of respect for Rymer. Joseph Spence, in his *Anecdotes, Observations, and Characters, of Books and Men* (1736; ed. 1820), records a conversation with Pope: '[Spence:] Rymer a learned and strict critic? [Pope:] Ay, that's exactly his character. He is generally right, though rather too severe in his opinion of the particular plays he speaks of; and is, on the whole, one of the best critics we ever had' (Quoted in Vickers (ed.), *Shakespeare*, ii. 70).

[49] As Gurr points out, the received date of 1576 is too late, and a professional theatrical activity can be dated to the 1560s. 1567 marks the date of the construction of the Red Lion. Andrew Gurr, *The Shakespearian Playing Companies* (Oxford: Clarendon Press, 1996), 4 and 24.

[50] See Gary Taylor, *Reinventing Shakespeare* (London: Hogarth Press, 1989), 25.

[51] Ibid. 26–8. For a discussion of *Hamlet*'s popularity amongst the Restoration public, both readers and audiences, see 'Hamlet is Discovered', ibid. 39–51. Taylor argues that *Hamlet* is the best 'single representative of the Restoration image of Shakespeare' (p. 39). It should be remembered that when Shakespeare's plays are said to have remained popular, what is being referred to is the Restoration adaptations of those plays.

[52] In his *Roscius Anglicanus* (1708), ed. M. Summers (1928), 21; quoted in *Hamlet*, ed. Hibbard, 17.

time; Rymer's comment about *Othello* agrees with recent research, which ranks that play, then *The Tragedy of Julius Caesar* and next *The Merry Wives of Windsor*, ahead of *Hamlet* in the number of performances.[53] Probably, therefore, Shaftesbury is not correct in his hesitant proposal, made in 1710, that, '[*Hamlet*] has perhaps been oftenest acted of any [plays] which have come upon our Stage', but his overestimation is evidence of the play's reputation.[54]

Theatrical critics concentrated on Prince Hamlet, as might be expected, given that he has the dominant role within the play. Less expected is the critics' concentration on the Prince's mixture of moods and changeability. To Sir Richard Steele, writing in the *Tatler* of 1709, young Hamlet is 'admirable' especially for his 'several Emotions of Mind and Breaks of Passion'[55] which in turn are able to move the emotions of the audience. This supposed ability to create dramatic persons who could call forth an emotional response in an audience was for Steele, and others, a strong proof of Shakespeare's artistic worth; its value as a quality (and so perhaps the argument that Shakespeare was capable of creating it) stemmed in part from the recent impact of Longinus' *On Sublimity* and the growth of the sentimental movement.[56]

As this praise suggests, neo-classical rules had less prescriptive force in more theatrically based criticism. The Prince's inconsistency came to be seen as his defining, and most praiseworthy, quality. So Aaron Hill, writing in the *Prompter* in 1735, begins by declaring that 'HAMLET is the *Play*, of all their dramatic Circulation, which may be oftenest seen without *Satiety*'.[57] This is despite its 'Errors and Absurdities *Self-contradictory* and *indefensible*' (iii. 35). For the Prince fascinates in his changeability:

> To what *Excess* then wou'd it not move were *Hamlet's Character* as strongly *represented* as *written*! The Poet has adorn'd him with a succession of the most *opposite* Beauties, which are *varied*, like *Colours* on the *Chameleon*, according to the *different Lights* in which we behold him. But the PLAYER, unequal to his *Precedent*, is for-ever *His unvaried* SELF. (iii. 35)

53 Taylor, *Reinventing Shakespeare*, 28–9.

54 In *Characteristicks of Men, Manners, Opinions, Times . . . Vol.1 . . . Soliloquy, or Advice to an Author* (1710); quoted in Vickers (ed.), *Shakespeare*, ii. 264. Further references to this book are given after quotations in the text.

55 Sir Richard Steele, the *Tatler*, 12 Dec. 1709; quoted in *Shakespeare*, ed. Vickers, ii. 210.

56 The impact of Longinus' *On Sublimity* at this time was, most basically, the result of Boileau's translation of it in 1674; that it was taken up so swiftly suggests the discontents felt with neo-classicism—*On Sublimity* provided a classical authority which was not neo-classical. *On Sublimity* fostered an expressive theory of literary creation which was part of English Romanticism; the Romantics, however, dismissed the treatise for its public and rhetorical aspects. See See M. H. Abrams, *The Mirror and the Lamp: Romantic Theory and Critical Tradition* (Oxford: Oxford University Press, 1953), 72–4; Jonathan Bate, *Shakespeare and the English Romantic Imagination* (Oxford: Clarendon Press, 1986), 22–31. For a discussion of the use of Longinus to champion the works of Shakespeare, see Taylor, *Reinventing Shakespeare*, 89–91. For a general account of the literary development of the sentimental movement see Part One of R. F. Brissenden, *Virtue in Distress: Studies in the Novel of Sentiment from Richardson to Sade* (London: Macmillan, 1974), 3–155.

57 Aaron Hill, 'No.100', *Prompter*, 24 Oct. 1735; quoted in Vickers (ed.), *Shakespeare*, iii. 35. Further references to this book are given after quotations in the text.

Again the Prince is seen in a Protean light, which suits his developing role as the prime example of Shakespeare's art; like his author, the Prince seems capable of transforming himself constantly. The Prince is variable, the player too constant. What is needed is a form of super-actor: 'the Double Capacity of *Mr.* WILKS, and *Mr.* BOOTH should *unite* in ONE Actor' (iii. 36). This changeability is rare; Thomas Purney in 1717 categorizes the Prince as one of the 'uncommon Characters' who are 'the only difficult ones to draw, the only Ones that shine on the Stage, and the only Ones I could never find in the *French* writers of Tragedy'.[58] The uncommonness of Hamlet thus deftly draws support from the anti-French feeling, which would increase throughout the century.[59] Purney, as many others, uses the Prince to typify Shakespeare's achievement, seeing both the prince and the achievement as the product of a particularly English genius, untrammelled by the rules of artifice.

In this way, theatre-based literary criticism paralleled the argument seen in more formal literary criticism. Shakespeare's ability to create dramatic persons, 'uncommon Characters', is again taken as one of the defining marks of his achievement. Hamlet the Prince and *Hamlet* the play again become the particular example of this ability. Once more, 'Who's there?' is asked, first of Shakespeare and then, in order to understand the answer, of Prince Hamlet. While at the same time, the mystery of Shakespeare's achievement not only remains, but is transferred onto the Prince; Shakespeare and the Prince merge in Proteus, and so in a symbol of language and human nature.

More formal literary critics, as has been seen, had begun to consider *Hamlet* as one of the major examples of Shakespeare's ability or inability to depict character, and so as a test case of Shakespeare's worth. Yet as such critics focused more closely on that play, so the problems posed for the defenders of Shakespeare by the criterion of consistency of 'character' grew more acute. Gildon, in *The Laws of Poetry* (1721), mentioned above, had pointed out the frailty of Dryden's response to Rymer; he went on to develop Rymer's attack on the characters, by attacking Shakespeare's use of the soliloquy, and in particular,

> That famous *soliloquy* which has been so much cry'd up in *Hamlet*. . . *To be, or not to be*, &c . . . . which as it was produc'd by nothing before, so has it no manner of influence on what follows after and is therefore a perfectly detach'd piece, and has nothing to do in the play.[60]

[58] Thomas Purney, Preface to *Pastorals. Viz. The Bashful Swain: And Beauty and Simplicity* (1717); quoted in Vickers (ed.), *Shakespeare*, ii. 318.

[59] The linking of Shakespeare with the anti-French feeling of the time is another factor in his increasing literary stature. This is discussed, in the context of the perceived Shakespearian nature of political caricature, in Bate, *Shakespearean Constitutions*, 20.

[60] Quoted in Vickers (ed.), *Shakespeare*, ii. 371. Further references to this book are given after quotations in the text.

The cogency of the charge that the soliloquy is curiously isolated within and detachable from the play is demonstrated by the number of times it has since been repeated by critics. *Hamlet*, and especially the Prince, are not easy to defend from charges of inconsistency.

One defender was the Reverend George Stubbes, who wrote in 1736 *Some Remarks on the Tragedy of Hamlet*—the first piece of formal criticism solely on *Hamlet*. His argument at first seems to be going beyond the pattern established in Cavendish's letter. For he begins by dismissing those rules 'established by Arbitrary Dogmatising Criticks' in favour of the 'Rules of Reason and Nature'. This dismissal will allow him to concentrate on that aspect which previous writers have 'the least insisted on', but which when insisted on 'will, however, put every Thing he [Shakespeare] has produc'd in its true and proper Light'. Stubbes recognizes a critical dialogue surrounding *Hamlet*, and recognizes that the dialogue has been inconclusive. To a degree, then, he recognizes 'the *Hamlet* Problem', which he offers to solve by directing the debate to the correct aspect of the play.

Yet the untalked-of area central to Shakespeare's art turns out to be the same one that Cavendish put forward, and has Dryden's (neo-classical) criterion of consistency:

> His particular Excellency consists in the Variety and Singularity of his Characters, and in the constant Conformity of each Character to itself from its very first setting out in the Play quite to the End. (iii. 40)

That positive sense of 'singularity' may recall Pope. However, though this 'particular Excellency' is the conclusion which Stubbes wants his discussion of *Hamlet* to substantiate, he produces perhaps the most comprehensive list so far of Shakespeare's inconsistencies in the depiction of 'character'. His honesty in so doing is as remarkable as it is destructive to the conclusion at which he aims. For, unlike Dryden or Pope, he refuses to remain at the level of general statement. He comments in detail on the play, and as he does so the neo-classical basis of his definition of character, very much the same as his predecessors', leads him constantly to find fault with the 'characters' in *Hamlet*: the Prince's 'assumption' of madness is too 'lightly managed' (iii. 54) to suit tragedy and 'too ludicrous for his character' (iii. 56); the conception of making him mad itself is 'injudicious' because it cannot help his revenge and so becomes an 'absurdity' (iii. 55) when used to explain his delaying; the Prince's speech over Claudius at prayer is 'so very Bloody . . . so inhuman . . . so unworthy of a Hero that I wish our Poet had omitted it' (iii. 59); Ophelia's madness is 'very shocking', the gravediggers 'very unbecoming' (iii. 61), and so on. As this list suggests, Stubbes's negative criticism initiates many critical debates, debates that arise from the argument of consistency. (He even suggests that many of the characters' inconsistencies stem from Shakespeare's use of an old play—an argument that underpins both Empson's and Bradshaw's discussions of

Hamlet.) Stubbes's criticism of *Hamlet*, as it tries to provide evidence for a positive evaluation of Shakespeare, makes even clearer the fragility of Dryden's and Pope's argument. For the replication of the traditional argumentative pattern, since it does not redefine 'character' or the terminology concerning it, now leads Stubbes to make *Hamlet* critically problematic as he seeks to defend it.

William Guthrie points the way forward for the defence of *Hamlet* and so of Shakespeare with *An Essay upon English Tragedy* (1747). Arguing as ever that Shakespeare's worth and distinction lay in the way he created character, he follows—whether intentionally or not—Gildon's (and so Rymer's) narrowing of the battleground. Where Gildon argues that the soliloquy, best exemplified by those in *Hamlet*, demonstrates most clearly Shakespeare's inability to create consistent characters, Guthrie argues that the soliloquy most clearly demonstrates that ability. Guthrie uses Joseph Addison's *Cato*, first produced in 1713, as the comparison through which to analyse *Hamlet*'s achievement:

> [Cato's soliloquy] is the language of doubting; but of such doubts as the speaker is prepared to cut asunder if he cannot resolve them. The words of Cato are not like those of Hamlet, the emanations of the soul; they are therefore improper for a soliloquy, where the discourse is supposed to be held with the heart, that fountain of truth. Cato seems instructed as to all he doubts: while irresolute, he appears determined; and bespeaks his quarters, while he questions whether there is lodging. How different from this is the conduct of Shakespeare on the same occasion![61]

For Guthrie, Hamlet is a supreme example of 'character' because his soliloquy creates him standing alone, independent of instruction, having his own soul. Once more, the sense is that the 'character' of the Prince manages to appear in some way real. Cavendish called this 'express[ing] to the Life': Pope described 'every single character in Shakespeare' as being 'as much an Individual as those in Life itself'. Guthrie, in agreement with this, attempts to describe more clearly how this lifelikeness was effected. Cato shows Addison to be one of Pope's 'multipliers of the same image'; Addison's 'characters' are made up from the laying-on of a set of received conventions, leading to the sense of his being 'instructed as to all he doubts'. Hamlet's doubts, by contrast, flow from his 'soul' and cannot be 'cut asunder' since they are part of who he is and who he is going to be. His questions over 'lodging' would not demonstrate a knowledge of their answers or 'quarters'. Guthrie has a conception of 'character' as a unit that is more than the sum of its parts or qualities, being organized from or around an interior point. Yet his understanding of how Shakespeare has produced this is vague; the Prince's 'character' is in some way internal and unique, where Cato's is external and received. Guthrie seems to use the negative definition of comparison because he cannot provide a positive description.

[61] In *An Essay upon English Tragedy. With Remarks upon the Abbe de Blanc's Observations on the English Stage*; quoted in Vickers (ed.), *Shakespeare*, iii. 202.

His redefinition of dramatic 'character' involves making its possession of this vague interior area—'soul' or 'heart'—almost its essence. This interior area, although it eludes precise description, is now the mark of Shakespeare's distinguishing ability to depict dramatic persons and so of his worth. Moreover, young Hamlet, particularly in his soliloquies, is the prime example of this.

Guthrie's argument had not, however, directly answered the charge of inconsistency. Rather it sidestepped the issue by refocusing the area over which the debate of consistency would be fought. Tobias Smollett, reviewing Joseph Warton's *Essay on the writings and Genius of Pope* in 1756, raises the issue of consistency once more, again to challenge the evaluation of Shakespeare:

> These [imperfections] his warmest admirers will not deny, and there are an hundred characters in his plays that (if we may be allowed the expression) speak out of character . . . The famous soliloquy of *Hamlet* is introduced by the head and shoulders. He had some reason to revenge his father's death upon his uncle, but he had none to take away his own life. Nor does it appear from any other part of the play that he had any such intention.[62]

Smollett's charge of inconsistency develops, in interior terms, Gildon's assertion that the Prince's soliloquy does not belong in the play. The novelty of this can be glimpsed in Smollett's hesitant parenthesis, worrying over the phrase 'out of character'—the *OED* records the first use of 'in character' in 1745 (sense 17b). Smollett argues that the Prince's soliloquy is inconsistent as it is unmotivated. Hamlet has reasons to debate vengeance, but none to debate suicide. In so doing, Smollett accepts Guthrie's contention that 'character' must possess an interior aspect. The charge of inconsistency is now seen in terms of the lack of motivation, as the terms of the debate are interiorized.

Samuel Johnson in his 1765 edition of *The Plays of William Shakespeare* also defends this soliloquy against the charge of inconsistency. In his note on the soliloquy he argues that it is 'connected rather in the speaker's mind than on his tongue'.[63] This is a dangerous argument. Not only does it concede that the soliloquy is inconsistent at a literal level, but also it goes behind or beyond the language of the soliloquy for evidence of consistency. This evidence is provided by the critic's own interpretation; Johnson creates a narrative, extrapolated from the rest of the play and from his belief in his knowledge of human nature, into which he fits Hamlet's soliloquy. It is this narrative which suggests both that the soliloquy has a train of thought and how that soliloquy might arise from Hamlet's situation. Johnson thus uses the interior domain as a gap on which to write his own explanatory reading of the play in order to refute the charge of inconsistency. So doing, he leaves himself open to Barker's and the

[62] Tobias Smollett, in *Critical Review*, I (1756), 226–40; quoted in Vickers (ed.), *Shakespeare*, v. 266.

[63] Samuel Johnson, *The Plays of William Shakespeare, in Eight Volumes, with the Corrections and Illustrations of Various Commentators; To which are added Notes by Sam. Johnson* (1765), viii. 207; quoted in Vickers (ed.), *Shakespeare*, v. 157.

Cultural Materialists' charge that in the interior of the Prince there is nothing, and that it is this absence that the critics have filled with their own interpretations and images.

In the preface to his edition, Johnson offers a more helpful rebuttal. Again the semantic nature of this critical debate becomes clear, as Johnson takes issue with what he sees as the previous overly narrow (or perhaps overly broad) neo-classic meaning of 'character'—as used by such critics as 'Rymer' and 'Voltaire'—under which all kings had to be heroes. Shakespeare's understanding of 'character' Johnson alleges to have been very different:

> [He] always makes nature predominate over accident; and if he preserves the essential character is not very careful of distinctions superinduced and adventitious. (v. 60)

'Essential character' is what Jonson perceives as the typically Shakespearian excellence. Previous antagonistic and narrowly neo-classical critics had incorrectly dwelt on 'adventitious' distinctions, a kind of sub-character, for their evidence of inconsistency.

What Johnson means by this distinction is made clearer when he discusses Polonius' speech to the King and Queen in 2. 2. Polonius, like young Hamlet, had been used often as evidence of Shakespeare's 'blundering maggot of self-contradiction'; Polonius' self-contradiction was seen in the contrast between the pompous and often pointless speech to the King and Queen, and the wise precepts that he had given to his departing son, Laertes, in 1. 3. William Warburton, in his edition of Shakespeare of 1757, had already defended the 'unity' of Polonius' 'character' by arguing that the minister's speech was 'a fine satire on the impertinent oratory then in vogue'. Warburton saw both the speech and precepts as results of Polonius' pedantic learning, and so repeated Pope's praise of Shakespeare's 'wonderful preservation' of 'character'.[64] Johnson, in turn keen to repeat—if with qualification—Pope's praise, discusses Warburton's account and agrees that it 'reconciles the seeming inconsistency'. Yet he believes that it subtly misrepresents Polonius:

> The commentator [Warburton] makes the character of *Polonius* a character only of manners, discriminated by properties superficial, accidental, and acquired. The poet intended a nobler delineation of a mixed character of manners and of nature. *Polonius* is a man bred in courts, exercised in business, stored with observation, confident of his knowledge, proud of his eloquence, and declining into dotage. (v. 156–7)

Johnson argues that Polonius, when he can draw on his past experience, can speak wisely to his son, but when he is forced to think about a new circumstance, as he is when confronted by Hamlet's apparent madness, his mind is exposed as having grown weak. 'Essential character' is here become a 'character . . . of nature'. Unlike 'adventitious character', it is not the product of

[64] William Warburton, *The Works of Shakespeare in Eight Volumes* (1747), viii. 160–1; quoted in Vickers (ed.), *Shakespeare*, iii. 247.

social position or role but of the routine stages and processes of life. Moreover, in the interaction between these two types of 'character' there is a clear sense of general 'character' being the product of the person's interaction with his or her circumstances. Yet such interaction is still rather formulaic; there is the sense that dotage mixed with certain 'manners' and 'properties' would produce a Polonius. Thus when the idea of the onset of 'dotage encroaching upon wisdom' is grasped it will, according to Johnson, 'solve all' of Polonius' seeming contradictions. Although he looks partly within Polonius to explain his words and deeds, Johnson has no sense of Polonius being unique, a lack which fits in with Johnson's dislike of the individual in literature, and his elevation of the species. Elsewhere in the preface he declares: 'In the writings of other poets a character is too often an individual; in those of *Shakespeare* it is commonly a species' (v. 57). Johnson's praise of the 'species' and dislike of the 'individual' focuses attention once more on the semantic battle over the group of words, central to literary criticism, centred on 'character'. Johnson's sense of 'individual' is of a 'character' that lacks 'representative' value; in this, as in the preface in general, Johnson's argument is seen to be a rather dated and conservative defence which is, at heart, neo-classical. Although Johnson redefines dramatic 'character' in order to make the interior the 'essential character', when he looks inward he finds not difference but similarity, a neo-classic constancy of composition almost as rigid or constraining as Rymer's external constancy. And while his sense of the combination of 'essential' and 'adventitious' 'character', of a shrewd wisdom in the past giving way to dotage, may explain why Polonius can utter words both wise and foolish, it does not seem likely to answer the list of Prince Hamlet's inconsistencies produced by Stubbes.

The praise of Shakespeare outside the domain of more formal literary criticism was less troubled. Pope's confident tone had been justified, for from the 1730s Shakespeare's cultural stature had increased at an exponential rate. The texts of his plays became widely available, as two publishers, Jacob Tonson and Robert Walker, fought a price-war over Shakespeare, bringing the plays out in cheap editions for the first time.[65] The plays were also performed far more frequently, not only because the popularity of the theatre increased, but also because much contemporary writing was suppressed by the Theatrical Licensing Act of 1737. In 1741 Shakespeare's cultural importance, and the nature of that importance, was demonstrated by the erection of his statue in Westminster Abbey. The decision to celebrate his birthday on St George's day had already been made. This praise became, by the 1760s, idolatry, the apotheosis of which was the Stratford Shakespeare Jubilee of 1769. Whatever else it may have achieved, it declared Shakespeare to be the national poet.[66]

[65] See Bate, *Shakespearean Constitutions*, 22–4.

[66] Another achievement, and an intended one, was the promotion of Garrick—the Jubilee's

Shakespeare had become 'The cheefe head | Of this post-hast, and Romage in the Land' (1. 1. 104–5).

Such a status influenced and was influenced by literary criticism, and Shakespeare enjoyed an unprecedented level of praise. Encomia went further than they had prior to the English Civil War; Shakespeare was now not simply heaped with general praise, but heaped with superlative praise as the literary genius of all time, as the glory of his nation. Within this mood, the arguments of the defenders of Shakespeare were accepted as uncontroversial truths, even if they had not answered the detractors. In terms of the area traced here, even a thoughtful critic and editor such as Edmund Capell was happy to note without qualification that the 'preservation of character' was as obvious a distinguishing feature of a Shakespearian play as any.[67] Capell, indeed, made explicit the myth that has already been seen to underlie descriptions of Shakespeare's ability to create 'character'; Capell describes Shakespeare as, 'this *Proteus*, who could put on any shape that either serv'd his interest or suited his inclination' (v. 320).

Shakespeare's worth no longer needed defending; it was accepted. *Hamlet* enjoyed a similarly assured value, both in criticism and in the theatre. In the theatre, its popularity seems to have increased; between 1751 and 1801 it became the second most performed play, after *Romeo and Juliet*, in the London patent theatres.[68] Yet in literary criticism the defenders of Shakespeare and *Hamlet*, when they moved from general praise to detailed argument, continued to struggle to dismiss his detractors and provide literary arguments to substantiate his immense cultural worth. Ironically, the area from which a main strand of Shakespeare's defence was begun, now threatened to become an obstacle that needed to be explained away before Shakespeare's literary worth could emerge. *Hamlet* had become a focus of this argument, and so the need to prove its consistency in the area of 'character' increased. Those who argued against such a consistency were now seldom detractors of Shakespeare, for however strongly the inconsistency was urged, it tended to be as the qualifier of praise, or as a momentary lapse of genius, a lapse to be regretted.

Francis Gentleman, writing on *Hamlet* in *The Dramatic Censor* (1770), is typical of the new mood:

> In respect of characters we are to lament that the hero, who is intended as amiable, should be such a heap of inconsistency: impetuous, tho' philosophical; sensible of

organizer—to the role of Shakespeare's chief advocate and interpreter. For a discussion of the Jubilee see Bate, *Shakespearean Constitutions*, 30–4; for a list of other references see Vickers (ed.), *Shakespeare*, v. 14. For arguments as to why Shakespeare should have become the national poet, see Dobson, *The Making of the National Poet*, *passim*.

[67] Edmund Capell, 'Introduction', *Mr. William Shakespeare his Comedies, Histories, and Tragedies*, 10 vols. (1768); quoted in Vickers (ed.), *Shakespeare*, v. 317. Further references to this book are given after quotations in the text.

[68] Bate, *Shakespearean Constitutions*, 97.

injury, yet timid of resentment; shrewd, yet void of policy . . . and yet from being pregnant with great variety . . . he is as agreeable and striking an object as any in the English drama.[69]

Gentleman, in paying attention to the passions of the mind, reflects and expresses the increasingly interior senses of 'character'. Unfortunately, as he acknowledges, this does not help to resolve the issue of the Prince's inconsistency; if anything, a more interior focus on the Prince as 'character' makes him seem less neo-classically consistent. This creates difficulties for Gentleman: first, he recognizes the importance of the category of 'character' in reaching critical evaluations; secondly, he believes *Hamlet* to be one of Shakespeare's great and most enjoyable plays, and so believes he must find the Prince worthy of praise, as the Prince's role is so central to the play. Gentleman wishes to praise, but cannot within the accepted critical terminology. This is a fundamental problem, and one that Gentleman recognizes in his solution; Hamlet is lauded not as a 'character', but as an 'object'—'as agreeable and striking an object as any in the English drama'. The problem with this solution is that 'object' has next to no meaning; 'object' merely allows Gentleman to praise Hamlet's greatness without stating his literary-critical criteria.

So, at the period when Shakespeare's reputation has been vindicated partly through a defence of his ability to create 'characters' which are in some special way '"personal" or "subjective"', one of his most famous 'characters' threatens to cease to be one, because the criterion of consistency still remains to be satisfied. George Steevens in 1772 makes this exceptional position of *Hamlet* clear; he sets an observation of Prince Hamlet's inconsistency against the 'universal encomium pronounced in this respect upon his [Shakespeare's] accurate preservation of *character*'.[70]

William Richardson's book of Shakespearian criticism, *A Philosophical Analysis and Illustration of some of Shakespeare's remarkable Characters* (1774), provided a way forward for the defence. In a sense, it represents the culmination of several of the developments within the literary debate that has here been traced. Richardson's book is the first published work devoted directly to the examination of Shakespeare's characters. 'Character' is clearly an important category, both in its own right and because of its significance within Shakespearian criticism; indeed, it is becoming the primary critical category. This is made explicit in Thomas Whately's *Remarks on Some of the Characters of Shakespeare*, a book which was begun before 1770, but only published posthumously in 1785. Whately opened his introduction by stressing 'character's' predominance over the more traditional categories:

[69] Francis Gentleman, in *The Dramatic Censor; or, Critical Companion*, 2 vols. (1770); quoted in Vickers (ed.), *Shakespeare*, v. 383. Further references to this book are given after quotations in the text.

[70] George Steevens, in *General Evening Post*, 1–2 Jan. 1772; quoted in Vickers (ed.), *Shakespeare*, v. 487.

The writers upon dramatic composition have, for the most part, confined their observations to the fable; and the maxims received amongst them, for the conduct of it, are therefore emphatically called, *The Rules of Drama* . . . there is, within the colder provinces of judgment and of knowledge, a subject for criticism more worthy of attention than the common topics of discussion: I mean the distinction and preservation of *character*.'[71]

For Richardson, part of the reason for the importance of 'character' is that he sees no useful distinction between literary and actual character; he uses Shakespearian 'characters' to clarify ethical issues: 'My intention', he says, 'is to make poetry subservient to philosophy, and to employ it in tracing the principles of human conduct.'[72] Shakespeare's 'characters' provide the material and the model for analysing human behaviour. Richardson is another who explains Shakespeare's ability to create such characters by invoking the figure of Proteus:

The genius of Shakespeare is unlimited. Possessing extreme sensibility, and uncommonly susceptible, he is the Proteus of the drama; he changes himself into every character, and enters easily into every condition of human nature. (vi. 118–19)

Prince Hamlet, however, remains a problem, as Richardson still accepts consistency as the defining mark of living 'characters'. So Richardson proposes the notion of intended inconsistencies: discussing young Hamlet's treatment of Ophelia, he argues,

Nor ought the pretended rudeness and seeming inconsistency of [Hamlet's] behaviour to be at all attributed to inconstancy . . . to confirm and publish this report [of his madness], seemingly so hurtful to his reputation, he would act in direct opposition to his former conduct and inconsistently with the genuine sentiments and affections of his soul. (vi. 122)

Recognizing the weight of evidence of the Prince's inconsistencies, Richardson agrees that they are there, and that the Prince acts 'in direct opposition to his former conduct'. However, this volte-face by the defence is not an admission of Shakespeare's blundering maggot of self-contradiction, as Rymer put it. For young Hamlet's inconsistencies are intended, only 'seemingly' inconsistent. They cloak his underlying purpose of revenge. With this assertion that the inconsistencies are intended, part of the artistic design, they become the especial proof of Shakespeare's excellence in creating dramatic 'characters'. The inconsistencies become the Prince's complexity, underlying which can still

[71] Thomas Whately, *Remarks on Some of the Characters of Shakespeare* (1785), 1–2; quoted in Vickers (ed.), *Shakespeare*, vi. 408.

[72] William Richardson, *A Philosophical Analysis and Illustration of some of Shakespeare's remarkable Characters* (1774), 43; quoted in Vickers (ed.), *Shakespeare*, vi. 119. For a list of references to the similar statements of other critics, see ibid. 19ff. Richardson, in his later essays and under the influence of Morgann, did make a distinction between dramatic and actual persons; e.g. his next series of essays was titled *Essays on Shakespeare's Dramatic Characters of Richard III, King Lear, and Timon of Athens* (1784). See Maurice Morgann, *Shakespearean Criticism*, ed. Daniel A. Fineman (Oxford: Clarendon Press, 1972), 17–18.

be found a consistency of purpose. Motives and passions are now divided into those put on for appearance and those which lie more deeply within. There is, to recall Johnson's terms, a sort of 'essential essential "character"'. The argument for consistency once more moves forward by developing a more interior definition of 'character'. So Whately, for example, asserts, 'No other dramatic writer could ever pretend to so deep and so extensive a knowledge of the human heart' (vi. 409).

Richardson's study of *Hamlet* is part of the final kind of critical practice in this period, a practice which developed in the last quarter of the eighteenth century—character criticism. Character criticism was not entirely new, but where it had previously been found in footnotes, periodicals, and as part of essays, now whole essays and books were devoted to this approach.[73] *Hamlet*, given its historical importance within the debate over Shakespeare's value, and given its theatrical success upon the stage, and the dominance of the Prince, was an obvious focus for this new criticism. Hamlet, alongside Falstaff, became the most studied character in this period.[74]

As Richardson's study makes plain, character criticism did not repudiate the argumentative pattern established by Cavendish. The critical debate over young Hamlet was still advanced through a dialogue, as one side sought to vindicate, and the other to denigrate, in relative terms, the Prince. Both sides still remained within neo-classical principles, accepting the demand for consistency in 'character'. Both sides still fought over the same area, seeing Hamlet, the play and the Prince, as a prime representative of Shakespeare's unique ability or inability to fashion dramatic persons, an ability central to his achievement. Richardson's assertion that a constant purpose underlay and produced the Prince's inconsistencies was a weakness in his argument. It satisfied the neo-classical demand for consistency more than it satisfactorily explained *Hamlet*. It sat awkwardly with the Prince's delaying of his revenge, which had already been emphasized by many critics. Richardson was aware of this, declaring that by the end of the closet scene 'all the business of the tragedy, in regard to the display of character, is here concluded . . . the succeeding circumstances of the play are unnecessary' (vi. 123)

Henry Mackenzie, in the article of 1780 quoted at the beginning of this chapter, noted the variety of literary-critical opinions concerning Shakespeare, and especially concerning Hamlet; the Prince, he argued, was the character of whom it was hardest to find a 'fixed or settled principle'. Mackenzie developed an argument similar to Richardson's:

> That *Hamlet's* character, thus formed by Nature, and thus modelled by situation, is often variable and uncertain I am not disposed to deny. I will content myself with the supposition that this is the very character which *Shakespeare* meant to allot him. (vi. 274)

[73] Brian Vickers, 'The Emergence of Character Criticism, 1774–1800', *SS* 34 (1981), 11–22.

[74] See Vickers (ed.), *Shakespeare*, vi. 21.

Mackenzie uses the same sense of 'character' as the product of 'essential' and 'adventitious' elements that was seen in Johnson. But where Johnson used the distinction to explain away inconsistency and uniqueness, Mackenzie sees it as the mechanism by which inconsistencies are produced. Instead of understanding how a 'character' has become what he or she is, we watch the process by which 'character' reaches expression, as it is 'modelled by situation'. Mackenzie finds the necessary consistency of character in the continual nature of young Hamlet's inconsistency.

This might seem to show a less interior focus than Richardson's argument, but it is interior in a different way. For if the Prince had a constant purpose such as 'vengeance', Mackenzie argues, the spectator would be interested in the success or lack of success of that purpose; his or her 'anxiety' would be 'for the event, not for the person' (vi. 274). Consistent inconsistency, then, makes the interior of the Prince the focus of the entire play, by evoking the audience's empathy. Moreover, the interior is now the area over which not only the critics but the Prince struggles, as 'character' becomes a process.

The incident of the *Ghost*, which is entirely the poet's own, and not to be found in the Danish legend, not only produces the happiest stage-effect but is also of the greatest advantage in unfolding that character which is stamped on the young prince at the opening of the play. In the communications of such a visionary being there is an uncertain kind of belief, and dark unlimited honour, which are aptly suited to display the wavering purpose and varied emotions of a mind endowed with a delicacy of feeling that often shakes its fortitude, with sensibility that overpowers its strength. (vi. 277)

'Stand & vnfold your selfe', Francisco had declared at the beginning of *Hamlet*; Mackenzie now sees such unfolding as central to the play, the attempt to identify the Ghost acting as a parallel and signal to the attempt to identify the Prince. Indeed, the play becomes a kind of collaborative effort, as Mackenzie sees the critics attempting a similar unfolding of the Prince to the Prince's unfolding of the Ghost, and to other dramatic persons' unfolding of the Prince. Mackenzie values the play and the Prince for doubting irresolution, 'uncertain kind of belief' and 'dark unlimited honour'. Elsewhere he calls this the 'indescribable charm in *Hamlet* which attracts every reader and every spectator' (vi. 275). Once more, then, while the inner quality of 'character' is redefined in answer to 'Who's there?', and while the importance of this quality is emphasized, its precise nature and the manner of its creation remains vague. Mackenzie, however, instead of finding this a difficulty or embarrassment, values this vagueness, allowing himself to be caught up in wonder. His inability to describe the 'charm' in *Hamlet* becomes the guarantee of Shakespeare's achievement.

Ham. What may this meane?
That thou dead Coarse againe in compleat steele,
Reuisits thus the glimpses of the Moone,
Making Night hidious? And we fooles of Nature,
So horridly to shake our disposition,
With thoughts beyond thee; reaches of our Soules.
(I. 4. 32–7)

The critical drama recalled in this chapter maintains a 'strict and most observant Watch' over *Hamlet.* The play and the Prince are continually on stage, and, as a key part of their evaluations of Shakespeare, the critics attempt to explain, primarily through notions of 'character', what they see before them. Yet their 'Who's there?' is never satisfactorily answered; unfolding the particular quality that distinguishes Hamlet, and so Shakespeare, eludes them. *Hamlet* begins to be celebrated for being beyond explanation; Shakespeare and his creations, it seems to these critics, somehow are Nature—and none of those creations more so than Prince Hamlet. Reverence and awe are the correct attitudes to strike; faith becomes a critical necessity.

This was not, of course, true of all critics; the critical drama never lost its dialogical nature. Some were unconvinced, for example, by Richardson's argument of intended inconsistency.[75] But in general these attitudes dominated; and Richardson's and Mackenzie's arguments were enthusiastically accepted and developed. Thomas Robertson added a refinement to the argument in 'An Essay on the Character of Hamlet, in Shakespeare's Tragedy of *Hamlet*' (1788). Looking as ever at the uncommonness of the Prince's depiction, he notes:

Now, in such an assemblage of qualities, combining to form the broad character of HAMLET, SHAKESPEARE appears to have seen that they were balanced in such an opposite manner that one class of them should counteract, and render inefficient the other. It is this that suffered nothing to be done; it is this that constantly impeded the action and kept the catastrophe back.[76]

Here then, not only is the focus of the play on the 'character' of Hamlet, but the inconsistencies of the interior area explain the movements of the plot. Gradually, each part of the play is seen to be expressive of the Prince's character. Robertson goes on to argue that that character is not only of significance as the supreme example of the distinguishing quality of Shakespeare's art, but also of historical significance. In this play, Robertson asserts, 'The world for the first time saw a *man of genius* upon the stage.'

To end with Maurice Morgann's *An Essay on the Dramatic Character of Sir John Falstaff* (1777) might seem a little peculiar. Morgann's subject, however, is not solely Falstaff; Morgann concludes his work by arguing that he has given the reader,

75 See, for instances, James Harris's *Philological Inquiries in Three Parts* (1781), or Thomas Davies' *Dramatic Miscellanies* of (1784); in Vickers (ed.), *Shakespeare*, vi. 310–13 and 370–84 respectively.

76 Thomas Robertson, 'An Essay on the Character of Hamlet, in Shakespeare's Tragedy of *Hamlet*', in *Transactions of the Royal Society of Edinburgh*, 2 (1788), 251–67; quoted in Vickers (ed.), *Shakespeare*, vi. 482.

An Essay professing to treat of the Courage of *Falstaff*, but extending itself to his Whole character; to the arts and genius of his Poetic-Maker, SHAKESPEARE; and thro' him sometimes, with ambitious aim, even to the principles of human nature itself.[77]

As that suggests, Morgann's *Essay* clearly articulates the central dynamics of the drama traced in this scene. A concentration on Falstaff leads to a concentration on 'whole character'; which in turn leads to an appreciation of the genius of the divinely creative Shakespeare; and from there to an appreciation of human nature itself. Morgann is an impressively self-conscious literary critic.[78] Morgann's essay is usually read as an argument that Falstaff is not a coward. As Daniel Fineman, the most recent editor of Morgann's works, points out, Morgann's argument—as his revisions make clear—attempts to trace the way in which Falstaff, as a dramatic character, is able to produce 'a mixed Effect' on the audience (p. 220); to show how the audience are led by their intuitive impression to see Falstaff as courageous, while also being led by their reasoning understanding to perceive his cowardice. This mixed effect is central to Morgann's appreciation of the play; he believes it creates the comic distance without which Falstaff could not be a dramatic success (p. 212).

Morgann, in other words, asks 'Who's there?' of Falstaff, and finds himself reaching contradictory and complex answers, which answers he takes to be definitively Shakespearian. He explains this by positing the presence of two types of character—'dramatic character' and 'whole character'. 'Dramatic character' is the result of the impression gained from the play; about four-fifths of the *Essay* is devoted to a close observation of Falstaff's actions and words within the plays. Far from being, as Morgann is often held to be, the originator of 'objectivism', that critical approach which decontextualizes a dramatic character and treats it as a living being (p. 80), Morgann insists on seeing Falstaff in context, in relation—or as he puts it, 'grouped'—with other dramatic characters. As a dramatic character, the audience see Falstaff as courageous. How, then, is Falstaff also seen to be cowardly? From what is the ambivalence of Falstaff's character created, which Morgann values so highly? 'Something', Morgann recognizes, 'should be said of the nature of *Shakespeare's* Dramatic characters; by what arts they were formed, and wherein they differ from those of other writers' (pp. 167–8). He goes on to attempt this in what is perhaps the most famous footnote in Shakespearian criticism.

Morgann begins with a statement which rests on the debate of the previous century and a half: 'The reader', Morgann asserts, 'must be sensible of some-

[77] Morgann, *Shakespearean Criticism*, ed. Fineman, 215. This discussion of Morgann's *Essay* is based on his revised manuscript as reconstructed by Fineman. Further references to this book are given after quotations in the text. Morgann's comment should not be taken to suggest that he does not value or take seriously his defence of Falstaff from the charge of cowardice; his humour does not lack seriousness. See ibid. 'Morgann's Attitude towards his Falstaffian Thesis', 44–52.

[78] The self-conscious nature of Morgann's criticism is clearest in his revisions of his 1777 essay. Fineman discusses these at length in his 'Critical Introduction' to Morgann, *Shakespearean Criticism*, *passim*.

thing in the compositions of *Shakespeare's* characters, which renders them essentially different from those drawn by other writers' (p. 167). Every dramatist creates dramatic character, as they must 'group' characters, that is create them through placing them in relation to the context of the play. However,

> There is a certain roundness and integrity in the forms of *Shakespeare*, which give them an independence as well as a relation, insomuch that we often meet with passages, which tho' perfectly felt, cannot be sufficiently explained in words, without unfolding the whole character of the speaker. (p. 167)

Morgann's sense of passages which, while 'perfectly felt' elude verbal description, is reminiscent of other critics' sense of wonder at the 'thoughts beyond the reaches of our souls' that *Hamlet* inspires. Morgann attempts to go beyond this, by 'unfolding the whole character of the speaker'. This is possible since, 'Those characters in *Shakespeare*, which are seen only in part, are yet capable of being unfolded and understood in the whole; every part being in fact relative, and inferring all the rest' (p. 168). The 'whole character' exists independently from the play, to be extrapolated or inferred from the more limited dramatic character which the audience is allowed to see. Through this interplay between whole and dramatic character Shakespeare achieves his unique effects of characterization. Morgann, using the Humean distinction between understanding and feeling, argues that the audience respond overwhelmingly to their felt intuition of Falstaff's dramatic character of a courageous man, while their reasoning understanding alerts them to his real character, that of a dislikeable coward.

Morgann is quite aware of the implications of his argument:

> If the characters of *Shakespeare* are thus *whole*, and as it were original, while those of almost all other writers are mere imitation, it may be fit to consider them rather as Historic than Dramatic beings; and when occasion requires, to account for their conduct from the *whole* of character, from general principles, from latent motives, and from policies not avowed. (p. 169)

To understand Shakespeare's characters, it is sometimes necessary to consider them 'rather as Historic than Dramatic beings'. This represents an expansion of the 'gap technique' of interpretation already seen in Johnson's explanation of young Hamlet's 'To be, or not to be' soliloquy. Johnson had rendered that soliloquy consistent with his conception of the Prince by producing a narrative that was supposed to lie behind it. Morgann now takes that 'gap', the space which must be filled before the character may be 'unfolded' and understood, as the quality (if an absence may be a quality) which distinguishes Shakespeare's 'characters'. In this way, Morgann explicitly defines the nature of Shakespeare's dramatic persons and of Shakespeare's achievement as the creation of 'characters' that demand to be treated as actual persons.

There was a widespread, often unacknowledged, use of Morgann's conclusion in criticism of *Hamlet* and its Prince. Robertson, for instance, in his study of 1788 mentioned above, suggests that: 'To understand the character of HAMLET we had best perhaps take it at two different times, before the death of his father and after that period.'[79] Morgann's model of the creation of dramatic persons, however, does not seem to have been used, perhaps because of its complexity. (Morgann's model was also not used by Romantic critics, who appear not to have known it; where Morgann saw Shakespeare's art to be his concealment of 'whole character' by 'dramatic character', the Romantic critic saw Shakespeare's art in the revelation of what Morgann would term 'whole character'.) Yet for all its subtlety, Morgann's sense of what 'whole character' is and how it is created relies on the same vagueness and wonder seen in previous critics. Shakespeare was able to create such dramatic persons through 'a wonderful facility of compressing, as it were, his own spirit into these images'. Once more Shakespeare is the divine-artificer, the Protean self-transformer. Quite what that 'facility' is, can only be defined by stating whose facility it is: 'Such an intuitive comprehension of things and such a facility, must unite to produce a *Shakespeare*.'[80] The quality is Shakespeare's own, and Shakespeare is the quality; there is no way into this recursively defining circle.

By 1801, then, the Jacobeans' prophecies of Shakespeare's immortality had been vindicated, though there had been times when it seemed, in formal criticism, that they would not be. Beginning with Cavendish's letter, one constant and significant consensus was seen to feature in the debate over Shakespeare's longevity and literary value. Shakespeare's ability—or inability—to create dramatic persons was agreed to be central to any evaluation of his work. 'Who's there?' was central to this debate, and at this time brought forth the answer, 'a character'. To the extent that there was a consensus over this area of debate, the '*Hamlet* Problem' is rather misleading. The presence of such a consensus, however, did not mean that the debate remained static; rather it moved forward through a series of definitions of 'character'. As the essential quality, or definition, of this area was sought, *Hamlet* became increasingly central to the argument. Shakespeare's reputation within literary criticism grew up together with the evaluation of *Hamlet*, the play and the Prince. Yet the critics who mounted so strict a watch over the play could not agree over the nature of the Prince, just as the watch in Denmark debated the nature of the Ghost. Neither group was able to speak satisfactorily to the object of their toil; both decided that, it 'being so Maiesticall' (I. I. 124), their attempts to catch it were 'vaine blowes, malicious Mockery' (I. I. 127). *Pace* Empson, 'the problem of the problem' therefore also overstates its case; Hamlet was seen to be critically problematic significantly before the end of the eighteenth century.

At the bottom of almost all the defences of Shakespeare lay the belief that his 'characters' were in some way real, where those of other dramatists were not;

[79] Thomas Robertson, 'An Essay on the Character of Hamlet', quoted in Vickers (ed.), *Shakespeare*, vi. 481.

[80] Fineman, p. 168.

and Prince Hamlet was the most real of Shakespearian 'characters'. This attempt to understand the 'realness' of Shakespeare's characters was bound up, as Morgann realized, with the attempt to understand human nature, what would now be called human personality. Yet Van Dyck's portrait of Suckling had claims to be the most impressive exploration of interiority. All the literary answers to 'Who's there?', when they tried to explain how 'character' was constructed, or what it was, relapsed into assertions of Shakespeare's mythic powers. Most commonly, Shakespeare was Proteus, the shape-changing god who knew the answer to everything, but would only give answers if caught. And Shakespeare, like Hamlet, and like the Ghost, could not be caught. He was beyond the natural, in some way he was Nature. The critics, by contrast, were left to play the 'fooles of Nature', grasping at 'thoughts beyond the reaches' of their souls.

5
A Wave o'th Sea

Enter Ghost againe.
Hor. But soft, behold: Loe, where it comes againe:
Ile crosse it, though it blast me. Stay Illusion.
(1. 1. 107–8)

THERE is no sharp break in the critical drama traced here after 1801. 'Who's there?' remains the central question, and *Hamlet* provides, with its Prince, the quintessentially Shakespearian answer, because he is seen as the greatest example of Shakespearian 'character'. The Prince is, as in the previous scene, akin to the Ghost; as a ghost, he keeps returning to torment and to perplex the watching critics. Yet Samuel Taylor Coleridge denies such a critical continuity. This chapter begins, in way of refutation, by locating Coleridge firmly as an actor within the critical drama seen in the previous chapter. Far from being radical or innovative, Coleridge's answers to 'Who's there?' are seen to be conservative, unable to progress, at their best, beyond the wonderment at Shakespeare's genius that Coleridge derides in his predecessors. William Hazlitt, by contrast, both sees himself within the critical drama and re-establishes the debate concerning 'character' on Montaignesque lines. Previous critics, including Coleridge, had approached 'that Within' Prince Hamlet in a Cartesian manner; 'that Within' they see as an area to be objectified and known, and 'character' as the product of self-mastery. Hazlitt, in distinction, sees 'that Within' the Prince as the ongoing and unmaintainable result of self-exploration, as 'a wave o'th sea'. In so doing, Hazlitt establishes the foundations of a constructivist and literary model of personality, a model well suited to analysing dramatic persons. It is this model, and this line of debate, that Part III develops.

[1] R. A. Foakes (ed.), *Coleridge on Shakespeare* (London: Routledge & Kegan Paul, 1971), 104. The text of this edition of the 1811–12 lectures is based on J. P. Collier's brochure transcripts, and so supersedes that in T. M. Raysor (ed.), *Shakespearean Criticism*, 2 vols. (2nd edn.; London: Dent, 1960) which is based on Collier's published and amended 1856 transcripts. For a discussion of the different versions of the lectures, and of the reasons for preferring the brochure transcripts, see the introduction to Foakes's edition. Foakes's tentative argument concerning the accuracy of Collier's transcription is given further substantiation in Georgianna Ziegler, 'A Victorian Reputation: John Payne Collier and His Contemporaries', *SS* 17 (1985), 209–34 (229–30). The Coleridgean text, being a transcript, is unstable. (Coleridge only published two essays of Shakespearian criticism—'The Specific Symptoms of Poetic Power', in *Biographia Literaria* (1817), ch. XV, and 'Essay on the Principles of Method', in *The Friend* (1818).) This instability is com-

If all that had been written upon Shakespeare by Englishmen were burnt for want of candles merely to read half of the works of Shakespeare, we should be gainers.[1]

Thus Coleridge, in his ninth lecture during the winter of 1811–12, demotes the critics of the previous scene from literary to literal illuminators.[2] Doing so, he asserts his decisive break from them, and so from the critical drama centring on *Hamlet*, the Prince and the play.[3] Coleridge derides that drama and its actors—he mentions Pope and Johnson by name—for their recourse to wonder: 'Coleridge', Collier records, 'went on to ridicule the modern commentators still further, asserting that they only exercised the most vulgar of all feeling—that of wonderment.'[4] Coleridge's attack on 'wonderment' is an attack on previous critics' answers to 'Who's there?'; their expressions of wonderment arose in response to that question, as they tried to explain what made Shakespeare's characters, and in particular Prince Hamlet, different from the characters of other dramatists. Coleridge, aware of the unconvincing nature of such answers, dislikes them. The profession of 'wonderment', even if offered honestly, is a device to confer respectability on the critic's simultaneous declaration both of the excellence of Shakespeare's works and of his own inability to explain that excellence within the terms of his own theoretical criteria. Coleridge wants to praise Shakespeare more compellingly, to show how Shakespeare's excellence demonstrates his 'judgement', how it is brought about 'by Laws . . . and not [by] acting without law as had been asserted' (p. 110). As Morris Weitz points out in *Hamlet and the Philosophy of Literary Criticism*, this is 'the fundamental thesis and theme' of Coleridge's Shakespearian criticism.[5]

pounded by the fact that J. P. Collier was the most successful and talented forger of Shakespeariana in history. (See Schoenbaum, *Shakespeare's Lives*, 245–65.) Foakes's argument of Collier's honesty in transcription is, however, convincing. Concerning the quotation, a similar attitude to previous critics can be found in Coleridge's notes for the fourth lecture, delivered on the 1 Apr. 1808, and in the report in the *Bristol Gazette* of the third lecture, 11 Nov. 1813; see R. A. Foakes (ed.), *Coleridge's Criticism of Shakespeare* (London: Athlone Press, 1989), 41, 75.

[2] Coleridge includes Scots in his reference to 'Englishmen'; Schlegel is the first critic 'to feel truly, and to appreciate properly [Shakespeare's] mighty genius'. Foakes (ed.) *Coleridge on Shakespeare*, 103. Coleridge is almost certain to have known of Richardson's and Mackenzie's work. See Raysor (ed.), *Shakespearean Criticism*, p. xx.

[3] The question of Coleridge's debt to earlier Shakespearian critics is large and much debated; this section concerns itself with this question only in respect to Coleridge's answer to 'Who's there?' The question as a whole was made a subject of critical debate by R. W. Babcock, *The Genesis of Shakespeare Idolatry 1766–1799* (Chapel Hill, NC: University of North Carolina Press, 1931), 211–39. Babcock, drawing on the work of Raysor and A. C. Bradley, and disagreeing with Nichol Smith, argued that no '*new*' criticism of Shakespeare can be found in Coleridge, merely the development of the critical approach established in the last third of the 18th c. Babcock's position achieved general acceptance until the 1950s, since when it has been increasingly challenged. For a brief critical history of this debate, and an argument for the 'new'-ness of Coleridge's critical approach, see M. M. Badawi, *Coleridge: Critic of Shakespeare* (Cambridge: Cambridge University Press, 1973).

[4] Foakes (ed.), *Coleridge on Shakespeare*, 102. Further references to this work are given after quotations in the text.

[5] Morris Weitz, *Hamlet and the Philosophy of Literary Criticism* (London: Faber and Faber, 1972; first pub. 1964), 168.

As Coleridge's attack on previous critics suggests, he is not starting the critical drama anew, but rather attempting a better answer to the same question. That answer runs along traditional lines. Previous commentators, Coleridge declares, have had to resort to the declaration of wonder, because they were unable 'to enter into his [Shakespeare's] peculiarities'.[6] The discussion of these peculiarities is held over for a later lecture, which has unfortunately not been recorded. However, in the 'Essay on the Principles of Method' (1818), Coleridge talks of 'Shakespeare's peculiar excellence'; this resides in the way that, 'Throughout the whole of his splendid picture gallery (the reader will excuse the confessed inadequacy of this metaphor), we find individuality everywhere, mere portrait nowhere.'[7] For Coleridge, the particular distinguishing mark and the particular excellence of Shakespeare's works is his ability to depict dramatic persons (I return to the distinction between individuality and portrait later). This is an argument familiar from the previous chapter, and with which Pope and Johnson would both agree (though Johnson might quibble with the use of 'individuality' as a term of praise). Similarly familiar are the criteria by which Coleridge judges Shakespeare's characters excellent: 'In all his various characters, we still feel ourselves communing with the same human nature, which is everywhere present as the vegetable sap in the branches' (p. 66). Shakespeare is able to create characters that are consistent with nature, a nature that is unchanging: '*Lear* and *The Merchant of Venice* were popular tales,' Coleridge argues, 'but so excellently managed, both were the representation of men in all ages and in all times' (p. 56). Coleridge's criteria are here difficult to distinguish from those of his neo-classical predecessors.

Coleridge's criticism of Shakespeare, in fact, repeats wholesale the fourfold pattern of critical argument first seen in Cavendish's letter. First, Coleridge sets out to defend Shakespeare from a critical attack—though such is the cultural prestige of Shakespeare by this time that the attack is one of inadequate praise. To fail to honour Shakespeare adequately is to fail as a critic: 'The Englishman', Coleridge says, 'who without reverence, a proud and affectionate reverence, can utter the name of William Shakespeare, stands disqualified for the office of critic.'[8] Secondly, Coleridge's defence takes Shakespeare's ability to create dramatic 'character' as a central proof of his particular excellence. Yet the defence also, thirdly, stays within its opponents' theoretical criteria, as it, fourthly, advances the argument by redefining the meaning of its opponents' terms.

The final substantiation of Coleridge's continuity comes in the centrality of *Hamlet*, the play and particularly the Prince, to Coleridge's criticism of Shakespeare. At the end of the third lecture of the 1813 series Young Hamlet is declared to be the supreme example of Shakespeare's 'peculiar excellence':

[6] Foakes (ed.), *Coleridge on Shakespeare*, 102.
[7] Foakes (ed.), *Coleridge's Criticism*, 65–6.
[8] Quoted in Nichol Smith (eds.), *Eighteenth Century Essays*, p. xix.

'Anything finer than this conception and working-out of a character is merely impossible.'[9] While at the beginning of the lecture's discussion of *Hamlet*, Coleridge is swiftly led to reproduce his general arguments about Shakespeare within the context of an explanation of the Prince's character:

The seeming inconsistencies in the conduct and character of Hamlet have long exercised the conjectural ingenuity of critics . . . The mystery has been too commonly explained by the very easy process of supposing that it is, in fact, inexplicable; and by resolving the difficulty into the capricious and irregular genius of Shakespeare.

Mr Coleridge . . . has effectually exposed the shallow and stupid arrogance of this vulgar and indolent decision. He has shown that the intricacies of Hamlet's character may be traced to Shakespeare's deep and accurate science in mental philosophy. That this character must have some common connection with the laws of our nature was assumed by the lecturer from the fact that Hamlet was the darling of every country where literature was fostered.[10]

What was 'wonderment' has become 'mystery', but otherwise Coleridge's charge remains; the previous critics' declaration of 'mystery' arises from an inability to make sense of the 'seeming inconsistencies' of character, and once more leads to the 'vulgar' declaration that Shakespeare was an 'irregular genius'. Coleridge (like Richardson and Mackenzie before him) will reveal the 'seeming inconsistencies' of the Prince to be the intricacies of Hamlet's character, by reference to the interior domain of the Prince's mind: 'Shakespeare's deep and accurate science in mental philosophy'. The intricacy of the character so depicted is still true to 'the laws of our nature' which are constant throughout the world. Ultimately, then, the refutation of the 'mystery' (or 'wonderment') of Prince Hamlet, and so—to a degree—the proof that Shakespeare's judgement is equal to his 'genius', lies in the ability to explain Shakespeare's capacity to create the interior domain of a character's mind—and particularly 'that Within' Prince Hamlet. Coleridge's continuity with the critical dialogue is thoroughgoing.

Hor. If thou hast any sound, or vse of Voyce,
Speake to me.
(I. I. 109–10)

Coleridge has two answers to 'Who's there?'—two conceptions of character, with which he attempts to challenge the Ghost of the critical drama; he believes both allow him to understand Hamlet's intricacies and define Shakespeare's particular excellence. One conception underpins what has since become known as 'the Romantic Hamlet' and is generally held to be the most influential version of the Prince in the nineteenth century.[11] (This version is usually taken to be the only Coleridgean Prince, and is also argued to be found

9 Foakes (ed.), *Coleridge's Criticism*, 70.
10 Ibid. 75.
11 See e.g. J. Bate (ed.), *The Romantics on Shakespeare* (Penguin: Harmondsworth, 1991), 2.

unchanged in the writings of Hazlitt and Lamb.) Coleridge gives a description of 'the Romantic Hamlet' in the third lecture of the 1813 series; he is,

> A man living in meditation, called upon to act by every motive human and divine, but the great purpose of life is defeated by continually resolving to do, yet doing nothing but resolve.[12]

The conception of character that underlies this Hamlet may be termed 'philosophic', for two reasons. First, it formed the foundation, so Coleridge believed, of his 'philosophical criticism':

> *Hamlet* was the play, or rather Hamlet himself was the character in the intuition and exposition of which I first made my turn for philosophical criticism, and especially for insight into the genius of Shakespeare, *noticed*.[13]

Secondly, it was the product of 'Shakespeare's deep and accurate science in mental philosophy' (quoted above). 'The Romantic Hamlet' is an example of the 'philosophic' conception of character since he is explicable from an idea or general principle; there is a kind of Platonic, ideal Prince Hamlet which the critic must grasp by 'intuition' before he can conduct an 'exposition' of the actual Prince Hamlet. This ideal principle is that the Prince, in 'continually resolving to do' does 'nothing but resolve'.

This ideal principle Coleridge elsewhere calls the 'germ' of a character. So, for example, he writes beside Johnson's notes on Hamlet's refusal to kill Claudius at prayer: 'Dr. Johnson's mistaking of the marks of reluctance and procrastination for impetuous, horror-striking fiendishness! Of such importance is it to understand the *germ* of a character.'[14] Coleridge, knowing the 'germ' of the Prince, has access to the true meaning which lies beyond the Prince's words and actions; Johnson, not knowing this, is misled into a more literal reading of the play. Though this philosophic conception of character may have got Coleridge's turn for criticism 'noticed', it is no more satisfactory than previous conceptions. To begin with it is dangerous, as it allows the literary critic to ignore the words of the text and produce instead a version of what the Prince 'really means'. Like Johnson's argument that the Prince's 'to be, or not to be' soliloquy was 'connected rather in the speaker's mind than on his tongue', Coleridge's 'philosophic character' relies on the critic inventing an ideal principle which he then uses to explain the text. Coleridge's conception of character, then, once again uses the gap technique; he takes the interior of the Prince to be an unexpressed area, and proceeds to fill this gap with his own reading, which reading he then uses to control what the Prince expresses. So doing, he leaves himself open—as did Johnson—to Barker's and the Cultural Materialists' charge that in the interior of the Prince there is nothing, and that it is this absence that critics have filled with their own words.

[12] Foakes (ed.), *Coleridge's Criticism*, 72.

[13] Raysor (ed.), *Shakespearean Criticism*, 16.

[14] Foakes (ed.), *Coleridge's Criticism*, 87. Further references to this book are given after quotations in the text.

Further, again in Johnsonian fashion, Coleridge's philosophic conception of character values generality above all. Coleridge argues that the ability to produce 'general truths' concerning human nature is what distinguishes Shakespeare from other dramatists. In the sixth lecture of the 1811–12 series, Coleridge noted that Shakespeare 'looked at every character with interest—only as it contains in it something generally true, and such as might be expressed in a philosophical problem' (p. 46). Indeed, Coleridge also saw this ability as the greatest glory of poetry, for in this lay its affinities to religion; having opened the eighth lecture of the 1811–12 series by observing that it was 'impossible to pay a higher compliment to Poetry than to consider it in the effects which it has in common with Religion', Coleridge gave the first such common effect as, 'To generalize our notions; to prevent men from confining their attention solely or chiefly to their own narrow sphere of action, to their own individualizing circumstances.'[15] Since Shakespeare is the prime example of this, he is the most properly religious of poets.[16] Similarly, since Prince Hamlet is the finest 'conception and working out of a character', he is one of Shakespeare's most instructive lessons, the greatest of all Shakespeare's 'philosophical problems'.

This conception of character (though it accords Prince Hamlet and Shakespeare a great cultural importance), is disappointingly reductive. Coleridge, believing the Prince to be a 'philosophical problem' with a moral lesson to teach, believes him to be solvable; Coleridge attempts to argue that all Young Hamlet's inconsistencies can be explained away by a single idea or '*germ*'. This becomes possible, of course, when the '*germ*' is allowed to control meaning; when the Prince's words do not fit the ideal principle, as when he watches Claudius at prayer, then it is the words which are to be discounted and not the ideal principle. Coleridge writes, when he discusses philosophic character, without any sense that the Prince or the play is problematic. In his account, Young Hamlet is not even a problem to himself, having a 'perfect knowledge of his own character'.[17] This Prince—'the Romantic Hamlet'—becomes merely a moral exemplum. The conclusion of the twelfth lecture of the 1812–13 series, after praising Hamlet as the finest conception and working out of a character, continues: 'Shakespeare wished to impress upon us the truth that action is the great end of existence—that no faculties of intellect, however brilliant, can be considered valuable, or otherwise than as misfortunes, if they

[15] Foakes (ed.), *Coleridge on Shakespeare*, 88.

[16] Coleridge is here refuting Johnson's famous statement, made in the preface to *The Plays of William Shakespeare*, that at times Shakespeare seems to write without moral purpose. Coleridge, by contrast, praises Shakespeare for '*keeping at all times the high road of life*. With him there were no innocent adulteries; he never rendered that amiable which religion and reason taught us to detest; he never clothed vice in the garb of virtue.' First lecture of the 1813 series, repr. in Foakes (ed.), *Coleridge's Criticism*, 55–6.

[17] Foakes (ed.), *Coleridge's Criticism*, 70. Further references to this book are given after quotations in the text.

withdraw us from, or render us repugnant to action' (p. 72). Under the philosophic conception of character, Shakespeare's ability to create dramatic character no longer inspires 'wonder' or 'mystery'; instead it leaves the bitter taste of moral triteness, sugared with the promise of religious importance. Coleridge's philosophic conception of character marks a lull in the critical drama; the conception, in its reductive and controlling aspects, produces a cruder, and less productive version of the Prince than the conceptions of the critics of the last quarter of the eighteenth century. For their conceptions of the interior of the Prince's character saw it as complex, developing, at tension within itself and thus producing real, if authorially intended, inconsistencies.

> *Hora.* If there be any good thing to be done,
> That may to thee do ease, and grace to me; speak to me.
> (I. I. 111–13)

The other conception of character used by Coleridge to try to make the Prince speak to him is an 'imaginative' conception of character. Often Coleridge uses this alongside his philosophic conception. So, for instance, it can be found in the third lecture of the 1813 series (which provided the opening example of the philosophic conception of character); within this imaginative conception of character, the Prince's mind,

> unseated from its healthy balance, is for ever occupied with the world within him, and abstracted from external things; his words give a substance to shadows, and he is dissatisfied with commonplace realities. (p. 76)

This description is, to an extent, philosophic, in its sense of the Prince's pre-occupation with thought; the idea of resolution being lost in resolving is not far away. However, the Prince is also seen here in more positive terms. Central to the imaginative conception of character is the phrase, 'the world within him'. All three extant versions of the lecture pick up on it, and repeat it.[18] Either Coleridge stressed it in delivery, or it impressed its auditors. Both are likely, as the phrase evokes the passage where Hamlet rejects his mother's use of 'seems', 'Seemes, Madam? Nay, it is: I know not Seemes' (I. 2. 76) and asserts in contradistinction that he has 'that Within, which passeth show' (I. 2. 86). (This was the passage which Barker and Cultural Materialists argued was traditionally used for evidence of the Prince's inner world.) Under this imaginative conception of character, the Prince is defined by his possession of 'the world within him', a world which is defined by the action of his imagination; dissatisfied with the commonplace, the Prince with his words effects a kind of transubstantiation, giving 'a substance to shadows'. The Prince, under this conception of character, is being defined by the creative activity of his imagination in general, and his verbal creativity in particular.

[18] See the transcripts of Collier, E. H. Coleridge, and the reporter of the *Bristol Gazette*; repr. in Foakes (ed.), *Coleridge's Criticism*, 70, 73, and 75 respectively.

This imaginative conception of character, and its subsequent version of the Prince as poet, though not as famous as 'the Romantic Hamlet', is of equal importance within Coleridge's criticism. In the seventh lecture of the 1811–12 series, Coleridge discusses *The Most Excellent and Lamentable Tragedy of Romeo and Juliet.* He begins by once more describing the various kinds of Shakespearian 'character', and selects Mercutio as one of the class of 'truly Shakespearian characters', since, 'Mercutio was a man possessing all the elements of a Poet: high fancy; rapid thoughts; the whole world was, as it were, subject to his law of association: whenever he wished to impress anything, all things became his servants' (p. 138). All 'Shakespeare's favourite characters', Coleridge argued, 'are full of such lively intellect' (p. 138). They, and Shakespeare's excellence in creating dramatic persons, are defined by the possession of an inner fountain of poetic expression.

In this way, Coleridge sites 'that Within' Hamlet at the centre of the Romantic poetic. Lying at the heart of English literary Romanticism was the belief in the central importance of the creative imagination,[19] and Hamlet's 'world within' is a definitive version of such creative imagination. Indeed, as Jonathan Bate argues in his study of Romantic responses to Shakespeare, the Romantic poetic may, in part, have been arrived at through the study of Shakespeare.[20] The imaginative Prince and the play are no longer the exception to critical criteria that they tended to be for neo-classical critics, but are instead seen as sources of those criteria. Coleridge, where he is concerned with his imaginative conception of character, has rewritten the notion of character within an expressive, not mimetic, poetic theory. However, in redefining Shakespeare's excellence in creating character in terms of his ability to confer the power of imagination on his dramatic persons, Coleridge has not fulfilled his promise to define 'that Within' clearly. Indeed, though he does not explicitly express the 'vulgar' wonder that he ridiculed in Pope and Johnson, he makes the interior and defining area of the Prince yet more wondrous. For, as the site of the imagination, it partakes of the inexplicableness of inspiration; by definition it is unfathomable. Moreover, Coleridge injects this interior area with metaphysical quality; the imaginative conception is seen to have its own kind of religious resonances. In the quotation from 'Essay on the Principles of Method' (1818) which was given early in this chapter, Coleridge made an analogy between Shakespeare's characters and a picture gallery, noting the 'confessed inadequacy' of the metaphor. The metaphor is inadequate as it falsifies Coleridge's imaginative conception of character; Coleridge dislikes both the way in which the metaphor pictures characters as passive and static, as simply the objects of the critics' gaze, or 'mere portrait' as he puts it. Earlier, in the ninth lecture of the 1811–12 series, Coleridge describes not only the

[19] See Abrams, *The Mirror and the Lamp*, *passim* (167–83). Coleridge, in his Shakespearian criticism, seems to meld the operations of imagination and fancy.

[20] See Bate, *Shakespeare and the English Romantic Imagination*, 17–19.

characters' active nature, but suggests that this in some way connects them with notions of a god-like eternity:

> [The characters] have the union of reason perceiving and the judgment recording actual facts, and the imagination diffusing over all a magic glory, and while it records the past, [it] projects in a wonderful degree to the future, and makes us feel, however slightly, and see, however dimly, that state of being in which there is neither past nor future, but which is permanent, and is the energy of nature.[21]

Shakespeare's characters, of which the prime example is Prince Hamlet, begin to offer not only unmediated access to nature, as if Shakespeare had the divine gift of creation, but also access to divinity itself, the condition of being eternal—'that state of being in which there is neither past nor future, but which is permanent, and is the energy of nature'.

> *Hora.* If thou art priuy to thy Countries Fate
> (Which happily foreknowing may auoyd) Oh speake.
> (I. I. 114–16)

William Hazlitt's Shakespearian criticism has a very different relationship to the critical tradition. Hazlitt's attempt to speak to the Ghost of the critical drama acknowledges its debts to the past. This is clearest in his *Characters of Shakespear's Plays* (1817), his chief work of Shakespearian criticism. In the opening lines of his preface, he sets out the nature of his continuity with the critical drama by offering his work as an explanation of some remarks of Pope (quoted in part in Chapter 4):

> It is observed by Mr. Pope, that
>
> 'If ever any author deserved the name of an *original*, it was Shakespear . . . The poetry of Shakespear was inspiration indeed: he is not so much an imitator, as an instrument of nature; and it is not so just to say that he speaks from her, as that she speaks through him.
>
> 'His *characters* are so much nature herself, that it is a sort of injury to call them by so distant a name as copies of her. Those of other poets have a constant resemblance, which shows that they received them from one another, and were but multipliers of the same image . . . But every single character in Shakespear, is as much an individual, as those in life itself; it is impossible to find any two alike . . . To this life and variety of character, we must add the wonderful preservation of it.'
>
> The object of the volume here offered to the public, is to illustrate these remarks in a more particular manner by a reference to each play.[22]

By choosing these two paragraphs from Pope's Preface to *The Works of Shakespeare* (1725), Hazlitt engages with Pope at the point where Pope was advancing the critical dialogue over character. Pope in these paragraphs was innovative

[21] Foakes (ed.), *Coleridge on Shakespeare*, 105.

[22] *The Complete Works of William Hazlitt*, ed. P. P. Howe, 21 vols. (London: J. M. Dent & Sons, 1930–34), iv. 171.

in his use of 'individual' as a positive term, yet left this innovatory stance undeveloped. Hazlitt, acknowledging the importance of Pope's observations by his quotation of them, goes on to make the development and 'illustration' of those observations the central 'object' of his volume. Hazlitt acknowledges his place within the critical drama and sets himself the task of examining in detail Shakespeare's excellence in creating dramatic persons. This, according to the preface, is the central aim of *Characters of Shakespear's Plays*.

Hazlitt, then, like Morgann, has a sense of the critical drama in which he is acting. (In the preface he goes on to explain his distinctness within this drama; he asserts his continuity with Pope to mark his antagonism—in this area—to Johnson, a critic whose generalizing and anti-individualist approach to literary criticism he dislikes.) Given such a self-conscious knowledge of the drama, it is to be expected that his essay on *Hamlet* should declare that play and the Prince to be the greatest example of Shakespeare's excellence: 'If *Lear* is distinguished by the greatest depth of passion, HAMLET is the most remarkable for the ingenuity, originality, and unstudied development of character.'[23] Yet this essay on *Hamlet*, which should in the preface's terms represent the culmination of the book, has been seen as atypical and disappointingly conventional by Hazlitt's recent critical champions.[24] Jonathan Bate, one of the most recent, praises the various innovatory aspects of *Characters of Shakespear's Plays* and is concerned especially to rescue Hazlitt from the line of decontextualizing character-criticism which Bate sees as running from Morgann, through Coleridge and the nineteenth century, and on to Bradley.[25] This is to an extent a wasted effort, as there is no such line; none of the critics mentioned decontextualize (in any simple sense) the dramatic persons of Shakespeare's plays. However, Bate's arguments still serve as a refutation of those who would wish to cast Hazlitt in such a tradition. The title of Hazlitt's work recognizes his interest in the whole of the plays; he does not deal with 'the characters' within the plays, but instead offers interpretations of the 'characters' of Shakespeare's plays. These twofold '*Characters*' contain new readings and emphases, seen most clearly, for Bate, in the essay on *Coriolanus*. In that essay, Bate values Hazlitt's explorations of Shakespeare's depiction of the people and the patricians, and his worrying over the related question of whether the language of poetry falls naturally in step with the language of power. Bate also values Hazlitt's political criticism, which he sees as radical in its resistance to appropriation by the state, and as impressively modern in attitude.[26]

[23] Ibid. iv. 233.

[24] See also J. Kinniard, *William Hazlitt: Critic of Power* (New York: Columbia University Press, 1978), 165–95.

[25] See Bate, *Shakespearean Constitutions*, 144.

[26] As John Lyon points out in his review of Bate's *Shakespearean Constitutions*, this radical strand within Shakespearian criticism refutes current arguments that seek to see Shakespeare's literary and cultural pre-eminence as 'ascribable merely to the political motivations of the Establishment'. See John M. Lyon, 'The Anxiety of Criticism', in *The Keats–Shelley Review*, 5 (1990), 105–17 (112).

Hazlitt's essay on *Hamlet* is, by contrast, disappointing to Bate as he believes it does decontextualize character, as well as reproduce 'the Romantic Hamlet' associated primarily with Coleridge's criticism. Worst of all for Bate, in this essay Hazlitt engages in a retreat from explicit political concerns into an unhelpful personal identification: 'The pull of Hamlet was such that when Hazlitt wrote of him he could not escape precisely the morbid egotism for which he so frequently castigated the poets of his own age.'[27] Bate is right in his sense that Hazlitt writes unusually on *Hamlet*. However, that difference does not represent a relapse into some kind of standard, morbidly egotistical Romantic reading; instead the essay is, in parts, one of the most innovatory and valuable pieces of Hazlitt's literary criticism. Its literary-critical radicalism (and to a lesser extent its political radicalism) lies in the way in which Hazlitt has developed Pope's sense of the individuality and inconstancy of Shakespearian 'characters', in the way in which he seeks to give his own sense of the 'very "personal" and "subjective" quality', as Rossiter phrased it, of *Hamlet*.

The essay opens as a response to an unasked question, a question similar to that which has driven the critical drama—that of 'Who's there?'; now this question is asked particularly of the Prince. Hazlitt gives his answer:

> This is that Hamlet the Dane, whom we read of in our youth, and whom we may be said almost to remember in our after-years; he who made that famous soliloquy on life, who gave the advice to the players, who thought 'this goodly frame, the earth, a steril promontory, . . . whom 'man delighted not, nor woman neither'; he who talked with the grave-diggers, and moralised on Yorick's skull; the school-fellow of Rosencraus and Guildenstern . . . the friend of Horatio; the lover of Ophelia; he that was mad and sent to England; the slow avenger of his father's death; who lived at the court of Horwendillus five hundred years before we were born, but all whose thoughts we seem to know as well as we do our own, because we have read them in Shakespear.[28]

This is not the answer of a decontextualizing character-critic, nor even of a standard character-critic, if by that phrase is meant those critics seen in the previous chapter. To begin with, Hazlitt is remarkably at ease with the Prince's many roles; to the implicit 'Who's there?', Hazlitt replies that Prince Hamlet is not only the soliloquizer, but the director, the melancholic, the graveyard moralizer, the schoolfellow, the friend, the lover, the exiled madman, the slow avenger, and the historical Prince as well. Hazlitt is untroubled by the multiplicity of Prince Hamlet's characters as he does not hold the neo-classical conception of character as predetermined role or roles; all Hamlet's roles, to Hazlitt, are the Prince's creation; he is not playing to a script. The Prince is the soliloquizer 'on life', the director 'who gave advice to the players', the melancholic 'who thought "this goodly frame, the earth, a steril promontory"'. Hazlitt's defining phrases and recourse to quotation is a way of insisting on

[27] Bate, *Shakespearean Constitutions*, 182.

[28] *Complete Works*, ed. Howe, iv. 232. Further references to this edition are given after quotations in the text.

Hamlet's irreducible uniqueness, a recognition that the Prince's actions or words are not reducible to a meaning, but rather are the meaning.

This sense of individuality runs close to making the jump to regarding the Prince as a living as opposed to a dramatic person, but Hazlitt never makes that leap. Instead, in his second paragraph Hazlitt moves immediately and explicitly to define the sense of Young Hamlet's 'realness' which he has implicitly developed:

> Hamlet is a name; his speeches and sayings but the idle coinage of the poet's brain. What then, are they not real? They are as real as our own thoughts. Their reality is in the reader's mind. (iv. 232)

Hazlitt is thoroughly aware of the fictive nature of Hamlet, but argues that this does not stop Hamlet being 'real' (as opposed to 'alive'). Our notion of reality, our sense of the world, Hazlitt argues, is in part a construct of our minds; our thoughts in part constitute our reality and so, since the Prince is a part of our thoughts, he is therefore a part of our world, 'real' in his effect on us. Hazlitt is advancing what would now be termed a constructivist or conventionalist argument. This is the theoretical context within which Hazlitt goes on to declare: 'It is *we* who are Hamlet' (iv. 232). This is often taken as the quotation which substantiates Bate's and others' hostile readings of the essay on *Hamlet*; it shows, so runs the argument, Hazlitt's Romantic, disabling, morbidly egotistical identification with the Prince. This interpretation quite misses Hazlitt's point. For, as Young Hamlet's 'speeches and sayings' are not only not idle coinage, but become real in our minds, so they produce those minds; through the opening part of the essay there runs the suggestion that the dramatic person creates our minds as our minds recreate him. Both grow up together; Hazlitt notes how the Prince is first read about 'in our youth', and then that we 'may be said almost to remember [him] in our after-years'. 'Remember' is being used in an unusual and specific sense here; the context ensures that the usual sense of the word is not available—Hazlitt is not saying that the readership 'almost' do not forget the Prince. Rather, the argument is that we may almost be said to 'remember' the Prince by 're-membering' him, bodying him forth in our own lives. This punning use of 'remember' may not be directly intended by Hazlitt, though the flag of 'may be said almost to' signals an unusual usage. (Similarly, the presence of 'after-years', a word which the *OED* records as being first used in 1814, lends support to the notion that Hazlitt is here trying to give expression to a notion he considers both new and important.) However, even if the pun is not intended, the meaning remains similar, as the sense of 'remember' would seem to be one of those given under *OED*'s sense 3, 'to commemorate' or 'record'. The suggestion is that our later years may almost be seen as giving witness to our reading of Hamlet, a commemoration that may presumably be seen in the Prince's influence on our actions.[29]

[29] According to the *OED*, the relevant meanings of sense 3 of 'remember' are obsolete at the

Hazlitt's point is not that we identify with the Prince, but that the Prince forms part of our identity. The essay, then, is the verbal equivalent of Van Dyck's visual analysis of the relationship between literature and life in his portrait of Sir John Suckling. Later, in 'On Personal Identity' (written in 1828), Hazlitt states his argument more explicitly: in the closing part of that essay he argues that the wish readers have to be any of the great poets is redundant, since,

> We have [the great poets] in our possession, enjoy, and *are*, by turns, in the best part of them, their thoughts, without any metamorphosis or miracle at all. . . . All that we know, think of, or can admire, in a manner becomes ourselves. We are not (the meanest of us) a volume, but a whole library.[30]

Within such a library, not all books are of equal importance. *Hamlet* is especially important for Hazlitt because it introduces a new area of writing and so of identity—as Van Dyck had shown. After asserting that, 'It is *we* who are Hamlet', Hazlitt continues: 'This play has a prophetic truth, which is above that of history' (iv. 232). Hazlitt's assertion of a 'prophetic truth' sounds worryingly reminiscent of the simplistic and crude aspects of Coleridge's philosophic notion of character. Yet Hazlitt's 'truth' is not a solution; he gives a further listing to explain his meaning:

> Whoever has become thoughtful and melancholy through his own mishaps or those of others, whoever has borne about with him the clouded brow of reflection . . . whose powers of action have been eaten up by thought, he to whom the universe seems infinite, and himself nothing . . .—this is the true Hamlet. (iv. 232–3)

The 'prophetic truth' turns out to be the exploration of a realm of the mind, an inner area of 'character', explored first by the Prince and since by others in life, and in fiction. 'The true Hamlet' is no single person or principle; instead he is many people and can be many more. Oscar Wilde, a literary-critical descendant of Hazlitt, puts this more memorably in his dialogue *The Decay of Lying* (1889), where Vivian says: 'Schopenhauer has analysed the pessimism that characterizes modern thought, but Hamlet invented it. The world has become sad because a puppet was once melancholy.'[31] Hamlet has created aspects of modern identity, aspects that the living may explore. It is the opening of this new aspect of identity that is prophetic, and yet 'above history', since it can, has, and may be repeated in each person's own history. Again Wilde makes a similar point about the multiplicity of this 'prophetic truth'; in another dialogue, *The Critic as Artist* (1890), Gilbert declares: 'In point of fact, there is no such thing as Shakespeare's Hamlet. If Hamlet has something of the definite-

time of Hazlitt's writing. In this case, it might well be that Hazlitt is using the word in a sense he perceives to be Shakespearian; the *OED* cites three such examples.

[30] In the *Monthly Magazine*, Jan. 1828; repr. in *Complete Works*, ed. Howe, xvii., 264–75 (274).

[31] *The Decay of Lying*, in *Complete Works of Oscar Wilde*, ed. Vyvyan Holland (London: BCA, 1976), 983.

ness of a work of art, he has also all the obscurity that belongs to life. There are as many Hamlets as there are melancholies.'[32]

Hazlitt argues, as would various of Wilde's persons, that the fictional Prince Hamlet is a part of the fashioning of a modern, personal identity. To criticize the play becomes difficult, under this argument, as it becomes an attempt at criticizing one's own sense of identity; the play becomes our play. Hazlitt opens the third paragraph by declaring, 'We have been so used to this tragedy that we hardly know how to criticize it any more than we should know how to describe our own faces.'[33] The Prince, as the analogy with 'our own faces' suggests, is seen as being a particularly intimate and important part of our self-image. It is also a place of burden, difficulty and sadness. Yet Bate's and others' sense of the essay's morbidity is misplaced, for Hazlitt's writing continues to be vigorous and excited, its exploratory and shifting argument expressive of the exploration, and the complexity of that exploration, which it describes. Hazlitt's sense of 'that Within' the Prince goes far beyond Coleridge's 'germ' idea of resolution being shown to lose itself in resolving, though that is there. But it is there as a part of the elements, feelings, and results of melancholy, reflectiveness, despair, rejection, grief, bitterness, and the loss of hopes. The Prince's inner variety mirrors the variety of his personal roles, each shaping the other. The sense of the 'growth', the processional nature of the Prince's character, becomes paramount.

The next section of Hazlitt's essay, which begins 'The character of Hamlet stands quite by itself', answers to Bate's charge of being commonplace. The style becomes rather pedestrian, and there is a summary feel to Hazlitt's account; at times he seems to be invoking Coleridge's philosophic conception of character, describing Hamlet as 'the prince of philosophical speculators' (iv. 234). The final paragraph, however, marks a return to the tone of the opening section, as Hazlitt declares that: 'We do not like to see our author's plays acted, and least of all, HAMLET' (iv. 237). Such a dislike of theatrical production is often seen as a Romantic prejudice, either to be damned for the incorrect novelistic approach it demonstrates or excused by reference to contemporary theatrical practices. Yet neither explains Hazlitt's objection. For he loved the theatre, owed his reputation to reviewing it, helped launch Edmund Kean's career, and in his essay on *Lear* in *Characters* held that actors 'are the best commentators on the poets' (iv. 256).[34] *Hamlet*, then, is a special case, which focuses worries that usually remain unspoken. The reason once again lies in the particular quality of the 'character' of the Prince, in 'that Within'.

[32] *The Critic as Artist*, ibid. 1034.

[33] *Complete Works*, ed. Howe, iv. 233. Further references to this edition are given after quotations in the text.

[34] See Bate, *Shakespearean Constitutions*, *passim*. For Hazlitt's support of Kean, see p. 38. Kinniard notes that Kean performances are drawn on over twenty times in *Characters of Shakespeare's Plays* (167).

There is no play that suffers so much in being transferred to the stage. Hamlet himself seems hardly capable of being acted. Mr. Kemble unavoidably fails in this character from a want of ease and variety. The character of Hamlet is made up of undulating lines; it has the yielding flexibility of 'a wave o' th' sea.' (iv. 237)

As often within Hazlitt's writing, he uses quotation to encapsulate and extend his argument. 'A wave o' th' sea' is Hazlitt's final attempt to express the nature of the composition of the Prince's interior area of character.

'A wave o' th' sea' refers the reader to Florizel's description of Perdita at the sheep-shearing festival in *The Winter's Tale.* Perdita is worried that her role as mistress of the feast is changing her disposition. Florizel reassures her:

When you speak (Sweet)
I'ld haue you do it euer: When you sing,
I'ld haue you buy, and sell so; so give Almes,
Pray so: and for the ord'ring your Affayres,
To sing them too. When you do dance, I wish you
A wave o'th Sea, that you might euer do
Nothing but that: moue still, still so:
And owne no other Function.

(4. 4. 136–43)

Florizel expresses his love for Perdita, declaring the perfection of her disposition. His only desire is that Perdita's present loveliness could in some way escape time and become endless and eternal. This desire is clear in his wish that she become 'A wave o'th Sea, that you might euer do | Nothing but that: move still, still so'. Florizel wants to capture the living loveliness of Perdita: he does not want to depict her statically, as she was lovely at a moment; rather, he wants to make her loveliness an unending moment. Yet, in its expression, his desire recognizes transience; for Florizel's vision of an endless, dynamic, ever-dancing love is fragile, pulled and shaped by the tides of time, as well as being sad in its insubstantiality—it prompts the thought of waves breaking, being lost on the shore.

The attempt to escape time and realize a vision of achieved, constant, and living love is central to *The Winter's Tale.* The play makes several attempts to achieve such a vision, the final providing a delicate and momentary success—when Hermione, as the statue, descends from her dais back into life. The play is as haunted and fragile as Florizel's description, one of Mamillius' 'sad Tale[s]', 'best for Winter' (2. 1. 27). Such a reading of the play may not be Hazlitt's, but Hazlitt's quotation of *The Winter's Tale* does ask the reader to bring a reading of the play to one's understanding of Prince Hamlet. If the reading advanced here is allowed, Hazlitt would seem to see this attempt to elude both time and stasis achieved in Hamlet. Hamlet is forever breaking and reconstituting himself, fluid yet centred, varied yet the same; he 'moves still, still so'. Like a dance, he is always progressing, while always remaining the same. In his character, art most clearly becomes life; for Hazlitt, as each of us 'remembers' Hamlet, so the statue descends again, and again.

This reading is lent support by Hazlitt's comparison of Chaucer's and Shakespeare's characters in 'On Shakespeare and Milton', the fourth of the *Lectures on the English Poets* (which were published the year after *Characters* in 1818). Hazlitt finds Chaucer's characters wanting, for while they are individuals in the sense of being distinct from one another, they are still 'too little varied in themselves', having 'a fixed essence of character' (v. 50–1). In Shakespearian characters, on the contrary,

> There is a continual composition and decomposition of its [the character's] elements, a fermentation of every particle in the whole mass, by its alternate affinity or antipathy to other principles which are brought into contact with it. Till the experiment is tried, we do not know the result, the turn which the character will take in its new circumstances. (v. 51)

Shakespearian characters are unfixed and lack essence, being defined by their processional nature, the product of actions in progress. And this is seen most clearly in Hamlet, whose character has 'the yielding flexibility of "a wave o' th' sea"'.

One result of this lack of fixity and essence is that the notion of a Coleridgean 'germ' or inner truth becomes irrelevant. The critic has no control over the dramatic person; within Hazlitt's approach, the Prince cannot be known or anticipated from an understanding of his 'germ', but must instead be watched and attended to. His words cannot be discounted by the critic's possession of his ideal principle. 'That Within' is a world to be explored, which exploration is less of a discovery than an invention. Self-knowledge is thus no more, as it was for Coleridge, a question of self-mastery, but of self-exploration. Hazlitt is re-establishing the terms within which the critical drama is described. Previous critics had employed what was—in its many variations—a Cartesian approach; by Cartesian is meant the stance, resultant from dualism, that divides and objectifies the body and mind in order both to achieve knowledge of them and to order them by the application of reason (reason, within the Cartesian context, being thinking according to the correct canons).[35] Such a stance sees 'character' as the product of self-mastery, a product which the person has a responsibility to know and to act so as to maintain. Within such a view, the Prince is, at best, a negative example of self-mastery and responsibility; Coleridge's philosophic prince was a moral lesson demonstrating the irresponsibility of allowing thought to predominate over action. His musings and actions were a waste of time, redeemed only by their poetic qualities. For Hazlitt, by contrast, Prince Hamlet's musings and actions were exciting,

[35] This discussion relies for the definition of its terms and its sense of historical framework on Charles Taylor, *Sources of the Self*. For a discussion of Cartesian and Montaignesque 'character' see ibid. chs. 8 and 10 respectively.

productive of 'character', a 'character' that was both original and modern. Hazlitt's processional conception of 'character', with its sense of 'character' as a continually changing product of self-exploration, is Montaignesque. Montaigne's argument concerning the constructed nature of identity, an argument that focused attention on the interrelation of literature and life, has already been examined in the discussion 'Of the institution and education of Children' in Chapter 2. Elsewhere Montaigne develops a notion of the variability of this constructed identity, and in particular on the inconstancy of his own personality. For example, at the beginning of the second chapter of his third book of *Essays*, Montaigne describes his attempt at self-portraiture: 'Others fashion man, I repeat him; and represent a particular one, but ill made . . . And though the lines of my picture change and vary, yet loose they not themselves. . . . *Constancy it selfe is nothing but a languishing and wavering dance*.'[36] 'The character of Hamlet', Hazlitt argued, 'is made up of undulating lines; it has the yielding flexibility of "a wave o' th' sea"'. The quotation invoked Perdita's dancing and Florizel's hope of its constancy. Hazlitt's essay on *Hamlet* seems at times to 'remember' Montaigne; and in its Montaignesque conception of character it finally gives the critical defence of Shakespeare a way of valuing the Prince's variety and multiplicity.

Hazlitt never explicitly compares Montaigne's *Essays* with Shakespeare's *Hamlet*, perhaps because he believed the *Essays* to have been first translated into English by Charles Cotton in the reign of Charles II.[37] But Hazlitt does, with his usual generosity, acknowledge the importance to his writing of Montaigne's *Essays*, and his praise of the Frenchman is often similar to his praise of Prince Hamlet. In 'On the Periodical Essayists', published in *Lectures on the English Comic Writers* (1819), Hazlitt argues that Montaigne is 'the father of this kind of personal authorship among the moderns' (vi. 95). His sense of Montaigne as the originator of a 'kind of personal authorship' parallels his sense of the Prince as the first explorer of the interior realm of character. Similarly, Hazlitt sees Montaigne as the same kind of moralist as Young Hamlet. For the Prince was, 'a great moralizer; and what makes him worth attending to is, that he moralizes on his own feelings and experience. He is not a common-place pedant' (iv. 233). This insistence on the correctness of evolving moral theory from experience, and the rejection of the received authority of the common-place is, for Hazlitt, a central and praiseworthy feature of Montaigne's *Essays*: the work 'does not deal in sweeping clauses of proscription and anathema, but in nice distinctions and liberal constructions. It makes up its general accounts from details, its few theories from many facts' (vi. 91–2). This represents an immense achievement: 'Nearly all the thinking of the two last centuries of that kind which the French denominate *morale observatrice* is to be found in

[36] Montaigne, iii. 21 (ch. 2).

[37] See *Complete Works*, ed. Howe, vi. 94. Further references to this edition are given after quotations in the text.

Montaigne's Essays. . . . There has been no new impulse given to thought since his time' (vi. 93–4). And it was an achievement that became possible by the simple expedient of displaying 'that Within': 'he did not set up for a philosopher, wit, orator, or moralist, but he became all these by merely daring to tell us whatever passed through his mind' (vi. 92). It is in this sense that Hazlitt goes on to praise Montaigne for being 'a most magnanimous and undisguised egotist', a description that would suit Hazlitt's Prince Hamlet (vi. 95). It is the Prince's magnanimous egotism that Hazlitt's essay explores, and that becomes an exploration of the construction of identity. This is quite different from a (morbid) egotistical identification.

Hazlitt's Montaignesque conception of character as 'a wave o' th' sea', and the related constructivist discussion of the 'real', offer productive ways forward for the critical drama. However, the description of 'that Within' still remains vague. Hazlitt, in this area, is willing to repeat unaltered previous scenes. He remains satisfied with Pope's notion, as quoted from his introduction above, that Shakespeare was able to gain direct access to nature: 'His *characters* are so much nature herself, that it is a sort of injury to call them by so distant a name as copies of her.' Similarly, Hazlitt advances the notion of Shakespeare as a kind of Proteus to explain this ability:

> The poet may be said, for the time, to identify himself with the character he wishes to represent, and to pass from one to another, like the same soul successively animating different bodies. By an art like that of the ventriloquist, he throws his imagination out of himself, and makes every word appear to proceed from the mouth of the person in whose name it is given.[38]

What remains, then, is the task of producing a vocabulary and methodology for discussing 'that Within'; a way, that is, of showing 'that Within' to be a textual construct, and not a critic's fiction—a way of tracing, placing and differentiating the undulating lines of the waves o'th sea.

[38] From 'Lecture IV—On Shakespeare and Milton', in *Lectures on the English Poets* (1818), repr. in *Complete Works*, ed. Howe, v. 50.

Part III

6
My Tables, My Tables

> *Hor.* Let vs impart what we haue seene to night
> Vnto yong *Hamlet*.
>
> (I. I. 149–50)

In Part III, *Hamlet* the play and Hamlet the Prince become primary objects of attention. The vistas of the past opened up in Parts I and II are not forgotten; rather, the critical issues and debates concerning 'that Within' are brought 'Vnto yong Hamlet'. Through a discussion of the Prince and the play, this chapter tries to advance those debates and, at the same time, to substantiate the second part of the assertion made at the beginning of Part I—that questions concerning the nature of identity and identification are central not only to New Historicist and Cultural Materialist criticism, but also to *Hamlet*.

As a preliminary, a summary of the previous chapters is useful to clarify on what grounds, and with what aims, the literary-critical debate staged here may be moved forward. This summary is structured around the various answers to 'Who's there?' A question-based structure is necessary as the answers are divergent, involving quite distinct debates over, most obviously, the nature of 'subjectivity' and 'character'. That these debates go under separate 'titles'—that is, use different key terms—is part of their proponents' arguments. The Cultural Materialist critic argues that Prince Hamlet is a 'subject'; in refusing to use the term 'character', the critic announces his or her refusal of the literary-critical criteria that underlie that term, and seeks to establish quite different, and irreconcilable, criteria. This is a quite different attitude from one neo-classical critic arguing with another neo-classical critic about whether Hamlet is, for example, well characterized or not; in this example both critics have a common ground of shared criteria, and so a ground for debate. The Cultural Materialist has no such ground for debate with the critic who uses the term 'character'; not having grounds for argument, there is no room for debate, but only for controversy. One argument may only be asserted against another, and the only measure of success is the loudness or dominance of a particular argument. For this reason, instead of the measured (if often ill-natured) debate that has been seen in more traditional criticism, the present arguments resemble a progression of rather shrill attacks and counter-attacks. Hence this book's title—'the controversies of self'.

These controversies share a terminological vagueness. A wide range of what should be quite distinct terms are 'collapsed' into the 'title' term: for example, the Cultural Materialist Belsey happily used 'the self', 'human nature', and the 'individual' interchangeably with the 'subject'; while the New Historicist Greenblatt collapses 'selves' into 'human identity' and that term into 'the human subject'. Each of these terms involves complex notions and they should be distinct, and distinct in important ways, from each other. Terminological vagueness has been a mark of the controversies of self. The first aim, for this chapter, is to clarify the terminology with which questions of identity and identification are discussed in an attempt to produce a more critically productive vocabulary. Ideally, this should also make debate, as opposed to controversy, once again possible.

In Shakespearian criticism up to the early nineteenth century, answers to questions of identity and identification became very quickly bound up with *Hamlet.* Unfolding the Prince became seen as the quintessential experience and pleasure of the Shakespearian text. Such unfolding of an inner area, or the impossibility of its being unfolded, was also taken to be the supreme proof of Shakespeare's worth. The answer to 'Who's there?' was 'character', which, in its meaning, underwent a gradual process of interiorization. Central to all such meanings of the word was the belief that as the Prince was a, and in a sense the, Shakespearian character, so he was a real person, independent of his author. Prince Hamlet was the liminal point at which art merged with life. He was the point of the most intense interrelationship between the fictive and the actual. And so the claim was made that Prince Hamlet was the first modern man, and (as Hazlitt developed it) a vital part of the armature on which individuals have since built up their identity.

Important to such a definition was the argument that the characters of other dramatists were not like this. However, when the inevitable questions of 'in what does this difference lie?', or 'what's unfolded?' were asked, the answers were unsatisfactory, demonstrating a range of responses from vagueness, to wonder, and finally, in Coleridge's and subsequent nineteenth-century critics' writings, to something very close to religious awe. The second aim which this situation suggests marks a development of the first; that is to produce a clear terminology which then allows a descriptive analysis of this previously vaguely defined area of Prince Hamlet. Ideally, such a terminology should also be able to describe the historical locatedness of this area. For only with such a historical ability can the claims of Shakespeare's originality be tested.

Cultural Materialists, recognizing the above tradition of criticism, and focusing on the Prince and the play, put forward a quite different answer to 'Who's there?' The Prince was to them 'no one', or, in the term they prefer, a 'subject'—as was every other dramatic personage. He was a subject as he was subject to social institutions and processes and also a subject made from the result of those social institutions and processes. He possessed no independent agency; 'that Within' was gestural, a vacant space; he was neither a 'character' nor an 'individual' as the previous tradition of criticism had defined those terms. Instead he was both a historically specific theatrical stage on which social tensions and competing arguments were articulated, and also a collection of dramatized literary types. In other words, the Prince was a kind of one-man secular morality play, an internalized Western. Such an answer represents a wholesale attack on the previous tradition (which is a very strong recommendation for the answer in Cultural Materialists' eyes). It attacks the notion of Shakespeare's pre-eminence. It attacks an entire way of interpreting drama, and seeks to site itself in relation to large questions of critical theory. It also hopes to attack and even change the present political state. For, and this is where a similarity with the previous criticism emerges strongly, if strangely, Cultural Materialists regard Prince Hamlet as real. Prince Hamlet's lack of 'that Within' is argued to give the reader insight into the true nature of being human. The absence of interiority within the Prince proves that notions of 'character' and 'individual' which argue that human nature possesses some form of interiority are the manipulative fictions of the bourgeois and capitalist state, by which that state persuades people they are free in the very act of harnessing them to its economic and political needs. As this in turn implies, Cultural Materialists are also aware of the way in which fictions can determine real lives; untold numbers of people since 1660, so they argue, have tried to live as 'characters' and 'individuals', with terrible results.

Yet the argument of their attacks is rather narrow, and the questions they have raised few. This is a result both of the near-repetitive cohesiveness seen in their various treatments of *Hamlet*, and the unproductive nature of their argument, much of which turns out to be either a quasi-religious polemic, disguised in a confusion of terms, or a poor use of out-of-date histories, or of out-of-date structuralist theories of cognitive development. Most of their arguments, in fact, serve no useful purpose other than to act as caveats. The strength of the Cultural Materialist argument centred on the proposal that, whether as the result of the historical context or as a deliberate authorial technique, 'that Within' Hamlet, his interiority, is nothing more concrete than a gap, or series of gaps, into which critics have ever since been rushing with their own beliefs. The third aim of this opening section is to ask whether or not this area, 'that Within', is constructed by the text and not the critics' imagination. This aim is a further development of the first and second aims. For clarifying the terminology used to discuss questions of identity and identification (the first aim) should, in allowing a descriptive analysis of the previously vaguely and wondrously defined inner area of Hamlet (the second aim), either refute or confirm the argument that Hamlet's interiority is the product of accidental or intended gaps.

New Historicists, in banishing the previous critical tradition rather as Gertrude did the memory of her first husband, gave a third answer, through which the unmentioned presence of *Hamlet* moved ghost-like. To the question of 'Who's there?' they also replied 'no one', yet did so for reasons different from those of the Cultural Materialists. Their belief that the Renaissance subject had no agency stems particularly from the influence of Greenblatt's interpretation of Lacanian notions of identity; identity is, as Greenblatt formulates it, the product of the intersection of authority and an alien. This left no area for agency or, in Michel Foucault's term, 'self-constituting interiority'. The prior and theoretical belief that it was and is impossible to self-fashion, underpins Greenblatt's work, and that of New Historicists generally. For New Historicists, then, identity is an expression of a crisis of authority, as it embodies the product of the intersection of authority and an alien. Identity becomes a form of political economy (as authority is taken to be ruling authority) whose principles are everywhere constant. For that reason, one depiction of such an identity, such as Hal's in *1 Henry IV*, can illuminate every other and become, for Greenblatt, the cultural key illuminating the circulation of power in Elizabethan or Jacobean England.

This approach to identity is not only considerably ahistorical but considerably acritical. For all identities are profoundly similar, and all literary depictions simply judged on their ability to disclose the underlying economy of the identity. 'No one' cannot be differentiated. The rigidly formulaic nature of this approach to identity is remarkable. Thus when New Historicism does turn to examine *Hamlet*, as Karin S. Coddon did in her '"Suche Strange Desygns": Madness, Subjectivity and Treason in *Hamlet* and Elizabethan Culture' (1989), the conclusions are predictable.[1] Hamlet's possible madness turns out to be the 'paradigmatic case' of madness, whose 'crisis of subjectivity . . . is *Hamlet*'s crisis of authority' (pp. 389, 395), and also the crisis of authority of Elizabethan culture. For Hamlet, the Prince and the play, can be read as an illumination of 'the offstage drama of disobedience and melancholy, treason and madness' (p. 399) provided by the Earl of Essex, Robert Devereaux, who himself was 'the embodiment of the Elizabethan *mal du siècle*' (p. 380). So subjectivity becomes interchangeable with authority, and Hamlet with Essex, and so with the *Zeitgeist* of the declining Elizabethan century. The New Historicist account of identity produces a fourth aim, a development of the third. For not only is it necessary to confirm whether or not there is an area within the Prince which is constituted of something more positive than gaps, but also to show that, if there is, then this area is significantly self-fashioned. The way forward, then, is to lay out a vocabulary capable of satisfactorily describing Prince Hamlet's 'that Within', and, if 'that Within' is more than the product of various gaps, to examine whether it is self-fashioned. This specific task may be put generally; it is to produce a way of describing the interiority of a literary person and, if there

[1] Karin S. Coddon, '"Suche Strange Desygns": Madness, Subjectivity and Treason in *Hamlet* and Elizabethan Culture', repr. in Susanne L. Wofford (ed.), *Case Studies in Contemporary Criticism: 'Hamlet'* (New York: St Martin's Press, 1994), 380–402. Further references to this essay are given after quotations in the text.

is such interiority, to describe how it is constituted. As the critical commentary surrounding the Prince shows, this is a difficult problem, and the literary-critical stakes are high.

Before attempting to satisfy these four aims, two other issues must be dealt with. The first is the substantiation of the assertion, made towards the end of Chapter 3, that the Cultural Materialist argument concerning the gestural nature of 'that Within' Prince Hamlet is hard to refute as there is no direct evidence within the play of a recognizably modern interiority. The second issue concerns the prevalence of critical vagueness over 'that Within'; this has been seen in the writing of critics up to the early nineteenth century, but it still needs to be seen whether such vagueness, typically observed in the reliance on a gap of wonder, is present in more contemporary critical writings.

First to the assertion that there is no direct evidence of interiority in *Hamlet*. 'Direct' is an important qualifier. Obviously, interiority cannot be produced or pointed to; it is not something that would physically exist inside Prince Hamlet, like a pair of kidneys, or a liver. Hamlet cannot discover it behind an arras, skewer it, and lug it out for show. Direct evidence, then, is not that direct. The direct evidence one might expect is rather a discussion of interiority in terms that are recognizably modern (in Francis Barker's term, 'post-Pepysian'), or that are recognizably relatable to modern terms. What one might expect to find, then, is a vocabulary of interiority.[2] But which interiority is being sought? For the moment it is that interiority Cultural Materialists have termed essentialist interiority; the Cartesian notion of interiority, that is, which is the object of the mainstream of the critical tradition traced in Part II, and with which Barker and others argue that Shakespeare has no connection. However, though Barker and other Cultural Materialist arguments do not mention it, there was and is another concept of interiority. This is seen at its earliest in the essays of Montaigne, later in the essays of Hazlitt and the dialogues of Wilde, and most recently (within this discussion) in Piaget's theories of cognitive development. This Montaignesque conception of interiority will be examined later; there will be all the more reason to return to it if the vocabulary of essentialist interiority is absent.

Such an absence would be remarkable. For the vocabulary of essentialist interiority has become intimately familiar. Its terms, on the one hand, are those which have been used and interpreted again and again within the controversies of self—'individual', 'character', 'personality', 'self', 'identity'. But its terms are also basic to the examination, interpretation, and evaluation of not

[2] For a discussion of the relationship between vocabularies and concepts, see Quentin Skinner, *The Foundations of Modern Political Thought*, 2 vols. (Cambridge: Cambridge University Press, 1978), i, p. x: 'The clearest sign that a society has entered into the self-conscious possession of a new concept is, I take it, that a new vocabulary comes to be generated, in terms of which the concept is then articulated and discussed.'

only literature, but also our world and ourselves. Indeed, they are so basic to our outlook that they are often referred to as if they had a physical existence. So while no one would argue that 'self', for instance, is an organ, it is often given the definite pronoun, and discussed as something quite distinct from one's body or one's mind.[3] Yet, remarkable though it is, such an absence is found within *Hamlet.* One problem with substantiating such a statement is that negative statements are always hard to argue in literature, unless one is willing to go through the play line by line, saying 'not here . . . not here . . . not here'. Even then such an argument lends itself to being tripped up with endless qualifications. Overall persuasiveness, then, not proof, must be the goal.

To begin with general supporting arguments, there are the main soliloquies. These, although often advanced as the defining marks of Prince Hamlet's inner nature, are remarkably general. So, in the most famous, 'To be, or not to be', 'I' or 'me' is not found once. The Prince instead subsumes himself in the common categories of the first person plural: 'and by a sleepe, to say we end | The Heart-ake,' and, 'what dreames may come, | When we haue shufflel'd off this mortall coile, | Must giue vs pawse' (3. 1. 63–4, 68–70). Or else he asks questions in the third person: 'who would beare the Whips and Scornes of time . . . when he himselfe might his *Quietus* make?' (3. 1. 72, 77) Whatever view is taken as to the meaning of the soliloquy—is the Prince debating his own self-murder? Or whether there is an afterlife?—the generality of the grammar cannot be denied. Indeed, this generality extends to the lack of any obvious narrative function. The soliloquy could come elsewhere. (Some productions have followed Q1's placement of the speech in 2. 2, after Polonius has read to the King and Queen Hamlet's letter declaring his love to Ophelia.)

Hamlet's other soliloquies do use the first person. Yet, again and again, they generalize outward where they might be expected to discriminate inward, and have a length far greater than that necessary for their narrative function. So, after having met the players in 2. 2, Hamlet begins: 'Now I am alone. | Oh what a Rogue and Pesant slaue am I?' (2. 2. 550–1) However, he soon moves to consider himself through a self-comparison with the player who has been declaiming the story of Priam's death:

> What would he doe,
> Had he the Motiue and the Cue for passion
> That I haue? He would . . .
>
> (2. 2. 561–3)

The Prince returns to consider himself directly in asking the question, 'Am I a Coward?' (2. 2. 572) But he answers it—in the affirmative—through the commonplaces of the theory of humours:

[3] For a philosophical discussion of the origins and influence of this tendency, see Anthony Kenny, *The Self* (Milwaukee: Marquette University Press, 1988).

for it cannot be,
But I am Pigeon-Liuer'd, and lacke Gall
To make Oppression bitter.

(2. 2. 577–9)

Here, with the theory of humours, there is a vocabulary of interiority which describes how a person's inner-life works. Yet this vocabulary does not provide the requisite direct evidence of Barker's essentialist interiority. The theory of humours is used often in *Hamlet.* Most obviously there is the issue of the Prince's melancholy. This issue is raised by the Prince later on in this soliloquy, when he wonders if the ghost may be the devil, intent on exploiting his 'Melanchollу' (2. 2. 602) in order 'to damne' him (2. 2. 604). Claudius, having overheard Hamlet's meeting with Ophelia, reflects that the Prince did not act madly but rather as if, 'There's something in his soule | O're which his Melancholly sits on brood' (3. 1. 167–8). The vocabulary of interiority which forms the theory of humours is capable of greater sophistication than is demonstrated in these uses of 'melancholy'. The mixture of a person's four cardinal humours—blood, phlegm, choler, and melancholy—determined their bodily 'temperament'—sanguine, phlegmatic, choleric, melancholic—and was reflected in their 'complexion'. Both 'temperament' and 'complexion', and the vocabulary associated with them, recur throughout *Hamlet.*[4] Yet the theory of humours, though capable of explaining and describing interiority (a capability attested to by its longevity) does so in common, impersonal terms.[5] Most importantly, it is a vocabulary founded on a physiology and not a psychology. 'That Within' in the physiological terms of humour theory is solely the product of combinations of humours; mental and physical constitution are linked and a self-constituting interiority possessed of agency is not countenanced. A similar situation is seen in relation to 'soul', the place in which Claudius locates Hamlet's possibly fertile melancholy. Although again an interior term, it lacks any sense of psychological or other individuation. 'Soul', used some forty times in *Hamlet,* has many meanings; most fundamentally, perhaps, it is the basic element of energy, what gives motion or life, either to the world or to a person; or it can be the quality that allows the person to feel, or to think; or it may represent the part of the person that is immortal, surviving after death, and here its religious nature is explicit. This derivative soul, given complete by God, was what Dollimore took as the foundation of 'Christian essentialism'.[6] It could be involved in dialogues with the body, yet its purpose was not to

[4] For words concerning the cardinal humours see: 1. 3. 7, 1. 3. 116, 2. 1. 35, 3. 2. 67, 3. 4. 68, Q2 4. 4. 9 + 52 (blood); 2. 2. 602, 3. 1. 168 (melancholy); 3. 2. 290, 3. 2. 294 (choler): for words based on 'temperament' see: 2. 2. 55, 3. 2. 8, 3. 2. 288, 3. 2. 325, 3. 4. 114, 3. 4. 131: and for those words based on 'complexion': Q2 1. 4. 18 + 11, 5. 2. 100.

[5] For a recent discussion of the theory of humours which includes a survey of previous writing on the subject, see Bert O. States, *'Hamlet' and the Concept of Character* (Baltimore and London: Johns Hopkins University Press, 1992), 63–86.

[6] Dollimore, *Radical Tragedy*, 155.

differentiate people from each other, but rather to show one the path that lead humankind to God.

These vocabularies, then, provide no evidence of essentialist and individual interiority, but reflect the more generalized sense of the person seen in the soliloquies, a generality reflected in the preponderance of impersonal verbs within the period.[7] Similarly surprising, perhaps, is the absence of a particular question from *Hamlet.* The absence is most clearly felt in Hamlet's soliloquy beginning 'How all occasions doe informe against me, | And spur my dull reuenge' (Q2 4. 4. 9 + 26–7).[8] In the soliloquy, Hamlet once more mulls over his delay:

> I doe not know
> Why yet I liue to say this thing's to doe,
> Sith I haue cause, and will, and strength, and meanes
> To doo't.
>
> (Q2 4. 4. 9 + 37–40)

The answer might seem quite obvious; it rests with 'who' Hamlet is. The question that Hamlet might be expected to ask at various moments throughout the play, then, is 'Who am I?', the near-equivalent of the Prince asking 'Who's there?' of himself. However, it is one of the few questions that the Prince never asks; instead, as here, he asks 'What is a man?' (Q2 4. 4. 9 + 27), or what is greatness. His questions are of the 'what' not 'who' variety.

What, then, of the passage usually put forward as direct evidence of an essential interiority, Hamlet's first speech of any length? This comes after his mother asks him to 'cast [his] nightly colour off' (1. 2. 68), reasoning, rather insensitively, that as death comes to all, the grief at its arrival for Old Hamlet should not 'seem . . . so particular' to her son (1. 2. 74). Gertrude's use of 'seem' has, here, the simple sense of 'appear', not the oppositional sense of 'appear (in opposition to what is)'. Gertrude is asking why Hamlet, alone amongst the court, should continue to grieve, and particularly to mark his grieving by dressing in black. Yet Hamlet seizes immediately on the oppositional sense of 'seem'. He begins by asserting that his grief is not a matter of appearance: 'Seemes Madam? Nay, it is' (1. 2. 76). Then, on a tangent to his mother's question, he expands to argue that his identity, though made up in part of external displays, is not defined by them:

> I know not Seemes:
> 'Tis not alone my Inky Cloake (good Mother)
> Nor Customary suites of solemne Blacke,
> Nor windy suspiration of forc'd breath,
> No, nor the fruitfull Riuer in the Eye,
> Nor the deiected hauiour of the Visage,

[7] See E. A. Abbott, *A Shakespearian Grammar* (London: Macmillan, 1905), sect. 297.

[8] The absence of this soliloquy will be argued in Ch. 8 to be an authorial revision.

Together with all Formes, Moods, shewes of Griefe,
That can denote me truly.

(1. 2. 76–83)

Hamlet's making of a question for himself (and implicitly for his mother)—in effect, 'What does denote one truly?'—is a measure of the importance of the issue of identity to him, and that his interest is announced in his first speech is a measure of its importance to the audience. Hamlet is come upon mid-thought, and his thoughts are on identity. The Prince next makes explicit the hierarchical relationship between a defining interior and a distrusted exterior, as he explains further the inferiority of the ways of 'seeming' that he has listed:

These indeed Seeme,
For they are actions that a man might play:
But I haue that Within, which passeth show;
These, but the Trappings, and the Suites of woe.

(1. 2. 83–6)

Hamlet, in making his public expressions of grief, clearly believes them to be of importance; at the same time, however, he allows such expressions little importance in denoting him truly because they are duplicable, they can be 'played'. 'That Within' is of value because it cannot be duplicated, it 'passeth show'.

Some critics, for example Harold Jenkins, argue that the last two lines express simply the commonplace notion that great grief is unutterable.[9] This sense is plausible only if the concluding lines are considered separately from those which have preceded them. The loose punctuation of Q2, which edition is most likely to preserve Shakespeare's own punctuation, makes this a grammatical possibility.[10] However, it would seem rather cussed to insist on such a divorce, when 'which passeth show' appears to set 'that Within' so clearly as an answer to what 'can denote me truly'. Q1 is interesting here. In that edition, Prince Hamlet's words do have the commonplace sense that Jenkins argues for:

My lord, ti's not the sable sute I weare:
No nor the teares that still stand in my eyes,
Nor the distracted hauiour in the visage,
Nor all together mixt with outward semblance,
Is equall to the sorrow of my heart,
Him haue I lost I must of force forgoe,
These but the ornaments and sutes of woe.

(Q1 179–85, 1. 2. 77–86[11])

[9] *Hamlet*, ed. Harold Jenkins (London: Methuen, 1982), 184.

[10] See *Hamlet*, ed. Philip Edwards (Cambridge: Cambridge University Press, 1985), 30–1; Stanley Wells and Gary Taylor (eds.) with John Jowett and William Montgomery, *William Shakespeare: A Textual Companion* (Oxford: Clarendon Press, 1987), 398–9.

[11] For a similar expression see *Richard II*, 4. 1. 295–8.

When Q1 is contrasted with the Folio, the Folio's greater complexity becomes apparent, and Jenkins's argument seems unsustainable. Moreover, the Folio's complexity is seen to be linked to the Prince's concern with identity that is brought into his answer with 'I know not seemes' and 'That can denote me truely'. The intriguing imprecision of 'that Within' is made clearer by the easy certainty of the more ornamentally poetic 'sorrow of my heart'. Hamlet's words in the Folio have a complexity of thought and a sense of difficulty with identity which is quite alien to Q1.[12]

This passage, however, does not provide direct evidence of essentialist interiority. For the meaning of Hamlet's 'that Within' remains vague; there is no vocabulary of essentialist interiority here to clarify or to begin to flesh out the phrase's intriguing imprecision, though it is perhaps the moment at which it would be most expected. 'That Within' is a signpost, pointing inwards. It might refer to an essentialist interiority, or it might not. It could refer to Hamlet's 'melancholy' or to his 'immortal soul'. The divide between an inward truth and outward expression is neither new nor remarkable; 'men', as Balthasar sings in *Much adoe about Nothing*, 'were deceiuers euer' (2. 3. 62). Hamlet, as Barker pointed out, does not describe 'that Within', apart from noting that it either betters, that is 'passeth', show, or goes beyond show, and so is indescribable.

In fact, a vocabulary of essentialist interiority cannot be found within *Hamlet* because it does not exist outside it; its absence in *Hamlet* is a reflection of its absence from the wider culture. Or rather, to be more precise, this vocabulary of meaning is not to be found; for some of the words are present, but without their interior meanings. So, within the play for example, while 'individual', 'personality', and 'identity' are not to be found, 'character' and 'self' are. Yet 'character' has no inner sense. In its two appearances in *Hamlet*, once as a verb and once as a noun, it has the sense of 'writing'. Polonius, as part of his good-bye to Laertes, exhorts him to 'Character' his 'few Precepts in thy memory' (1. 3. 58–9), while Claudius, in answer to Laertes' question whether he knows 'the hand' of the letter the messenger has brought, states ''Tis *Hamlets* Character' (4. 7. 49, 50). 'Character' does, elsewhere in Shakespeare, and within Elizabethan language, have the beginnings of a more interior sense, as when Viola says of and to the Captain in *Twelfe Night, Or what you will*, 'thou hast a minde that suites | With this thy faire and outward charracter' (1. 2. 46–7). The connection is here made between the outward form and the inner state. The *OED* quotes this line as its first location for this sense (sense 10). From this connection many of the later essentialist senses will develop. Indeed, this connection is also, according to the 'cultural graphology' advanced by Jonathan Goldberg, implicit in the sense of 'character' as writing.[13] Goldberg argues that

[12] The arguments over the nature of Q1 are discussed in Ch. 8. Here, Q1 is taken to be a memorial reconstruction; within a memorial reconstruction one might expect such a difficult and radical passage to be rendered commonplace.

[13] Jonathan Goldberg, *Writing Matter: From the Hands of the English Renaissance* (Stanford, Calif.:

the arrival of the italic hand in England in the sixteenth century initiated a momentous shift in history of handwriting. Within this shift the development of a repeatable signature 'serves as a mark of the person, as differentiated, repeatable, and therefore self-identical' (p. 239). 'Character' as writing becomes representative of the differentiated 'I'. The secretary's closet, the particular site of writing, 'represent[s] the locus through which a modern individuality emerges, with extensions to all who write' (p. 9).

'Charactery' and 'characterism' might seem to offer other more modern senses. Ben Jonson, in *The New Inn* (1629), prefaces his play with (amongst other things) 'some short characterism of the chief actors'. Yet his descriptions are general, suggesting the type of person that will be dealt with. In this the descriptions are of the same nature as Jonson's charactonymic naming: 'Good-stock', 'Ferret', 'Lovel' (Love-ill or Love-well?).[14] Indeed, 'charactery' and 'characterism' are in general bound up with the upsurge at the beginning of the seventeenth century of the literary genre of the character sketch; this was seen in, for instance, Bishop Joseph Hall's *Characters of Virtues and Vices* (1608), Sir Thomas Overbury's *Characters* (1614), and John Earle's *Microcosmography: or A Piece of the World Discovered in Essays and Characters* (1628).[15] Again, it is tempting to translate 'character' here in its modern sense. But these characters are social types; Earle's contents page, for instance, starts off with 'A Child', 'A Young raw Preacher', 'A Grave Divine', 'A Modest Man', and so on. Their interest lies in their wit, unity, and concision of depiction, not in any concern with an individual 'I'.[16] What none of these senses of 'character' possess are meanings bound up with the notion of interiority. This was the area of meaning which was seen (in Part II) to develop within literary criticism around the word 'character'. This is the sense the *OED* gives as, 'a personality invested with distinctive attributes and qualities by a novelist or dramatist' (17a), listing as its first

Stanford University Press, 1990), 2. Further references to this book are given after quotations in the text.

[14] As Lovel's name makes plain, these charactonyms are not transparent; they do not, in any simple sense, express their bearers. In fact, neither names nor characters demonstrate the direct expression of a type that can be seen in *Every Man Out of His Humour* (1599), where the onlooker Mitis, because he was 'a person of no action', was afforded 'no Character' by Jonson in the prefatory material. (These sketches of the dramatic persons are perhaps the first collection of Characters in English, pre-dating as they do those of Hall.) The characters and names in *The New Inn* develop the naturalism Jonson first employed significantly in *The Alchemist* (1610). See Barton, *Ben Jonson*, 189–93, 274–6.

[15] These, though influenced by Theophrastus' *Characters* (4th–3rd c. BC), are distinct from them. See the introduction to Thomas Overbury, *The Overburian Characters*, ed. W. J. Paylor (Oxford: Basil Blackwell, 1936), pp. v–xvi.

[16] There is a succinct statement of 'What A Character Is' from the ninth edition of Overbury's *Characters* (1616) onward. (Only a small number of the *Characters* are by Overbury, the rest being in the main anonymous.) This statement suggests three aims for 'A Character': it should make 'a deep impression'; it should provide a 'shorte Embleme; in little comprehending much'; and it should be 'quaintlie drawn in various collours, all of them heightned by one shadowing'. See *The Overburian Characters*, ed. Paylor, 92.

location Dryden's 1664 dedication to his *Rival Ladies*. (The *OED*'s first locations, however, are not to be taken as authorative, but indicative.) None of these recognizably modern senses of 'character' are available to Shakespeare.

The use of 'self' does not provide direct evidence either. The culminating precept of the 'few precepts' that Polonius gives to his son seems to have an interior sense: 'This aboue all; to thine owne selfe be true' (1. 3. 78). Yet such evidence is deceptive. For Polonius' precept means nothing more than his reprimand, fifteen lines later, to Ophelia. In criticizing his daughter for spending time with Prince Hamlet, Polonius argues that such behaviour demonstrates that: 'You doe not vnderstand your selfe so cleerely, | As it behooues my Daughter, and your Honour' (1. 3. 96–7). Here, as the following line makes clear, understanding 'your selfe' means simply that Ophelia must understand 'herself' as the product of her place in a system of relationships based upon her position as daughter to Polonius, and her obedience to the external value-system of honour. To 'vnderstand your selfe' is the equivalent of 'to know one's place'. The *OED* quotes this example as an illustration of this sense (1d). To a modern reader, however, such an exterior meaning does not seem to allow for the weight of the gap between 'your' and 'selfe'. For 'your self' hints at a substantive sense to 'self' that 'yourself' does not. However, in the Folio and Quartos 'myself', 'yourself' and 'him- or herself', and so on, are all commonly printed as two words. As such they are simply examples of, in the *OED*'s phrase, 'the pronominal notion expressed substantively' (C.I.1). It might be objected that Polonius' advice to his son is slightly different, for the gap between 'thine' and 'selfe' is emphasized by the interpolation of 'owne'. (The gap is given greater emphasis by modernized versions of the text, which print 'your self' as 'yourself', and 'my self' as 'myself', and so on, thereby making the gap between 'thine' and 'selfe', in 'thine own self' unique and striking.) However, such an intrusion of 'owne' is again common; as the *OED* notes, 'self', when expressing a pronominal sense substantively, is, 'often qualified by an adj., either emphasising, as *my own self, his very self,* or descriptive, as *your dear self*' (C.I.1a). What Polonius' precept amounts to, then, is an exhortation to 'be true to *yourself* only'. Once again, as with 'that Within', this is simply a signpost pointing inwards. 'Yourself' is composed, as Polonius understands it and makes clear in his advice to his daughter and his instructions to Renaldo, of one's place, one's family, or of an externally given code of honour and morality, and so on.

Once more it is worth noting that, as with 'character' there is a more interior sense of 'self' available to the time. In *The Tragedie of Troylus and Cressida*, Cressida says to Troilus, 'I haue a kinde of selfe recides with you: | But an vnkinde selfe, that it selfe will leaue' (3. 2. 144–5). Here 'self', the *OED* argues, means 'an assemblage of characteristics and dispositions which may be conceived as constituting one of various conflicting personalities within a human being' (C.I.4b). (Spenser this time provides the first location, in his 1595 collection of sonnets, the *Amoretti*.) Just as with 'that Within', 'self' needs to be located within its vocabularies of meaning to be more fully understood; what it does not provide, according to the *OED*, is the sense of 'self' that would provide direct evidence of interiority: '3. Chiefly *Philos.* That which in a person is really and intrinsically *he* (in contradistinction to what is adventitious); the ego (often identified with the soul or mind as opposed to the body); a permanent subject of successive and various states of consciousness' (C.1.3). The first location of such a 'post-Pepysian' sense is given as 1674.

The *OED*'s first locations, as has been said, are not authoritative. However, it would seem that one of the reasons why no direct evidence of an inner, post-Pepysian vocabulary is to be found is that one does not, at the date of *Hamlet*, exist. If the other words on our basic list are examined, the words, that is, that were not present at all in *Hamlet*, a similar pattern is observed; the words only develop their, now dominant, interior sense well after Shakespeare's time. 'Individual', for instance, as Raymond Williams pointed out so influentially in *Keywords*, is present in Elizabethan English, but, whether as an adjective or noun, it has a range of meanings centred on that of 'indivisible'.[17] It is only from 1646, according to the *OED*, that a more modern sense with a connotation of interiority can be found ('interiority' itself comes into the language in 1701): only then could an individual man mean a man, 'distinguished from others by attributes of [his] own; marked by a peculiar and striking character' (A.4). Williams puts the arrival of modern senses of 'the individual' later, in the late eighteenth century. 'Identity' is an older word than 'individual', its first location being given as 1570. But at the beginning of the seventeenth century it means simply 'The quality or condition of being the same in substance . . . absolute or essential sameness; oneness' (1a)—meanings which would today be given to 'identical'. 'Identity' starts being applied to people from 1638, in the sense of 'the condition or fact that a person or a thing is itself and not something else; individuality, personality' (2a). Here the interrelated web that these words form begins to come to prominence, 'identity' summoning 'individuality' and so 'individual' to gloss itself. 'Personality', the word the dictionary yoked with 'individuality' to straddle the meaning of identity, turns out to be another word whose interior senses come later; 'personality' only gains the sense of 'that quality or assemblage of qualities that makes a person what he is, as distinct from other persons; distinctive personal or individual character' in 1795 (2a). Before that date, its senses were bound up with discriminating between persons and things.

What this interrelated web of words also suggests is that a debate about interiority can be traced within the etymologies of words. To return to 'self', for example, the *OED* records that compounds using 'self-', having more or less died away in the medieval period, began to be coined again in the sixteenth century, and were 'greatly augmented' in the mid-seventeenth century, 'when

[17] See Ch. 2, p. 37.

many new words appeared in theological and philosophical writing, some of which had apparently a restricted currency of about 50 years (e.g. 1645–1690), while a large proportion became established and have a continuous history down to the present time'. One may even see rivalries between vocabularies, as they negotiate their new senses. So, for example, 'soul' begins to be used in ways that might register more individuating senses in the fifteenth century, as a way to express the defining trait of a person ('a dull soul'), and then in the sixteenth century there is a flurry of compound words using verbal nouns and present participles (*OED* senses 22 and 23), suggesting that 'soul' is moving into more secular and particular domains of meaning. However, while 'self' and its compounds have flourished, 'soul' has become marginalized, left now possessing only archaic or theological senses. It is part of Foucault's purpose to surprise us, in *Discipline and Punish*, when he suggests that we are still governed by souls—and it is still the given and un-self-constituting senses of 'soul' that make the word of use to him. A similar rivalry might be seen between 'character' and 'complexion'; 'complexion', like 'character', made a link between interior world and external appearance, but increasingly lost such interior senses in the seventeenth centuries, until it is now used primarily to refer only to the appearance of the skin. (In phrases such as 'a healthy complexion', the older, more sophisticated medical senses can be glimpsed.)

Too much reliance should not be placed on the *OED*; examining the usage of the time for Barker's essentialist vocabulary of meaning is an extremely valuable, if huge task. It is one Anne Ferry set herself in *The Inward Language: Sonnets of Wyatt, Sidney, Shakespeare, Donne* (1983). Drawing on a large range of texts, she is quite certain of her conclusion; she argues that sixteenth- and early seventeenth-century writers are 'without modern vocabularies for describing what we call the *real self* or the *inner life*'.[18] These vocabularies, Ferry argues, came into being as a consequence of the theoretical formulation of inward experience represented by texts such as Locke's *Essay* of 1689 (p. 7). She looks at the words above, and adds more which are either not present or lack their now dominant interior meanings, such as 'personal', 'awareness', 'consciousness', 'introspection', and 'inward'.

There is not, then, in *Hamlet*, because there cannot be, direct evidence of the vocabulary of meaning of essentialist interiority. Yet this does not imply such an essentialist interiority did not exist or was not possessed. Ferry, for instance, goes on to consider the question of whether sixteenth- and early seventeenth-century writers 'nevertheless conceived of inward experience in any sense to which our terminologies can intelligibly be applied' (p. xi). She answers 'yes', crediting Sidney and Shakespeare with inventing such a sense of inward experience in their sonnets, before it was theoretically formulated by the

[18] Anne Ferry, *The 'Inward' Language: Sonnets of Wyatt, Sidney, Shakespeare, Donne* (Chicago: University of Chicago Press, 1983), p. xi. Further references to this book are given after quotations in the text.

philosophers. (Ferry also asserts that Shakespeare developed this sense in *Hamlet* through the figure of the Prince.) The poets invented this sense by having the persons in their works recognize that, 'There is an inescapable difference between inward states and their rendering in language' (p. 250). Ferry sees Hamlet's recognizably and innovatory interiority, then, as stemming from his insistence on the gap between what 'Seemes' and 'that Within'.

Ferry's argument, in fact, suggests that direct evidence of inward experience can never be satisfactorily found. Her assertion that, 'there is an inescapable difference between inward states and their rendering in language', cuts to some extent against the thrust of her argument. To ask Prince Hamlet to speak about 'that Within' , it would seem, is not only to ask him to describe something which is indescribable because of his historical location (before the development of a vocabulary of essentialist interiority), but also to ask him to describe something which is by its nature, when strictly considered, indescribable. Hamlet is himself aware of this; as he notes, 'that Within . . . passeth show'.[19] To say this is not, however, as Ferry assumes, to say that interiority cannot be expressed positively in ways that are cognitively meaningful; for language, working at its height, possesses the resources to describe the indescribable, to 'gesture' beyond its current vocabularies of meaning in a cognitively significant way. It does this through the use of metaphor.[20]

To say so is to dismiss substitutive and emotive theories of metaphor. Metaphor is not an ornament, speaking of one thing in terms of another (as are, for instance, metonymy and synecdoche). Nor is it a defamiliarizing generator of emotion through unusual combinations of sense. Instead, it is, in Janet Soskice's definition, a 'unique cognitive vehicle enabling one to say things that can be said in no other way'.[21] Such a cognitive view is based upon I. A. Richards's sense of metaphor and its meaning as the new product of an interaction of thoughts: 'when we use a metaphor we have two thoughts of different things active together and supported by a single word or phrase, whose meaning is a resultant of their interaction' (p. 45). Richards defined these two

[19] There are logical arguments for such inexpressibility based on the nature of language. Many are reflections of Wittgenstein's point that any language requires another language to unpack its meanings fully, which in turn requires another language and so on. Meaning can never be fully unpacked, and this is of particular importance when dealing with a non-physical object such as the concept of interiority which is constituted through language. However, from this fact about the nature of language, it cannot be argued that because something cannot be defined or expressed satisfactorily it does not exist. For a discussion of the post-structuralist misuse of this problem of language see Taylor, *Sources of the Self*, 34–5, 524.

[20] For an argument that often runs parallel to this, see Raymond Williams's discussion of the 'structure of feeling' as a way of describing what cannot be expressed. This occurs in a series of interviews led by Perry Anderson, Anthony Barnett, and Francis Mulhern at Cambridge in June–November 1977, in *Politics and Letters*, 156–72.

[21] Janet Martin Soskice, *Metaphor and Religious Language* (Oxford: Clarendon Press, 1985), 24. Further references to this book are given after quotations in the text.

thoughts as those of the 'tenor' and the 'vehicle'. Take, for example, the last line from George Herbert's 'Prayer (I)': 'The land of spices; something understood'. The 'tenor', which is never mentioned, is the nature of prayer, and the 'vehicle' the 'land of spices'. The metaphor offers a model of prayer as the land of spices; that is, it offers to schematize the unknown—the mysterious and indefinable nature of prayer—through the known, if exotic—the eastern land of spices. The different thoughts, in Richards's term, 'interact'. Of course, this is not a 'true' statement; prayer is not a land of spices, no more than it was the Church's banquet, the soul in paraphrase, the heart in pilgrimage, or any other of the many vehicles which Herbert assembles, all without a main verb, to constitute his poem. Yet the metaphor of the land of spices communicates something of the nature of prayer; it does not define prayer, but gives a partially adequate description, a model through which to gain some sense of what prayer may be. As Soskice puts it, 'A good metaphor may not simply be an oblique reference to a predetermined subject but a new vision, the birth of a new understanding, a new referential access. A strong metaphor compels new possibilities of vision' (p. 58). Such a use of metaphor to model a field of knowledge is a common practice: science, for example, relies on a multiplicity of such models, such as 'light waves' or 'magnetic fields'. Both these metaphors are, strictly speaking, inaccurate (Soskice speaks of their 'partial adequacy'). However, both were vital to the understanding of their scientific field, and enabled more precise theoretical formulations, and better metaphors, to be developed. Indeed, within scientific thought it is a highly contentious issue whether these models can be replaced with theoretical formulations (pp. 99–144).

In Herbert's 'Prayer (I)', each metaphor gives 'a new vision', compelling 'new possibilities of vision'. At the same time, the poem insists on its humanity through its repeated and open acknowledgement of its partial adequacy. The repeated gestures of metaphors, their reaching into the unknown through the known, cannot build up a complete whole; all that can be gained by such knowledge, as all that can be gained by prayer, is 'something understood'. Those last lines of Herbert's poem, in both summing up the progress and process of the poem and also giving the final description of prayer in a form which suggests that prayer is itself in some sense metaphorical, suggest the metaphoric nature of man's relationship to God. For a Christian, in talking to or of God, is faced with the need to know the unknown and unknowable, or define the indefinable. That this has continuously been attempted through the resources of metaphor is Soskice's main argument. Hamlet's position in having to define the indefinable in order to express his interiority is not unique. Medieval mystics, for instance, in trying to express their experience of God, were faced with similar problems. The mystics took recourse to the gestural nature of language, that 'play of meaningfulness among words', as R. P. Blackmur describes it, 'which cannot be defined in the formulas in the dictionary, but which is defined in their use together'.[22] Metaphor, then, offers Hamlet the possibility of a cognitively meaningful verbal expression of his interiority, even if he lacks a developed vocabulary of essentialist interiority; this possibility is explored in the next chapter. Ferry's sense of Hamlet's interiority as stemming from his insistence on the gap between what 'Seemes' and 'that Within' is a little crude; it is also an example of the literary-critical use of the concept of the gap to explain 'that Within' the Prince. It is to the use of the concept of the gap in the twentieth century—the second preliminary issue—that this chapter now turns.

Bert O. States's *'Hamlet' and the Concept of Character* (1992) is a useful place to start considering whether the gap has flourished in the twentieth century, as it is both fairly recent and, as its title suggests, focuses on many of the same areas of concern as this discussion. States continues many of the critical traditions examined in Part II. He chooses *Hamlet* as his textual example as 'it does not seem . . . far-fetched to think of *Hamlet* as the quintessential drama of character'.[23] 'The play' thus offers 'an ideal opportunity to see how the impression of psychological depth is created' (p. xix). For States, though he acknowledges that there are differing types and aims of characterization, the most impressive acts of characterization, and the most Shakespearian, are those that demonstrate the most 'psychological depth'. His study has the traditional assumption, therefore, that an analytic definition of what character is will explain how 'psychological depth' is created.

As this may suggest, States is relatively untroubled by the troublesome nature of 'character'. One of the lessons to be drawn from Part II was that words concerning interiority need to be used very carefully ('interiority' included), because our critical vocabulary of interiority is being applied retrospectively when it is being applied to Prince Hamlet, or any Elizabethan or Jacobean dramatic person. The cavalier use of words such as 'character' or 'individual' produces a form of anachronistic modernization. States does, however, define his use of 'character'. He points out usefully that there are two concepts of 'character'; one, a 'hard' concept, is based on typology, as exampled by 'Charactery' (the charactery of Hall, Overbury, and Earle), and the other, a 'soft' concept, is the more modern concept that States is interested in.

Almost immediately States's attempt at analytic definition runs into a traditional problem: 'And this is the astonishing and simple point about character. Character keeps deferring its essence and foundation as one tries to move around "in" it analytically' (p. 5). States comes up against the vagueness that has been seen so often. He presses ahead by invoking the concept of the 'trait'. 'Character', States argues, is in fact made up from 'traits', seen in the

[22] R. P. Blackmur, *Language as Gesture: Essays in Poetry* (London: George Allen & Unwin, 1954), 6.

[23] States, '*Hamlet*', p. xix. Further references to this book are given after quotations in the text.

moments when 'character' issues into action (p. 3). By examining Hamlet's traits one can glimpse the consistency that marks the existence of character. As this suggests, States's traditionalism extends to a neo-classic insistence on the importance of consistency to character: 'Character,' he argues, must be 'something which persists recognizably in each new appearance' (p. xv). As that 'recognizably' suggests, it is up to the critic to decide which actions are traits, and so demonstrate consistency with the character that has been seen before, and which are not. Those that do not demonstrate such consistency are not traits at all but aberrations. For example, States argues that Hamlet's cruelty to Ophelia is condition- and situation-specific; it is brought about by a remarkable chain of circumstance and so is an aberration. Whereas Hamlet's generosity is not context-dependent, but ever-present, even when it is not manifest, and so is a trait.

The objection to this is the argument that every action is a product both of the situation and the person. States is aware of this; a problem with 'drawing distinctions between traits and other kinds of behavioural response,' he says, 'is that there must be some dispositional, or character, basis in any response whatsoever, since not all people respond to the same things in the same way' (p. 52). This problem is provoked by the very structure of *Hamlet*, which in its pairings continually asks us to make comparisons between different persons' responses to similar stimuli. To understate the matter, Laertes' response to the death of his father is different from Hamlet's response to the death of his. How then is a critic to decide, as States does, that Hamlet's cruelty to Ophelia is an isolated aberration, and not a trait which can also be seen in his sending off to execution his old schoolfriends Rosencrantz and Guildenstern, in his desire to send off to hell his uncle, and in his taunting of Polonius? The answer lies in the personal choice of the critic. As with Coleridge's philosophic conception of character, the critic simply decides which actions fit the character and so demonstrate consistency, and which actions do not. The conception of character, of course, is itself the product of the critic's decision as to what are traits and what aberrations.

Having set up this system, States moves on to give his account of the culminating triumph of characterization—the production of psychological depth of character. He is certain of this part of his argument: 'One thing seems clear, however: "depth" of character begins along the crevice between permanently established traits and these sometime "habits"' (p. 51).[24] Once again, then, the inner depths of character are the product of gaps. (Indeed, States had earlier discussed the 'gap between motive and intensity' (p. 46).) But this time the critic is actually creating those gaps, and not finding them. For it is the critic who has decided which actions are the manifestation of traits and which the aberrations of 'sometime "habits"', and so has determined where the 'crevices'

[24] States uses 'habits' here to refer to the sequence of aberrant responses a situation and event may call forth from a character.

are to be found. Certainly, in States's case, the use of vague and wondrous 'gaps' to explain Shakespeare's achievement is not only present but flourishing. States's work demonstrates the strong relationship between a literary critic's conception of character and a critic's chosen psychological theory of personality. When one turns to examine that relationship, the importance of choosing a suitably literary theory of personality becomes clear.

States's conception of character, in relation to Hamlet the Prince and *Hamlet* the play, is not only critically unpersuasive but also descriptively unsatisfactory. The conception of character, for example, with its insistence on consistency as the defining criterion of character, has no place for change. States recognizes this, discounting change and distrusting related words such as 'development' (p. 8). 'What we mean', he says, 'when we refer to character development is largely the development of our intimacy with a character' (p. 18). The character, for States, is always already there, and it is the audience who learn new information about it. Indeed, he even argues that when characters are seen learning, even learning about themselves, this does not amount to development or change, for, 'If we confuse what the character learns with what he is we have no word, or concept, for the thing the actor plays and what we, in reading, sense as a constancy in Hamlet's evolving search for commitment and selfhood' (p. 17). Yet such a sense of constancy within an evolving search for commitment and selfhood does not answer to 'our' experience of Prince Hamlet—as that experience has been manifested in the critical commentary.

States's critical approach, as he acknowledges, is based closely on trait theory; this is a body of personality theory that argues that traits (and often, to be more precise, five traits) are the fundamental building-blocks of personality.[25] An introductory text to such theories, such as Lawrence A. Pervin's *Personality: Theory and Research* (1993), notes the objections which have been made to this approach.

> Over the past two decades trait theory has come in for considerable criticism because of its emphasis on stable and enduring properties of the person. In particular, critics of trait theory argue that behaviour is much more variable from situation to situation than trait theorists suggest [. . . Trait theory] is strangely lacking in regard to a theory of personality change.[26]

States's literary approach, then, shares the limitations of its psychological model. More, it is a psychological model whose limitations make it particularly unsuited to analysing Prince Hamlet.

[25] There is no one theory of traits. Rather there is a body of theories based on the works of Gordon W. Allport, H. J. Eysenck, and Raymond B. Catell. See Lawrence A. Pervin, *Personality: Theory and Research*, (6th edn.; New York: John Wiley & Sons, 1993), chs. 9, 10. For the five-factor model of personality and the linked fundamental lexical hypothesis, see pp. 306–9. A sense of the closeness of the relationship between States's criticism and trait theory can be seen in the way States's ch. 4, 'The Theory of Humours', develops or mirrors Eysenck's 1975 article, 'The Relationship of Two Dimensions of Personality Derived from Factor Analysis to Four Greek Temperamental Types' (an article extracted in Pervin, 284).

[26] Pervin, *Personality*, 328, 334.

The use of trait theory to analyse a dramatic person raises, once again, the vexed question of the relationship between literature and life; to apply a personality theory to a dramatic person is, in effect, to treat a dramatic person as a real person. Oddly, given his critical practice, States warns against just such a conflation of real and dramatic persons. Anxious to avoid being drawn into the 'energetically disputed' controversies of self, and aware, perhaps, of the complexities and confusions that the tendency to treat Hamlet as real has led to within those controversies, he argues that literature and life, or more specifically literary character and human character, are quite distinct: 'Literary or dramatic character is not a representation of real character but an illusion of character.'[27]

As a response to the question of, 'What is the difference between a literary and a real character?' this is not persuasive. The difference between 'representation' and 'illusion' is unclear; perhaps a representation may be perceived, and an illusion imagined? Such an explanatory distinction is as tenuous as States's original statement, but suggests what would seem (from the rest of the book) to be the belief that underlies States's argument—that representation would present character whole, while literary character is an illusion, built, as it is, upon a technique of gaps. But is the phenomenon of an illusion of literary character possible? States illustrates his belief in the positive nature of such illusion through analogy, explaining that his notion of character is, 'a variation on Henry James's notion about ghosts in the Preface of *The Turn of the Screw*; if you want to create a good convincing ghost, don't tell us what it is or why it is there' (p. 208). This analogy works only at first sight. James's ghost does generate its interest, fearfulness, and believableness because it is unknowable. However, its unknowableness generates these and other qualities not because it is an illusion founded on a gap, but because it is a reflection of others' perceptions and consciousness; the story is presented as the manuscript of a governess, and the unreliability of the first-person narration makes our uncertainty concerning the ghost also an uncertainty concerning the characters. By the end, we are uncertain whether the ghost existed at all, or whether—and this adds the bite to James's story—the ghost might have been the invention of the neurotic and manipulative governess, an invention with which she terrifies Miles, the young boy in her care, to death.

As the *The Turn of the Screw* demonstrates, illusion relies on our knowing the thing invoked. A ghost can be created through techniques of illusion because we know what is implied by the general category of a ghost. Similarly, when the chorus asks in the Prologue to *The Life of Henry the Fifth*, whether casques, kings, armies, and years can be crammed 'Within this Woodden O' (l.13), the answer is yes, because all these things are known to the audience and so can be summoned with a word or an action or a costume. Yet only character in its sense of stock type, in the sense, that is, associated with the charactery of Over-

[27] States, '*Hamlet*', p. xv. Further references to this book are given after quotations in the text.

bury and Earle, can be summoned in this way. An illusion of an individual literary character or a unique 'psychological depth' of character is not possible, because uniqueness is the product of a recognition both of familiarity and difference, and the distinctions that produce difference cannot plausibly be argued to stem from gaps. A gap cannot generate the simultaneous recognition of familiarity and difference that uniqueness requires.

The failure of States's attempt, via his concept of illusion, to separate literary character from real character does not establish that all attempts must fail. Yet it is very hard to establish any ground of distinction, and very easy to point to interrelationships. For literary interiority has had its own demonstrable impact on life. Literary persons have produced real personalities, a process that might be described as producing the 'texture' of personal life. Hazlitt's witnessing to this texture—'We are not (the meanest of us) a volume, but a whole library'—has been examined. Oscar Wilde, who developed a Hazlittean position with regard to Prince Hamlet, also develops his own sense of this texture; in *De Profundis* he asserts, 'Of course Culture has intensified the personality of man. Art has made us myriad-minded.'[28] Wilde's use of the compound word, 'myriad-minded', recalls Coleridge's famous description of 'our myriad-minded Shakespeare'.[29] In this way, Wilde enacts the process he describes; he weaves the shaping influence of Shakespeare upon our personality by describing our minds through a descriptive compound adjective intended to celebrate Shakespeare's mind.

More recently Harold Bloom, while continuing this tradition, has widened its frame of reference:

> The tragic hero in Shakespeare, at his most universally moving in Hamlet, is a representation so original that conceptually *he contains us*, and has fashioned our psychology of motives ever since. Our map or general theory of the mind may be Freud's, but Freud, like all the rest of us, inherits the representation of the mind, at its most subtle and excellent, from Shakespeare.[30]

This is a challenging statement which Bloom leaves unargued. Particularly interesting is its assertion that Freud derived his representation of the mind from Shakespeare's analysis. If true, and supporting evidence can be found in other critics' writings, it would partly remove (and also complicate) the charge of anachronism from Freudian interpretations of Shakespeare, and explain why Freudian approaches have been so productive.[31] Support for such an

[28] Oscar Wilde, *De Profundis*, repr. in *Complete Works of Oscar Wilde*, ed. Holland, 927.

[29] Coleridge draws attention to the phrase within the text by an erudite footnote. Samuel Taylor Coleridge, *Biographia Literaria: Or Biographical Sketches of my Literary Life and Opinions* (London: Dent, 1975; first pub. 1817), 175 (ch. XV).

[30] Harold Bloom, *Ruin the Sacred Truths: Poetry and Belief from the Bible to the Present* (Cambridge, Mass.: Harvard University Press, 1989), 58.

[31] See e.g. Marjorie Garber, *Shakespeare's Ghost Writers: Literature as Uncanny Causality* (London: Methuen, 1987).

argument can be seen in R. S. White's parallel argument that Marx, 'confusing Shakespeare's construction of character with the "real life" of Shakespeare's England', derived his theory of alienation in part from an analysis of the relationship between capital and human behaviour in Shakespearian texts, and in particular *Timon of Athens*.[32] This leads White to conclude that 'as with Freud's theories, Shakespeare has directly influenced some of the most important non-literary, theoretical models of the twentieth century'.[33]

Shakespeare's importance to psychoanalytic thinking is maintained in the work of Lacan. In his 1959 seminars, 'Desire and the Interpretation of Desire in *Hamlet*', Lacan put forward an interpretation of Hamlet as a particularly modern hero, differentiating his analysis from that of Freud's by arguing that the Prince was distinguished from Oedipus by his awareness of his situation.[34] Lacan argued that *Hamlet* analysed the functions of the object of desire and need more instructively than any other work or person: 'It would be excessive, perhaps, if I were to say that the tragedy of Hamlet took us over the entire range of those functions of the object. But it definitely does enable us to go much further than anyone has ever gone by any route.'[35] More, it was in these seminars on *Hamlet* that Lacan advanced what has become one of his most famous definitions of the Other.[36]

The argument these statements concerning the texture of life support, then, is the notion that real interiority is in part constructed from literary interiority; or, perhaps, that interiority is a *literary* part of us, as our limbs are a *physical* part of us. Real character and literary character are not distinct, and do not, as States's formulation implied, exist on different levels. Rather 'that Within' is a place which may be literally literary. This strange cross-over is reflected everywhere in the language of psychoanalysis; as Shoshana Felman has pointed out, psychoanalysis constantly uses literary situations and persons—for instance the Oedipus complex and Narcissism—to describe its own senses of interiority:

> Literature, in other words, is the language which psychoanalysis uses in order to *speak of itself*, in order to *name itself*. Literature is therefore not simply *outside* psychoanalysis, since it motivates and *inhabits* the very names of its concepts, since it is the *inherent reference* by which psychoanalysis names its findings. . . . In the same way that psychoanalysis points to the unconscious of literature, *literature, in its turn, is the unconscious of psychoanalysis*.[37]

There is, it seems, no simple difference to be established between interpreting dramatic and actual persons. It is this equality that gives force to, and which is

[32] R. S. White, 'Marx and Shakespeare, *SS* 44 (1991), 89–100 (94). [33] Ibid. 100.

[34] J. Lacan, 'Desire and the Interpretation of Desire in *Hamlet*', trans. James Hulbert, *Yale French Studies*, 55/56 (1977), 11–52 (19). For Freud's analysis of *Hamlet* see 'The Material and Sources of Dreams' in his *The Interpretation of Dreams*, ed. and trans. James Strachey (London: George Allen & Unwin, 1954), 264–6. This interpretation was expanded by Ernest Jones, *Hamlet and Oedipus* (London: Victor Gollancz, 1949).

[35] Lacan, 'Desire', 29.

[36] See Hulbert's note, ibid. 25.

[37] Shoshana Felman, 'To Open the Question', *Yale French Studies*, 55/56 (1977), 5–10, (9–10).

expressed by, the particularly Elizabethan metaphor of the world as a stage, and the person as an actor.[38] More recently, Irving Goffman's work has demonstrated how profitable it can be to view and interpret people as actors.[39]

One of the consequences of viewing the interiority of literary and real persons as indistinguishable is that it suggests that writers and psychologists are engaged in similar tasks. This is the subject of Kenneth J. Gergen's article on 'Textual Considerations in the Scientific Construction of Human Character'. As he concludes, both writer and psychologist are 'engaged in the literary process of rendering human character both interesting and intelligible'.[40] There is, then, nothing theoretically troublesome with States's use of trait theory, bar the fact that it is unproductive in defining, in his term, 'psychological depth'. Indeed, States's use of trait theory is to be welcomed in that it begins to bring into use theories—other than those of Freudian or Lacanian psychoanalysis—designed to interpret personality. In doing so, States begins to redress the 'shocking cultural lag', explored by John V. Knapp, between the writings of literary critics on personality and those of psychologists.[41] The difficulty lies not in the use of theory, but in States's choice of theory. For different theories have different focuses of convenience; they aim to explain different aspects of identity. Trait theory, as has been said, is relatively unsatisfactory at explaining change within personality and at explaining 'that Within' Prince Hamlet. What is wanted is a theory which copes well with the literally literal aspects of personality and with change.

George A. Kelly (1905–66) was an American psychologist whose clinical work led him to develop personal construct theory, a theory which he expounded in *The Psychology of Personal Constructs*, published in 1955.[42] At a time when psychology was dominated by approaches based on essentialist notions of human nature, Kelly advanced an approach which refused to accept the notion that

[38] See Righter, *Shakespeare and the Idea of the Play*, *passim*.

[39] See e.g. Irving Goffman, *Frame Analysis* (Penguin: Harmondsworth, 1975).

[40] Kenneth J. Gergen, 'Textual Considerations in the Scientific Construction of Human Character', *Style*, 24 (1990), 365–79, (377).

[41] John V. Knapp, 'Introduction: Self-Preservation and Self-Transformation: Interdisciplinary Approaches to Literary Character', *Style*, 24 (1990), 349–64 (356).

[42] See George A. Kelly, *The Psychology of Personal Constructs*, 2 vols. (2nd edn.; London: Routledge, 1991; first pub. 1955). Kelly later extracted the first three chapters of this as *A Theory of Personality: The Psychology of Personal Constructs* (New York: Norton, 1963). This introductory text omits the detail of Kelly's scientific methodology and clinical practice, but explains well the philosophical underpinnings and theoretical postulates of personal construct theory. As it is widely available, quotations have been taken from the abridgement wherever possible. For a short biography of Kelly, who guarded his privacy, see Fay Fransella, *George Kelly* (London: Sage, 1995), ch. 1. The most autobiographical of his essays is 'Confusion and the Clock', in *Personal Construct Psychology 1977* (London: Academic Press, 1978), 209–33. This essay, like most of his later writing, is in first-draft, lecture-paper form. The University of Reading, in association with the Centre for Personal Construct Psychology, London, is in the process of establishing the Fransella Personal Construct Psychology Collection.

there might be stable truths to be known about man as a psychological subject. Instead Kelly saw man as 'a form of movement', which movement was guaranteed by man's temporal nature; man, for Kelly, is the 'only connecting link' between the 'two universes' of past and future—only man anticipates, snatching 'handfuls from each of the two worlds in order to bring them together and subject them to the same stern laws'.[43]

Anticipation, as the attempt to render intelligible and meaningful the stream of events that is life, is the central and inescapable human activity for Kelly. The person is seen as an inherently active process; and so Kelly discards such terms as 'motive' and 'motivation' (as well as, among others, 'drive', 'stimulus', and 'response', or 'purpose' and 'need')—terms which he dislikes both because they presuppose man, in his psychological aspects, as inert until acted upon, and because of their normative and pseudo-objective nature. As that may suggest, although Kelly himself was generally perceived as a conservative figure by those around him, his theory and its political implications are in no way innately conservative.

To make clear the distinctive qualities of personal construct theory, Kelly at times suggests, with a characteristic modest humour, that his psychology might be seen as 'a jackass theory', because, as he put it, his approach explicitly refuses both the pitchforks of push theories, and the carrots of pull theories, focusing instead on the animal in the middle.[44] This animal Kelly standardly referred to as 'man-the-scientist', a characterization designed in part to differentiate Kelly's approach from those of his contemporaries, and in particular behaviourist approaches. (Kelly had a far greater respect for Freudian approaches, for when he first began practising as a psychotherapist, he had been converted to a Freudian position. This he found surprising, as he had been quite unpersuaded by Freud when he had first studied him; however, as he later recalled: 'Now that I had listened to the language of distress, Freud's writings made a new kind of sense. That fellow Freud, he was indeed a clinician! He too must have listened to these same cries echoing from deep down where there are no sentences, no words, no syntax.'[45] What made Kelly dissatisfied with Freudian theory was his later discovery that his own, un-Freudian interpretations could be equally helpful to clients in distress.) 'Man-the-scientist' stresses Kelly's rejection of the notion, particularly strong in behaviourist approaches, that the psychologist is in some way superior to his human subject, and capable of testing the subject in more-or-less objective ways. Kelly insists on the mutually interactive nature of psychology—on how, for example, the psychologist's physical or methodological presence shapes the

[43] Kelly, 'Man's Construction of his Alternatives', in *Clinical Psychology and Personality: The Selected Papers of George Kelly*, ed. Brendan Maher (New York: Robert E. Krieger, 1979), 66–93 (p. 86). Kelly's insistence that man must be placed in time as well as space is one of the most distinctive aspects of his psychology. See also 'The Strategy of Psychological Research' in Maher, 114–32.

[44] Kelly, 'Man's Construction', 81.

[45] Kelly, 'The Autobiography of a Theory', in *Clinical Psychology*, ed. Maher, 46–65 (51).

subject's behaviour, as the subject seeks to understand the behaviour of the psychologist. In this way, then, both are 'scientists', both involved in similar tasks, if at different levels of competence and complexity. As Montaigne put it when musing over his games with his cat: 'When I am playing with my Cat, who knowes whether she have more sport in dallying with me, than I have in gaming with her? We entertaine one another with mutuall apish trickes.'[46] For Kelly, psychology is simply a particular form of anticipation with its own range of relevance; personal construct theory, in this way, is a reflexive theory, in that its explanatory force explains its own development. In this sense it can be seen as a metatheory, a theory about theories; so, for example, Robert. B. Ewen closes a summary of personal construct theory noting, 'to some psychologists (e.g., Fiske, 1978, p. 39), Kelly's approach provides the key to understanding all theories of personality: they represent the personal constructs of their creators, albeit ones that are more systematic and explicit than those of most people'.[47]

Most importantly, however, Kelly's use of 'man-the-scientist' centres attention on his contention that man constantly seeks ways to improve his ability to predict, and so control and render meaningful, that which he sees around him.[48] Man does this by producing intelligible representations of reality, which he then tries out on his world; if these are predictively successful, then they are retained, and if they are not, they are abandoned or adapted—at least this is the procedure in a psychologically healthy person. As the scientist develops theories to explain the physical world, then, so the person interprets and reinterprets (in Kelly's terms construes and reconstrues) their environment, with the aim of making it increasingly meaningful.

The foregoing view of the person as scientist is encapsulated in, and derives from, what Kelly termed the 'fundamental postulate' of his theory: 'a person's processes are psychologically channelized by the ways in which he anticipates events'.[49] The implications of this postulate are explained through a further eleven corollaries, and together these provide the formal content of Personal Construct Theory.[50] As has already been seen, Kelly is concerned with the person (and not the group or society) in his psychological aspect, the person being regarded as a process. What the reference to the person's anticipation of *events* is designed to emphasize is that, although there can be no unmediated access to the physical world, that world does exist separately from the person's

[46] Montaigne, ii. 144 (ch. 12).

[47] Robert B. Ewen, *An Introduction to Theories of Personality* (5th edn.; Mahwah, NJ: Lawrence Erlbaum, 1998), 374.

[48] Kelly, *A Theory*, 4.

[49] Ibid. 46.

[50] These are the construction, individuality, organization, dichotomy, choice, range, experience, modulation, fragmentation, commonality, and sociality corollaries. Kelly writes with an often elegant clarity; however, if an introductory text is wanted, the standard work is Don Bannister and Fay Fransella, *Inquiring Man: The Psychology of Personal Constructs* (3rd edn.; London: Routledge, 1986).

representations or constructions of it, and may validate or invalidate the predictions made about it. In this way, then, the representations of reality both render experience of the world meaningful, and are derived from a mediated experience of the world. Since man's attempts to control and render intelligible the world may also change what his world is (the most obvious example here being the achievements of the physical sciences), so those attempts may also change what man is; there is an interrelationship between man's changing construal of the world, and the changing nature of the world which is being construed. Indeed, since man is increasingly able to transform the world thanks to his technologies (technologies of prediction, it might be said), so his own processional nature may in effect speed up, a process Kelly terms 'ontological acceleration'.[51]

Kelly is alert to the darker implications of this view, and the Manhattan Project lingers in the background of some of his essays.[52] More generally, however, Kelly emphasizes the liberating nature of this view of the person and world, which view he termed 'constructive alternativism', and which is now referred to more simply as a 'constructivist'[53] approach. As that might suggest, Kelly's model of 'man-the-scientist' has similarities to Piaget's description of the learning child, discussed in Part I (and this model will also be seen to be within the Montaignesque and Hazlittean tradition argued for above). As with the Piagetian approach, so in the Kellyan, man, though a construct, is not a constructed product of the surrounding world, but a constructor, a producer of himself. The possible relationship between Piagetian and Kellyan approaches has been explored, usually with the aim of giving personal construct theory a developmental model—the omission of which has been one focus of criticism of Kelly's theory.[54] Yet it may be that Kelly, who had extensive clinical experience of working with children, omitted a developmental model because he saw no interesting or productive difference between the processes of construal in

[51] Kelly, 'Ontological Acceleration', in *Clinical Psychology*, ed. Maher, 7–45.

[52] Ibid.

[53] 'Constructive Alternativism' is the title and subject of the first chapter of *A Theory*. Fransella suggests that the use of the term 'constructivism' is derived from Kelly's 'constructive alternativism'. See Fransella, *George Kelly*, 130. Fransella notes that Joseph Rychlak has argued that Kelly is best seen as a 'Kantian constructivist'. See Rychlak, *Introduction to Personality and Psychotherapy: A Theory-Construction Approach* (2nd edn.; New York: Houghton Mifflin, 1981), 745. Kelly is well aware of the long philosophical traditions on which he draws for his own theory of personality.

[54] For discussions of the issue of this relationship, see Bannister and Fransella, *Inquiring Man*, 66–8, and Phillida Salmon, *Psychology for Teachers: An Alternative Approach* (London: Hutchinson, 1988). Allan Davisson suggests that the academic success of Piaget's and Chomsky's writing may have been what allowed Kelly's theory to flourish in America, having remained a relatively minor voice during the 1950s and 1960s. See his 'George Kelly and the American Mind (Or Why Has He Been Obscure for So Long in the U.S.A. and whence the New Interest?)', in Fransella (ed.), *Personal Construct Psychology 1977*, 25–34. Kelly, however, is unlikely to have been sympathetic to Piaget's developmental stages. Davisson also discusses the much quicker take-up of Kelly's *Personal Construct Psychology* in the UK. He advances Don Bannister's proposal that this may have been because of the UK's greater tradition of interest, within psychology, in the individual case and personal perspective.

the child and the man. For Kelly's 'man-the-scientist', if psychologically healthy, should always be like a young, Piagetian child in the adventurous nature of its desire to understand his world as meaningfully as possible through its imaginative constructions of it. 'No psychologist', similarly, according to Kelly, is 'all that he might be', 'until he has undertaken to join the child's most audacious venture beyond the frontiers of social conventions and to share its most unexpected outcomes.'[55] The sense of human potential is a constant within Kelly's writings, and he was keenest to identify his theory as a humanist one.[56] The task of the psychologist was not only to explore man in his psychological aspects, but in so doing to develop the possibilities of what it is to be human: the psychologist was

> Not simply to tabulate the categorial ways in which men presently behave . . . but to engage himself with fellow men in exploring the uncharted realms into which the human quest may be expanded . . . So now, in order to survive, psychology must invent as well as discover. That will make it a discipline disconcertingly alien to the one in which most of us were once trained.[57]

The Kellyan psychologist and client are involved in a constantly changing experiment, which has no objective, or discoverable, limits.

In contrast with trait theory, then, Kelly's approach—in its humanist and constructivist aspects—lends itself to an account of the literally literary aspects of personality and with change. The process of producing an intelligible representation of reality, for example, is closely analogous to the production of literature. This is most obviously so, perhaps, in the functions of myth or folklore. Kelly does not directly formulate this analogy, but he does note that stories, providing as they do an articulate and easily usable representation of reality, are 'a powerful tool in child psychotherapy and one which, incidentally, has amazingly escaped systematic treatment by psychologists'.[58] What Kelly does directly explore, in what was intended to be the epilogue to his second book (to be entitled *The Human Feeling*), was the issue of the extent to which dramatic persons may be real in Hazlitt's and Wilde's sense; the sense, that is, of creating aspects of identity that the living may explore. Kelly argues that Mozart's Don Giovanni is such a dramatic person: 'Mozart's image of Don Juan was a correct one. Here was an image that projected itself into the future, moment by moment, scene by scene . . . as we continue to look we see that others found it was, or could be, their image too.' Mozart's version of Don Juan

[55] Kelly, 'Ontological Acceleration', 8.

[56] See particularly Kelly, 'Humanist Methodology in Psychological Research', in *Clinical Psychology*, ed. Maher, 133–46. Kelly rejected the description of his theory as cognitive, refusing to divide the person into the threefold Aristotelian categories of mind, will, and emotion. However, owing to the increasingly flexible use of the term 'cognitive', many commentators now place Kelly's theory both as an initiator of, and within, cognitive theories of psychology.

[57] Kelly, 'Ontological Acceleration', 16–17.

[58] Kelly, *A Theory*, 162.

had and has a prophetic truth, 'still foretelling what lies ahead along the dark paths we walk'.[59] Kelly's account of Mozart and Don Giovanni is also a telling of the Pygmalion story, and it is with that story that the parallels between scientific and artistic endeavours culminate in Kelly's work. (Kelly's thinking may have been taking a literary turn in what proved to be the final years of his life.)[60] Indeed, Kelly's 'man-the-scientist' might be reformulated as 'man-the-poet', if it were not for the fact that 'poet' has lost its Renaissance and earlier senses of prediction and control. These were the senses recalled by Puttenham in the third and fourth chapters of the first book of his *The Arte of English Poesie.* They were, respectively, 'How Poets were the first priests, the first prophets, the first Legislators and politicians of the world', and 'How the Poets were the first Philosophers, the first Astronomers and Historiographers and Oratours and Musitiens of the world'.[61]

Personal construct psychology, then, sees man as an active, self-producing subject exploring the external and internal worlds through a series of representations or construals designed to anticipate and to render intelligible his path through the flow of time. The importance of construal gives a central place to the imagination's constructive powers, so uniting the fields of activity of psychologist, scientist, and poet (as it may do the lunatic, the lover, and the poet). At the same time the approach quite rejects essentialist notions of what it is to be a person; for man may continuously construe and reconstrue his world. If we turn now to look more closely at the detail of Kelly's notion of construal, its usefulness to literary persons is again apparent.

Kelly argued that a person construed the world through a framework made up of constructs. A construct is a way of perceiving events, made up from an oppositional pair which contain a similarity–contrast comparison. (Although a construct need not be verbalized, it usually is.) For example, good–bad is a construct. A construct, once formed and employed, becomes applicable to its employer. It becomes part of a hierarchical system of constructs, which system, Kelly argues, is its employer's personality, as the construct system 'control[s] the role one plays in life'.[62] It is also his or her philosophy, for it includes the ways in which he or she views and values the world. So Kelly says, 'if we examine a person's philosophy closely, we find ourself staring at the person himself. If we reach an understanding of how a person behaves, we discover it in the manner in which he represents his circumstances to himself' (p. 16).

Psychotherapy becomes necessary when a person becomes unable to reconstrue the world, continuing to use a construct although it is clear that it is

59 Kelly, 'Epilogue: Don Juan', in *Clinical Psychology*, ed. Maher, 333–51 (348).

60 See also 'The Language of Hypothesis', ibid. 147–62. This and the Epilogue date from 1964 and 1966 respectively.

61 Puttenham, *The Art of English Poesie*, 6, 8.

62 Kelly, *A Theory*, 135. Further references to this book are given after quotations in the text. Kelly differentiates between several kinds of construct, and has his own, restricted, definition of 'role'.

not predictively useful.[63] Take, as an example of the processes involved, a Westerner who has gone to live in Japan. This person regards himself as 'friendly towards new people' as opposed to 'hostile towards new people'; that is, he places himself at the 'friendly' end of his 'friendly or hostile towards new people' construct. This construct subsumes others, such as 'will shake hands or will not shake hands' and 'maintains eye-contact or avoids eye-contact'. What this person soon discovers, however, is that although he cheerily strides up to the Japanese he meets, looking them in the eye and firmly shaking their hands, they treat him coldly, as if he had acted hostilely towards them. His belief that he is a friendly person, and that friendly people look you in the eye and shake your hand, is not validated by experience.

This makes him anxious (or rather, more anxious than normal, for anxiety is a part of anticipation for Kelly), and he feels a sense of threat, recognizing that his framework for ordering and understanding the world is under pressure; there is, obviously, a need for change and reconstrual. This may happen in different ways. When threatened, the temptation is simply to switch the poles of a construct; so this person, wishing to keep his understanding of himself as one of being friendly to new people, may try not shaking hands and avoiding eye-contact. In this particular context, this will probably help matters. More positively, the person needs to elaborate his construct system ; 'bowing or not bowing' might be added or, probably higher up the hierarchy of constructs, 'in a non-Western or in a Western' country. The latter might well turn out to be predictively very useful. (The ability to elaborate, Kelly sees as dependent on a creativity cycle, during which people move from loose to tight construing.)

The person in need of psychotherapy, however, cannot reconstrue his representation of reality in this way, but will insist on maintaining his previous constructs, so displaying hostility in Kelly's terms. He may make new hypotheses designed to support those constructs, as, for example, that all Japanese are unfriendly to foreigners, which he validates by shaking their hands harder and looking them directly in the eye longer. This is in no sense wrong, but it prevents the person from achieving his aim of being friendly towards new people, and if this causes him distress—for suddenly people have become far more opaque to him than before, and he finds that unpredictability to be dangerous and isolating—then he may seek to utilize the psychotherapist as one of his tools for enabling the reconstruction of his world. What the therapist may then need to discover is the meaning of shaking hands for this person. For meaning, Kelly insists, is a contextual matter; it is only within the person's systems of value that it can be reasonably understood.[64] Thus it may be that

[63] See Kelly, *Psychology*, ii. 193.

[64] An impressive example of this insistence on the locality of meaningfulness comes in Fransella and Meshoulam's work with persons who stutter. This explored the meaningfulness of stuttering for the clients—the way in which it allowed the clients to exert predictive control on their lives—and the relative paucity, by comparison, for the clients of the meaningfulness of the construct of

'shaking hands or not shaking hands' is a construct itself subsumed under what may be the immensely strong construct (constellatory in Kelly's terms) of 'like father or not like father', and the person may have organized his system of constructs in order to be able to place himself consistently at the 'like father' pole of this construct. Shaking hands for this person may be one of the central acts of identification with the chief authority figure in his life.

The therapist's job, then, to understand his client, is to understand how the client construes his world, and so to understand his construct system; to do this, the therapist must 'compile a lexicon' of the client's constructs (p. 141). The therapist's aim in compiling a lexicon is to facilitate the 'human readjustment to stress' (p. 12). For having gained some knowledge of the construct system, the therapist may be able to suggest realistic alternative constructs. The aim remains to find 'better ways to help a person reconstrue his life so that he need not be the victim of his past' (p. 23). So he can, in fact, once again re-establish his predictive control on the future. Kelly developed his own assessment technique to compile this lexicon of constructs; this was the Role Construct Repertory Test, generally referred to as the Rep test. It is a technique that has been much used, sometimes with modifications, and often outside personal construct theory. The client is offered a list of figures believed to be important to all people—mother, father, teacher, neighbour, manager, and so on. The client then identifies these figures with people from his or her own life. The therapist then selects three figures and asks the subject which two are alike, and which one unlike. In this way the similarity and contrast poles of constructs become evident, and the answers can also be subjected to factor analysis.[65]

The Rep test is often the first move in the attempt to compile a lexicon of the client's constructs (and so to understand the meaningfulness of his acts). Another method Kelly developed was 'self-characterization', in which the client is asked to write a sympathetic account of himself in the third person, which the therapist then analyses. The purpose of compiling this lexicon is to allow the psychologist to 'help the person formulate new and rather basic constructs' (p. 134). The client is then encouraged to play with these new constructs and to see if he enjoys them—to put them on and see if they fit. In some cases, particularly if the client and therapist do not appear to be experimenting usefully within their clinical relationship, the therapist may try 'fixed-role therapy'. For this, the therapist will write a characterization of the client tangentially related (as opposed to diametrically opposed) to the client's own self-characterization. This will then be shown to the client, and—if the characterization is found credible and likeable—the client will be asked to play this role for perhaps two weeks, the aim being for the client to recognize new responses and understand this other, decentred person he or she is bringing

fluency. See Bannister and Fransella, *Inquiring Man*, 121–4.

[65] See also Fay Fransella and Don Bannister, *A Manual for Repertory Grid Technique* (London: Academic Press, 1977).

into being. As Pervin summarizes, 'Fixed-role therapy encourages clients to *represent themselves in new ways*, to *behave in new ways*, to *construe themselves in new ways*, and thereby to *become new people*.'[66]

Kelly's theory does not explain Hamlet the Prince or *Hamlet* the play; indeed, Kellyan theory rejects the notion of explanations of the Coleridgean, Freudian, or trait-theory kind.[67] A Kellyan analysis of the Prince would be aimed at trying to understand as fully as possible the meaningfulness of his behaviour, both verbal and physical—which behaviour is seen more as a series of questions than answers. However, although such an analysis will be outlined here, the particular focus is the relevance of Kelly's approach to the area of concern described previously in this discussion—on how personal construct psychology facilitates an understanding of the production and process of Hamlet's sense of interiority.

On a simple level, Hamlet is a very suitable client for a Kellyan approach. *Hamlet* is a play full of past thoughts and past deeds, and the Prince has become a victim of the past. The Ghost of Old Hamlet is the most potent symbol of the continuing presence of the past in the Prince's present, and its controlling influence on his actions and judgements. Even before the Ghost's arrival, his mother's recent and over-hasty marriage, and Claudius' assumption of the throne, have made Prince Hamlet question his previous ways of construing his family and society. With the Ghost's arrival, the Prince's sense that his ability to render the world intelligible is under wholesale threat is confirmed; indeed, it seems to him that he must try to begin to construe his world anew, casting off all his old values, experiences, and beliefs, founding a new construction of the world on the Ghost's 'commandment'.

> Yea, from the Table of my Memory,
> Ile wipe away all triuiall fond Records,
> All sawes of Bookes, all formes, all presures past,
> That youth and obseruation coppied there;
> And thy Commandment all alone shall liue
> Within the Booke and Volume of my Braine.
>
> (1. 5. 98–104)

As the Prince discovers (and Kelly would agree), such wholesale reconstruing is easier to state than carry out. One cannot immediately change all one's beliefs and values; one cannot conduct a wholesale reinterpretation of one's memories and associations. The attempt to do so borders, like the Prince, on madness. To Kelly, indeed, the backward-looking nature of the attempt to cancel out previous constructs is unlikely to succeed. This is compounded by the nature of

[66] Pervin, *Personality*, 257.

[67] A. E. St G. Moss analyses the meaningfulness of the act of writing *Hamlet* to Shakespeare in Kellyan terms. Moss has an untroubled sense of the relationship between author and work. See 'Shakespeare and Role-Construct Therapy', and 'Hamlet and Role-Construct Theory', in *British Journal of Medical Psychology*, 47 (1974), 235–52 and 253–64 respectively.

the Ghost's command, 'remember me', for that too is a command to live in the past. In asking for atonement and compensation, the Ghost would make the possibility of reconstruction unlikely, and indeed it would seem that the Prince fails to re-establish predictive control on the world around him to any meaningful degree, rather choosing to restrict the ways in which he renders intelligible his world.[68]

To understand that struggle, the audience as psychologist need an equivalent of a Rep test, and this is provided by Hamlet's soliloquies. This equivalence is on occasion remarkably exact. In the Prince's first soliloquy, 'Oh that this too too solid Flesh, would melt' (1. 2. 129), there is a triad of comparison: Claudius, Gertrude, and Old Hamlet are compared. Old Hamlet 'was to this', this being Claudius, 'Hiperion to a Satyre' (1. 2. 139–40). A construct is introduced, then, working on the poles of god and beast. Shortly, Hamlet places himself within the same construct and triad, when he returns to compare his father with his uncle; Claudius, he says, 'is no more like my Father, Then I to *Hercules*' (1. 2. 152–3). Hamlet does not directly call himself a satyr, but he is clearly towards that pole of the construct and far from the near-godly Hercules. Hamlet is here, then, applying a construct to himself, which was part of the process of creating personality. He is also suggesting a degree of commonality with Claudius, with whom he shares an end of the construct, which would seem uncomfortable; it reflects and is reflected in the pained and disordered nature of Hamlet's thinking. Gertrude, the wife of both brothers, has been at both poles of the construct. On the one hand she 'followed my poore Fathers body | like *Niobe*, all teares' (1. 2. 148–9), having loved him 'As if encrease of Appetite had growne | By what it fed on' (1. 2. 144–5). On the other hand, since her marriage to Claudius proved that 'like' to connote not similitude but disguise, she is also a beast, or worse: '(O Heauen! A beast that wants discourse of Reason | Would have mourn'd longer).' (1. 2. 150–1). Her moving from one pole to another dramatizes the pressurized, slot-rattling reconstruing (in Kelly's term) that Hamlet is engaged in, only being capable of moving from one end of the construct to the other. Such triads of comparison feature in two of the other three long soliloquies of the play in Q2 (and so in one of the other two soliloquies in the Folio). For instance, 'Oh what a Rogue and Pesant slaue am I?', begins with the Prince contrasting the player's relationship to Hecuba—'What's *Hecuba* to him, or he to *Hecuba*, | That he should weepe for her?' (2. 2. 559–60)—with his own relationship to his father: 'Yet I . . . can say nothing: No, not for a King' (2. 2. 566–9). Here one of the triad's persons is 'mythical'; the triangular relationship is made up of Hamlet, the player, and Hecuba/Old Hamlet, who both occupy one point. The player is defined by enacted motive, Hamlet by unacted motive.[69]

[68] See Kelly, *Psychology*, ii. 194.

[69] In a similar fashion, in 'How all occasions doe informe against me' (Q2 4. 4. 9 + 26) the triad is given by Hamlet, Fortinbras, and Old Hamlet/Poland.

Constructs need not, however, involve persons, or triads. They can be discussed independently of the processes that gave rise to them. This is the case with the 'To be, or not to be' soliloquy, where the Prince is seen debating between the relative merits of each of this construct's poles. Kelly places himself in the tradition of using the Prince to illustrate life; he takes a quotation from the 'To be or not to be' soliloquy as his example of the way in which persons choose between the poles of their constructs (pp. 64–5). The radical nature of Hamlet's construing is demonstrated here, as with the Prince's earlier double-placement of Gertrude, by the tendency of the construct's poles to lose their distinction. Hamlet begins by opposing existence with non-existence, and suggests as their markers the misfortunes of life versus the calm of death. Then, however, he is led to imagine that death may have its own misfortunes, if, like sleep, it is filled with dreams and fears. As the distinction between the two poles—existence and non-existence—collapses, Hamlet is left only with fear; fear of what is known versus the greater fear of what is unknown. Such fear Hamlet metamorphoses into conscience, 'Thus Conscience does make Cowards of vs all' (3. 1. 82), and finally into thought, 'And thus the Natiue hew of Resolution | Is sicklied o're, with the pale cast of Thought' (3. 1. 83–4).

What Kelly's approach helps us to recognize, then, is how such general constructs are capable of expressing individual difference and how they constitute a unique personality. Moreover, such constructs as conscience are 'high-level'; they are towards the top of the hierarchical system that goes to make up personality. 'To be or not to be', therefore, is remarkably and fundamentally personal in its generality; it allows the audience to build up their lexicon of Hamlet's constructs, and so the lexicon of his personality. This provides some of the soliloquies with their dramatic function; for while they are, to greater or lesser extents, non-narrative, they are important to the play as they give near-direct access to Hamlet's personality in process.[70] 'To be or not to be', then, gives us a portion of Hamlet's philosophy of the world—a philosophy which, within Kelly's theory, is Hamlet's personality.

This suggests a rather different definition of 'soliloquy' from that which is usually given. The definition of soliloquy is usually composed of formal and functional aspects. A formal definition usually provides the starting-point: a soliloquy is a speech made by a dramatic person when he or she is either alone or thinks him- or herself to be alone—'To be or not to be', for example, may be overheard by Claudius and Polonius. Functional definitions are used to refine such formal definitions. S. S. Hussey, in his *Literary Language of Shakespeare*

[70] Their lack of narrative role should not be used as a negative criticism, though it has often been so used. For instance, G. R. Hibbard, in his edition of *Hamlet*, argues that the Folio omits the 'How all occasions do inform against me' soliloquy as it does 'nothing to advance the action' (Hibbard, 362). Many of Shakespeare's most imaginative and arresting scenes have little narrative function. The scene where the flower-crowned Lear meets Edgar and Gloucester would be a famous example.

(1992) illustrates this process well: he defines four kinds of Shakespearian soliloquy, of which the last is Shakespeare's culminating triumph.[71] The first and weakest kind of Shakespearian soliloquy provides the audience with an exposition of what is happening and what the dramatic person plans to do; it is through the latter exposition that the soliloquy distinguishes itself from a monologue. This kind of soliloquy Shakespeare developed, through the figure of Richard III, into the second category, a speech which demonstrated an interpreting viewpoint and a process of thought, usually through the use of characterizing imagery and syntax. Next came, with Brutus in *Julius Caesar*, the portrayal of a mental state, and finally, with Hamlet, the portrayal of moral choice and moral dilemma. This is taken to be the 'best' and most Shakespearian kind of soliloquy.[72]

This description of the soliloquies as the portrayal of moral choice and moral dilemma does not suit the interpretation offered here. Such a portrayal suggests a static conception of who the Prince is; he has to decide which choice to make—the dilemma and choice is external to him. Whereas, if the soliloquies are moments of construing, moments in which the Prince attempts to reconstrue himself and become to an extent a new person, they are above all the demonstration of the fluidity and processional nature of the Prince. The soliloquies do not portray a choice or dilemma, though there may be choices and dilemmas within them, but rather a part of the speaker's representation of life, in the process of construction. In this sense they are not distinguished by being dramatized thinking, though they certainly demonstrate such, but rather by being the drama of thought. Such soliloquies are not uniquely Shakespearian. They are, however, remarkably difficult to make dramatically effective. Abstract concepts, such as conscience or thought, are far less obviously dramatic than dilemmas, whether those be a choice between good and evil or between competing goods. In a large measure it is the quality of their expression, their poetry, which makes them dramatic, and this achievement is rare.[73]

Kelly's approach provides a way of describing clearly and productively the construction of an inner area of identity, an area which literary criticism often refers to as character. This was Kelly's aim. For he set out to confront a situation prevalent in psychology which is similar to that seen within literary criticism; he sought to escape 'the vagueness so often associated with attempts

[71] S. S. Hussey, *The Literary Language of Shakespeare* (London: Longman, 1992), 181–202.

[72] The Shakespearian nature of this is hard to discriminate. The opening soliloquy of Marlowe's *Dr Faustus*, for example, provides an example of Hussey's last type of soliloquy, with Faustus choosing between that learning which is allowable to man and that which is not (a moral choice made unmissable by Marlowe's use of the good and bad angels). The play's closing soliloquy, in contrast, provides a brilliant example of Hussey's penultimate type, as Faustus wonders whether he can repent and be saved.

[73] A comparison with Lovel's Neoplatonizing in Jonson's *The New Inn* shows how hard it is to render the abstract dramatically effective.

to understand the inner man'.[74] Kelly would not have been impressed with States's 'astonishing and simple point about character', the point that 'character keeps deferring its essence and foundation as one tries to move around "in" it analytically'.[75] As has been seen, this is not to say that 'the inner man' is in any way essentialist under Kelly. The idea of construing the world and oneself is itself deeply inimical to essentialist outlooks. Kelly sees personality, the construct system, as constantly subject to change, as the predictive efficiency of one's constructs are validated or invalidated by the outcomes of events. Nor is this system logic-tight; constructs may exist in tension with one another, offering quite different readings of the same event, and subsuming or being incorporated into other constructs as they are seen to be more or less useful. The slipperiness of Hamlet's constructs causes Kelly no surprise. Man, for Kelly, is an active process, and Kelly's aim is to try 'to catch the sense of man going about his business of being human, and what on earth it means to be a person'. This description of man's 'personal adventure' suits both Shakespeare's achievement in the soliloquies of *Hamlet* and Prince Hamlet's own aims.[76]

At the same time as it is radically non-essentialist, Kelly's approach also gives to man a radical degree of agency. One can free oneself from old constructs and enslave oneself to new constructs, again and again. This is the process seen being repeatedly attempted in the soliloquies. Kelly gives us, then, a model which sees personality as an active process which is self-built, and not as a quasi-concrete, unchanging and yet unrecoverable antecedent substance. At the same time, he gives us reasons why literature should create so powerfully and so well the effect of personality; since literature may be, like personality, an argued, philosophical representation of the world. Some literary works, of course, may offer representations that are quite un-Kellyan in their tenor, just as different philosophical schools produce carrot and stick, and not jackass, theories. Other literary works, by contrast, might delight in exploring constructivist notions of personality and the world. Kelly reaches for *Hamlet*, as has been seen, at a significant moment in his explanation of a person's use of constructs. Although *Hamlet* is not mentioned elsewhere in Kelly's work, his reaching for that example suggests, I believe, not only the literariness of Kelly's approach, but its Shakespearian nature; and this might be turned around to argue for the constructivist nature of Shakespearian, as opposed, say, to Jonsonian drama.[77] The preface to *The Psychology of Personal Constructs* supports

[74] Kelly, *Psychology*, 183.

[75] States, *Hamlet*, 5.

[76] Kelly, *Psychology*, 183.

[77] In respect to notions of dramatic personality, the most influential single article is perhaps Thomas M. Greene, 'Ben Jonson and the Centred Self', *Studies in English Literature*, 10 (1970), 325–48. Greene's article shared and explored the general sense of a Jonson of fixed ideals which had been dominant at least since the Herford and Simpson edition. With the recent challenge to this view, notably in the works of Anne Barton and Ian Donaldson, it may be time to reconsider

this sense of a Shakespearian Kelly. The preface makes generous acknowledgement to the 'nearly a hundred persons' who gave their reactions to the book. Thirty-five are mentioned by name, eighteen as participants, eight for their ideas, and seven whose writings are quoted. Only then comes the final and culminating acknowledgement: 'and, of course, that distinguished and insightful colleague of all personal-construct theorists, Mr. William Shakespeare'.

Kelly's approach, then, begins to satisfy the aims stated at the beginning of this chapter. He provides a method of analysing interiority and its construction. However, his approach is not historically descriptive—it does not offer a historical picture of the changes in constructs and construing over the centuries (though it is aware that there must be such a history of change). Nor does it have degrees of innerness, in the senses discussed here. Before remedying these deficiencies, the following section returns to look at the literary-critical vagueness over 'that Within', and the use of the technique of the gap.

The technique of the gap was seen to be flourishing within Ferry's and States's quite different literary criticism. The presence of this technique can be found in many other critical approaches to *Hamlet*. States, as far as he was able, rigorously stuck to the task of examining 'soft' character. Peter Ure, by contrast, employs both concepts of character in the collection of his writings in *Elizabethan and Jacobean Drama*, talking of 'hard' character under the term of 'role'. In his first two chapters, he explores the interplay between character and role, and finds that it is through the gap between the two that the dramatic situation 'becomes profound and exciting, and permits rich inferences about what the hero's inward self is like'.[78] Others have employed approaches to explaining 'that Within' which avoid character, though not the technique of the gap. Joel Fineman, for instance, argues, as did Ferry, that Shakespeare in the *Sonnets* invented a new kind of subjectivity which, 'has historically established itself as the hallmark and the all-encompassing paradigm of literary subjectivity in general'.[79] Fineman examines the grammatical and figural relationships that are set up within the sonnets, and argues that the gap or difference between I and you, or between the praiser and the praisee, or

Jonson's notion of dramatic personality, and his relationship in this respect to Shakespeare. See Anne Barton, *Ben Jonson, Dramatist*, and Ian Donaldson, *Jonson's Magic Houses: Essays in Interpretation* (Oxford: Clarendon Press, 1997). For a preliminary move towards such a reconsideration, indebted to the above, see my 'On Reading *The Tempest* Autobiographically: Ben Jonson's *The New Inn*', *Shakespeare Studies* (Tokyo), 34 (1996), 1–26. For a much fuller reconsideration, exploring the dramatic potential of gaps as topoi of unknowable inwardness, see Maus, *Inwardness and Theater*, ch. 5.

[78] Peter Ure, *Elizabethan and Jacobean Drama*, ed. J. C. Maxwell, (Liverpool: Liverpool University Press, 1974), 30. John Bayley employs a similar approach in his *Shakespeare and Tragedy* (London: Routledge & Kegan Paul, 1981), 181–4.

[79] Joel Fineman, *Shakespeare's Perjured Eye*, 81.

between the ideal vision and the verbal representation, become the focus of the poet's, that is the 'I''s, attention and experience: 'the subject of Shakespeare's sonnets experiences himself as his difference from himself'.[80]

Graham Bradshaw employs a thematic approach. Again, he is traditional in his claim for the importance of Shakespeare's achievement, arguing that Hamlet 'was and probably still is the most complex character ever to have appeared on an English stage'.[81] This complexity is, he argues, the result of 'Shakespeare's habit of creative interiorization' (p. 22). 'Creative interiorization' is the product of locating thematic conflicts within the Prince: so, for instance, 'the collision between the opposed views of Nature and value [. . . becomes] internalized, to an unprecedented degree, so that the protagonist's own fractured view of the nature of Nature is at the centre of the play's nervous system' (p. 6). Shakespeare's ability to create 'that Within' characters here rests on the gap between two opposed views of the world. This is, like States's, Ure's, and Fineman's approaches, illuminating. Bradshaw's approach, for instance, points up how Shakespeare's dramatic persons are intimately enmeshed in the conflict of values within his plays, and how those conflicts orchestrate our own critical controversies. Bradshaw calls this quality of Shakespeare's plays their 'perspectivism'; it is an extremely rewarding notion, advancing as it does beyond Keats's 'negative capability' and Rabkin's productive analogies with duck–rabbit pictures.

More recently, Katharine Eisaman Maus has historicized the technique of the gap, focusing on the English Renaissance and examining 'the epistemological anxieties that gap generates, the social practices that are devised to manage it, and the sociopolitical purposes it serves'.[82] Maus fulfils many of the New Historicists' declared aims, providing a thick description of the meaningfulness of gaps to several of the cultures of the English Renaissance. (In Maus's account the gap is the recognition of an absent presence in the form of the unknowable interior, the 'inwardness *topos*'.) As Maus is aware, however, in doing so she rejects the assumptions and conclusions of most of the New Historicist and Cultural Materialist writing on subjectivity 'in the past decade'.[83] Crucially she realizes, as they do not, that the fictional nature of notions of interiority does not deny them actual and observeable effects on their surrounding world. Her book, *Inwardness and Theater in the English Renaissance*, may come to mark a return of a productive and innovative historicism.

The 'gap', then, is still in widespread, and sometimes very productive use. Yet, as an analysis of the constitution of interiority, the technique of the gap is perhaps at its least useful. Indeed, reading through the varieties of approach

[80] Ibid. 25.

[81] Bradshaw, *Shakespeare's Scepticism*, 103. Further references to this book are given after quotations in the text.

[82] Maus, *Inwardness and Theater*, 2.

[83] Ibid. 2, 26–7, 32.

which use the gap to try to account for the construction of interiority, one sometimes has the sense of the belief in 'the more gaps the merrier'. So, for example, Kenneth Muir, in 'Shakespeare's Open Secret', sets out to answer the question of how Shakespeare creates characters more lifelike than those of other dramatists. He turns to Hamlet, and argues that it is no longer enough to investigate the Prince's actions, his words about himself and others, or the words of others about him, his speech patterns, or his silences. Rather grandly, Muir terms such approaches 'a *reductio ad absurdum* of the old method of character analysis', which 'no one would now regard . . . as adequate'.[84] Instead, Muir pursues, as well as these, a series of conflicts which he reviews at the conclusion of his argument:

> What I am arguing is that the conflicting impressions of a character which we get from all the factors I have been discussing—the disparity between source and play, the disparity between what different characters say about each other, the contrast between metaphysical and psychological motives, the shattering of stereotypes, the complicating effect of the poetry, the poet's presumed identification with some of his characters more than with others, the difference between one production and another, between one actor and another—these conflicting impressions are the means by which we are convinced that the characters are real, not *real* people, but startlingly natural.[85]

A complex inner life, it would seem, is the product of a complex arrangement of gaps.

Gaps, then, have been pursued and discovered by the critical tradition in an attempt to gain access to 'that Within' Prince Hamlet. (In the twentieth century this received a boost from Freud's influential theoretical formulation of the significance of what is not said.) Gaps have been seen as the key to the understanding and construction of the Prince's interiority or, in States's phrase, psychological depth. To picture interiority as a gap is the equivalent of picturing interiority as a well; this equivalent image makes sense of, and is derived from, gap-critics' attachment to terms such as depth. Yet a gap is an unusual well; it is bottomless, having only sides. Its depth is unknowable—gap-critics would say profound.[86] The possibility of that latter sense has suited critics who wish to protect and emphasize Prince Hamlet's inner life.

To picture gaps as unsoundable wells makes clear that they cannot exist in a cumulative relationship to each other. More wells, contrary to Muir's and others' suggestion, do not equal deeper. Also, such a picture of interiority as a well is static. A well or gap cannot change; it either is there or it is not. Kelly's personal construct theory argued that personality could be seen as a framework of self-chosen constructs through which threats in the world could be

[84] Kenneth Muir, 'Shakespeare's Open Secret', *SS* 34 (1981), 1–10 (3). [85] Ibid. 9.

[86] For this reason, a gap is not the equivalent of a gesture. A gesture, as for instance a metaphor, provides a 'bottom' in the shape of a vehicle. This struggles both to locate and suggest the scope of the tenor. A gesture might be thought of as putting its audience at the bottom of a well, in order to focus their attention on, and give a sense of, the light at the top.

rendered intelligible. Personality, in this sense, was a complicated activity, a process of testing, ordering, and producing constructs. This activity was at its height in *Hamlet*, where the murder of Old Hamlet by his brother, and that brother's subsequent marriage to his sister-in-law, Gertrude, forced Prince Hamlet into a wholesale reconstrual of his world and so himself.

Kelly's theory provided a model for seeing and describing interiority not as an expressive gap, but as a verbally constructed possession. In this way, by focusing on the possessed nature of interiority, as opposed to its directly expressed nature, the absence of our contemporary vocabulary for the description of interiority was not seen to be an insoluble problem. However, this picture of interiority was relatively flat, lacking obvious degrees of innerness. What had in effect been lost was the metaphoric knowledge of interiority as depth. Kelly's picture of interiority had instead a scale of the importance of constructs to prediction. This picture was also ahistorical.

Charles Taylor's *Sources of the Self: The Making of the Modern Identity* (1989) provides a means of making Kelly's construct theory descriptive both of historical change and of relative degrees of innerness for literary texts. It offers a way of making a virtue out of the spatial nature of the flatness of Kelly's theory. Taylor is concerned to trace the development of the senses of inwardness in Western culture, which he does through an authoritative interpretative study of the answers to 'Who's there?' Taylor's study is interpretative in that it examines certain key answers to this question, instead of trying to present a historical account of the development of the senses of inwardness; it gives historical authority and explanation to what has already been seen in *Hamlet*. In that play, the Prince always seemed to be on the verge of asking 'Who am I?', but in fact came out with questions and arguments based upon the radically distinct question of 'What am I?' Taylor notes that, in our contemporary society, 'Who am I?' is assumed to be the way of going about answering the question of 'Who's there?' But he goes on to make clear that such a question is historically located: 'This question would not have been phrased so in earlier centuries . . . Talk about identity in the modern sense would have been incomprehensible to our forebears of a couple of centuries ago.'[87]

This is an important qualification of the timeless nature of gaps; it goes, for instance, against Ferry's assertion that Hamlet possesses a modern inwardness. Hamlet's interiority may have modern aspects but it must also be different, and significantly different, from interiorities which are available in the twentieth century. It is tempting to forget this difference, a tendency which this discussion might be thought to endorse by concentrating on the innovative aspects of Hamlet's interiority. The next chapter re-establishes balance, by examining an aspect of the historical difference between the interiorities available to *Hamlet* and those available today.

87 Taylor, *Sources of the Self*, 28. Further references to this book are given after quotations in the text.

Taylor demonstrates the historical locatedness of talk about identity with an example which parallels the previous discussion of Polonius' advice to Laertes. Taylor looks at a common Greek injunction, most famously inscribed above the oracle at Delphi: 'Know thyself.' He points out that the meaning of this depends not on the vocabulary (which tempts us simply to assign modern senses to the words), but on the vocabulary of meaning available at the time. As Taylor points out, 'thyself' has none of the modern connotations of 'thy self', no more than did Polonius' 'to thine own self be true'; the Greeks 'didn't normally speak of the human agent as "ho autos", or use the term in a context which we would translate with the indefinite article' (p. 113). To understand what the Greeks, or Polonius meant, one has to understand the linguistic web of meanings in which the particular utterance is made. In carrying out such an analysis, whether within *Hamlet* or at other moments in the evolution of Western culture, one is carrying out a task New Historicists proclaim to be very dear to their hearts.[88] For what is being attempted is an analysis of a language of, in Clifford Geertz's term, 'thick description'.[89] It is a language particularly dense with meaning and particularly culturally bound, as it makes sense of the actions and feelings of a person within their culture. Taylor, in producing a chronological framework within which to discuss the development of this language, has performed one of the New Historicists' most talked-about projects.

Taylor's analysis of this language of inwardness is structured around his examination of the different meanings various cultures, as represented by various authors, have given to the inner–outer divide. These different meanings are the product of this divide's differing relationship to the person's moral goods. To understand what moral goods are, and how they are an essential part of a person's inwardness, it is necessary to explain Taylor's picture of the person.

The fundamental premiss of Taylor's argument is that every person has an inescapable need for 'strong evaluation';[90] that is, every person feels the need to ask questions about what are their moral goods. Taylor defines moral in this context in a wide sense; morality is not only concerned with questions of what it is right to do, but also with questions of what it is good to be. Moreover, a moral good must have a communal aspect; it must not be 'rendered valid by [a person's] own desires, inclinations or choices, but rather stand independent of these and offer standards by which they can be judged' (p. 4). Every person, then, will have a range of moral goods, and those goods will have some kind of communal aspect. The person will also need to know in what relation he or she

[88] See e.g. Greenblatt, *Renaissance Self-Fashioning*, 3–4.

[89] See Clifford Geertz, *The Interpretation of Cultures* (New York: Basic Books, 1973), 3–30. As Geertz points out when introducing it, the phrase comes from the work of Gilbert Ryle, who talks of the need for 'thick descriptions' of actions.

[90] Taylor, *Sources of the Self*, 4. Further references to this book are given after quotations in the text.

stands to those goods. The self, in Taylor's definition, is the point of perspective formed by our questioning of what our goods are and our decision as to how we are positioned in relation to them. The self is, then, a point of perspective.

Being the result of the person's own decisions, the self is also constructed by and of self-agency. At the same time, it exists in relationship to one's goods, dependent on them though distinct from them. Taylor describes as his 'entire way of proceeding' the 'mapping' of 'connections between senses of the self and moral visions' (p. x). Such a self, as a point of perspective by which one's relationship to one's values is articulated, is important to identity. It is not identity's equivalent, but an area within identity, specifically verbal, and bound up with the interpretation of actions and events. Taylor sums up this three-sided relationship: 'The notion of the self which connects it to our need for identity is meant to pick out this crucial feature of human agency, that we cannot do without some orientation to the good, that we each essentially are (i.e., define ourselves inter alia by) where we stand on this' (p. 33). Thus, by charting the differing relationship of the inside–outside divide to various authors' moral goods, Taylor is charting the development of the (re)sources of the self and so is charting moments in the making of the modern identity. His title is complex and precise.

How, then, does this make a virtue of Kelly's limitations? Taylor himself suggests no such connection, taking pains to distinguish his picture of the person from psychological views. His concept of the self, he argues, is quite un-Freudian, as it is quite unlike the concept of the Ego, which Taylor argues is simply, in its ideal state, a lucid calculator of pay-offs, unconnected with the good or identity (p. 34). Similarly, Taylor distinguishes himself from Rogerian phenomenological approaches, which see the self actively seeking to fulfil its (already present) shape, drawing its purposes, goals, and life-plans out of itself (p. 38). For Taylor, there is no pre-existent shape to the self which needs fulfilling.

His picture of the person, however, in this and in other areas is compatible with Kelly's. Taylor's view of the inward aspects of identity as a vitally important, but non-essential construct which is dependent on one's own agency as well as a web of communal relations, parallels Kelly's view. So does the importance his account attaches to cognition, creation, and process. Where Kelly pictures the person as a scientist-philosopher, Taylor would view the person as an ethical-philosopher. The match is not exact, but it has many points and areas of overlap. Most importantly, Taylor's goods, as sources of self, are analogous to Kelly's constructs, which were sources of personality. Taylor's chronology of those sources, then, provides a way of locating Hamlet's constructs in history. This chronology, incidentally, refutes—from the standpoint of another discipline—the various but coherent historical accounts of the self or subjectivity advanced by New Historicists and Cultural Materialists.

Taylor discusses, as has been said, the development of the resources of inwardness through the use of the relationship of the inner–outer divide to reason and moral goods. Taylor begins his historical analysis with a prelude, designed to show just how different previous languages of inwardness can be from contemporary languages. He begins by examining the writings of Homer. As Bruno Snell pointed out in *The Discovery of the Mind* (1953), the Homeric hero has no unitary place of consciousness; instead of words which could be translated as 'mind', there is instead a multiplicity of mind locations—the spirit, the heart, the lungs. The hero's consciousness can be said to be fragmented. More, there is an unsettling—to a modern reader—lack of personal responsibility or personal volition. When a hero carries out some particularly remarkable deed, or makes a disastrous mistake, this is ascribed to the influence of a god.[91]

Taylor begins his own analysis with Plato's very different picture of the person. Within Plato's writings, the mind is a unitary space, and one of the basic aims of reason is to achieve self-mastery. For Plato, life was something to be lived in accordance with a set of goods which existed externally of the person, the discovery of which demonstrated one's ability to think rationally. 'Plato', Taylor argues, 'offers what we can call a substantive conception of reason. Rationality is tied to the perception of order; and so to realize our capacity for reason is to see the order as it is.'[92] The most famous example of the exterior nature of this order of goods is Plato's theory of ideal forms.

Augustine marks a radical change from this view, a view which is dominant in the classical world. Augustine believes that the order of goods, which is explicitly the order of God, is to be discovered by looking within: 'Noli foras ire, in teipsum redi; in interiore homine habitat veritas'[93] ('Do not desire to search outwards, but rather return into yourself; truth dwells within man'). Augustine insisted on the importance of the first-person standpoint to the search for truth and on the importance not only of the thing experienced but on the activity of seeing. Taylor describes this change as a turn to 'the inwardness of radical reflexivity', as opposed to Plato's reflexivity of looking after one's self or soul (p. 131). This insistence on the activity of perception represents the attempt to 'become aware of our awareness, try to experience our experiencing, focus on the way the world is *for* us' (p. 130).

Augustine is writing some one thousand years before the Cultural Material-

[91] Bruno Snell, *The Discovery of the Mind: The Greek Origins of European Thought* (Oxford: Basil Blackwell, 1953), 6–22. For a development of Snell's arguments with reference to Greek tragedy, and an exploration of the difficulty that such differing conceptions of the mind and will provide, see 'Intimations of the will in Greek tragedy', in Jean-Pierre Vernant and P. Vidal-Naquet, *Tragedy and Myth in Ancient Greece*, trans. Janet Lloyd (Brighton: Harvester, 1981), 28–62. Snell's argument is based upon a strong metaphor theory akin to that of Soskice.

[92] Taylor, *Sources of the Self*, 121.

[93] Augustine, *De Vera Religione* 34. 72; quoted in Taylor, *Sources of the Self*, 129. Further references to this book are given after quotations in the text.

ists' magical date of 1660, after which interiority is said to have become possible. Yet Augustine, as Michel Foucault also pointed out in his *Technologies of the Self*, clearly had a profound interest in, and a complex understanding of, interiority.[94] The interior of man became a hallowed space for Augustine, as the place through which one could truly understand oneself; the place, that is, where one could understand one's nature before God. The mention of Michel Foucault makes clear another way in which Taylor's work should be of interest to New Historicism. For *Sources of the Self* can be seen as the fulfilment of the task Foucault set up for himself in *Technologies of the Self*; Taylor produces what Foucault had hoped to—an account of the ways in which people's self-agency has developed.

Yet though Augustine does have a sense of interiority, he does not have one which has available all the modern sources of inwardness. Although Augustine's order of goods is internal to the person, it is still given by God. In a sense, the person looks (with)in to look out. Descartes changes this. For Descartes, the perception of the order of goods is no longer the proof and criteria of rational thought. Instead, such an order is arrived at by thinking according to correct methods. The order of goods is thus the product of thinking; rationality has become procedural and not, as it was for Plato, substantive. 'What has happened,' Taylor argues, is 'that God's existence has become a stage in *my* progress towards science through the methodical ordering of evident insight. God's existence is a theorem in *my* system of perfect science.'[95] The order of goods, then, is no longer given, but internally constructed.

Moreover, Descartes's criteria of rationality, and his premiss that one had to be free of the illusion which mingles mind with matter, led to a new model of rational self-mastery which presents it as a matter of instrumental control. For, 'to be free from the illusion which mingles mind with matter is to have an understanding of the latter which facilitates its control. . . . The hegemony of reason is defined no longer as that of a dominant vision but rather in terms of a directing agency subordinating a functional domain.'[96] As Taylor points out, this instrumental possibility to remake oneself parallels, though it has no causal relationship to, the wider and more rigorous application of discipline through a variety of fields which Foucault charted.[97] Locke is seen to interiorize the self further, by identifying it purely with the instrumental power to remake, and seeing it as a perfectly detachable consciousness. Taylor calls Locke's version of the self 'the punctual self', the image of the point being used to convey Locke's sense that 'the real self is "extensionless"; it is nowhere but in this power to fix things as objects'.[98]

Taylor carries on his study to the twentieth century. However, his account

[94] Foucault, *Technologies of the Self*, 14.

[95] Taylor, *Sources of the Self*, 157.

[96] Ibid. 149.

[97] See e.g. Foucault, *Discipline and Punish*, *passim*.

[98] Taylor, *Sources of the Self*, 172.

of the sources of the self up to Locke provides a chronological perspective against which *Hamlet* could be placed in order to develop a sense of the cultural resources of the self available to Shakespeare. Yet such an approach would remain in the history of ideas mould, and not allow the possibility of innovation or differentiation to the play. It is still not clear how Taylor's approach helps to render the approach derived from Kelly's personal construct theory descriptively fluent both in history and degree.

Kelly's theory, as was said, saw personality as the product of a framework of constructs. The constructs were internally constitutive, as one viewed oneself through them. For example, when Hamlet viewed his father as a god, and Claudius as a beast, he placed himself along the line which can be thought to connect these poles; upsettingly and confusingly for the Prince, he placed himself towards the bestial end, akin with Claudius. Hamlet's sense of self, then, could here be represented as a point on a line (though it was in no Lockean sense punctual). It was not a gap, but a point. This had the great advantage of allowing it to be talked about clearly and specifically, but at the same time lost any sense of degrees of innerness, or of the depth associated with gaps. Taylor talks about the self as being the perspective, or orientation, one has to one's moral goods. To express the need for this orientation he uses the analogy of a map; just as it is no good simply having a map of the landscape you occupy, so it is no good to know simply what your moral goods are. You need to know where on the map you stand, and in which direction you are facing, before you can progress forward, make a decision, and so on.

Now, noting the analogy between Taylor's goods and Kelly's constructs, one could place either on this map. So, for instance, there could be a lake representing bestiality and a mountain representing godliness. One's self, according to Taylor, would be derived from taking a bearing first from one of these features, and then from the other. This would produce two lines, at whose intersection one would find one's point of perspective or self. This 'triangulation' is implicit in Kelly's use of triads of persons to uncover the bipolar nature of constructs. One could imagine the point on the line between the poles of the construct being extended perpendicularly. Another line extended from another construct, that perhaps of the existence–non-existence construct of the 'To be or not to be' soliloquy, would give an intersection.[99] This would both locate and orientate Hamlet on such a map. The intersection would be his sense of self, that is the place or area of self-agency within identity.

Interiority, conceived through this metaphoric model of a map, is not a gap, nor a point, but an intersection. Seeing it thus provides a way of describing

[99] Although Taylor does not note this, one is unlikely to occupy a single point on the map. As one can have, and nearly always does have, relationships with goods or constructs which are in conflict with each other, such a bearing-taking would not result in a perfect intersection on the map. Rather one would have several points on the map. This could be thought of as delimiting an area of perspective.

both the constructed and relational aspects of interiority. The map can in turn be made historically descriptive, by providing some basic features of a symbolic landscape. Like a medieval map, it would have a centre, in this case not Jerusalem, but Locke's punctual self. The border of the land mass around this point would be the inner–outer divide. The land mass would represent 'that Within', the ocean that without.

Where would Plato's point of perspective be located? Plato's moral goods—as they were external and given—would be located outside the land mass, in the ocean; they could be represented as islands. His point of perspective would be closer to the shore than Homer's, for example, as Plato had a greater sense of self-agency. Augustine's moral goods, by contrast with Plato's, would be features of the landscape of the main land mass, as they were to be found 'in interiore homine'. They would produce intersections in the interior of the land mass that is 'that Within'. Similarly Descartes's moral goods, being both interior and self-constructed, would exist in a very close relationship to the epicentre of the land mass, and Locke's punctual self, being the continuity of consciousness alone, would be in the centre.

Such an analogy is productive in broad outline only. However, such a map is descriptive both of historical location and degrees of interiority. Interiority, within this more spatial metaphor, is not only not a gap but an intersection, but also not a well but a continent. Depth is replaced by distance. Moreover, as an intersection and not a gap, interiority is not a series of static absences, but a central area created through a web of relationships. 'That within' can now be seen to be textually produced, and historically located, and to be no critics' invention.

To place Hamlet on this map, would be to locate both his interiority in its historical position, and to express the innerness of his interiority. Placing Claudius and Gertrude on the same map would also produce a comparative sense of the difference between the Prince's inner world and that of those around him. Hamlet's 'that Within' speech and its context provide a productive starting-point. Hamlet's speech comes in response to his mother's request to put off his 'nightly colour'. The Queen ends her persuasion with a question:

> Thou know'st 'tis common, all that liues must dye,
> Passing through Nature, to Eternity.
> *Hamlet.* I Madam, it is common.
> *Queen.* If it be;
> Why seemes it so particular with thee.
>
> (I. 2. 72–5)

Hamlet, as has been argued, does not answer this question, but rather seizes on and denies the allegation he sees in his mother's use of 'seemes'. However, the Queen's question is interesting in itself. It makes no allowance for what one would imagine to be the obvious answer; that death seems 'particular' to

Hamlet because it was his father, in particular, who died. This is not merely evidence of the Queen's obtuseness, though it may in part be that. More interestingly, the question actively works to deny the value of the obvious answer. For 'particular' is set up as one term of a rational distinction, or pole of a construct. The other is 'common'. The linguistic web it is set into devalues 'particular', while establishing 'common' as the criteria for rational and socially valued behaviour. The 'common' course is that of 'Nature', which is in turn the god-given course, leading as it does to 'Eternity'. 'Particular' is thus unnatural and ungodly.

Claudius uses a similar construct, with the same associations though more heavily stressed, in reply to Hamlet's answer to his mother. The Prince's continued and unique grief is,

> a fault to Heauen,
> A fault against the Dead, a fault to Nature,
> To Reason most absurd, whose common Theame
> Is death of Fathers.
>
> (I. 2. 101–4)

Where, then, would Claudius and Gertrude appear on the map which has been outlined? Their moral goods, along with Plato's, are not on the land of 'that Within' but in the ocean. The 'Reason' that Hamlet should act in accordance with is not something arrived at through the individual's experience, but rather a common and inherited tradition of action and thought, which can be understood by the reasonable study of 'Nature'. One's relationship to these goods is, as it is for Plato, a question of recognizing the pre-existent, ideal scheme of things. Notions of the discreteness or uniqueness of the 'I' is frowned upon, devalued.

Hamlet, however, does not argue from the same basis. He does not argue, as he might, that Gertrude's and Claudius' reasoning has misunderstood 'Nature'. Instead, he puts forward a quite different construct in his answer to his mother, implying a quite different relationship to differently placed moral goods. The Prince, as has been seen, has as the poles of his construct 'Seemes' and 'that Within', and identifies himself with the latter:

> Seemes Madam? Nay, it is: I know not Seemes.
> 'Tis not alone my Inky Cloake (good Mother)
> . . . . .
>
> Together with all Formes, Moods, shewes of Griefe,
> That can denote me truly. These indeed Seeme,
> For they are actions that a man might play:
> But I haue that Within, which passeth show.
>
> (I. 2. 76–85)

Hamlet, then, in seizing on the issue of identity unintentionally implicit in his mother's use of seems, discusses what denotes him in terms of an inner–outer construct. This, it is important to note, is quite different from the King's and the Queen's use of a common–particular construct.

The Prince's identity, his 'I', is not 'alone' constructed from features in the common, external and visible world; his goods, in terms of the map, are not predominantly in the ocean. Rather, what he values especially, and what he feels crucially defines his identity, is his relationship with his inner world, his relationship to the landscape of his island. In valuing the 'I' in this way, Hamlet is not valuing the 'particular'. For it is not the 'I''s contradistinction to the common that gives it its value to the Prince. Rather it is the 'I''s unique separateness, and its ability to be its own source of value, that the Prince asserts. Such a stance, more modern than Claudius' and Gertrude's, is also rhetorically weaker. For Hamlet cannot bring the weight of common-senses or human commonality to his side. It no longer makes sense for him to appeal to Nature or his natural qualities, as does Claudius in reply to the Prince:

> 'Tis vnmanly greefe,
> It shewes a will most incorrect to Heauen,
> A Heart vnfortified, a Minde impatient,
> An Vnderstanding simple, and vnschool'd.
>
> (I. 2. 94–8)

The sense of Claudius switching into a standard argument is strong here, and such rehearsed common arguments dwarf—in their length, lucidity, and argumentative force—Hamlet's own fragile assertion of 'that Within'.

Hamlet's inner landscape remains barely described by contrast, though clearly valued, as the Prince continually, repetitively, returns to it. His soliloquy after the court has left the stage allows us to locate more accurately the position of his self on the map. What is immediately clear is that Hamlet, while he does not care for 'seeming' in its sense of put on appearance, knows, and is profoundly interested in, the seeming of interpretation:

> O God, O God!
> How weary, stale, flat, and vnprofitable
> Seemes to me all the vses of this world.
>
> (I. 2. 132–5)

That 'to me' is important. 'To me' is the Prince's own tag; it reflects his awareness that he is construing and his concern with the activity and the transformative nature of his understanding. This concern is made clear by what is in a way a repetition and expansion of this passage, the passage where Hamlet explains to the recently arrived Rosencrantz and Guildenstern what troubles him:

> and indeed, it goes so heavenly with my dispositi-
> on; that this goodly frame the Earth, seemes *to me* a ster-
> ill Promontory; this most excellent Canopy the Ayre,

> . . . why it appears no other thing
> *to mee*, then a foule and pestilent congregation of vapours. What a piece of work is a man! How Noble in
> Reason? how infinite in faculty?
> . . . and yet *to me*, what
> is this Quintessence of dust? Man delights not me.
> (2. 2. 298–309; my emphasis)

Hamlet, in focusing on the activity of his perception, mirrors Augustine's turn 'in interiore homine'. Doing so, he demonstrates the same 'radical reflexivity', to use Taylor's term, and one could indeed describe Hamlet through Taylor's description of Augustine: Hamlet, like Augustine, is making the attempt to 'become aware of our awareness, try to experience our experiencing, focus on the way the world is *for* us'.[100]

Hamlet, in fact, goes further towards the interior of the I than Augustine. For he countenances the idea that thought constitutes the goods themselves. Earlier in his conversation with his boyhood friends, he compares Denmark to a prison. They object, and he concedes that it is not then a prison to them:

> For there is nothing
> either good or bad, but thinking makes it so: to me it is
> a prison.
> (2. 2. 250–3)

The Prince here matches the disengaged subject seen in the writings of Descartes. Denmark can be a prison to Hamlet alone—the commonwealth of interpretation, the commonality of family, such externals have no say in the matter. Hamlet is an island to himself. Denmark is a prison, and Hamlet a prisoner, because Hamlet thinks it so. It is tempting to describe such a position as Cartesian, so placing Hamlet at the beginning of the development of modern sources of the self, and also possessed of such sources. However, such a move would be over-hasty.

Hamlet's self, his place on the map, is far further than Gertrude's or Claudius' into the middle of the landscape of his island, as are his goods. Or rather, one strand of the Prince's thinking is. For, as has been seen, the Prince also employs older versions and views of interiority, such as the theory of humours. It is important to remember that the sources of the self do not fade away. Even the Homeric senses of self, for instance, are present to the modern sense of self, in phrases such as, 'he's beside himself'. The sources of the self, in fact, might be thought of as being residual, dominant, and emergent, in Raymond Williams's terms. Indeed, the Prince may switch to a more exterior concept of the sources of the self after his return from his sea voyage, in Act 5. In that act, Hamlet pays far less attention to the shaping powers of his perception, the action of his understanding. Instead, he registers a sense of a given intendedness of life.

[100] Taylor, *Sources of the Self*, 130.

It is tempting to see this as Hamlet's acceptance of providence, the god-given ordering of life. *Hamlet* is, from its beginning, not only full of specifically religious language, but intent on making religious questions central to the audience's understanding of what takes place.[101] Most obviously, there is the nature of the Ghost and of the religion of the court at Elsinore, about which so much has been written.[102] So when Hamlet declares, 'There's a Diuinity that shapes our ends, | Rough-hew them how we will' (5. 2. 10–11), or when he dismisses his sense of foreboding at the forthcoming fencing match with Laertes with the words, 'Not a whit, we defie Augury; there's a speciall Prouidence in the fall of a sparrow' (5. 2. 165–6), it is tempting to see him accepting a Christian, and perhaps particularly Calvinist, belief. (The mention of a sparrow's fall is a reference to Matthew 10: 29, the importance of which verse Calvin insisted on.) Yet, as Alan Sinfield has pointed out, *Hamlet* often explores the overlap between Protestantism and the stoicism of Seneca. And as Calvin noted, it was especially the doctrine of special providence that some attacked as being a form of stoicism: 'Those who cast obloquy on this doctrine [of special providence], calumniate it as the dogma of the Stoics concerning fate.'[103] The Prince's comment concerning the sparrow, according to Sinfield, focuses attention on the play's exploration of areas of known dissatisfaction with Protestant theology.

Whichever tradition of thought it derives from or confirms, Hamlet in Act 5 is more aware of a given quality to his life—as he might be, considering the fortuitous events of his sea voyage. This change in Hamlet is signalled strongly in his willingness to identify himself with his name as he steps forward to declare himself at Ophelia's burial: 'This is I, *Hamlet* the Dane' (5. 1. 254–5). Such an assertion of identity as a grammatic, familial, and national location does not mean that the issues of identity and identification have ceased to be important for the Prince, in that he has solved them. There is no sense in which the Prince has arrived at self-knowledge. There is no point at which the Prince tells us what he has learnt about himself. All the questions that he has raised remain. Indeed, his musings over the nature of man continue. His declaration of himself follows on from his pondering over the nature of man's mortality initiated by the gravedigger's unearthing of Yorick's skull.

Rather than suggesting self-mastery, in asserting the grammatic unity of

[101] A. C. Bradley noted the insistently religious nature of *Hamlet* long ago in his published lectures. See A. C. Bradley, *Shakespearean Tragedy: Lectures on 'Hamlet', 'Othello', 'King Lear' and 'Macbeth* (Macmillan & Co., 1904; repr. Harmondsworth: Penguin, 1991), 127–66 (164–6).

[102] For the former (and latter) see J. Dover Wilson, *What Happens in Hamlet* (3rd edn.; Cambridge: Cambridge University Press, 1970; first pub. 1935); B. L. Joseph, *Conscience and the King* (London: Chatto & Windus, 1953), 32–6; Eleanor Prosser, *Hamlet and Revenge* (Stanford, Calif.: Stanford University Press, 1967), 97–117; Barbara Everett, '*Hamlet*: A Time to Die', *SS* 30 (1977), 117–34; Arthur McGee *The Elizabethan Hamlet* (New Haven, Conn.: Yale University Press, 1987), *passim*; John S. Wilks, *The Idea of Conscience in Renaissance Tragedy* (London: Routledge, 1990), 100–24.

[103] Quoted in Sinfield, *Faultlines*, 229.

'I', and the clear familial location of '*Hamlet* the Dane', the Prince seems to accept that his questions must remain, and decides not to worry actively after them. (He has adopted the attitude, that is, that Keats labelled 'negative capability'.)[104] He has accepted the 'I' as an inescapable place, whose continuity provides its own form of identity. If the Prince has not come to self-knowledge, then neither has he achieved self-mastery, the one relying on the other as it does. Indeed, the terms seem rather inappropriate to describe the Prince, and this inappropriateness gave rise to the hesitation in describing the Prince as Cartesian. Self-mastery and self-knowledge are terms which are linked to an instrumental, cause and effect view of identity which, as the Prince discovers, cannot describe him satisfactorily. The critical tradition has overwhelmingly employed such Cartesian approaches, as was seen in Part II. To offer such a theory is to cast oneself in the role of Claudius or Polonius, a casting whose unsatisfactoriness is made plain in those characters' attempts to describe the Prince. Claudius, for instance, tells Rosencrantz and Guildenstern of '*Hamlets* transformation' (2. 2. 5) and asks them to find out 'What it should bee . . . that thus hath put him | So much from th'vnderstanding of himselfe' (2. 2. 7–10). Polonius searches along similar lines, assuring the king that he has found 'The very cause of *Hamlets* Lunacie' (2. 2. 49).

Yet to understand Hamlet is not the same as understanding a series of cause and effect relationships. Guildenstern tries to sound the Prince, as Hamlet himself points out, as if he were a musical instrument; as if, that is, Hamlet is nothing other than a 'machine', as he describes his body in his love-letter to Ophelia. Indeed, Guildenstern makes of the Prince something less than a musical instrument, since he is willing to try to sound the Prince, but refuses to try to get a sound out of the recorder Hamlet offers him. As Hamlet points out,

> Why looke you now, how vnworthy a thing you make of me: you would play vpon mee; you would seeme to know my stops: you would pluck out the heart of my Mysterie; . . .
> Why do you thinke, that I am easier to bee plaid on, then a Pipe?
>
> (3. 2. 350–8)

Hamlet is not only not easier to play than a pipe, but he cannot be understood as a set of regulated actions. He is rather a 'Mysterie'. Whether 'mystery' is taken in its non-theological senses, as 'a hidden or secret thing, a matter unexplained or inexplicable; something beyond human knowledge', or whether it carries also its theological associations of 'a religious truth known only from divine revelation' (*OED* II.5a. and I.2), it is certainly something more valued and complex than a scheme of cause and effect. Of course, if it is taken

[104] See Keats's letter to his brothers George and Tom of 21/27 (?) Dec. 1817. *The Letters of John Keats 1814–1821*, ed. Hyder Edward Rollins, 2 vols. (Cambridge, Mass.: Harvard University Press, 1958), 195.

in its theological sense, then it begins to open up the questions of direct expression and metaphor mentioned above. The Prince would seem to be self-consciously gesturing towards the area which I invoked as a parallel to explain his predicament. Such a use of the expressive resources of metaphor will be considered in the next section.

Hamlet is also inadequately explained in terms of self-knowledge and self-mastery because his location on our map continually changes. His constructs keep on collapsing their terms. If one plotted the points of perspective that the Prince occupied on the map, he would be seen to be wandering over it. His soliloquies and conversations make clear that the clarity of a single location never remains available to him for long. His soliloquies, in fact, rather than portraying a developing and clarifying chain of thought, are more like the diary entries of his life. Hamlet's soliloquies are analogous to diary entries because they partake of a diary's 'peculiar truth', as Mary Warnock puts it in her book *Memory* (1987); 'the demand that each day be written as it comes'.[105] Hamlet's soliloquies capture this immediacy. They also partake of Warnock's other defining feature of a diary, that it should not be interchangeable with a conversation, for the diarist has no one to manipulate apart from himself.

To picture the soliloquies in these terms is to note the importance of memory within them. They are all moments of memory; in their various ways, they all echo (one perhaps 'pre-echoing') the soliloquy of the Prince after he has talked with the Ghost, a soliloquy already quoted:

> Remember thee?
> I, thou poore Ghost, while memory holds a seate
> In this distracted Globe: Remember thee?
> Yea, . . .
>
> (I. 5. 95–8)[106]

Indeed, this soliloquy becomes almost a literal diary entry at its ends when Hamlet notes, 'My Tables, my Tables; meet it is I set it downe' (I. 5. 107–8). In calling for a book here, Hamlet has provided problems for many producers, who are very unwilling to allow a book so dramatically to take centre stage.[107] Yet the act of writing deserves such prominence, because it captures and encapsulates Hamlet's diarist-like desire for truth through the acts of memory. Here, as elsewhere in the Prince's soliloquies, as in a diary, the desire for understanding commingles with the desire for expression.

This interest in memory should not be surprising; as Warnock points out,

[105] Mary Warnock, *Memory* (Faber: London, 1987), 109.

[106] Frances A. Yates would argue that the Globe theatre itself was a physical realization of a Renaissance memory system. See particularly the chapter on 'Fludd's Memory Theatre and the Globe Theatre' in her *The Art of Memory* (London: Pimlico, 1992; first pub. 1966), 310–29. If this is accepted, Hamlet's reference to 'this distracted Globe' becomes yet richer in meaning.

[107] See e.g. Steven Berkoff's discussion of this scene in *I am Hamlet* (London: Faber and Faber, 1989), 44–5.

memory and personal identity are 'twin subjects' whose relationship has been a topic 'central to philosophy for centuries'.[108] The play is full of direct references to memory; no other Shakespearian play, in fact, has so many references to 'memory', 'remembrance', and variant words. The soliloquies, however, in their repetitive nature, in their returning to the same object of description, the Prince himself, are memory in action. They are moments not only of memory but of recollection; typically, the spur to soliloquize is given by something that recalls Hamlet to the demands of the past (and in particular the Ghost's demand for revenge). They are moments, that is, in which memory realizes that memory is being experienced. Warnock describes such recognition in terms of pleasure (p. 145); as the Prince realizes, memory can also be a place of sorrow, and, in Kelly's terms, threat. Having seen the passion of the player recounting Priam's slaughter, Hamlet must recollect the murder of his own father, and his own response to it. This is not a pleasure, but rather a burden, leading to his reflection: 'Oh what a Rogue and Pesant slaue am I?' (2. 2. 551).

The soliloquies, in their repetitive return to the same object of description, the Prince himself, in their return to wonder at this 'I', become a form of autobiography. They create a continuity of this inner 'I'. They express, in Warnock's words, 'the continuity that constitutes a human person' (p. 125). In so doing they create a story for Hamlet, the story that is his life. As Warnock puts it, 'the pleasures of memory are here brought to bear, to make up the story of a life' (p. 125). The Prince's self may, then, be seen as a story, and the soliloquies as a formal experiment to express such an inner narrative. If this is so, why should Hamlet's understanding of 'that Within', his self, be understood not predominantly in terms of self-mastery but rather in terms of self-creation? His soliloquies would not be expected to present an analysis of Hamlet, but would rather *be* him. The Prince's self would be a particular form of story, a form which is quite distinct from all the other forms of personal stories within the play.

It is now time to bring back on stage Hazlitt's Montaignesque conception of character. Taylor's work is again helpful here, facilitating a clearer description of this character and, at the same time, of the Prince's self as a particular, historically innovative, form of story.[109] Taylor argues that a fork occurs in the sources of the self after Augustine, a fork which occurs at around the time of Descartes and which leads to the production of a second kind of radical reflexivity. This, Taylor argues (substantiating Hazlitt's assertions), can be seen in the writings of Montaigne. Montaigne set out, as he explains in his foreword to the *Essays*, to leave a literary record of himself for his family and friends.

[108] Warnock, *Memory*, pp. vii, 53. Further references to this book are given after quotations in the text.

[109] The central importance of Taylor's work to the controversies of self is being increasingly recognized. See e.g. David Aers, 'A Whisper in the Ear of Early Modernists', in Aers (ed.), *Culture and History 1350–1600* (London, 1992), 177–202 (183), and Hanson, *Discovering the Subject*, 152. Hanson cites Aers.

'Thus,' Montaigne says in his introduction, 'my selfe am the groundworke of my booke.'[110] Taylor, as has been mentioned previously, notes that Montaigne began with the hope that this picture of his inner world would serve to discover a stable core of being: 'This is the virtually unanimous direction of ancient thought: beneath the changing and shifting desires in the unwise soul, and over against the fluctuating fortunes of the external world, our true nature, reason, provides a foundation, unwavering and constant.' With such a belief, Taylor also notes, 'the modern problem of identity remains unintelligible'.[111]

What Montaigne discovered in his interior, however, was a landscape of 'terrifying inner instability'.[112] The interior of his 'groundwork' in the *Essays* is made up to such a degree of flux that it appears more akin to an ocean. So in Montaigne's first chapter, 'By Divers Meanes Men Come Unto a Like End', he is led to note, 'Surely, man is a wonderfull, vaine, divers and wavering subject: it is very hard to ground any directly-constant and uniforme judgement upon him.'[113] This oceanic image is ever-present through his works. In the first chapter of the second book, 'Of the inconstancie of our actions', Montaigne notes that even good authors 'doe ill, and take a wrong course, wilfully to opinionate themselves about framing a constant and solide contexture of us' (ii. 6). For in man, 'all is but changing, motion, and inconstancy . . . We float and waver between divers opinions: we will nothing freely, nothing absolutely' (ii. 7). And so, 'If I speake diversly of my selfe, it is because I looke diversly upon my selfe' (ii. 10).

Nothing certain of this inner land, bar this fact of inconstancy, is learnt throughout the three books. What then is their point? It is that which Montaigne's foreword sets out. For his form, the essay, sought to express this inner diversity, and so express the author himself, his oceanic groundwork.[114] So, at the beginning of the second chapter of his third book, 'Of Repenting', Montaigne writes those lines already quoted in relation to Florizel's wish for Perdita to be a 'wave o'th sea':

> Others fashion man, I repeat him; and represent a particular one, but ill made; and whom were I to forme a new, he should be far other then he is; but he is now made. And though the lines of my picture change and vary, yet loose they not themselves. . . . *Constancy it selfe is nothing but a languishing and wavering dance.* (iii. 21)

Montaigne keeps on describing his diversity, not as a catalogue, but because diversity is what he finds in 'that Within'. As his use of the image of the picture suggests, this is the equivalent of shifting perspectives on the same basic shape;

[110] Montaigne, i. 12 ('The Author to the Reader').

[111] Taylor, *Sources of the Self*, 178.

[112] Ibid. 178.

[113] Montaigne, i. 16. Further references to the *Essays* are given after quotations in the text.

[114] This aim was recognized by his readers, some of whom also seem to have recognized the innovatory achievement the *Essays* represent. So Samuel Daniel, in his prefatory poem to Florio's translation of the *Essays*, writes: 'This Prince *Montaigne* (if he be not more) | Hath more adventur'd of his owne estate | Then ever man did of himself before' (i. 6).

it is always within the frame, and recognizable as a whole, though the proportion of every line has changed. This is suggestive of the sense of the journeying of the Prince's self, a sense derived from the use of the metaphor of a map. (The self as point of perspective, it will be remembered, kept on changing locations.) This similarity is confirmed as Montaigne carries on his declaration,

> I cannot settle my object; it goest so unquietly and staggering, with a naturall drunkennesse. I take it in this plight, as it is at th'instant I ammuse my selfe about it. I describe not the essence, but the passage; not a passage from age to age, or as the people reckon, from seaven yeares to seaven, but from day to day, from minute to minute . . . Were my mind setled, I would not essay, but resolve my selfe. (iii. 21)

The repetitive nature of the essay is the formal device by which Montaigne represents the truth, as he sees it, that life is not being—'essence'—but becoming—'passage'.

This attempt to express the accreted particularity of an individual life, this attempt to map the journey of self-exploration, is quite in contrast to Descartes's route towards self-mastery. Where Cartesianism, in Taylor's words, 'gives us a science of the subject in its general essence', Montaigne's approach aimed 'to identify the individual in his or her unrepeatable difference'. Montaigne's repetitive viewing of the subject did this by providing 'a critique of first-person self-interpretations, rather than by the proofs of impersonal reasoning'.[115] Moreover, Montaigne's approach suggests that part of one's 'passage' or voyage in this ocean of the self is the essay itself. In other words, the essays are in part constitutive of Montaigne; a part of Montaigne's inner world literally is literary. This is the position that Hazlitt, Oscar Wilde, and others have already been seen expressing. Montaigne formulates this position in the eighteenth chapter of his second book, 'Of giving the lie':

> In framing this pourtraite by my selfe, I have so often beene faine to frizle and trimme me, that so I might the better extract my selfe, that the patterne is thereby confirmed, and in some sort formed. Drawing my selfe for others, I have drawn my self with purer and better colours, then were my first. I have no more made my booke, then my book hath made me. A book consubstantiall to his Author: Of a peculiar and fit occupation. A member of my life. (ii. 400)

Hamlet's repetitions, his soliloquies, are essays which share in Montaigne's techniques.[116] They are his attempts to capture himself, showing his frustration at his inability to capture a solid picture of that self. Shorn of Montaigne's moments of formal self-consciousness, they are the dramatized moment of Montaigne's reflections. Hamlet, like Montaigne, is also dissatisfied with the 'proofs of impersonal reasoning', progressing instead through 'a critique of

[115] Taylor, *Sources of the Self*, 182.

[116] The question of whether this is the result of Montaigne's influence upon Shakespeare is too large to be considered here. For an introductory discussion of this debate see Harold Jenkins's introduction to *Hamlet*, 108–10.

first-person self-interpretations'—through a variety of the ways in which things 'seem to' him.

Hamlet's soliloquies, mirroring the formal techniques of Montaigne's essays, are the members of his life, the points, secured by memory, on the indeterminate map of his inner world. They are his diary, the moments when he has noted down the particular form of his 'natural drunkenness', which, when held together in a chain, give the structure of his passage, identifying the individual in his 'unrepeatable difference', and creating the narrative shape of his inner life. (Like Hamlet's soliloquies, Montaigne's *Essays* would fulfil Warnock's criteria for both diary and autobiography.) One may say that the Prince's interiority is more modern than Claudius' and Gertrude's in that it is Montaignesque. This is to interpret the Prince in terms of self-exploration and self-discovery, part of a line quite different from that of the theorists of self-mastery. It is to refuse an empirical tradition of factual statement devoid of any figurative nature, a line that finds it hard to talk in any meaningful sense about interiority at all. Fashioning, so central to Greenblatt's thinking on identity, and its related instrumental stance, is irrelevant to this approach. Creation, exploration, mapping is all.

Such a self-portrait, whether that of Montaigne or of Shakespeare's Hamlet, inaugurates 'the search for the self in order to come to terms with oneself', as Taylor puts it, a search which has 'become one of the fundamental themes of our modern culture'. For,

> There is a question about ourselves—which we roughly gesture at with the term identity—which cannot be sufficiently answered with any general doctrine of human nature. The search for identity can be seen as the search for what I essentially am. But this can no longer be sufficiently defined in terms of some universal description of human agency as such, as soul, reason, or will. There still remains a question about me, and that is why I think of myself as a self. This word now circumscribes an area of questioning. It designates the kind of being of which this question of identity can be asked.[117]

Shakespeare's Hamlet is this kind of being.

The aims stated at the beginning of the chapter are now satisfied. A clear terminology, borrowed from the disciplines of cognitive psychology and of moral philosophy, has been provided in which to describe 'that Within', and this terminology is capable of describing the historical placing of 'that Within'. Through this terminology, and as part of developing it, several approaches have been offered which describe clearly the self-constituted, though not self-fashioned, nature of Hamlet's interiority. Hamlet's interiority is not gestural. It is not the product of a critic's wish. Moreover, and importantly, it is at times Montaignesque, and recognizably modern. The several approaches which have been offered can be divided into two kinds. The first progressed through

[117] Taylor, *Sources of the Self*, 183–4.

an examination of the Prince's relationship to his constructs and his goods, which were seen to be his sources of self. The second progressed by picturing the Prince's self as a form of story. This section closes by showing how these two approaches are naturally linked, and, at the same time, gives its sense of the nature of *Hamlet* as a tragedy.

The critical problems of *Hamlet* are often argued to be the result of Shakespeare's entrapment within the revenge drama form of his source, the now vanished *Ur-Hamlet*. Yet the idea of Shakespeare being entrapped just this once by a source is inherently unlikely; Holinshed, Plautus, and Plutarch provided no such problems. Revenge drama is rather the perfect form for Shakespeare's concerns, as they have here been argued, as it is a literary form which naturally raises issues of ethics and so of identity.[118] Particular forms of story are dependent on and expressive of particular ethical relationships and so of particular identities. One can reverse this, and talk of identity as being a narrative concept. Such a narrative concept of personal identity is advanced by Alisdair MacIntyre, in *After Virtue* (1985). Under such a concept, as MacIntyre points out, 'the unity of a human life is the unity of a narrative quest'.[119] That quest is for the good. This idea of life as a narrative quest for the good is strongly reminiscent of Charles Taylor's account of the importance of 'moral goods' to identity for the simple reason that Taylor, as he acknowledges, takes MacIntyre as one of his guiding lights. MacIntyre, in fact, deals with an area within Taylor's analysis; MacIntyre captures the darkness of that history of the sources of the self which Taylor chooses not to treat.

MacIntyre advances his narrative concept of identity in the context of his thesis that the language of morality, a language central to the narrative quest for identity, suffered a catastrophic collapse between the fifteenth and seventeenth centuries, with the result that the present is a moral dystopia. This collapse occurred when moral statements became non-functional; when saying that something was good ceased to mean that it was good for something (p. 56). This, in turn, was the result of the concept of man becoming non-functional, when to be a man no longer designated acting in any particular way. 'It is only when man is thought of as an individual prior to and apart from all roles that "man" ceases to be a functional concept' (p. 56). This represents a decisive separation of the self from traditional modes of thought, and so from the virtues; for, 'there is no way to possess the virtues except as part of a tradition in which we inherit them and our understanding of them from a series of predecessors' (p. 119).

[118] The etymology of 'ethics' reinforces this link with identity that Taylor and this discussion argue for: as Alasdair MacIntyre points out in his *After Virtue*, 'ethics' (a Greek word) and the Latin word 'moralis' (which was invented by Cicero to translate the Greek word) both have as their root meaning 'pertaining to character'. Alasdair MacIntyre, *After Virtue: A Study in Moral Theory* (2nd edn.; Duckworth: London, 1985), 38.

[119] MacIntyre, *After Virtue*, 219. Further references to this book are given after quotations in the text.

Separated from an intelligible narrative of the goods or virtues, from external criteria of goods, morality becomes the expression of pure will. Each person had to invent his or her own goods, and construct his or her own narrative. This is an immensely impoverished and sad position to be in, MacIntyre suggests. *Hamlet*, the play, in seeing the Prince in tragic terms, agrees. For the availability to the Prince of new sources of the self is not an occasion of joy, but rather a wholesale loss seen in terms of the arrival of a terrible burden; in *Hamlet* the Prince is seen being forced to make up his own narrative.

The Prince's story, which I have suggested is of a new kind, is a story of growing up. However, as Montaigne notes, it cannot be told in the old ways in terms of a passage 'from age to age, or as the people reckon, from seaven yeares to seaven'. Such old communal stories do not hold for Hamlet; his growing up must be an expression of 'that Within', a discovery carried out 'from day to day, from minute to minute'. It is appropriate, if unintended, that Hamlet's age and dress is so particularly indeterminate, for the Prince cannot find satisfaction with the traditional roles and stories that are offered him. For others it is not so. Laertes can play the son and revenger quite happily. For him, the story is clear, pre-existent:

> To hell Allegeance: Vowes, to the blackest diuell.
> Conscience and Grace, to the profoundest Pit.
> I dare Damnation: to this point I stand,
> That both the worlds I giue to negligence,
> Let come what comes: onely Ile be reueng'd
> Most throughly for my Father.
>
> (4. 5. 129–34)

Laertes can locate himself in a way Hamlet is incapable of doing. As there were residual, dominant, and emergent sources of self, so are there stories. Hamlet, by contrast, is driven out from the past, from traditional schemes of values, and so from his own story, his self (and himself). The Ghost coming to Hamlet, as has been mentioned, is one of the many irruptions of the past into the present. Less commented on is the way in which these irruptions actively destroy the past for the Prince. The Ghost, in apparently confirming the murder of Old Hamlet, murders Hamlet's past, by proving Hamlet's knowledge of the world false—at least to the Prince it seems to:

> Remember thee?
> Yea, from the Table of my Memory,
> Ile wipe away all triuiall fond Records,
> All sawes of Bookes, all formes, all presures past,
> That youth and obseruation coppide there;
> And thy Commandment all alone shall liue
> Within the Booke and Volume of my Braine.
>
> (1. 5. 97–103)

Memory destroys memory. It happens again, when Rosencrantz and Guildenstern arrive. These are Hamlet's childhood friends, and in betraying him now, they practice a particularly intimate betrayal; they prove false not only his knowledge of the present world but also the world of his childhood.

As the play progresses, Hamlet is left more and more in the present, searching for the thread of his story out of which to make sense of his life. He values Horatio, a friend from his more recent past as a student, particularly for his value as a recorder; constantly Hamlet is shown narrating his history to Horatio, or asking him if he recalls what he has said. One of MacIntyre's comments is illuminating of the Prince's predicament: 'The story of my life is always embedded in the past; and to try to cut myself off from the past, in the individualist mode, is to deform my present relationships' (p. 221). Hamlet does not try to cut himself off from the past, but is cut off from it, the truth of his memories proved false. Cut off in this way from the values and traditions out of which the narrative quest for life is sustained, Hamlet can find no story to render satisfactorily intelligible his life.

This is his tragedy. This lack provides the sadness which registers throughout the tragedy. For the tragedy of Hamlet does not lie in the Prince's death in the final scene. Rather it inheres in the Prince's life, in his struggle to find an identity or story that will express him. For though the soliloquies, in creating a form of autobiography, give the Prince a story, it is a story *manqué*, unsatisfactory—though fascinating—both to him and us. As he lies dying, the Prince, still Young Hamlet, tries to make good this lack:

> You that looke pale, and tremble at this chance,
> That are but Mutes or audience to this acte:
> Had I but time (as this fell Sergeant death
> Is strick'd in his Arrest) oh I could tell you.
>
> (5. 2. 286–9)

But the Prince's claim is made apostrophe by the approach of that fell sergeant, Death—he never has the opportunity to tell us, and we doubt, on what has been seen, that he could.

The hurt this lack of narrative causes him, so much more than the loss of his life, becomes clear in his desperate insistence that Horatio does not follow him:

> Oh good *Horatio*, what a wounded name,
> (Things standing thus vnknowne) shall liue behind me.
> If thou did'st euer hold me in thy heart,
> Absent thee from felicitie awhile,
> And in this harsh world draw thy breath in paine,
> To tell my Storie.
>
> (5. 2. 298–301)

MacIntyre points out that narrative forms provide the sources of identity for the age; he is another who recognizes the literally literary nature of identity.[120] Hamlet, dying so, unintelligible to himself, provides what has become a distinctively modern story and so a modern sense of self. Both have been repeated many times since. One such repetition is in Kafka's *The Trial*. *The Trial* tells the story of Joseph K, a sub-manager at a bank. Joseph K's life suddenly becomes unintelligible, as he is put on trial for a crime he has committed in the past, though what this is he does not know. For the life of him, Joseph K cannot regain control or authority over his life. And so he loses it, having first given up trying to render intelligible what is happening to him. He is killed by two men he does not know in a small quarry, with a butcher's knife, as he says with his last words, 'Like a dog'.

Every literary approach, like every theory, has its own focus of convenience. Put more negatively, every approach has its limitations. What, then, are the limitations of the approach described and followed above? The picture of the Prince's interiority is by and large unemotional in a broad sense; the Prince's passions are given a minor role in his description. This limitation is, as is to be expected from the argument concerning States and trait theory, in part a reflection of an aspect of Kelly's personal construct theory.[121] Kelly's 'man-the-scientist' is emotional, but in a rather narrow sense; his emotions are anxieties, predominantly thoughtful, and his metaphorical heart is very clearly a part of his mind. However, this focus of convenience suits *Hamlet*; the Prince is far more thoughtful than he is emotional. Indeed, it is his lack of either emotion or remorse at some of his actions—his killing of Polonius, his treatment of Ophelia, his sending of Rosencrantz and Guildenstern to their deaths—that impresses. Motivation, also, has not been treated. Again this reflects Kelly's theory, in which motive has no meaningful existence. The concept of 'character', by contrast, although it has been seen to have little descriptive purchase on interiority, is more capable of talking about motive. If, that is, the concept's seemingly inherent insistence on producing a metatextual and consistent core self out of a dramatic figure's actions is allowed. One of the reasons why critics have wanted to discover 'character', in fact, is to recover motive. The picture of Hamlet given above is also active; what, then, has happened to the Prince's famous delay? Delay is seen rather as a frantic activity, which leads to no result. This again seems to suit Hamlet the Prince and *Hamlet* the play.

Most obviously perhaps, there is within this approach no sense of a solution. Instead what is given is, to return to Kelly's words, an impression of a man 'going about his business of being human', which is in this case the active exploration of 'what on earth it means to be a person'.[122] In the Prince's case this is particularly the case of learning how to live with the big words, or rather,

[120] MacIntyre argues that it is modern and remarkable even to try to separate art from life, and particularly story-telling from the form of human life. Ibid. 226.

[121] For short summaries of the perceived strengths and weaknesses of Kelly's theory, see Pervin, *Personality*, 266–9, and Ewen, *Theories of Personality*, 373–6. For a fuller treatment of criticisms, and some of the responses, see Fransella, *Kelly*, 112–32.

[122] Kelly, *Psychology*, 183.

perhaps, of learning how to live without them. By the big words I refer to those in which our moral values inhere. Words such as 'love', 'reason', 'beauty', and so on. What Hamlet discovers is that these words are not given things, but instead are part of, and involve him in, the complicated business of being human. Wittgenstein makes this point neatly in relation to aesthetic words:

In order to get clear about aesthetic words you have to describe ways of living. We think we have to talk about aesthetic judgements like 'This is beautiful', but we find that if we have to talk about aesthetic judgements we don't find these words at all, but a word used something like a gesture, accompanying a complicated activity.[123]

[123] L. Wittgenstein, 'Lectures on Aesthetics', pt. I, sect. 35, in *Lectures and Conversations on Aesthetics, Psychology and Religious Belief: Compiled from Notes taken by Yorick Smythies, Rush Rhees and James Taylor*, ed. Cyril Barrett (Oxford: Basil Blackwell, 1966), 11.

7
A King of Infinite Space

King. But now my Cosin *Hamlet*, and my Sonne?

(I. 2. 64)

SHAKESPEARE'S Prince Hamlet has a self which is both a part of, and important to, his sense of identity. The last chapter put forward two complementary ways of describing and following this self. 'That Within' the Prince was seen to be an area discrete, though not separate, from his society, and that discreteness was seen to have been self-created; the Prince was seen to possess a self-constituting, as opposed to a self-fashioning, agency. Such an argument refutes the basic thrusts of the arguments of Cultural Materialists and New Historicists concerning English Renaissance literary subjectivity. It also concentrates on the similarities between the Prince's senses of self and more modern senses of self. However, at the heart of the descriptive approaches to self put forward in Chapter 6 is an insistence on the non-essentialist nature of self; Prince Hamlet's senses of self must be historically sited, distinct in various ways from our contemporary senses of self. Prince Hamlet must have aspects of his sense of self that make him of his time; to a point, he must acknowledge Claudius' claim of kinship in this, as in familial matters—no matter how distasteful that kinship may be to him. This chapter focuses on one aspect of this kinship, and so on one difference between the senses of self within *Hamlet* and modern senses of self. During the Elizabethan and Jacobean periods, it is argued, there is a rhetorical sense of self. Such a rhetorical sense of self is examined as it can be seen within some of Shakespeare's plays, and is placed in relation to Prince Hamlet's senses of self.

The meaning of 'rhetorical', as used above, may need explanation. 'Rhetoric' is used here in the sense broached by C. S. Lewis in the introductory chapter to his *English Literature in the Sixteenth Century Excluding Drama*: 'Rhetoric', Lewis noted, 'is the greatest barrier between us and our ancestors.'[1] This is a rather grand statement, according 'rhetoric' a great and wide-ranging importance in all aspects of culture. Lewis leaves this assertion of importance rather unsubstantiated. On the one hand, he gives as example the sixteenth century's (to his mind) deplorable enjoyment of rhetorical figures for their own sake, and on the other he speaks (very positively) of a different, rhetorical, way of

[1] C. S. Lewis, *English Literature in the Sixteenth Century Excluding Drama* (Oxford: Clarendon Press, 1954), 61.

thinking, evidenced by the sixteenth century's ability to talk about the humdrum and the profound in the same breath. Each example is given baldly, as might be expected in the introduction to a literary guide.

Lewis's use of 'rhetoric' has the virtue of making immediately plain what 'rhetoric' does not mean; 'rhetoric', as Lewis used it and as it is here used, does not have its currently dominant sense of an ornamental patterning added to language, which is often seen as marking out that language as deceptive and specious.[2] 'Rhetoric' is something far larger, far more important, and far more positive than that. What that was in the English Renaissance[3] has been the subject of a large body of critical work, carried out over the last forty-five years, and on which the following discussion relies. Central to nearly all of this work is the recognition that 'rhetoric' is not a simple or single activity, but a system. What follows is an outline of the manner in which that recognition came about, and of the critical implications of that recognition.

The recognition that rhetoric was a system emerged first with the piecing-together of the sixteenth-century pedagogy of rhetoric.[4] This did not stop at the teaching of *elocutio*, that is the teaching of the use of figures and tropes. Also taught were *inventio* and *dispositio*, the means of discovering and organizing arguments respectively, as well as *memoria*, the art of memory, and *pronunciatio*—the art of delivering speeches.[5] To refer to 'rhetoric', then, was to refer to all of these categories of activity. They could all be yoked together, as together they dealt with every aspect of communication. But each also represented and

[2] Such a negative sense was also current during the English Renaissance, and became more pronounced at the end of the 16th c., with the rise of satire and the plain anti-courtly style, now particularly associated with John Donne. So, to choose an example at random, the Princess Agripyne, in Thomas Dekker's *Old Fortunatus*, can talk of a soldier's wooing as 'home-spun stuff' because 'there's no outlandish thread in it, no rhetoric. A soldier casts no figures to get his mistress' heart.' (In *Thomas Dekker*, ed. Ernest Rhys (London: Vizetelly & Co., 1887), 3. 1, p. 339.) However, in Dekker, as in Shakespeare, the use of a copious style of rhetoric does not in general mark the speaker out as untrustworthy, as it begins to do in the plays of Ben Jonson and others. For a discussion of this see Neil Rhodes, *The Power of Eloquence and English Renaissance Literature* (Hemel Hempstead: Harvester Wheatsheaf, 1992).

[3] For an account of the relationship between Renaissance, medieval and classical rhetorics, see Kristeller, *Renaissance Thought*, esp. ch. 5.

[4] The initiator of this line of research was T. W. Baldwin. His *William Shakespeare's Small Latine and Lesse Greeke*, 2 vols. (Urbana, Ill.: University of Illinois Press, 1944) carried out the monumental task of piecing together rhetoric's central place within the curriculum of Elizabethan schools. W. S. Howell's *Logic and Rhetoric in England: 1500–1700* (Princeton: Princeton University Press, 1956) looked at the competing systems of rhetoric in the period, with more emphasis on the practice of rhetoric in universities. Hugh Kearney examined the social role that such an education played within the university curriculum of England, Scotland, and Ireland in his *Scholars and Gentlemen: Universities and Society in Pre-Industrial Britain 1500–1700* (London: Faber and Faber, 1970). Brian Vickers, *In Defense of Rhetoric* (Oxford: Clarendon Press, 1988), surveys the practice and intellectual dominance of rhetoric within the English Renaissance (noting, for instance, that one of the few changes to the Statutes of Cambridge University at the beginning of Elizabeth I's reign was to replace the study of mathematics with rhetoric (p. 182)).

[5] For the Ramistic reforms which challenged this approach, see Howell and Vickers, n. 4 above. The reforms' impacts were felt after Shakespeare had completed his schooling.

generated its own field of knowledge. *Inventio*, as the means of discovering arguments, considered questions of the nature of thought and methods of thinking, and so of origin and originality, and authority and authorship.[6] *Dispositio*, as the means of arranging arguments, considered questions of logic, on the one hand, and audience on the other; and of what types of logic appealed to what audiences. Decorum was a central concept to most of the five categories of rhetoric. *Elocutio*, as well as being the occasion for long lists of figures and tropes, generated many debates concerning the nature of language;[7] was it given by God, or made by man? Were words intimately or arbitrarily related to things?[8] What gave words their power? What was a trope? *Memoria* not only offered methods for facilitating memory, but considered the nature of the mind and the way in which thought is preserved within it.[9] *Pronunciatio* investigated the physical and visual nature of expression: the impacts of tones of speech, of the speaker's appearance, and the importance of gesture.[10] Yet these concerns were only the beginning of rhetoric's field of interest. For if rhetoric had one defining aim, it was to produce language that was persuasive and so offered power in a civic context.[11] As such, rhetoric insisted on the importance of those trained in it being able to analyse social context, whether that involved a person, a group, or a social institution.[12] For only then could one discover the best means to influence one's audience.

All these various concerns can be seen in two kinds of publication which

[6] David Quint discusses the later debates as constituent moments in the emergence during the Renaissance of the sense of historical relativism necessary for the appreciation of the concept of originality. See his *Origin and Originality in Renaissance Literature: Versions of the Source* (New Haven: Yale University Press, 1983).

[7] Jane Donawerth provides a general survey and source-book of these debates. See the first three chapters of her *Shakespeare and the Sixteenth-Century Study of Language* (Urbana, Ill. and Chicago: University of Illinois Press, 1984). Marion Trousdale traces the different pleasures of language fostered by a rhetoric, and so the different textual expectations of Renaissance readers and auditors. See her *Shakespeare and the Rhetoricians* (Chapel Hill, NC: University of North Carolina Press, 1982).

[8] Richard Waswo argues that there was a semantic shift in the 16th c., similar to that seen at the beginning of the 20th c. This shift involved a move from a conception of words as signs, to a conception that words created meaning by virtue of their relationship to each other; that is to a constitutive view of the relationship between language and meaning. See his *Language and Meaning in the Renaissance* (Princeton: Princeton University Press, 1987).

[9] See Yates, *The Art of Memory*.

[10] See David Bevington, *Action is Eloquence* (Cambridge, Mass.: Harvard University Press, 1984).

[11] See Frank Whigham, *Ambition and Privilege: The Social Tropes of Elizabethan Courtesy Theory* (Berkeley: University of California Press, 1984).

[12] This aspect of rhetoric's activity is represented most clearly in works of 'institution literature' such as Niccolo Machiavelli's *The Prince* (1513), Sir Thomas More's *Utopia* (1516), Baldassare Castiglione's *Il Libro del Cortegiano* (1528), Sir Thomas Elyot's *Boke named the Governour* (1531), Roger Ascham's *The Scholemaster* (1570), and Henry Peacham's *The Compleat Gentleman* (1622). The term 'institution literature' is useful in focusing attention on the importance of social context within these works. It is taken from Thomas Greene, 'The Flexibility of the Self in Renaissance Literature' in Peter Demetz, Thomas Greene, and Lowry Nelson, Jr. (eds.), *The Disciplines of Criticism: Essays in Literary Theory, Interpretation, and History* (New Haven: Yale University Press, 1968), 241–64.

flourished in the sixteenth century, and which are most obviously representative and constitutive of rhetoric's fields of knowledge; these are the manuals of rhetoric and the genre of courtesy literature.[13] The difference between these two kinds is their relative emphases. The manuals are mainly concerned with propounding the categories of rhetoric, and dealing with the questions raised by those categories. Courtesy literature focused mainly on analysing the two-way relationship between the person and his (and less frequently her) social context. Yet both are related. This relationship is clear at the level of stated concern. On the one hand, manuals of rhetoric argue—typically in an introductory overview—about rhetoric's power and usefulness in a civic context.[14] On the other, works of courtesy literature constantly refer to the importance of eloquence and a literary education.[15] But more important is an unstated relationship; both kinds of literature argue for a tactical presentation of oneself and one's arguments, a presentation which must be tailored to one's context.

This relationship is glimpsed succinctly in George Puttenham's description of allegory as 'the Courtly figure' in his *The Arte of English Poesie* (1589).[16] Allegory is courtly for Puttenham in that it disguises what it presents in order to win its ends. In that sense, this trope is the literary device that represents the courtier's role, which role 'is in plaine termes', Puttenham says in his conclusion, 'cunningly to be able to dissemble . . . whereby the better to winne his purposes and good aduantages' (pp. 250–1). Allegory becomes for Puttenham not only one of the most important and widely used tropes, but also a symbol of the nature of rule:

> the vse of [allegory] is so large, and his vertue of so great efficacie as it is supposed no man can pleasantly vtter and perswade without it, but in effect is sure neuer or very seldome to thriue and prosper in the world, that cannot skilfully put in vse, in somuch as not onely euery common Courtier, but also the grauest Counsellour, yea and the most noble and wisest Prince of them all are many times enforced to vse it . . . Qui nescit dissimulare nescit regnare. [Who refuses to dissemble refuses to rule] (p. 155)

[13] The term 'courtesy literature' is a competitor of 'institution literature' as both cover many of the same texts. So, of the texts listed in n. 12, only *Utopia* is unlikely to be considered as courtesy literature. See Whigham, *Ambition and Privilege*, ch. 1, for a productive use of the term. 'Courtesy literature', though perhaps not so helpful a term as 'institution literature', is by far the most commonly used.

[14] So, to take as example the most popular manual of rhetoric in English (by reprints), Thomas Wilson in the Epistle to his *Art of Rhetorique* (1553) asks: 'If the worthinesse of Eloquence maie moove vs, what worthier thing can there bee, then with a word to winne Cities and whole Countries?' Thomas Wilson, *Arte of Rhetorique*, ed. G. H. Mair (Oxford: Clarendon Press, 1909; first pub. 1560), A.ii.b. Lazarus Pyott's *The Orator* of 1596 provides another example: 'The use [of rhetoric] whereof in every member in our commonweale is as necessary, as the abuse or wilfull ignorance is odius . . . In reasoning of private debates, here maiest thou find apt metaphors, in incouraging thy souldiers fit motives . . . briefly every private man may be in this partaker of a general profit.' Quoted in Baldwin, *William Shakespeare's Small Latine*, ii. 45.

[15] See e.g. Baldassare Castiglione, *The Book of the Courtier*, trans. Sir Thomas Hoby (London: Dent, 1928; first pub. 1561), 56–74.

[16] Puttenham, *English Poesie*, 155. Further references to this book are given after quotations in the text.

What is becoming clear, here, is that to refer to 'rhetoric' is not only to refer to the practices that map out a field of knowledge which, composed of many other fields, sought to analyse the world in order to gain power over it. Rhetoric's field of knowledge, and so its analyses, are also constitutive of that world, and the persons within it. It is in this sense that one may refer to a rhetorical world, and a rhetorical person. One might think of 'rhetoric', in fact, as the equivalent of contemporary science, and so as a 'technology of power' in the Foucauldian sense.[17] 'Rhetoric' understood as such a field of knowledge makes sense of Lewis's statement of its being 'the greatest barrier between us and our ancestors'. The meaning of 'rhetoric' is not amenable to the formulated definitions of the dictionary; 'rhetoric' is another of those words, as Wittgenstein said, 'used something like a gesture, accompanying a complicated activity'.

One would expect the rhetorical nature of persons within such a rhetorical world to be of import to the controversies of self, and previous literary-critical work has recognized connections between the two topics. Michael McCanles, in his *The Text of Sidney's Arcadian World* (1989), puts forward an argument which he sees as complementary to Greenblatt's argument concerning self-fashioning, as that is given in *Renaissance Self-Fashioning*. Where Greenblatt examines the role of social and political codes in constituting identity, McCanles looks at the shaping influence of 'rhetorical figuration' on identity. McCanles, invoking the strong Whorf–Sapir thesis once more, argues that human reality 'is constituted from the linguistic codes made available by culture itself', and that these codes are at this time the figures of rhetoric.[18] McCanles's concept of identity, like Greenblatt's, has no place for self-constituting agency, nor any sense of degrees of innerness.[19]

[17] The Foucault, that is, of *Discipline and Punish*. Rhetoric could be well described by Foucault's genealogical approach, for it is clearly a discipline which fashioned its subjects through a micro-physics of power. This, however, is not the place for such an analysis. It is also tempting to describe 'rhetoric' by an earlier term of Foucault's, that is as an 'episteme'. An episteme is 'the total set of relations that unite, at a given period, the discursive practices that give rise to epistemological figures, sciences, and possibly formalize systems' (*The Archaeology of Knowledge*, trans. A. M. Sheridan Smith (London: Tavistock, 1972; first pub. as *L'Archeologie du Savoir*, Paris: Editions Gallimard, 1969), 191). This captures nicely the importance of rhetoric as a system of thought. However, Foucault uses episteme precisely and problematically in *The Order of Things*; he divides up the period from the Renaissance into four remarkably (and unconvincingly) discontinuous epistemes. It would thus be contradictory in Foucault's terms to talk of a rhetorical episteme in the Renaissance period. Also, the rigidity and discontinuity suggested by 'episteme' does not suit the remarkable power and presence of rhetoric as a field of knowledge or 'technology' throughout history, descending from Aristotle (and earlier) to the middle of the 18th c.

[18] Michael McCanles, *The Text of Sidney's Arcadian World* (Durham: Duke University Press, 1989), 187.

[19] The same points may be made about Christy Desmet's *Reading Shakespeare's Characters: Rhetoric, Ethics, and Identity* (Amherst, Mass.: University of Massachusetts Press, 1992); Desmet dismisses the notion of self, innerness, and historical difference in the first page of her introduction, pursuing instead a de Mannean- and Burkean-inspired reading of the reader's identification with character (see also p. 27). This different perspective apart, Desmet's book has many of the same concerns as this thesis, and her discussions of those concerns are valuable.

McCanles's approach, in its concentration on language and most especially on figures, that is on *elocutio*, represents a development of the most common form of critical attempt to understand the rhetorical nature of literature. For, rather disappointingly, when single literary texts are examined, the attempt to recover and examine the systemic nature of rhetoric tends to be abandoned. Thus, concerning *Hamlet*, George T. Wright argues that the use of hendiadys is particularly expressive of the play's fascination with false unions;[20] while Georgio Melchiori finds the key figure to be oxymoron, and Patricia Parker puts forward a more general concern with figures of copula and sequitur reflecting the play's concern with political succession.[21] Neil Rhodes, however, in *The Power of Eloquence and English Renaissance Literature* (1992), insists on a wider sense of rhetoric as an approach to the world (if not as a field of knowledge) and does so as a corrective to Greenblatt's arguments, again in *Renaissance Self-Fashioning*, concerning the person's lack of agency. Rhodes argues that there was a rhetorical identity which he terms 'the bravery of the self'. ('Self' rather blurs into 'identity' in Rhodes's account.) By 'bravery', Rhodes invokes that word's Renaissance senses of boasting and swaggering. For this concept of identity is one 'which stresses the demonstrative personality rather than the integrity of the inner self, and which recognizes the central importance of eloquence in creating such a personality'.[22] Rhodes insists, then, on the sense, ever-present in Renaissance manuals of rhetoric and courtesy literature, as well as in such famous texts as Pico della Mirandola's *Oration*, that the person fashions himself through acting. He reasserts the claims of a large body of Renaissance literature and of literary criticism which Greenblatt set himself against when he failed to find self-fashioning in the Renaissance.

Yet Rhodes still examines rhetoric's impact on identity only in external terms; he leaves aside the possibility of an inner self altogether, and so does not consider what might be the rhetorical nature of that self. This is neither necessary nor logical. For, whether or not one accepts the existence of a self, rhetoric, as a field of knowledge, is bound to structure the way in which Renaissance persons think; it is bound, that is, to structure them internally. Walter J. Ong makes clear the logic of this relationship in his *Rhetoric, Romance and Technology* (1971):

> Human thought structures are tied in with verbalization and must fit available media of communication; there is no way for persons with no experience of writing to put their minds through the continuous linear sequence of thought such as goes, for example, into an encyclopedia article.[23]

[20] George T. Wright, '*Hamlet* and Hendiadys', *PMLA* 96 (1981), 168–93.

[21] Georgio Melchiori, 'The Rhetoric of Character Construction: *Othello*', *SS* 34 (1981), 61–72; Patricia Parker, *Literary Fat Ladies: Rhetoric, Gender, Property* (London and New York: Methuen, 1987), 120. Donald K. Hedrick argues that such figure-spotting is a pointless game at which one cannot lose: '"It is No Novelty for a Prince to be a Prince": An Enantiomorphous Hamlet', *SQ* 35 (1984), 62–76.

[22] Rhodes, *The Power of Eloquence*, 40.

[23] Walter J. Ong, *Rhetoric, Romance, and Technology: Studies in the Interaction of Expression and Culture* (Ithaca, NY: Cornell University Press, 1971), 2.

Ong's conception of rhetoric as a system of communication parallels the sense of rhetoric, advanced here, as a field of knowledge. Both conceptions of rhetoric see it as shaping thought, and so shaping the person's constitution of the world, and of him- or herself. This, then, is the logical argument for the existence of a rhetorical sense of self.

However, our sense of what that rhetorical sense of self might be, how it might appear in a play, is still undefined. 'Rhetoric' has so far been examined in rather abstract terms, in order to insist on its systemic nature. It is time to turn to the effects produced by this field of knowledge, to ask what might identify a sense of self as being rhetorical. Erasmus' *De Copia* (1512) was the most influential manual of rhetoric in the sixteenth century. It opens with an image of what rhetoric could both produce and be: 'The speech of man is a magnificent and impressive thing when it surges along like a golden river.'[24] Erasmus does not attempt a description of the various parts and aspects of rhetoric, but rather uses an image as a model of rhetoric's effects. That is, to recall the discussion of the use of metaphor in Chapter 6, Erasmus uses the simile of speech as a surging golden river to schematize a certain area of the activity that constitutes rhetoric's field of knowledge. (The difference between simile and metaphor in this respect is that simile has no catachretic function.)

Erasmus' model is primarily an expression of his understanding of one aspect of rhetoric's effect. The image of speech as a surging river captures the sense of the smooth and yet irresistibly powerful force that one's arguments, when properly produced, may attain. Such a river would carry away the objections of others. At the same time, the image suggests the beauty and awe that such speech may generate in its hearers; it is a 'golden' river. That 'golden' also suggests the value of such speech, holding the promise of personal success and power in the secular world. However, Erasmus' image, as such a model, may allow further understandings of rhetoric to be developed; such models, if they are profitable, allow one to think through the domain they describe.[25] For instance, the image of speech as a 'surging' river has suggestions of inhuman volume, of elemental power, and destructive force. If rhetoric produces such powerful speech, what is to stop it being used destructively and not magnificently? To argue through Erasmus' image in this way is to exploit the dramatic potential of his model of rhetoric and so of his manual of rhetoric. Most manuals denied this potential, by insisting on a link between morality and eloquence. This link derived its authority from the manuals of the classical teachers of rhetoric. Quintilian's *Institutio Oratoria*, the most influential of these, put this link thus: 'bene dicere non possit nisi bonus' ('no man can speak well

[24] Desiderius Erasmus, *De Copia*, trans. Betty I. Knott, 3rd edn. (1534) in *Collected Works*, 86 vols. (Toronto: University of Toronto Press, 1974–1993), xxiv. 296.

[25] For an argument that our conceptual system is itself metaphorical in nature, and so that metaphor is central to understanding (and an understanding of culture), see George Lakoff and Mark Johnson, *Metaphors We Live By* (Chicago: University of Chicago Press, 1980).

who is not good himself').[26] Yet Shakespeare (and other dramatists) quite ignored this undramatic proposition. Within his plays, those who use speech powerfully often use it destructively; Iago and Richard III are obvious examples. Shakespeare, then, is no academic user of a manual of rhetoric, following its rules and employing its figures (though he does of course also do this). Rather he argues about and explores rhetoric, exploiting the manuals, as he exploited every other source-book, for their dramatic potential.

How, then, does this relate to a rhetorical sense of self? The chapter began with the aim of identifying what might make an Elizabethan sense of self of its own period and different from later senses of self. One of the largest differences between that world and our own was bound up with the rhetorical nature of the Elizabethan world. Rhetoric, it was argued, is a complicated activity which constitutes a field of knowledge; logically, such a field of knowledge ought to structure the persons within it. The external impact of rhetoric on persons was seen already to have been the focus of literary criticism. However, as a field of knowledge it was argued that rhetoric should have an internal impact as well—it should structure the self, as well as other aspects of identity. Given that rhetoric is such a complicated and wide-ranging domain of activity, only a particular aspect of its impact can here be explored—only one aspect, that is, of what might make a sense of self rhetorical and so historically sited. In the search for such an aspect, Erasmus' use of water imagery to model the impact of rhetoric as speech was examined. This, it was suggested, although not the only model used to schematize rhetoric's impact, could be used to explore that impact. Moreover, Erasmus' choice of water imagery is typical; the impact of rhetoric, as Ong noted, is usually expressed through such imagery: 'Rhetoric is typically an overwhelming phenomenon, implemented by what the classical world and the Renaissance called *copia*, abundance, plenty, unstinted flow. . . . Its world is commonly and aptly described in . . . water symbolism.'[27] Rhetoric's world, it seems, is somehow liquid. If that is true, it seems possible that a rhetorical sense of self should share this liquidity.

In Chapter 6, metaphor was argued to offer an expressive resource for a person's sense of self, even a self which lacked a modern vocabulary of interiority. It would seem likely that a rhetorical sense of self would express and explore itself through the same complex of imagery which is used to express and explore the nature of rhetoric. If this is so, one might expect to find images of a person's self, within Shakespeare's plays, as images of water. This line of thought can be developed through Erasmus' image. If speech is a river, what then is the speaker? Some form of reservoir whose interior is also made up of the same water that composes its world. Such a liquid sense of self might strike us as unlikely; but then one might expect to find particularly unfamiliar a sense of self different from our own.

[26] Marcus Fabius Quintilian, *Institutio Oratoria*, trans. H. E. Butler, 4 vols. (London: William Heinemann, 1920), i. 315 (Bk. II, ch. xv, 35).

[27] Ong, *Rhetoric, Romance and Technology*, 14.

Ant. I to the world am like a drop of water,
That in the Ocean seekes another drop,
Who falling there to finde his fellow forth,
(Vnseene, inquisitiue) confounds himselfe.
So I, to finde a Mother and a Brother,
In quest of them (vnhappie a) loose my selfe.
(1. 2. 34–40)

These lines with their unfamiliar image come from Act 1 scene 2 of *The Comedie of Errors*. Antipholus of Syracuse, having just arrived at Ephesus in search of his mother and long-lost identical twin brother, pauses before entering the city. For a moment before the play's confusions of identity begins he is alone, and in that moment he suddenly tells the audience of his fears that he is losing his personal identity. He compares himself to a drop of water. This image does not match exactly the argument developed from Erasmus' image of speech as a river, but it is close. Antipholus pictures himself and his world as made up from water; both, that is, are constituted of the same element (which element, as Ong points out, is typically used to express the rhetorical nature of the world). The difference between himself and his world, a discreteness that Antipholus values highly, is expressed through the physical shape of the water-drop. The water-drop is discrete from the ocean not because of any act of 'bravery'—to invoke Rhodes's term for the external impact of rhetoric—but because it is centred on itself. The image contains no suggestions of acting or audience.

The image of a water-drop, in fact, well expresses aspects of self as those were previously defined. Like a water-drop, self depends not on any essential quality, but is constructed from the world which surrounds it. Like the forces that produce a water-drop, self orientates and shapes identity. Most important and dramatic, however, is the intense fragility conferred upon identity by picturing it as a construct of water, as the world as ocean threatens to submerge, or render it indistinct. Antipholus' fear that he is losing his identity is the fear, now unfamiliar, of the dissolution of self. 'One', as Ong notes, 'may drown in rhetoric.'[28] To us, such drowning and dissolution may be unfamiliar, but such fears were not unfamiliar to that time. Similar water imagery recurs at other moments of personal crisis. So, for example, a little later within Shakespeare's plays, when Richard II, having been taken prisoner by Bolingbroke, is brought to answer the articles against him—a scene located by the Arden edition in Westminster Hall—Richard wishes that he were 'a Mockerie, King of Snow' so that, 'Standing before the Sunne of Bullingbrooke', he might 'melt my selfe away in Water-drops' (*The life & death of King Richard the Second*, 4. 1. 250–2). The image's concern with matters of identity is made sharper by the passages that precede and follow it. In the lines immediately before Richard expresses his desire to melt, he bemoans the fact

[28] Ibid.

that he has 'worn so many Winters out' but knows 'not now, what Name to call my selfe' (4. 1. 248–9). In the lines immediately after, he calls for a mirror, 'That it may shewe me what a Face I haue, Since it is Bankrupt of his Maiestie' (4. 1. 256–7). When the mirror arrives, Richard cannot reconcile the face he still sees in it with his nameless, dissolved sense of himself. So he smashes the mirror, producing a more representative image of a face 'in an hundred shiuers' (4. 1. 279). Richard's wish for dissolution can be paralleled with that of Faustus in Marlowe's and his collaborator's *The Tragicall History of D. Faustus* (1588–9). At the end of the play, when the devils are about to enter to take his soul down to hell, he cries: 'O soul, be changed to little water drops | And fall into the ocean, ne'er be found!' (5. 7. 118–19).[29] Faustus's desire for dissolution is associated particularly with his desire that his soul escape; in the preceding lines he begged the stars to 'draw up Faustus like a foggy mist | Into the entrails of yon labouring cloud', where his body might be consumed by lightening, allowing his soul to 'ascend to heaven' (5. 7. 91–5). A soul is not a self, as has been seen, but Marlowe is using water imagery to express an inner aspect of identity.[30]

Richard and Faustus wish for a dissolution they cannot achieve, where Antipholus fears a dissolution that seems all too possible. This is not to suggest that one attitude predominates over the other. Antipholus' fears are also shared by others outside Shakespeare's plays. For instance, Morose, the lover of silence in Ben Jonson's *Epicoene, Or the Silent Woman* (1609–10), describes the arrival of his relatives as threatening to drown him:

> Oh, the sea breaks in upon me! Another flood! An inundation! I shall be o'erwhelm'd with noise. It beats already at my shores.
>
> (3. 6. 2–4)

These are two quite different attitudes to drowning, but both become possible as fears or hopes within a rhetorical world. That world itself seems, at times, threatened by inundation. So, for instance, the opening of 'An Homelie of Whoredome and Unclenness' deplores a situation where, 'Above other vices the outragious seas of adultery, whoredome, fornicacion and unclennesse have not onleye braste in, but also overflowed almoste the whoole worlde.'[31]

This rhetorical sense of self, expressed through water imagery, is neither constantly present nor constantly constituted within Shakespeare's plays.

[29] This passage is the same in both the A- and B-text; it is cited from the A-text of David Bevington's and Eric Rasmussen's edition.

[30] For another example of the desire for dissolution, see Beatrice-Joanna's request—at the end of Thomas Middleton's and William Rowley's *The Changeling* (1622)—that her defining life-blood be mingled in 'the common sewere' and so be taken 'from distinction' (5. 3. 153). This is cited from N. W. Bawcutt's edition.

[31] *Certain Sermons or Homilies (1547) and A Homily against Disobedience and Wilful Rebellion (1570): A Critical Edition*, ed. Ronald B. Bond (Toronto: University of Toronto Press, 1987), 174.

Antipholus' sense of dissolution is simple and his fear of it mild. This is partly due to the impersonal, overtly poetic nature of his image and partly due to the comic nature of the play. Antipholus may fear dissolution, but it is unlikely, as this is comedy, that he would drown. Antony's sense of dissolution in *The Tragedie of Anthonie, and Cleopatra* is, by contrast, complicated and immensely painful. After his final defeat at Alexandria, Antony drowns.

Enter Anthony, and Eros
Ant. Eros, thou yet behold'st me?
Eros. I Noble Lord.
Ant. Sometime we see a clowd that's Dragonish,
A vapour sometime, like a Bear, or Lyon,
A toward Cittadell, a pendant Rocke,
A forked Mountaine, or blew Promontorie
With Trees vpon't, that nodde vnto the world,
And mocke our eyes with Ayre.
Thou hast seene these Signes,
They are blacke Vespers Pageants.
Eros. I my lord.
Ant. That which is now a Horse, euen with a thoght
the Racke dislimes, and makes it indistinct
As water is in water.
Eros. It does my Lord.
Ant. My good Knaue *Eros*, now thy Captaine is
Euen such a body: here I am *Anthony*,
Yet cannot hold this visible shape (my Knaue).

(4. 15. 1–14)

Antony's drowning, his sense that he 'cannot hold this visible shape' is painful. This is registered particularly in the embarrassment of seeing the once magnificent Antony flounder in public: his question, '*Eros*, thou yet behold'st me?' is on one level absurd. Eros and the audience can quite plainly see Antony. However, Antony's 'me' refers to more than his physical presence; it refers also to his sense of his self, a sense so important to Antony that it is dominant over his sense of his own corporeality. Thus when Antony loses this sense, when his picture of his self becomes as 'indistinct | As water is in water', he cannot believe his 'visible shape' remains.

The image with which Antony represents his sense of his dissolution is layered. To begin with, Antony pictures himself as a particularly shaped cloud, whose shape is in a moment 'dislimed', that is 'dislimned', and rendered indistinct in the mass of clouds. There is a degree of corporeality to this part of the image, particularly if the pun of dislimns/dislimbs is allowed, which expresses the violence that Antony feels has been done his identity. (The reason why one might not allow this pun is the *OED*'s date of first recorded usage for 'dislimbs' as 1662.) This cloudy Antony was torn apart on a rack, rent limb from limb to his constituent parts. However, this corporeality is itself fluid, made up as it is from clouds. (Clouds were related, in Elizabethan thought—as in our meteorology—to the ocean. So, for example, Richard III laments, at the beginning of *The Tragedy of Richard the Third*, that 'all the clouds that lowr'd vpon our House' are 'In the deepe bosome of the Ocean buried' (1. 1. 3–4).) This fluidity is reinforced first by Antony's varying his first image of himself as a cloud with a parallel image of himself as a 'vapour'. The discrimination between the two is a fine one. However, 'vapour', in its senses of 'mist' and 'fog', as well as its scientific sense of an evaporated substance, focuses attention more closely on the liquid nature of the substance.[32] This sense of the liquid nature of the image is reinforced further when Antony expands his image by exampling the loss of distinction it portrays as the indistinctness of 'water . . . in water'.

Each layer of the image pictures inner identity as constituted out of an external element, as something given a transient self-definition by its shape, a shape which is at any moment capable of flowing away. This sense of outlines, and of the self-constituted nature of these, emerges most clearly in the use of 'dislimns' (a word which also demonstrates the immense precision and effort of Antony's use of language here). According to the *OED*, the word is a neologism, not used again until used imitatively in the nineteenth century. The *OED* gives its meaning as 'to obliterate the outlines of (anything limned)'. Clearly, as a neologism, one would expect the word's meaning to suit the context, for the compiler of the dictionary's entry will have this as their aim. However, the word's precision is also seen in its invocation of the positive sense of 'limn'. To 'limn' here carries two areas of relevant meaning. 'Limning', in its older sense, referred particularly to the art of illuminating manuscripts; that is, to a form of illustration based around the use of water-colours. At around the turn of the sixteenth and seventeenth centuries it came to refer specifically to painting in water-colours.[33] The idea of water-colour painting suits Antony's image, and does so in several ways. Water-colours are, in a sense, paintings in clouds, or of water in water. Typically they make much of the fragility of their form. 'To limn the water, limn (something) on water' became, by 1620 according to the *OED*, a proverbial expression said of something transient or futile. Antony's use of 'dislimns' might here be thought to invoke it (and also the sense of vapour as 'something unsubstantial' (*OED* 2c)).

Also, in the sixteenth and seventeenth centuries, limning had come to refer particularly to the art of miniature painting. Recently, much emphasis has been placed on Henry VIII's and Elizabeth I's use of miniatures as political icons; as public representations of an ideal image of the ruler. Yet they could

[32] It may also be related to the theory of humours.

[33] See *OED*, 'limn' *v.*, senses 1, 3, and 5. The *OED* also credits Shakespeare with the first use of 'water-colour' in *The First Part of Henry the Fourth*: 'And neuer yet did Insurrection want | Such water-colours, to impaint his cause' (5. 1. 79–80).

also be intensely personal paintings, intended for the closet as well as the box of display on a courtier's arm. Intimacy was the key to their style, and they attempted to generate such intimacy by capturing transient moments particularly expressive of personality. So, for instance, Nicholas Hilliard, the most famous English proponent of the miniaturist's art, writes in his *A Treatise Concerning the Arte of Limning* that miniatures should attempt to capture the, 'louely graces wittye smilings, and thosse stolne glances wch sudainely like lighting passe and another Countenance taketh place'.[34] Both senses of miniature as icon and glimpse of intimacy are, perhaps, invoked by Antony's use of 'dislimnd'. Antony's sense of self is represented for a moment as a miniature (which being oval or round has the same shape as a drop of water[35]) which becomes 'unpainted'—a peculiar, quasi-magical and mysterious process in its un-creative aspect. One could imagine the effect of bleach on a water-colour, dissolving away the artist's work to the continuous texture of the canvas. Antony is thus un-painted. He loses sight of the precious picture of himself that he has valued and created through his life. He merges with his surroundings, losing his sense of his 'visible shape'. He has flowed back into the element from which he was created.

Such fluidity of form is suggestive of the figure of Proteus, who might be called the Shakespearian god, in the light of literary critics' use of Proteus to attempt to define Shakespeare's ability to create character (seen in Part II). Proteus, as has been noted, achieved especial prominence during the Renaissance: in classical myth, Proteus had been a minor sea-god who served Poseidon and had, according to Homer, both the power to change his shape and a vast knowledge; in the Renaissance, Proteus gained in importance as he came to be seen as a symbol of a defining aspect of man's nature. This aspect of Proteus was formulated strikingly by Juan Luis Vives in his *Fabula de homine* (after 1518), which itself draws on Giovanni Pico della Mirandola's more influential and innovative *De dignitate hominis* (written 1486). In Vives's fable, the world is created as a theatre and play for the gods, and by Jupiter as an after-dinner surprise for the guests at Juno's birthday party. The gods, when they have finished eating, take their seats for the performance, and soon begin discussing who is the best actor on the planet before them. Soon it becomes clear that man deserves the title; he acts different parts with each of his entrances. He can live as insensibly as a plant; or as cunningly as the fox, or as

[34] Nicholas Hilliard, *A Treatise Concerning the Arte of Limning*, ed. R. K. R. Thornton and T. G. S. Cain (Northumberland: Mid Northumberland Arts Group, 1981; unpub. previously, wr. 1589–1603). Roy Strong argues that the attempt to capture the personality of the sitter is a humanist ideal, first brought to England by Hans Holbein the Younger. See Roy Strong, *Holbein: The Complete Paintings* (London: Granada, 1980), 6. Hilliard took Holbein as his example; Holbein's was the 'manner of limning I haue euer imitated & hold it for the best'. See Hilliard, 69.

[35] Thornton and Cain argue that the shape of the frame was particularly important to Hilliard, who exploited the tension between the frame's formal pattern and the realism of the portrait within. See Hilliard, *Treatise*, 63.

lustfully as a sow; or he can live justly and prudently with others, in the society of a city. What really impresses the gods is man's next entrance as a god; they declare man 'to be that multiform Proteus, the son of the Ocean', and they call for him to join them.[36] When he does he is acting the part of Jupiter himself, and so well that some of the gods think he is Jupiter.

Vives's fable casts man as Proteus to recognize the power of his free choice; he may choose what he wishes to be. It is this near-divine ability to form and transform himself that distinguishes man from every other creature on earth. In casting man as Proteus, Vives, following Pico, argues that man's dignity rests not in his place at the centre of creation or in his nature as the microcosm of the macrocosm, but in his being without a given nature and capable of moving through the hierarchies of creation. Man's unfixity, his 'indeterminate nature' as Pico phrases it, is his greatness; in this lies his worth.[37] This nature also gives him his goal; on the one hand, he must attempt to ascend to the nature of a god, and on the other he must beware that he does not become a beast.

Viewed in this way, the image of man as Proteus, as a shape-changer, is overwhelmingly positive; its negative aspects are minor, though dangerous. The figure of man as Proteus neatly captures the rhetorical sense of self. Proteus' element is the water, and his nature partakes of the ocean's fluidity. Proteus' element is also language, for language, as has been seen, is often pictured in water-based images. Proteus is the figure that links water, language, and human nature together, celebrating the divinity of change and the power of language. Such a positive sense of a Protean or rhetorical sense of self, however, has not been seen within Shakespeare's plays. Shakespeare, just as he dismissed the undramatic insistence of the manuals of rhetoric that only the good may speak persuasively, dramatizes the troubling aspects of the Protean sense of self. In doing so he draws on another tradition of interpreting Proteus, a darker tradition distrustful of the ability to change.[38] A. Bartlett Giamatti, in *Exile and Change in Renaissance Literature* (1984), describes these two different traditions as the difference between those who saw Proteus as a symbol of the one truth lying behind the many, and those who saw Proteus as a symbol of the many that are to be found in the one. Giamatti cites Montaigne as an example of the latter.[39]

Montaigne's descriptions of man and himself, quoted in Chapter 6, were full of oceanic imagery. So, for instance, Montaigne described man as a 'wonder-

[36] Juan Luis Vives, 'A Fable About Man', trans. Nancy Lekeith, in *The Renaissance Philosophy of Man*, ed. Ernst Cassirer, Paul Oskar Kristeller, and John Herman Randall, Jr. (Chicago: University of Chicago Press, 1948), 389.

[37] Giovanni Pico Della Mirandola, 'Oration on the Dignity of Man', trans. Elizabeth Livermore Forbes, in Cassirer *et al.*, *The Renaissance Philosophy*, 224.

[38] For a succinct overview of the anti-theatrical form of this darker tradition as it has descended from Plato's writings, see Desmet, *Reading Shakespeare's Characters*, 17–24.

[39] A. Bartlett Giamatti, 'Proteus Unbound: Some Versions of the Sea God in the Renaissance', in *Exile and Change in Renaissance Literature* (New Haven: Yale University Press, 1984), 115–50 (118).

full, vaine, divers and wavering subject', and noted that within this subject 'all is but changing, motion, and inconstancy . . . We float and waver between divers opinions: we will nothing freely, nothing absolutely'. As Thomas Greene points out, the variation within personality that Montaigne found was negative in the respect that it precluded transformation, whether that was a transformation, in Pico's terms, up to the godhead or down to the beast.[40] In Montaigne's *Essays* there is a horizontal multiplicity of expression, a variation which, though it spurs and shapes the formal expression of the *Essays*, can become fatiguing and wearisome. Shakespeare exploits this more negative tradition of interpretation of Protean identity more dramatically. The terror that lies within Pico's 'indeterminate nature' is staged; dramatic persons struggle constantly to be determinate, and occasionally fail, losing hold on their fluid selves, flowing into the invisibility of indeterminacy.

Shakespeare's Prince Hamlet draws on this Protean, rhetorical sense of self. Hamlet begins, one might say, where Faustus left off. The opening lines of his first soliloquy are a wish for dissolution (here of the flesh) as a means to escape his present predicament: 'Oh that this too too solid Flesh, would melt, | Thaw, and resolue it selfe into a Dew' (1. 2. 129–30). Hamlet desires the watery nature of a rhetorical self which the solidity of his flesh denies him. His predicament is less pressing than Faustus's; no bell is immediately to sound twelve, and no devils wait to drag the Prince down to hell—though a ghost (after the bell has sounded twelve unheard) will soon come to him, and make the Prince wonder whether he is being tempted to his own damnation. This sense of his over-solid nature is paralleled by Hamlet's sense of a lack of words; the soliloquy which begins with the desire to melt ends with his recognition that, because of the situation he finds himself in, he cannot say what he would wish to, but must keep his words contained: 'But breake my heart, for I must hold my tongue' (1. 2. 159).

This initial desire for words is soon contradicted. In Act 2, when he is alone after having heard and seen the players' recital of the death of Priam, the Prince upbraids himself at some length for his inaction. Then he turns on himself for giving his feelings verbal expression:

> I sure, this is most braue,
> That I, the Sonne of the Deere murthered,
> Prompted to my Reuenge by Heauen, and Hell,
> Must (like a Whore) vnpacke my heart with words.
>
> (2. 2. 584–7)

There is a sense here that the Prince is disillusioned with words themselves, as in his reply, earlier in the same scene, to Polonius' question as to what he reads—'Words, words, words' (2. 2. 194). Indeed, the Prince, as Lawrence

[40] Greene, 'The Flexibility of the Self', 260.

Danson argues in *Tragic Alphabet*, might be said to be disillusioned with language itself, and is certainly keenly aware of its limitations.[41]

This is not to say that language, in *Hamlet*, is seen as in any sense impotent, or dominated by the expressive resources of the unsaid. Nor is it to say that Hamlet's use of language, and that of other dramatic persons, is ineffective. The reverse is truer; as Inga-Stina Ewbank argues, words and the dramatic persons' use of words are prime movers within the play. Again and again words are seen to persuade, and Ewbank suggests the play be seen as 'a complex study of people trying to control each other by words'.[42] Though Ewbank never mentions 'rhetoric', her description of the dramatic persons' use of language shows them to be good rhetoricians, in the sense that they follow the manuals' advice in paying attention to their audiences:

> The characters of the play, then, are on the whole very self-conscious speakers, in a way which involves consciousness of others: they believe in the word and its powers, but they are also aware of the necessity so to translate intentions and experiences into words as to make them meaningful to the interlocutor.

Prince Hamlet uses a wider range of language more effectively than anyone else within the play, and yet he is, at the same time, disillusioned and actively scornful of language. Aware of rhetoric's powers, he is also aware of its deceits and tricks, that 'marriage vowes' may be 'Dicers Oathes', and 'sweete Religion . . . | A rapsidie of words' (3. 4. 43–7). Prince Hamlet, in fact, has become dissatisfied with rhetoric.

To understand this dissatisfaction and its implications, Hamlet's first meeting with the Ghost must be returned to again. After the Ghost has left, as the glow-worms fade in the beginnings of the day, Hamlet says:

> Remember thee?
> Yea, from the Table of my Memory,
> Ile wipe away all triuiall fond Records,
> All sawes of Bookes, all formes, all presures past,
> That youth and obseruation coppied there;
> And thy Commandment all alone shall liue
> Within the Booke and Volume of my Braine
>
> (1. 5. 95–103)

As has been said, the Ghost's return forces the Prince to abandon his memories of the past by proving them (as the Prince thinks) false. The Ghost's return also causes the Prince to try to abandon rhetoric, by abandoning one of the

[41] See the introduction and ch. 2 of Lawrence Danson, *Tragic Alphabet: Shakespeare's Drama of Language* (New Haven and London: Yale University Press, 1974). For a related argument see also John Paterson, 'The Word in *Hamlet*', *SQ* 2 (1951), 47–56.

[42] Inga-Stina Ewbank, '*Hamlet* and the Power of Words', *SS* 30 (1977), 85–102, (88). See for a related discussion of language's expressive abilities within Shakespeare, Anne Barton, 'Shakespeare and the Limits of Language', *SS* 21 (1974), 19–30.

founding techniques of its system of knowledge—the commonplace book. For it is as a commonplace book, here, that the Prince conceptualizes his mind. Commonplace books tend now to be thought of as random collections of commonplace literary extracts collected as a matter of personal choice. However, in the sixteenth century they were an essential part of a rhetorical education.[43] The books took their name from the way in which they were divided up into common-places, that is into common subject-headings or topics. These 'topics' derived from the categories of classification as set out by Aristotle, 'place' being the English translation of the Greek 'topos'. A commonplace book, then, was not so called to designate its contents, but rather to designate its particular form of structural division.

Into the appropriate section the student would note particularly brilliant aphorisms—the 'sawes of Bookes' as Hamlet refers to them—and well-expressed arguments that he (or she) came across in her reading or 'observation'.[44] Commonplace books provided storehouses of knowledge; they were intended, to use a more modern image, as memory-banks. They provided a way of anatomizing literature: they provided a means of breaking down the information contained within a literary work into constituent parts and then of storing it, with the purpose of facilitating its retrieval and later use within one's own arguments or thoughts. As that suggests, the commonplace book was influential in sixteenth-century strategies of reading, writing, and thinking. Ann Moss argues that the commonplace book 'might be considered a paradigm of Renaissance literature', for, 'Renaissance literature of the imagination is at its most typical when accumulating variations round a commonplace theme and playing textual allusions against each other.'[45] The habits of thought of Renaissance literature, that is, are the habits or techniques of the commonplace book. The commonplace book is central to the discursive practices which constitute the field of knowledge that is rhetoric.

Within *Hamlet*, Polonius, as Alan Fisher has argued, exemplifies the strengths and limitations of such a system, particularly in his farewell to his

[43] The following account of the role and importance of commonplace books is based upon a paper, entitled 'Commonplace Books', given by Dr Ann Moss to the British Section of the International Society of the History of Rhetoric on 6 Mar. 1993. Quotations are given from a printed copy of this. See also Ann Moss, *Printed Commonplace-Books and the Structuring of Renaissance Thought* (Oxford: Clarendon Press, 1996).

[44] Moss quotes Erasmus' description of this process: 'After you have prepared yourself a sufficient number of headings and have arranged them in whatever order you prefer, and have next subdivided them one by one into their appropriate sections and have labelled these sections with commonplaces, . . . then whatever you come across in any author, particularly if it is especially striking, you will be able to note it down immediately in its appropriate place, . . . This will ensure both that what you read will stay fixed more firmly in your mind, and that you will learn to make use of the riches you have acquired by reading . . . Finally, whenever occasion demands, you will have ready to hand a supply of material for spoken and written composition, because you will have, as it were, a well-organized set of pigeon-holes from which you may extract what you want' (p. 13). Moss argued that 'exactly the same prescriptions are enunciated by paedagogic theorists throughout the sixteenth century' (p. 2).

[45] Ibid. 19.

son.[46] Though Polonius' thinking, as it is seen in the play, is neither perceptive nor very wise, the precepts that he gives as a parting gift, though perhaps too many, are impressive. The commonplace system preserves acknowledged wisdom well (while at the same time tending to mould new experience into old categories).[47] It explains the contradiction between Polonius' thoughts and the wisdom of his general advice, 'the seeming inconsistency' as Johnson put it, 'of so much wisdom with so much folly'.[48] Twentieth-century critics have hardly remarked on the disparity between Polonius' thoughts and his precepts, often seeing the two as complementary; the wise-saws are the clichés of the foolish counsellor. This change of critical attitude reflects the impact of mass printing and, more recently, of the electronic storage of information. As Ong points out, only a culture which is assured that it is able to preserve its knowledge deprecates sententiae and cliché.[49]

The commonplace book, then, was not only an image for the mind, as Hamlet uses it, but an image of the sixteenth-century rhetorical mind. It is that rhetorical system and body of knowledge that the Prince declares that he will 'wipe away'. Abandoning the received authorities of his childhood, and the learning gleaned from his studies, is a possible, if tragic course. Yet to step outside the system through which he has in some measure constructed himself is barely conceivable. However dissatisfied the Prince may be with rhetoric, he cannot simply replace that, or any, self-structuring system of thought in one go. Instead, the Ghost's command to revenge will be copied 'all alone' into 'the Booke and Volume' of his brain; the book itself will not itself be abandoned.

Disillusioned with rhetoric, then, and yet unable to escape its constitutive field, Hamlet is dissatisfied in many ways with his sense of self. The previous chapter touched on that dissatisfaction as it traced the Prince's loss of his narrative of self. This chapter has examined one aspect of the sources of self available to the Prince—the Protean rhetorical sense of self. Shakespeare's Prince, however, goes beyond dissatisfaction with a rhetorical sense of self; though he cannot abandon the 'Booke' of his brain, he introduces a new

[46] Alan Fisher, 'Shakespeare's Last Humanist', in *Renaissance and Reformation*, 26: 1 (1990) 37–47. Fisher sees Polonius as 'representative of a whole manner of thinking of which the play is aware and which it examines critically', which manner of thinking Fisher labels humanist. 'Humanist', I would argue, is here a misleading term, for Fisher is referring to the impact of rhetoric within humanist educational techniques and ideals. Fisher also treats the mind as a commonplace book, though he goes on to make assumptions as to the authority of the subject within such a way of thinking that the arguments advanced in this thesis reject.

[47] Ann Moss notes how 'Every new text, every new discovery, every new observation, it seems, could be dismembered, fitted into the corpus of received wisdom, and rendered harmless by assimilation among the "endoxa" of universally sanctioned probabilities supported by dialectical argumentation' (p. 21).

[48] Samuel Johnson, from his notes to his edition of Shakespeare, in *Samuel Johnson on Shakespeare*, ed. H. R. Woudhuysen (Harmondsworth: Penguin, 1989), 239.

[49] Ong, *Rhetoric, Romance and Technology*, 20.

metaphor, and so begins to develop a new understanding, of self. It is with this beginning that this chapter closes.

When Hamlet first meets Rosencrantz and Guildenstern, he welcomes them to a Denmark he describes as a prison. His former friends argue with this description of the kingdom, and Rosencrantz maintains that Denmark only seems a prison to the Prince because of his ambition—the kingdom, ''tis | too narrow for your minde' (2. 2. 253–4). Rosencrantz sets up a Tamburlaine-like sense of the Prince, whose ambitious thoughts encompass far greater kingdoms of the earth than Denmark. Hamlet reverses this, and in doing so puts forward an image for the self which is not based on water, but on a more modern sense of self as area or extension. Hamlet replies to Rosencrantz:

> O God, I could be bounded in a nutshell, and
> count my selfe a King of infinite space; were it not that
> I haue bad dreames.
>
> (2. 2. 255–7)

The kingdom that Hamlet desires to rule is that of his sense of self; his sense of self is the 'I' that could be bounded in a nutshell. That kingdom is both impossibly small and infinitely large, containing all possible kingdoms. This sense of self is no longer constituted from water, nor is its constructed identity pictured in terms of shape; rather it is being pictured as a paradox of extension. Moreover, it is an area which has become mysterious and ungovernable; the 'I' has 'bad dreams', and yet the 'I' cannot control those dreams. Hamlet's sense of himself as a mysterious paradox of extension is not offered as cause for celebration, but as a reason for his grief. The metaphor parallels his sense of his unintelligibility to himself, and his lack of coherent narrative for his life. His loss of narrative is a loss of his ability to trace himself in time. Cut off from the past, unable to gain control over his future, his present moment extends infinitely. His sense of self becomes spatialized, offering him the opportunity of becoming king of infinite space; and yet 'bad dreams' mock this king with the memory of memories.

8
The Princes Hamlet

In Part III it has been argued that senses of self are both an issue and at issue within *Hamlet*, the play. This debate is generated primarily through a presentation of the Prince's dissatisfaction with received or available senses of self. In their place Young Hamlet is given self-constituting formal strategies and the self-expressive resources of metaphor. The quality of this debate concerning the sense of self, the quality, that is, of the play's intellectual argument about and analysis of self (and so of the composition of identity and subjectivity), can be seen in the profound impact the play has had and continues to have on subsequent discussions of the issue. Clearly this debate within *Hamlet*, involving as it does the presentation of competing conceptions of the nature of subjectivity, parallels at many points the controversies of self. One might say that the controversies of self are internal to *Hamlet*. Yet this debate over the nature of subjectivity is given no role within either New Historicist or Cultural Materialist discussions of the nature of English Renaissance subjectivity. The result of (or perhaps the reason for) this omission is to see *Hamlet*, as well as other plays, as static, unthinking objects that must demonstrate a certain, set, and single view of subjectivity. Under such a view, the play is rendered subject, its voices silent under the discourse of the critic. However, the play is in this respect, as in others, a voluble argument, an argument held both within itself and with its culture. It is this argument that generates the dynamic contingency between the play and its culture, a contingency which New Historicists and Cultural Materialists claim to value highly. It is also this argument which ensures that the play eludes causal historical explanation, another linchpin of New Historicists' and Cultural Materialists' stated approaches. The reasons for such a surprising critical forgetting have already been surveyed.

The play of this book (in three acts, not five) draws to a close by listening to this argument in another way. As is fitting, perhaps, the protagonist is called forward to deliver a brief epilogue. However, as he does so, that protagonist is seen to be double; for when Prince Hamlet steps forward, it becomes clear that there is not one Prince Hamlet, but two. There are two Princes Hamlet because the verbal variants between the Q2 and Folio texts of *Hamlet* create two versions of the Prince, each with a different sense of self. This chapter concludes this book by arguing that not only *Hamlet* but also Shakespeare can be seen debating the controversies of self; Shakespeare can be seen, in the Quarto–Folio variants, creating different senses of self for his Princes Hamlet.

To argue that Shakespeare can be seen creating different senses of self for Prince Hamlet in the Q2 and Folio texts is to accept and support the theory of authorial revision. This theory is contestable, and has been of late much contested, though as a topic of literary–critical debate it is in no way new; as Paul Werstine notes in 'The Textual Mystery of *Hamlet*' (1988), this debate had a previous heyday in the nineteenth century.[1] There are few matters of certainty in the arguments for and against authorial revision; no one argument can convince, rather it is the cumulative weight of many arguments which persuades one either to accept or reject the theory. At present it would seem that the arguments for authorial revision outweigh those against it; each of the last three editors of *Hamlet* has come out in favour of the theory. Though these editors each give different accounts concerning the means and times of revision, all argue that Q2 represents an earlier version of the play, the revisions of which can be seen in the Folio text.[2] These editors also agree in accepting the general consensus, current since G. I. Duthie's *The Bad Quarto of Hamlet* (1941), that Q1 is a memorial reconstruction. Although this view of the nature of Q1 has recently begun to be questioned, it is accepted here, and Q1 put aside.[3] This is not to say Q1 has no authority, but that what it has to say is not of relevance to the textual variation discussed below.

Central to the editors' arguments for authorial revision is the analysis of variant passages. The arguments start from the recognition that the omission or addition of passages to the texts damage neither metre, sense, nor drama; these passages cannot plausibly be seen to be the result of any of the many accidents of transmission and publishing. The arguments go on to trace the ways in which the omissions or additions can be seen to have significant dramatic effects. These effects are further argued to have a cumulative dramatic coherence; one change reinforces another, until a series of such changes

[1] Paul Werstine, 'The Textual Mystery of *Hamlet*', *SQ* 39 (1988), 1–26 (1).

[2] The editors are Edwards (1985), Wells (1986), and Hibbard (1987). Their respective arguments are discussed by Taylor (and Wells) in Wells, *William Shakespeare: A Textual Companion*, 396–402. (The Norton Shakespeare, based as it is upon Wells's text, has not been considered as a new edition in respect to its textual matter.) Most arguments concerning the ordering of the versions of the play assume revision takes place fairly shortly after the original composition. Roslyn L. Knutson, however, spreads the revision out over eight or so years. She argues that the 'little Yases' (2. 2. 339) passage, which is not present in Q2, refers not to the War of the Theatres, but is rather a warning to the Children of Blackfriars whose political daring in 1606–8 put the theatrical community as a whole at risk. See Roslyn L. Knutson, 'A New Date and Commercial Agenda for the "Little Eyases" Passage in *Hamlet*', *SQ* 46 (1995), 1–31.

[3] A survey of the debate concerning the nature of Q1 can be found in Thomas Clayton (ed.), *The 'Hamlet' First Published (Q1, 1603): Origins, Form, Intertextualities* (Newark, Del.: University of Delaware Press, 1992), 26–9; and in Grace Ioppolo, *Revising Shakespeare* (Cambridge, Mass.: Harvard University Press, 1991), who also surveys the issue of revision as a whole, arguing against the conclusions drawn by New Historicists from the acceptance of revision. See also J. M. Nosworthy, *Shakespeare's Occasional Plays: Their Origin and Transmission* (London: Arnold, 1965), ch. 12; and Leah S. Marcus, *Unediting the Renaissance* (Routledge: London, 1996), who proposes a Hamlet caught moving between oral and literary cultures.

can be said to produce a text of the play which is coherently distinct from another text of the play.[4] This coherence shows the variants to be informed by a guiding principle, to have a deducible literary dramatic purpose. Again, such a coherence between the dramatic effects of variants cannot plausibly be seen as the result of chance. The presence of an informing principle is a strong argument for seeing the textual variants as revisions. The principle argued for here is that the textual variations between Q2 and Folio texts of *Hamlet* change the Prince's sense of self.

Such arguments from variant passages are still very far—and usually much further than is admitted—from presenting a conclusive case for authorial revision. It may be more likely that an author, as opposed to anyone else, would carry out connected revisions to his or her own text. Yet others, whether a single person or a group of actors, might and did similarly revise someone else's text. The argument for authorial revision is strengthened if the variant passages are surrounded by single-word variants, and if those single-word variants support the dramatic effects produced by the addition or omission of the variant passages. John Kerrigan argues in 'Revision, Adaptation, and the Fool in *King Lear*' that at the beginning of the seventeenth century only authors revising their own work make single-word and indifferent alterations; authors who are revising the work of others make only large-scale alterations, adding or deleting passages. *Hamlet* has very many such single-word and indifferent variants, and satisfies Kerrigan's criteria for authorial revision.[5]

Yet still one cannot be certain that the revisions are authorial. Kerrigan's argument is not conclusive. *Hamlet* might, for example, have been revised by Shakespeare and another or others; Shakespeare may be responsible for most of the single-word variants, and the others for the additions and omissions of passages. Moreover, arguments that single-word variants support the dramatic effects of variant passages tend to be rather unconvincing, since they are so easily produced; single-word variants, by nature of their small size, are easily manipulable to a critic's narrative. A critic who bases his argument on single-

[4] So e.g. G. R. Hibbard, the editor of the Oxford single-volume *Hamlet*, argues that the major variants in the Folio are all part of a general aim to quicken the perceived pace of the play (Hibbard, 126). Philip Edwards, in a more illuminating discussion, argues that the changes between Q2 and Folio resolve local confusions present in Q2, and generally improve the play. His discussion of the end of 3. 4, where Hamlet is saying goodbye to his mother after killing Polonius, is particularly good (Edwards, 16). Paul Werstine (who denies that the variants can be attributed to any particular author) argues that the Folio both shows a Laertes who is stronger, more reflective, and more worthy of the respect that Hamlet shows him in 5. 2 than the Laertes of Q2; and provides a different representation of the contest between Hamlet and Claudius (Werstine, 3–23). These types of arguments were developed most recently in discussions of the texts of *King Lear*. See e.g. Roger Warren, 'The Folio Omission of the Mock Trial: Motives and Consequences', 45–58; Michael Warren, 'The Diminution of Kent', 59–74; John Kerrigan 'Revision, Adaptation, and the Fool in *King Lear*', 195–245—all in Gary Taylor and Michael Warren (eds.), *The Division of the Kingdoms: Shakespeare's Two Versions of 'King Lear'* (Oxford: Clarendon Press, 1983).

[5] Kerrigan, ibid. 213.

word variants and does manage to convince is John Jones, in *Shakespeare at Work* (1995); though it should be noted that Jones, in his various and brilliant arguments, is not arguing for revision but for a notion of the 'creative confirmation' of the play's 'personality'. Yet, finally, whether or not one accepts the theory of authorial revision remains the result of a weighing-up of probabilities. Shakespeare is described as revisor in the discussion that follows as both the weight of previous evidence and the present analysis of the textual variants seem to merit that ascription. Indeed, it seems inherently unlikely that anyone other than Shakespeare made the revisions; those who argue against authorial revisions never say who the revisions are by, preferring to lose the author or authors in a theoretical maze of possibilities and practices. However, the chapter's argument does not stand or fall by the ascription of the revisions to Shakespeare. It makes little difference whether Shakespeare, some other dramatist, or an actor, revised *Hamlet* and created a different sense of self for the Prince. Whoever is responsible for the revisions, the debate over the nature of subjectivity heard between the Q2 and Folio Princes is equally audible.

According to the *Textual Companion*, 'Of all the two-text plays, *Hamlet* comes closest to *Lear* in the scale and complexity of the textual variation apparently resulting from authorial revision.'[6] The Folio *Hamlet* omits some 230 lines present in Q2, which are mostly accounted for by the removal of sixteen passages; and it adds some seventy lines, the majority of which can be found in three passages.[7] On top of these variant passages are a large number of single-word textual variants, which are conveniently listed in the *Textual Companion*.[8] The most obvious point to be made about this listing of revisions was made by W. W. Greg: 'the omission of 225 lines out of nearly 4,000 [the total number of lines in the Folio] is not very much and does not suggest any serious attempt to shorten the play'.[9] The revisions are made for purposes other than abridgement.

Of the nineteen variant passages, nine involve Hamlet, and it is the difference their presence or absence makes to *Hamlet* the play (or more accurately *Hamlet* the plays) that this chapter examines. Two caveats are born in mind. The first has already been mentioned, and concerns the manipulable nature of single-word variants; for this reason, little weight is put on single-word variants in what follows. The second caveat is advanced by Thomas Clayton in the introduction to *The 'Hamlet' First Published* (1992) and concerns the use of variant passages. These are more resistant to critical manipulation than single-word variants, but, Clayton warns, they are not immune. Clayton outlines the tell-tale signs of such manipulation.[10] Typically, quite innocuous

[6] Wells and Taylor, *Shakespeare: A Textual Companion*, 401–2.

[7] Wells's and Taylor's counting of passages is followed here.

[8] Ibid. 402–20.

[9] W. W. Greg, *The Shakespeare First Folio* (Oxford: Clarendon Press, 1955); quoted in *Hamlet*, ed. Hibbard, 108.

[10] See 'Introduction: *Hamlet*'s Ghost' in Clayton, *The 'Hamlet' First Published*, 40–3.

passages—which are either additions or omissions—appear centrally within the textual critic's narrative; these are then claimed to be of pivotal importance, and so to resolve textual problems and sway the movement of the play as a whole. Clayton suggests a practical test for the plausibility of such claims; if the passage is important, 'criticism would probably have made much of it already, and students would notice it regularly'.[11]

The first 'princely cut', that is omission by the Folio of lines spoken by the Prince in Q2, passes Clayton's test easily. The cut occurs in I. 4, where the Prince waits with Horatio and the others for the Ghost to appear. A kettle drum and trumpet sound out Claudius' drinking of a pledge, and Horatio asks if such behaviour is customary. The Folio Prince observes that the custom was one 'More honour'd in the breach, then the obseruance' (I. 4. 18). The Q2 Prince is less succinct, going on to note:

This heauy headed reueale east and west
Makes vs tradust, and taxed of other nations,
They clip vs drunkards, and with Swinish phrase
Soyle our addition, and indeede it takes
From our atchieuements, though perform'd at height
The pith and marrow of our attribute,
So oft it chaunces in particuler men,
That for some vicious mole of nature in them
As in their birth wherein they are not guilty,
(Since nature cannot choose his origin)
By their ore-grow'th of some complextion,
Oft breaking downe the pales and forts of reason,
Or by some habit, that too much ore-leauens
The forme of plausiue manners, that these men
Carrying I say the stamp of one defect
Being Natures liuery, or Fortunes starre,
His vertues else be they as pure as grace,
As infinite as man may vndergoe,
Shall in the generall censure take corruption
From that particuler fault: the dram of eale
Doth all the noble substance of a doubt
To his owne scandle.

(Q2 I. 4. 621 + 1–22)

The editors of the Oxford and New Cambridge *Hamlet*s offer their reasons for this cut. G. R. Hibbard suggests that the passage is cut so that the audience is not 'tantalized with a repetition of one of the stock "complaints" of the Elizabethan satirist: the drunkenness of the Danes', when what the audience wants to see is the Ghost.[12] Such an argument is weak, and could equally well be reversed. J. Dover Wilson argued that the delay before the Ghost's arrival

[11] Ibid. 42–3.
[12] *Hamlet*, ed. Hibbard, 356.

was a good example of Shakespeare's dramatic astuteness; 'tantalizing' audiences is usually a mark of dramatic success.

Moreover, though the complaint against the Danes may be stock, the thesis that Hamlet advances from it, beginning 'So oft it chaunces in particuler men', is not. Indeed, the concerns of this passage are central to the play. Focusing on its vocabulary alone produces a list of what have become key words within critical accounts: 'nature', 'reason', 'habit' (q.v. 'custom'), 'fortune', and 'corruption'. Rather than being, as Edwards suggests in the New Cambridge *Hamlet*, an unimportant passage with a difficult textual crux (the 'dram of eale'), this is an important passage.[13] It has demonstrated that importance, as Clayton would expect, by recurring within criticism of the play. In particular, critics have noted how central these lines are to our understanding of Prince Hamlet. For instance, Molly Mahood argues in *Shakespeare's Word-Play* that these lines are 'vital to our understanding of Hamlet's dilemma'.[14] Wolfgang Clemen similarly believes that these lines touch 'upon that *leitmotif* of the whole play; [Hamlet] describes how human nature may be brought to decay . . . the balance of the powers in man is the theme here, and "corruption", a basic motif in the whole play, already makes its appearance.'[15] Ifor Evans, in *The Language of Shakespeare's Plays*, goes further: 'It could be urged,' he writes, 'that in this sentence Shakespeare defines the conception of character which is illustrated through the protagonists of his tragedies.'[16]

Evans overstates his case; Shakespeare, as has been seen, does not have a single, as Evans calls it, 'conception of character'. But Evans is quite right to point out that the Prince is here advancing a concept of the way in which personality functions and is providing a picture of a certain sense of self. In fact, the Q2 Prince here advances several related concepts of the functioning of personality. He sums these up in the image of 'the stamp of one defect', which certain men can be found 'carrying'. As that 'carrying' and 'stamp' suggests, there is little sense of agency or self-constituting interiority in the way in which the Prince discusses personality; here personality is pictured in external and impersonal terms. So, for instance, this Prince begins his analogy between Denmark and a man by noting how certain men are born with 'some vicious mole of nature in them', for which 'they are not guilty, | (Since nature cannot choose his origin)'. Personality is a given quality. Next the Prince attributes a person's behaviour to the 'ore-grow'th of some complextion'. 'Complextion', as has been seen, is a technical term, part of the physiological vocabulary that articulates the theory of humours, describing the interior areas of personality in common, impersonal terms. Finally the Prince notes how one vicious 'habit'

[13] *Hamlet*, ed. Edwards, 14.

[14] Molly M. Mahood, *Shakespeare's Word-Play* (London: Methuen, 1957), 116.

[15] W. H. Clemen, 'The Imagery of *Hamlet*' in *Shakespeare: 'Hamlet'*, ed. John Jump (London: Macmillan, 1968), 72.

[16] Ifor Evans, *The Language of Shakespeare's Plays*, (3rd edn.; London: Methuen, 1964), 119.

may come to taint the rest of a man's praiseworthy behaviour. 'Habit' may have its modern sense here or may, as Jenkins suggests in the Arden edition, have the older sense of 'habit as a manifestation of nature'; neither sense allows room for an area of self-constituted interiority within identity.

This passage offers an intense presentation, by Young Hamlet, of external and impersonal theories of personality. Moreover, it does so towards the beginning of the play and in memorable language. Evans claims that these lines are 'the most sustained period in blank verse to be found anywhere in the plays'.[17] Perhaps this is so; there is no denying the power of phrases such as 'some vicious mole of nature', and 'the stamp of one defect'. Such a use of external and impersonal theories of personality should not surprise. In Chapter 6, the Prince was seen to use various versions and views of interiority; although, that is, he discovered instrumental, cause and effect views of identity to be unsatisfactory in describing himself, he still, at moments, used them. The point was made that previous concepts of interiority remained available when other concepts arose; Raymond Williams's sense of the residual, dominant, and emerging categories of culture was appropriate to describe the available senses of self. However, the balance between the Prince's senses of self shifts with the presence and absence of this passage. Present, it gives us an unforgettable glimpse of a Hamlet more as the New Historicists and Cultural Materialists would have him, believing, with Guildenstern and (at moments) Coleridge, that it is possible to 'pluck out the heart' of someone's 'mystery'. The Q2 Prince here is seen believing in cause and effect explanations of personality. This complicates his sense, articulated elsewhere in Q2, of the inadequacy of these explanations. With the passage absent, the Folio Prince's sense of the unique nature of his mystery is far more dominant, and the audience's attention is more clearly focused on the Prince's frustrated attempts to discover narratives that will render intelligible the pattern of his life.

The Folio's toning-down of the Q2 Prince's expression of impersonal and external concepts of personality continues through the next two princely cuts. These come in 3. 4, where Hamlet reprimands his mother for her incestuous and swift remarriage to Claudius. The first cut comes as Hamlet asserts that his mother cannot use the excuse of love for her actions, as she has reached the age when judgement should predominate over 'the hey-day in the blood'. Looking at two paintings, presumably miniatures, one of Old Hamlet and another of Claudius, Hamlet asks his mother, 'what Iudgement | Would step from this, to this?' (3. 4. 69–70)[18] In the Folio, he does not pause for answer, but goes straight on to another question, 'What diuell was't, | That thus hath cousend you at hoodman-blinde?' (3. 4. 70–1). But in Q2, he does take the time for an answer, though it is his own:

[17] Ibid. 118.

[18] Jenkins reviews the various opinions concerning the exact nature of the 'pictures'. '*Hamlet* Then Till Now', 516–19.

Sence sure youe haue
Els could you not haue motion, but sure that sence
Is appoplext, for madnesse would not erre
Nor sence to ecstacie was nere so thral'd
But it reseru'd some quantity of choise
To serue in such a difference.

(Q2 3. 4. 70 + 1–5)

Hamlet here invokes the idea, deriving from Aristotle according to the commentary, that any creature capable of movement ('motion') must have external senses.[19] His mother's five senses, he argues, must in some way be completely dysfunctional ('appoplext'), or else she could never have married Claudius. This line of argument is amplified in the second half of this cut, which comes after Hamlet's 'What diuell was't?' (3. 4. 70). In Q2, the Prince lists each of the five senses, arguing that any of them would have prevented his mother from marrying, had they been working:

Eyes without feeling, feeling without sight,
Eares without hands, or eyes, smelling sance all,
Or but a sickly part of one true sence
Could not so mope.

(Q2 3. 4. 71 + 1–4)

Again, the Q2 Prince is offering an impersonal conception of personality which denies the person agency; Gertrude thought as she did because of a failure in her five senses. Once more, the presence or absence of this passage alters the balance of the notions of self that the Prince uses. The Q2 Prince again finds external, given explanations satisfactory, while the Folio Prince keeps his counsel.

The second cut in this scene intensifies the Folio Prince Hamlet's silence. The Prince, having forced a confession of wrongdoing from his mother, now urges her to live a purer life. He asks her not to share Claudius' bed, and so to 'Assume a Vertue, if you have it not' (3. 4. 151). In the Folio he continues by pointing out that such abstinence will become successively more easy:

refraine to night,
And that shall lend a kinde of easinesse
To the next abstinence.

(3. 4. 152–4)

The Q2 Prince, between these two quotations, provides a theoretical explanation of the way in which such 'assuming' works:

That monster custome, who all sence doth eate,
Of habits deuill, is angel yet in this
That to the vse of actions faire and good,

[19] Jenkins quotes C. S. Lewis to this effect. Ibid. 323.

He likewise giues a frock or Liuery
That aptly is put on.

(Q2 3. 4. 151 + 1–5)

'Custome', this Prince Hamlet theorizes, is able to shape people for good or ill, emphasizing its external and impersonal nature by his personification of it as 'that monster'. He expands on this in the second half of the cut passage, which comes after line 154. As the first abstinence makes the second easier, so does the second make,

the next more easie:
For vse almost can change the stamp of nature,
And either [shame] the deuill, or throwe him out
With wonderous potency.

(Q2 3. 4. 154 + 1–3)

The Q2 Prince suggests that impersonal custom can almost change the givenness of nature. With the phrase 'the stamp of nature' the first princely cut is recalled; the phrase combines 'the vicious mole of nature' and 'the stamp of one defect'. 'Nature' is now presumed to be a 'vicious mole', its 'stamp' being that of the devil. Indeed, this cut passage recalls, in its emphasis on 'Custome', 'habit', 'use', and 'nature', the way in which that first passage invoked many critical key words, so strengthening the sense that the removal of both passages displays a related concern.

The next princely cut comes towards the end of 3. 4, as the Prince is taking his leave of his mother. He reminds her that he must go to England, an arrangement that Gertrude acknowledges: ''Tis so concluded on' (3. 4. 185). In Q2 the Prince goes on to analyse the situation and outline his plans:

Ham. Ther's letters seald, and my two Schoolefellowes,
Whom I will trust as I will Adders fang'd,
They beare the mandat, they must sweep my way
And marshall me to knauery: let it worke,
For tis the sport to haue the enginer
Hoist with his owne petar, an't shall goe hard
But I will delue one yard belowe their mines,
And blowe them at the Moone: o tis most sweete
When in one line two crafts directly meete.

(Q2 3. 4. 185 + 1–9)

Edwards discusses the impact of the omission of this passage well.[20] As he points out, the cut removes a number of niggling problems raised by its presence; how does Hamlet know that his friends are accompanying him to England? How does he know that Claudius is intent on killing him (particularly when Claudius has yet to tell the audience of this)? Why does he believe that his 'Schoole-

[20] *Hamlet*, ed. Edwards, 14–16.

fellowes' are willing accomplices in this plan? More significant is the impact the presence or absence has on our view of Hamlet. The Q2 Prince here announces a plan that he carries through to the letter. This sits uncomfortably with his later assertion to Horatio that the events on board the ship demonstrate that 'There's a Diuinity that shapes our ends' (5. 2. 10); is the Prince here labouring to conceal the coldness of his calculations? How is his assertion that 'They are not neere my Conscience' (5. 2. 59) to be read?

Edwards argues that this omission improves the play: 'The Hamlet whose experiences and thoughts have been with us for three acts is lessened and limited by the plan and threat which he issues in the quarto version of the speech.'[21] Whether or not Edwards's qualitative judgement is considered correct, the omission of this passage significantly changes the perspective within which the audience view the Prince. The Folio Prince's motives are less known than the Q2 Prince's; he is again quieter.

However, though this is a significant revision, it is not a revision aimed at changing the Prince's sense of self. The revision produces two Prince Hamlets, but differentiates them not on the grounds of their senses of self but on the grounds of their motivation (an area bound up particularly with the literary-critical concerns of character). The final princely cut achieves a similar effect; the Folio, in cutting the messenger's delivery of Gertrude's request for Hamlet to 'vse some gentle entertainment | to *Laertes*, before you fall to play' (Q2 5. 2. 154 + 11–12), makes his subsequent attempt at a reconciliation with Laertes his own choice.[22] The Folio cuts an external explanation for its Prince's actions, and in so doing increases the agency the Prince is seen to have. More, the Folio provides a motive for the Prince's attempt at reconciliation; for earlier in the same scene the Folio Prince expresses his regrets to Horatio concerning his earlier treatment of Laertes:

> but I am very sorry good *Horatio*,
> That to *Laertes* I forgot my selfe;
> For by the image of my Cause, I see
> The Portraiture of his.
>
> (5. 2. 76–9)

The Folio Prince is given more mystery with regard to his intentions, as a result of the first omission, and a greater degree of agency and self-motivation, as a result of the second omission and Folio addition.

These changes effected by the Folio revisions create a different Prince; it is tempting to see them as further examples of the revisions altering the Princes' senses of self. However, it must be said again, motive, intentions, and agency are not self. The most that can be argued is that these omissions and additions

[21] Ibid. 16.

[22] Taylor makes this and the following point in Wells and Taylor, *Shakespeare: A Textual Companion*, 400.

demonstrate a principle of revision which, though strictly speaking different from the revisions aimed at changing the Prince's sense of self, are in sympathy with it. In other words, as one might expect, other constitutive aspects of the Prince's identity are being altered at the same time as his sense of self is being altered.

There remain four further variant passages which concern Prince Hamlet. Two of these have no relevance to the principle of revision being argued for here. One is the omission of about half of Hamlet's mocking banter with Osric (Q2 5. 2. 106 + 1–25). The other is the addition of the passage concerning the children's company, the 'little | Yases' (2. 2. 337–62). Both of these variants are of local dramatic effect. The dramatic effects of the second omission, by contrast, go beyond the scope of this chapter. This is the omission from the Folio of most of 4. 4, and in particular Hamlet's soliloquy which begins, 'How all occasions doe informe against me, | And spur my dull reuenge.' (Q2 4. 4. 9 + 26–7). The desire to alter the Prince's sense of self does not explain this cut, for its dramatic effects are far more complicated and widespread than that. However, the cut does have that effect amongst others. This was the passage which contains the Prince's clearest and most distancing example of a 'what?' not 'who?' question, already discussed in 3. 1. It was here that when the Prince asked himself 'Why yet I liue to say this thing's to doe?' (Q2 4. 4. 9 + 38), he returned to an answer, unexpected to a modern audience, in terms of the question 'What is a man?' (4. 4. 9 + 27). Cutting this soliloquy again produces a Folio Prince who is quieter on matters concerning his sense of self, and less given to explanations in external terms.[23]

There remains, then, a final addition, which has been discussed in Chapters 6 and 7. Hamlet welcomes his old friends, Rosencrantz and Guildenstern, on their arrival at Elsinore. He asks them if they have any news of interest of foreign affairs, and Rosencrantz replies that they have none, except 'that the World's growne honest' (2. 2. 238–9). Hamlet is unconvinced: 'Then is Doomesday neere: But your newes is | not true' (2. 2. 240–1). The Q2 Prince went straight on to ask, 'But in the beaten way of friendship, what make you at *Elsonoure*?' (2. 2. 270–1). The Folio Prince, however, goes on to 'question more in particular' (2. 2. 241), asking what his friends have done to deserve being sent 'to Prison hither?' (2. 2. 243). Rosencrantz and Guildenstern disagree and, in reply to Rosencrantz's suggestion that it is his ambition which makes Denmark seem a prison to him, Hamlet replies with his image of the self as a paradox of extension: 'O God, I could be bounded in a nutshell, and | count my selfe a Kinge of infinite space; were it not that I haue bad dreames' (2. 2. 255–7).

This chapter closes with the sight of two Princes Hamlet on its stage. The Q2 Prince is more vociferous, more willing to use external, given theories of self. The Folio Prince is seen as quieter, less willing to think through such normative

[23] Jones argues that the inclusion of this soliloquy by Lewis Theobald in his 1733 edition of Shakespeare, the first conflated edition of *Hamlet*, prompted the debate over the Prince's delay.

systems; but he is not silent, speaking—in ways his brother does not—of 'that Within'. Side by side, the Princes Hamlet stage between them different notions of the sense of self. Doing so, they may be seen to play the drama of Shakespeare's own controversies of self. This book has been, all along, an attempt, as Greenblatt has urged, to listen to voices; it has tried to bring critics and literary works to speak on its stage. The book's critical drama is, in the end, most like an eavesdropping scene. The voices of the past cannot be heard perfectly, for a variety of reasons. Yet those voices must be listened to as best they can be; for such a listening is part of giving to the past the respect that it deserves, without which the present is a much quieter, and a duller place. The past is no child to be seen and not heard. Its answers to the question that lies at the heart of our controversies of self—'Who's there?'—should provide the starting-point for our own critical enquiries. Within *Hamlet*, and between *Hamlet*s, and between Princes Hamlet, the argument concerning the nature of self is heard, extending out into the play's surrounding cultures and times. To listen attentively to those voices, to try to register their tone and understand their gestures, is to preserve the differences of those voices from our own and to locate them in history. Without such a location, our own voices lose their sense of position, their point of perspectives. Silence, within such a view, is death.

Yet no single answer will be overheard on this subject of self; no consensus will resolve the controversies of self. The controversies are to be listened to and described. Unless, that is, the answer is Benedick's in *Much adoe about Nothing*. Benedick is the luckiest of listeners. He finds love through his eavesdropping, but as he does so he realizes that he is compromising almost everything he has declared that he believes in. Wisely, he decides not to worry; 'for man', he says, 'is a giddy thing, and this is my conclusion.'

References

PRIMARY TEXTS

Hamlet, Prince of Denmark, ed. Philip Edwards (Cambridge: Cambridge University Press, 1985)

Hamlet, ed. G. R. Hibbard (Oxford: Oxford University Press, 1987)

Hamlet, ed. Harold Jenkins (London: Methuen, 1982)

The Three-Text 'Hamlet', ed. Bernice W. Kliman (New York: AMS Press, 1991)

William Shakespeare: The Complete Works, ed. Stanley Wells, Gary Taylor, *et al.* (Oxford: Oxford University Press, 1986)

Mr. William Shakespeares Comedies, Histories, & Tragedies [ed. Edward Knight and Ralph Crane?] (London: Jaggard, Blount, Smithweeke and Aspley, 1623; facsimile edn. prepared by Helge Kökeritz and Charles Tyler Prouty, Oxford: Oxford University Press, 1955)

ANON., *The Life and Death of Iacke Straw* (London: William Barley, 1593)

CASTIGLIONE, BALDASSARE, *The Book of the Courtier*, trans Sir Thomas Hoby (London: Dent, 1928; first pub. 1561)

A Catalogue of the Contents of Strawberry Hill (London: Smith and Robins, 1842)

CAVENDISH, GEORGE, *The Life and Death of Cardinal Wolsey*, ed. Richard S. Sylvester (London: EETS, 1959)

Certain Sermons or Homilies (1547) and A Homily against Disobedience and Wilful Rebellion (1570): A Critical Edition, ed. Ronald B. Bond (Toronto: University of Toronto Press, 1987)

DONNE, JOHN, *John Donne: The Complete English Poems*, ed. A. J. Smith (Harmondsworth: Penguin, 1971)

ERASMUS, DESIDERIUS, *De Copia*, trans. Betty I. Knott (3rd edn., 1534) in *Collected Works*, 86 vols. (Toronto: University of Toronto Press, 1974–93), xxiv

HILLIARD, NICHOLAS, *A Treatise Concerning the Arte of Limning*, ed. R. K. R. Thornton and T. G. S. Cain (Northumberland: Mid Northumberland Arts Group, 1981; unpub. previously, wr. 1589–1603)

JONSON, BEN, *Ben Jonson*, ed. C. H. Herford and Percy Simpson, 11 vols. (Oxford: Clarendon Press, 1925–52)

—— *The New Inn*, ed. Michael Hattaway (Manchester: Manchester University Press, 1984; first performed 1629)

MARLOWE, CHRISTOPHER and collaborator, *The Tragicall History of D. Faustus*, ed. David Bevington and Eric Rasmussen (Manchester: Manchester University Press, 1993; first performed 1588–9)

MIDDLETON, THOMAS, and ROWLEY, WILLIAM, *The Changeling*, ed. N. W. Bawcutt (Manchester: Manchester University Press, 1958; first performed 1622)

MONTAIGNE, MICHAEL, *The Essays of Montaigne*, trans. John Florio, 3 vols. (3rd edn., 1632; London: Nutt, 1892–3)

Overbury, Thomas, *The Overburian Characters*, ed. W. J. Paylor (Oxford: Basil Blackwell, 1936; first pub. 1614)

Pico (Giovanni Pico Della Mirandola), 'Oration on the Dignity of Man', trans. Elizabeth Livermore Forbes, in Cassirer, *et al.*, *The Renaissance Philosophy of Man*, 215–54

Quintilian, Marcus Fabius, *Institutio Oratoria*, trans. H. E. Butler, 4 vols. (London: William Heinemann, 1920)

Vives, Juan Luis, 'A Fable About Man', trans. Nancy Lekeith, in Cassirer, *et al.*, *The Renaissance Philosophy of Man*, 385–93

Webster, John, *The Tragedy of the Duchess of Malfi*, ed. Elizabeth M. Brennan (3rd edn., London: A. C. Black, 1993; first performed 1613–14)

Wilson, Thomas, *Arte of Rhetorique*, ed. G. H. Mair (Oxford: Clarendon Press, 1909; 2nd edn. of 1560)

SECONDARY TEXTS

Abbott, E. A., *A Shakespearian Grammar* (London: Macmillan, 1905)

Abrams, M. H., *The Mirror and the Lamp: Romantic Theory and Critical Tradition* (Oxford: Oxford University Press, 1953)

Aers, David, *Community, Gender, and Individual Identity: English Writing 1360–1430* (London: Routledge, 1988)

——'A Whisper in the Ear of Early Modernists', in Aers (ed.) *Culture and History 1350–1600* (London: Harvester Wheatsheaf, 1992), 177–202

Althusser, Louis, 'Ideology and Ideological State Apparatuses', in *Lenin and Philosophy and Other Essays*, trans. Ben Brewster (London: NLB, 1971), 121–73

Babcock, R. W., *The Genesis of Shakespeare Idolatry 1766–1799* (Chapel Hill, NC: University of North Carolina Press, 1931)

Badawi, M. M., *Coleridge: Critic of Shakespeare* (Cambridge: Cambridge University Press, 1973)

Baldwin, T. W., *William Shakespeare's Small Latine and Lesse Greeke*, 2 vols. (Urbana, Ill.: University of Illinois Press, 1944)

Bannister, Don and Fransella, Fay, *Inquiring Man: The Psychology of Personal Constructs*, (3rd edn.; London: Routledge, 1986).

Barber, C. L., *Shakespeare's Festive Comedy: A Study of Dramatic Form and its Relation to Social Custom* (Princeton: Princeton University Press, 1959)

Barker, Francis, *The Tremulous Private Body: Essays in Subjection* (London: Methuen, 1984)

——and Hulme, Peter, 'Nymphs and Reapers Heavily Vanish: The Discursive Contexts of *The Tempest*', in Drakakis (ed.), *Alternative Shakespeares*, 191–205

Barton, Anne, 'Shakespeare and the Limits of Language', *SS* 21 (1974), 19–30

——*Ben Jonson, Dramatist* (Cambridge: Cambridge University Press, 1984)

——'Perils of Historicism', *NYRB*, 28 March 1991, 51–4

——'Comic London', in *Essays, Mainly Shakespearean* (Cambridge: Cambridge University Press, 1994), 329–51

——'London Comedy and the Ethos of the City', in *Essays, Mainly Shakespearean*, 302–28

BATE, JONATHAN, *Shakespeare and the English Romantic Imagination* (Oxford: Clarendon Press, 1986)

——*Shakespearean Constitutions: Politics, Theatre, Criticism 1730–1830* (Oxford: Clarendon Press, 1989)

——(ed.), *The Romantics on Shakespeare* (Penguin: Harmondsworth, 1991)

BAYLEY, JOHN, *Shakespeare and Tragedy* (London: Routledge & Kegan Paul, 1981)

BELSEY, CATHERINE, *The Subject of Tragedy: Identity and Difference in Renaissance Drama* (London: Methuen, 1985)

——'Literature, History, Politics', in Wilson and Dutton (eds.), *New Historicism*, 33–44

BERKOFF, STEVEN, *I am Hamlet* (London: Faber and Faber, 1989)

BEVINGTON, DAVID, *Action is Eloquence* (Cambridge, Mass.: Harvard University Press, 1984)

BLACKMUR, R. P., *Language as Gesture: Essays in Poetry* (London: George Allen & Unwin, 1954)

BLIGH, JOHN, 'Shakespearean Character Study to 1800', *SS* 37 (1984), 141–53

BLOOM, HAROLD, *Ruin the Sacred Truths: Poetry and Belief from the Bible to the Present* (Cambridge, Mass.: Harvard University Press, 1989)

BOOTH, STEPHEN, 'On the Value of *Hamlet*', in Norman Rabkin (ed.), *Reinterpretations of Elizabethan Drama* (Columbia University Press: New York and London, 1969), 137–76

BOSSY, JOHN, *Giordano Bruno and the Embassy Affair* (Vintage: London, 1992; first pub. 1991)

BRADLEY, A. C., *Shakespearean Tragedy: Lectures on 'Hamlet', 'Othello', 'King Lear' and 'Macbeth'* (Macmillan & Co., 1904; repr. Harmondsworth: Penguin, 1991)

BRADSHAW, GRAHAM, *Shakespeare's Scepticism* (Brighton: Harvester Press, 1987)

——*Misrepresentations: Shakespeare and the Materialists* (Ithaca, NY: Cornell University Press, 1993)

BRISSENDEN, R. F., *Virtue in Distress: Studies in the Novel of Sentiment from Richardson to Sade* (London: Macmillan, 1974)

BURFORD, E. J., *Bawds and Lodgings* (London: Peter Owen, 1976)

BURNET, GEORGE, *Bishop Burnet's History of His Own Time*, 2 vols. (London: T. Ward, 1724–34).

BUSHNELL, REBECCA W., *Tragedies of Tyrants: Political Thought and Theater in the English Renaissance* (Ithaca, NY: Cornell University Press, 1990)

CAIN, TOM, 'Ralegh's Roles', *EIC* 24 (1974), 286–94

CASSIRER, ERNST, KRISTELLER, PAUL OSKAR and RANDALL, JOHN HERMAN JR. (eds.), *The Renaissance Philosophy of Man* (Chicago: University of Chicago Press, 1948)

CLAYTON, THOMAS (ed.), *The 'Hamlet' First Published (Q1, 1603): Origins, Form, Intertextualities* (Newark, Del.: University of Delaware Press, 1992)

CLEMEN, W. H., 'The Imagery of *Hamlet*', in *Shakespeare: Hamlet*, ed. John Jump, 64–77

CODDON, KARIN S., '"Suche Strange Desygns": Madness, Subjectivity and Treason in *Hamlet* and Elizabethan Culture', in Wofford (ed.), *Case Studies in Contemporary Criticism: 'Hamlet'*, 380–402

COHEN, WALTER, 'Political Criticism of Shakespeare', in Howard and O'Connor (eds.), *Shakespeare Reproduced*, 18–46

COLEMAN, CHRISTOPHER and STARKEY, DAVID (eds.), *Revolution Reassessed: Revisions in the History of Tudor Government and Administration* (Oxford: Clarendon Press, 1986)

Collier, Peter and Ryan, Helga Geyer (eds.), *Literary Theory Today* (Oxford: Polity Press, 1990)

Conklin, Paul S., *A History of 'Hamlet' Criticism 1601–1821* (New York: Humanities Press, 1968)

Cressy, David, 'Foucault, Stone, Shakespeare and Social History', *ELR* 21 (1991), 121–33

Daniell, David, '*Hamlet*', in Wells (ed.), *Shakespeare: A Bibliographical Guide*, 201–21

Danson, Lawrence, *Tragic Alphabet: Shakespeare's Drama of Language* (New Haven and London: Yale University Press, 1974)

Davisson, Allan, 'George Kelly and the American Mind (Or Why Has He Been Obscure for So Long in the U.S.A. and whence the New Interest?)', in Fransella (ed.), *Personal Construct Psychology 1977*, 25–34

de Grazia, Margreta and Stallybrass, Peter, 'The Materiality of the Shakespearean Text', *SQ* 44 (1993), 255–83

——and Quilligan, Maureen (eds.), *Subject and Object in Renaissance Culture* (Cambridge: Cambridge University Press, 1996)

Demetz, Peter, Greene, Thomas, and Nelson, Lowry Jr. (eds.), *The Disciplines of Criticism: Essays in Literary Theory, Interpretation, and History* (New Haven and London: Yale University Press, 1968)

Derrida, Jacques, *Of Grammatology*, trans. Gayatri Chakravorty Spivak (Baltimore: Johns Hopkins University Press, 1974; first pub. as *De la grammatologie*, Paris, 1967)

Desmet, Christy, *Reading Shakespeare's Characters: Rhetoric, Ethics, and Identity* (Amherst, Mass.: University of Massachusetts Press, 1992)

Dews, Peter, *Logics of Disintegration: Post-Structuralist Thought and the Claims of Critical Theory* (London: Verso, 1987)

Dietrich, Julia, *'Hamlet' in the 1960s: An Annotated Bibliography* (New York: Garland, 1992)

Dobson, Michael, *The Making of the National Poet: Shakespeare, Adaptation and Authorship, 1660–1769* (Oxford: Clarendon Press, 1992)

Dollimore, Jonathan, *Radical Tragedy: Religion, Ideology and Power in the Drama of Shakespeare and his Contemporaries* (Brighton: Harvester Press, 1984)

——'Critical Developments: Cultural Materialism, Feminism and Gender Critique, and New Historicism', in Wells (ed.), *Shakespeare: A Bibliographical Guide*, 405–28

——and Sinfield, Alan (eds.), *Political Shakespeare: New Essays in Cultural Materialism* (Manchester: Manchester University Press, 1985)

Donaldson, Ian, *Jonson's Magic Houses: Essays in Interpretation* (Oxford: Clarendon Press, 1997)

Donawerth, Jane, *Shakespeare and the Sixteenth-Century Study of Language* (Urbana, Ill., and Chicago: University of Illinois Press, 1984)

Drakakis, John (ed.), *Alternative Shakespeares* (London: Methuen, 1985)

During, Simon, *Foucault and Literature: Towards a Genealogy of Writing* (London: Routledge, 1992)

Dutton, Richard, 'Postscript', in Wilson and Dutton (eds.), *New Historicism*, 219–32

Eagleton, Terry, *William Shakespeare* (Oxford: Basil Blackwell, 1986)

Edwards, Catherine, 'Beware of Imitations: Theatre and the Subversion of Imperial Identity', in Jas Elsner and Jamie Masters (eds.), *Reflections of Nero: Culture, History and Representation* (Chapel Hill, NC: University of North Carolina Press, 1994), 83–97

ELLMANN, RICHARD, *Oscar Wilde* (London: Hamish Hamilton, 1987)
ELTON, G. R., *The Tudor Revolution in Government* (Cambridge: Cambridge University Press, 1953)
EMPSON, W., '*Hamlet*', in David B. Pirie (ed.), *Essays on Shakespeare* (Cambridge: Cambridge University Press, 1986), 79–136 (first pub. in *Sewanee Review*, 61 (1953), 15–42, 185–205)
EVANS, IFOR, *The Language of Shakespeare's Plays*, (3rd edn.; London: Methuen, 1964)
EVERETT, BARBARA, '*Hamlet*: A Time to Die', *SS* 30 (1977), 117–34
EWBANK, INGA-STINA, '*Hamlet* and the Power of Words', *SS* 30 (1977), 85–102
EWEN, ROBERT B., *An Introduction to Theories of Personality* (5th edn.; Mahwah, NJ: Lawrence Erlbaum, 1998)
FELPERIN, HOWARD, *The Uses of the Canon: Elizabethan Literature and Contemporary Theory* (Oxford: Clarendon Press, 1990)
FERRY, ANNE, *The 'Inward' Language: Sonnets of Wyatt, Sidney, Shakespeare, Donne* (Chicago: University of Chicago Press, 1983)
FINEMAN, JOEL, *Shakespeare's Perjured Eye: The Invention of Poetic Subjectivity in the Sonnets* (Berkeley: University of California Press, 1986)
——'The History of the Anecdote: Fiction and Fiction', in Veeser (ed.), *The New Historicism*, 49–76
FISH, STANLEY, 'Commentary: The Young and the Restless', in Veeser (ed.), *The New Historicism*, 303–16
FISHER, ALAN, 'Shakespeare's Last Humanist', *Renaissance and Reformation*, 26: 1 (1990) 37–47
FISHER, SHEILA and HALLEY, JANET E. (eds.), *Seeking the Woman in Late Medieval and Renaissance Writings: Essays in Feminist Contextual Criticism* (Knoxville, Tenn.: University of Tennessee Press, 1989)
FOAKES, R. A. (ed.), *Coleridge on Shakespeare* (London: Routledge & Kegan Paul, 1971)
——*Coleridge's Criticism of Shakespeare* (London: Athlone Press, 1989)
FOUCAULT, MICHEL, *Madness and Civilization: A History of Insanity in the Age of Reason*, trans. Richard Howard (London: Tavistock, 1967; first pub. as *Histoire de la folie à l'âge classique*, Librairie Plon, 1961)
——*The Archaeology of Knowledge*, trans. A. M. Sheridan Smith (London: Tavistock, 1967; first pub. as *L'Archeologie du savoir*, Paris: Editions Gallimard, 1969)
——*Discipline and Punish: The Birth of the Prison*, trans. Alan Sheriden (Harmondsworth: Penguin, 1991; first pub. as *Surveiller et punir: Naissance de la prison*, Paris: Editions Gallimard, 1975)
——'Nietzsche, Genealogy, History', in *The Foucault Reader*, ed. Paul Rabinow (Harmondsworth: Penguin, 1991; first pub. New York: Random House, 1984), 76–100
——*The History of Sexuality: An Introduction*, trans. Robert Hurley (Harmondsworth: Penguin, 1990; first pub. as *La Volonté de savoir*, Paris: Editions Gallimard, 1976)
FRANSELLA, FAY (ed.), *Personal Construct Psychology 1977* (London: Academic Press, 1978), 25–34.
——and BANNISTER, DON, *A Manual for Repertory Grid Technique* (London: Academic Press, 1977)
——*George Kelly* (London: Sage, 1995)
FREUD, SIGMUND, *The Interpretation of Dreams*, ed. and trans. James Strachey (London: George Allen & Unwin, 1954; first pub. 1900)

GALLAGHER, CATHERINE, 'Marxism and The New Historicism', in Vesser (ed.), *The New Historicism*, 37–48

GARBER, MARJORIE, *Shakespeare's Ghost Writers: Literature as Uncanny Casualty* (London: Methuen, 1987)

GARDNER, HOWARD, *The Quest for Mind: Piaget, Levi-Strauss and the Structuralist Movement* (London: Quartet, 1976)

GEERTZ, CLIFFORD, *The Interpretation of Cultures: Selected Essays* (New York: Basic Books, 1973)

GERGEN, KENNETH J., 'Textual Considerations in the Scientific Construction of Human Character', *Style*, 24 (1990), 365–79

GIAMATTI, A. BARTLETT, *Exile and Change in Renaissance Literature* (New Haven: Yale University Press, 1984)

GIBBONS, BRIAN, *Jacobean City Comedy* (2nd edn.; London: Methuen, 1980)

GLANVILLE, PHILIPPA, 'Cardinal Wolsey and the Goldsmiths', in Gunn and Lindley (eds.), *Cardinal Wolsey*, 131–48

GOFFMAN, IRVING, *Frame Analysis* (Penguin: Harmondsworth, 1975)

GOLDBERG, JONATHAN, *Writing Matter: From the Hands of the English Renaissance* (Stanford, Calif.: Stanford University Press, 1990)

GRADY, HUGH, *The Modernist Shakespeare* (Oxford: Clarendon Press, 1991)

GREENBLATT, STEPHEN J., *Sir Walter Ralegh: The Renaissance Man and his Roles* (New Haven: Yale University Press, 1973)

——*Renaissance Self Fashioning: From More to Shakespeare* (Chicago: University of Chicago Press, 1980)

——*Shakespearean Negotiations: The Circulation of Social Energy in Renaissance England* (Oxford: Clarendon Press, 1988)

——*Learning to Curse: Essays in Early Modern Culture* (London: Routledge, 1990)

——(ed.), *Genre*, 15 (1982)

GREENE, THOMAS, 'The Flexibility of the Self in Renaissance Literature' in Demetz, Greene, and Nelson (eds.), *The Disciplines of Criticism*, 241–64

GRIFFITHS, ERIC, 'To Care & Not to Care', *TLS* 28 May 1993, 13–14

GUNN, S. J., and LINDLEY, P. G. (eds.), *Cardinal Wolsey: Church, State and Art* (Cambridge: Cambridge University Press, 1991)

GURR, ANDREW, *The Shakespearian Playing Companies* (Oxford: Clarendon Press, 1996)

GWYN, PETER, *The King's Cardinal: The Rise and Fall of Thomas Wolsey* (London: Barrie & Jenkins, 1990)

HANSON, ELIZABETH, *Discovering the Subject in Renaissance England* (Cambridge: Cambridge University Press, 1998)

HARRIS, LAURIE LANZAN, *Shakespearean Criticism: Excerpts from the Criticism of William Shakespeare's Plays and Poetry from the First Published Appraisals to Current Evaluations*, 7 vols. (Detroit, Mich.: Gale, 1984–), vol. i

HEDRICK, DONALD K., '"It is No Novelty for a Prince to be a Prince": An Enantiomorphous Hamlet', *SQ* 35 (1984), 62–76

HIRST, DEREK, *Authority and Conflict: England 1603–1658* (London: Edward Arnold, 1986)

HOLSTUN, JAMES, 'Ranting at the New Historicism', *ELR* 19 (1989), 189–225

HONIGMANN, E. A. J., *Shakespeare's Impact on his Contemporaries* (London: Macmillan, 1982)

HOULBROOKE, RALPH (ed.), *English Family Life, 1576–1716: An Anthology from Diaries* (Basil Blackwell: Oxford, 1988)

Howard, Jean E., 'The New Historicism in Renaissance Studies', *ELR* 16 (1986), 13–43
——and O'Connor, Marion F. (eds.), *Shakespeare Reproduced: The Text in History and Ideology* (Methuen: New York, 1987)
——*The Stage and Social Struggle in Early Modern England* (London: Routledge, 1994)
Howe, P. P., (ed.), *The Complete Works of William Hazlitt*, 21 vols. (London: J. M. Dent & Sons, 1930–34)
Howell, W. S., *Logic and Rhetoric in England: 1500–1700* (Princeton: Princeton University Press, 1956)
Hunter, G. K., '*Hamlet* Criticism', *The Critical Quarterly*, 1 (1959), 27–32
Hussey, S. S., *The Literary Language of Shakespeare* (2nd edn.; London: Longman, 1992)
Ioppolo, Grace, *Revising Shakespeare* (Cambridge, Mass.: Harvard University Press, 1991)
Ives, E. W., 'The Fall of Wolsey', in Gunn and Lindley (eds.), *Cardinal Wolsey*, 286–315
Jenkins, Harold, '*Hamlet* Then Till Now', *SS* 18 (1965), 34–45
Jones, Ernest, *Hamlet and Oedipus* (London: Victor Gollancz, 1949)
Jones, John, *Shakespeare at Work* (Oxford: Clarendon Press, 1995)
Joseph, B. L., *Conscience and the King* (London: Chatto & Windus, 1953)
Jump, John (ed.), *Shakespeare: 'Hamlet'* (London: Macmillan, 1968)
Kearney, Hugh, *Scholars and Gentlemen: Universities and Society in Pre-Industrial Britain 1500–1700* (London: Faber & Faber, 1970)
Kelly, George A., *The Psychology of Personal Constructs*, 2 vols. (2nd edn.; London: Routledge, 1991; first pub. 1955)
——*A Theory of Personality: The Psychology of Personal Constructs* (New York: Norton, 1963)
——'Epilogue: Don Juan', in Maher (ed.), *Clinical Psychology*, 331–51.
——'Humanistic Methodology in Psychological Research', in Maher (ed.), *Clinical Psychology*, 133–46.
——'The Autobiography of a Theory', in Maher (ed.), *Clinical Psychology*, 46–65.
——'The Language of Hypothesis', in Maher (ed.), *Clinical Psychology*, 147–62.
——'Man's Construction of his Alternatives', in Maher (ed.), *Clinical Psychology*, 66–93.
——'Ontological Acceleration', in Maher (ed.), *Clinical Psychology*, 7–45.
——'The Strategy of Psychological Research', in Maher (ed.), *Clinical Psychology*, 114–32.
——'Confusion and the Clock', in Fransella (ed.), *Personal Construct Psychology 1977*, 209–33.
Kenny, Anthony, *The Self* (Milwaukee: Marquette University Press, 1988)
Kermode, Frank, 'The High Cost of New Historicism', *NYRB* 19 June 1992, 43–6
——'Toe-Lining', *London Review of Books*, 22 January 1998, 9–10
Kerrigan, John, 'Revision, Adaptation, and the Fool in *King Lear*', in Taylor and Warren (eds.), *The Division of the Kingdoms*, 195–245
Kinniard, J., *William Hazlitt: Critic of Power* (New York: Columbia University Press, 1978)
Knapp, John V., 'Introduction: Self-Preservation and Self-Transformation: Interdisciplinary Approaches to Literary Character', *Style*, 24 (1990), 349–64
Knutson, Roslyn L., 'A New Date and Commercial Agenda for the "Little Eyases" Passage in *Hamlet*', *SQ* 46 (1995), 1–31
Kristeller, Paul Oskar, *Renaissance Thought: The Classic, Scholastic and Humanist Strains* (New York: Harper & Row, 1961)

Lacan, J., 'Desire and the Interpretation of Desire in *Hamlet*', trans. James Hulbert, *Yale French Studies*, 55/56 (1977), 11–52

Lakoff, George, and Johnson, Mark, *Metaphors We Live By* (Chicago: University of Chicago Press, 1980)

Lee, John, 'The Man who Mistook his Hat: Stephen Greenblatt and the Anecdote', *EIC* 45 (1995), 285–300

——'Correction', *EIC* (1998), July, 290

—— 'On Reading *The Tempest* Autobiographically: Ben Jonson's *The New Inn*', *Shakespeare Studies* (Tokyo), 34 (1996), 1–26.

Lentricchia, Frank, *After the New Criticism* (London: Athlone, 1980)

——'Foucault's Legacy—A New Historicism?', in Veeser (ed.), *The New Historicism*, 231–42

——and McLaughlin, Thomas (eds.), *Critical Terms for Literary Study* (Chicago: University of Chicago Press, 1990)

Levin, Richard, 'Unthinkable Thoughts in the New Historicizing of English Renaissance Drama', *New Literary History*, 3 (1990), 433–48

Lewis, C. S., *English Literature in the Sixteenth Century Excluding Drama* (Oxford: Clarendon Press, 1954)

Lewis, Wilmarth Sheldon, *Horace Walpole* (London: Rupert Hart-Davis, 1961)

——and Riely, John (eds.), *The Yale Edition of Horace Walpole's Correspondence*, 48 vols. (Oxford: Oxford University Press, 1937–83)

Lindley, P. G., 'Playing Check-Mate with Royal Majesty? Wolsey's Patronage of Italian Renaissance Sculpture', in Gunn and Lindley (eds.), *Cardinal Wolsey*, 261–85

Loades, D. M., *The Tudor Court* (London: Batsford, 1986)

—— *The Tudor Court* (London: Historical Association, 1991)

Lockyer, Roger, *The Early Stuarts: A Political History of England, 1603–1642* (Harlow: Longman, 1989)

Lovejoy, Arthur O., *The Great Chain of Being: A Study of the History of an Idea* (Cambridge, Mass.: Harvard University Press, 1936)

Lyon, John M., 'The Anxiety of Criticism', *The Keats-Shelley Review*, 5 (1990), 105–17

McCanles, Michael, 'The Authentic Discourse of the Renaissance', *Diacritics*, 10:1 (1980), 77–87

—— *The Text of Sidney's Arcadian World* (Durham: Duke University Press, 1989)

MacFarlane, Alan, *Marriage and Love in England: Modes of Reproduction 1300–1840* (Oxford: Basil Blackwell, 1986)

McGee, Arthur, *The Elizabethan Hamlet* (New Haven: Yale University Press, 1987)

McGinn, D. G., *Shakespeare's Influence on the Drama of his Age* (New Brunswick: Rutgers University Press, 1938)

MacIntyre, Alasdair, *After Virtue: A Study in Moral Theory* (2nd edn.; London: Duckworth, 1985)

McMullan, Gordon and Hope, Jonathan (eds.), *The Politics of Tragicomedy: Shakespeare and After* (London: Routledge, 1992)

Marcus, Leah S., *Unediting the Renaissance* (London: Routledge, 1996)

Maher, Brendan (ed.), *Clinical Psychology and Personality: The Selected Papers of George Kelly* (New York: Robert E. Krieger, 1979)

Mahood, Molly M., *Shakespeare's Word-Play* (London: Methuen, 1957)

MARTIN, LUTHER H., GUTMAN, HUCK, and HUTTON, PATRICK H. (eds.), *Technologies of the Self: A Seminar with Michel Foucault* (London: Tavistock, 1988)

MAUS, KATHARINE EISAMAN, *Inwardness and Theater in the English Renaissance* (Chicago: University of Chicago Press, 1995)

MELCHIORI, GEORGIO, 'The Rhetoric of Character Construction: *Othello*', *SS* 34 (1981), 61–72

MONTROSE, LOUIS, 'Renaissance Literary Studies and the Subject of History', *ELR* 16 (1986), 5–12

——'Professing the Renaissance: The Poetics and Politics of Culture', in Veeser (ed.), *A New Historicism*, 15–36

MORGANN, MAURICE, *Shakespearean Criticism*, ed. Daniel A. Fineman (Oxford: Clarendon Press, 1972)

MOSS, ANNE, 'Commonplace Books', unpub. paper given to the International Society of the History of Rhetoric on 6 March 1993

—— *Printed Commonplace-Books and the Structuring of Renaissance Thought* (Oxford: Clarendon Press, 1996)

MUIR, KENNETH, 'Shakespeare's Open Secret', *SS* 34 (1981), 1–10

MUNRO, J., (ed.), *The Shakspere Allusion-Book: A Collection of Allusions to Shakespeare from 1591 to 1700*, 2 vols. (London: Oxford University Press, 1932)

NEELY, CAROL THOMAS, 'Constructing the Subject: Feminist Practice and the New Renaissance Discourses', *ELR* 18 (1988), 5–18

NEWTON, JUDITH LOWDER, 'History as Usual? Feminism and the "New Historicism"', in Veeser (ed.), *The New Historicism*, 152–67

NORBROOK, DAVID, *Poetry and Politics in the English Renaissance* (London: Routledge & Kegan Paul, 1984)

NOSWORTHY, J. M., *Shakespeare's Occasional Plays: Their Origin and Transmission* (London: Arnold, 1965)

ONG, WALTER J., *Rhetoric, Romance, and Technology: Studies in the Interaction of Expression and Culture* (Ithaca, NY: Cornell Univesity Press, 1971)

PALFREY, SIMON, *Late Shakespeare: A New World of Words* (Oxford: Clarendon Press, 1997)

PARKER, PATRICIA, *Literary Fat Ladies: Rhetoric, Gender, Property* (London and New York: Methuen, 1987)

PATERSON, JOHN, 'The Word in *Hamlet*', *SQ* 2 (1951), 47–56

PATTERSON, LEE, *Negotiating the Past: The Historical Understanding of Medieval Literature* (Madison, Wis.: University of Wisconsin, 1987)

—— 'Literary History', in Lentricchia and McLaughlin (eds.), *Critical Terms for Literary Study*, 250–62

PERVIN, LAWRENCE A., *Personality: Theory and Research* (6th edn.; New York: John Wiley & Sons, 1993)

PLOWDEN, A., *The Elizabethan Secret Service* (Hemel Hempstead: Harvester Wheatsheaf, 1991)

POLLOCK, LINDA A., *Forgotten Children: Parent–Child Relations from 1500 to 1900* (Cambridge: Cambridge University Press, 1983)

PROSSER, ELEANOR, *Hamlet and Revenge* (Stanford, Calif.: Stanford University Press, 1967)

PUTTENHAM, GEORGE, *The Arte of English Poesie* (Menston: Scolar Press, 1968; first pub. 1589)

QUINT, DAVID, *Origin and Originality in Renaissance Literature: Versions of the Source* (New

Haven: Yale University Press, 1983)

——*Montaigne and the Quality of Mercy: Ethical and Political Themes in the Essais* (Princeton: Princeton University Press, 1998)

RALLI, AUGUSTUS, *A History of Shakespearean Criticism*, 2 vols. (London: Oxford University Press, 1932)

RAYSOR, T. M. (ed.), *Shakespearean Criticism*, 2 vols. (2nd edn.; London: Dent, 1960)

REES, JOAN, 'Sir Walter Ralegh; The Renaissance Man and his Roles', *RES* 26 (1975), 70–1

RHODES, NEIL, *The Power of Eloquence and English Renaissance Literature* (Hemel Hempstead: Harvester Wheatsheaf, 1992)

RIBNER, IRVING, *The English History Play in the Age of Shakespeare* (Princeton: Princeton University Press, 1957)

RIGHTER, ANNE, *Shakespeare and the Idea of the Play* (London: Chatto & Windus, 1962)

ROBINSON, RANDAL F., *'Hamlet' in the 1950s: An Annotated Bibliography* (New York: Garland, 1984)

ROGERS, MALCOLM, 'The Meaning of Van Dyck's Portrait of Sir John Suckling', *Burlington Magazine*, 120 (1978), 741–5

ROSSITER, A. P., *Angel with Horns: Fifteen Lectures on Shakespeare*, ed. Graham Storey (Harlow: Longman, 1989; first pub. 1961)

RYCHLAK, J. F., *Introduction to Personality and Psychotherapy: A Theory-Construction Approach* (2nd edn.; New York: Houghton Mifflin, 1981)

SAID, EDWARD, *Orientalism* (Harmondsworth: Penguin, 1985; first pub. New York: Pantheon, 1978)

SALINGAR, LEO, 'Shakespeare and the Ventriloquists', *SS* 34 (1981), 51–60

SALMON, PHILLIDA, *Psychology for Teachers: An Alternative Approach* (London: Hutchinson, 1988)

SCHOENBAUM, S., *Shakespeare's Lives* (Oxford: Clarendon Press, 1991)

SHARPE, J. A., *Early Modern England: A Social History 1550–1760* (London: Edward Arnold, 1987)

SHARPE, KEVIN, and LAKE, PETER (eds.), *Culture and Politics in Early Stuart England* (London: Macmillan, 1994)

SINFIELD, ALAN, *Faultlines: Cultural Materialism and the Politics of Dissident Reading* (Oxford: Clarendon Press, 1992)

SKINNER, QUENTIN, *The Foundations of Modern Political Thought*, 2 vols. (Cambridge: Cambridge University Press, 1978)

SMART, BARRY, *Michel Foucault* (London: Routledge, 1985)

SMITH, D. NICHOL (ed.), *Eighteenth Century Essays on Shakespeare* (2nd edn.; Oxford: Clarendon Press, 1963)

SNELL, BRUNO, *The Discovery of the Mind: The Greek Origins of European Thought* (Oxford: Basil Blackwell, 1953)

SOSKICE, JANET MARTIN, *Metaphor and Religious Language* (Clarendon Press: Oxford, 1985)

SPENCER, CHRISTOPHER, 'Introduction', *Five Restoration Adaptations of Shakespeare* (Urbana, Ill.: University of Illinois Press, 1965)

SPENCER, T. J. B., 'The Decline of Hamlet', *Stratford Upon Avon Studies*, 5 (1963), 185–99

STARKEY, DAVID (ed.), *The English Court: From the Wars of the Roses to the Civil War* (Harlow: Longman, 1987)

STATES, BERT O., *'Hamlet' and the Concept of Character* (Baltimore: Johns Hopkins

University Press, 1992)
STEINER, GEORGE, *Language and Silence: Essays 1958–1966* (London: Faber, 1967)
—— *The Portage to San Cristobal of A. H.* (London: Faber, 1981)
STONE, LAWRENCE, *The Causes of the English Revolution, 1529–1641* (London: Routledge & Kegan Paul, 1972)
—— *The Family, Sex and Marriage in England, 1500–1800* (London: Weidenfeld & Nicolson, 1977)
STRONG, ROY, *The Cult of Elizabeth: Elizabethan Portraiture and Pageantry* (London: Thames and Hudson, 1977)
—— *Holbein: The Complete Paintings* (London: Granada, 1980)
TAINE, HIPPOLYTE, *History of English Literature*, trans. H. Van Laun, 4 vols. (London: Chatto & Windus, 1877; first pub. 1864)
TAYLOR, CHARLES, *Sources of the Self: The Making of Modern Identity* (Cambridge: Cambridge University Press, 1989)
TAYLOR, GARY, *Reinventing Shakespeare* (London: Hogarth Press, 1989)
—— and WARREN, MICHAEL (eds.), *The Division of the Kingdoms: Shakespeare's Two Versions of 'King Lear'* (Oxford: Clarendon Press, 1983)
TENNENHOUSE, LEONARD, *Power on Display: The Politics of Shakespeare's Genres* (London: Methuen, 1986)
THOMAS, BROOK, *The New Historicism: And Other Old-Fashioned Topics* (Princeton: Princeton University Press, 1991)
TILLYARD, E. M. W., *The Elizabethan World Picture* (London: Chatto & Windus, 1943)
—— *Shakespeare's History Plays* (London: Chatto & Windus, 1944)
—— *Shakespeare's Problem Plays* (London: Chatto & Windus, 1950)
TROUSDALE, MARION, *Shakespeare and the Rhetoricians* (Chapel Hill, NC: University of North Carolina Press, 1982)
TZVETAN, TODOROV, *The Conquest of America: The Question of the Other*, trans. Richard Howard (New York: Harper Collins , 1984)
URE, PETER, *Elizabethan and Jacobean Drama*, ed. J. C. Maxwell (Liverpool: Liverpool University Press, 1974)
VEESER, H. ARAM (ed.), *The New Historicism* (New York: Routledge, 1989)
—— 'Introduction', in *The New Historicism*, pp. ix–xvi
VERNANT, JEAN-PIERRE, and VIDAL-NAQUET, P., *Tragedy and Myth in Ancient Greece*, trans. Janet Lloyd (Brighton: Harvester, 1981)
VICKERS, BRIAN, (ed.), *Shakespeare: The Critical Heritage*, 6 vols. (London: Routledge & Kegan Paul, 1974–81)
—— 'The Emergence of Character Criticism, 1774–1800', *SS* 34 (1981), 11–22
—— *In Defence of Rhetoric* (Oxford: Clarendon Press, 1988)
—— *Appropriating Shakespeare: Contemporary Critical Quarrels* (New Haven: Yale University Press, 1993)
WALLER, MARGUERITE, 'The Empire's New Clothes: Refashioning the Renaissance', in Fisher and Halley (eds.), *Seeking the Woman*, 160–83
WARNOCK, MARY, *Memory* (London: Faber, 1987)
WARREN, MICHAEL, 'The Diminution of Kent', in Taylor and Warren (eds.), *The Division of the Kingdoms*, 59–74
WARREN, ROGER, 'The Folio Omission of the Mock Trial: Motives and Consequences', in Taylor and Warren (eds.), *The Division of the Kingdoms*, 45–58

WASWO, RICHARD, *Language and Meaning in the Renaissance* (Princeton: Princeton University Press, 1987)

——'How To Be (or Not to Be) a Cultural Materialist', *The European English Messenger*, 6 (1997), 59–67

WAYMENT, HILARY, 'Wolsey and Stained Glass', in Gunn and Lindley (eds.), *Cardinal Wolsey*, 116–30

WAYNE, DON E., 'Power, Politics, and the Shakespearean Text: Recent Criticism in England and the United States', in Howard and O'Connor (eds.), *Shakespeare Reproduced*, 47–67

WEITZ, MORRIS, *Hamlet and the Philosophy of Literary Criticism* (London: Faber and Faber, 1972; first pub. 1964)

WELLS, STANLEY, (ed.), *Shakespeare: A Bibliographical Guide* (Oxford: Oxford University Press, 1990)

——, TAYLOR, GARY, JOWETT, JOHN, and MONTGOMERY, WILLIAM (eds.), *William Shakespeare: A Textual Companion* (Oxford: Clarendon Press, 1987)

WERSTINE, PAUL, 'The Textual Mystery of *Hamlet*', *SQ* 39 (1988), 1–26

WHIGHAM, FRANK, *Ambition and Privilege: The Social Tropes of Elizabethan Courtesy Theory* (Berkeley: University of California Press, 1984)

WHITE, HAYDEN, 'New Historicism: A Comment', in Veeser (ed.), *The New Historicism*, 293–302

WHITE, R. S., 'Marx and Shakespeare, *SS* 44 (1991), 89–100

WILKS, JOHN S., *The Idea of Conscience in Renaissance Tragedy* (London: Routledge, 1990)

WILLIAMS, RAYMOND, *Marxism and Literature* (Oxford: Oxford University Press, 1977)

——*Politics and Letters: Interviews with New Left Review* (London: NLB, 1979)

——*Keywords: A Vocabulary of Culture and Society*, (rev. edn.; London: Fontana Press, 1983)

WILLIAMSON, C. C. H., *Readings on the Character of Hamlet; 1661–1947* (New York; Gordian Press, 1972; first pub. 1950)

WILSON, J. DOVER, *What Happens in Hamlet* (3rd edn.; Cambridge: Cambridge University Press, 1970; first pub. 1935)

WILSON, RICHARD, 'Introduction: Historicising New Historicism', in Wilson and Dutton (eds.), *New Historicism*, 1–18

——and DUTTON, RICHARD, (eds.), *New Historicism and Renaissance Drama* (London: Longman, 1992)

WITTGENSTEIN, L., *Lectures and Conversations on Aesthetics, Psychology and Religious Belief: Compiled from Notes taken by Yorick Smythies, Rush Rhees and James Taylor*, ed. Cyril Barrett (Oxford: Basil Blackwell, 1966)

WOFFORD, SUSANNE L. (ed.), *Case Studies in Contemporary Criticism: 'Hamlet'* (New York: St Martin's Press, 1994)

WOUDHUYSEN, H. R. (ed.), *Samuel Johnson on Shakespeare* (Harmondsworth: Penguin, 1989)

WRIGHSTON, KEITH, *English Society: 1580–1680* (London: Hutchinson, 1982)

WRIGHT, GEORGE T., '*Hamlet* and Hendiadys', *PMLA* 96 (1981), 168–93

WILDE, OSCAR, *Complete Works of Oscar Wilde*, ed. Vyvyan Holland (London: Book Club Associates, 1976)

YATES, FRANCES A., *The Art of Memory* (London: Pimlico, 1992; first pub. 1966)

ZIEGLER, GEORGIANNA, 'A Victorian Reputation: John Payne Collier and His Contemporaries', *SS* 17 (1985), 209–34

Index

DATE DUE